MICHAEL ROSE

Industrial Behaviour

Research and Control

Penguin Books

PENGUIN BOOKS

Published by the Penguin Group
27 Wrights Lane, London W8 5TZ, England
Viking Penguin Inc., 40 West 23rd Street, New York, New York 10010, USA
Penguin Books Australia Ltd, Ringwood, Victoria, Australia
Penguin Books Canada Ltd, 2801 John Street, Markham, Ontario, Canada L3R 1B4
Penguin Books (NZ) Ltd, 182–190 Wairau Road, Auckland 10, New Zealand

Penguin Books Ltd, Registered Offices: Harmondsworth, Middlesex, England

First published by Allen Lane 1975
Published in Penguin Education 1978
Reprinted 1981, 1983
Reprinted in Pelican Books 1985
Second edition 1988

Made and printed in Great Britain by
Cox and Wyman Ltd, Reading, Berks
Filmset in Plantin (Linotron 202) by
Rowland Phototypesetting Ltd, Bury St Edmunds, Suffolk

Industrial Behaviour

After graduating in anthropology and economics from Cambridge University in 1962, Michael Rose joined the University's Department of Applied Economics as a fieldworker, contributing to a landmark study of how prosperity altered work attitudes and behaviour in the post-war boom period. (He also wrote successful satirical reviews at this time and reluctantly turned down a career in television.) In the late 1960s he carried out the first major inquiry in Britain into the coming information revolution. His *Computers, Managers and Society*, a bestselling Pelican, renewed the 'two cultures' controversy over the effect of science on society. He was based at Bath University from 1970, where he lectured on the European continent and carried out international comparative research, producing his acclaimed survey of culture and economic growth in France, *Servants of Post-Industrial Power?* This was followed by one of the first inquiries into nationalism and trade unions in western Europe and has featured in Open University films. At the same time he completed the first edition of *Industrial Behaviour*. As Reader in Economic Life at Bath he organized the 'Sunrise City' inquiry in the 1980s into the effect of social and cultural change on work. He had first explored this theme in 1985 in *Reworking the Work Ethic* – a study tipped to become a social science classic. He has recently held posts in Paris and at Oxford, and has travelled widely in several countries. His other interests include painting and mycology.

For
SOC 201/2
BU 1971–88

Contents

PART IV: IMPERATIVES OF THE MACHINE

PART V: ACTION THAT MEANS SOMETHING

PART VI: DIVIDING THE LABOURERS

CONCLUSION

Foreword

Like the first edition, this enlarged *Industrial Behaviour* tries to meet three main needs. To begin with, it gives an account of the most influential approaches to work behaviour and the workplace since 1900. It also tries to show how economic conditions, social philosophies, and other background influences have affected these various approaches – not in order to prove any trite theory that ideas directly mirror historical circumstances, but to show how the relationship between ideas and everyday life can itself vary over time.

Second, it gives interpretations, or re-appraisals, of many different studies of the workplace, and of some personal reputations. Some of the studies selected are recognized classics, and all are in some way exemplary. This examination, which draws attention to the role of research method, throws light on some potential, but unrecognized, classics. It also provides a number of examples to *avoid* following.

These two features should enable students and non-specialists to get their bearings in the field. Their needs, based on ten years' feedback from readers, have been kept in mind in preparing this enlarged edition.

The third aim combines naturally with the first two, but can be treated as quite distinct from them. The still far from finished mission to build an economic system that produces efficiently and distributes rewards justly also calls for an effort to understand economic life more fully. This intellectual drive has constantly been thwarted. Work, the workplace, and people at work are complex and changeable. Even careful observers misread them.

Equally honest ones, under the influence of some intoxicating doctrine or other, impose a reading on them.

The understanding to be gained by looking, sympathetically but unsentimentally, at past attempts to explain work behaviour can contribute to the underlying task of discovering better forms of control over economic life. Such a task should not be narrowly shaped by the immediate concerns of professional controllers, yet account should be taken of the dilemmas that all forms of control throw up. Again, familiarity with the history of that effort can be rewarding for its own sake. Studies of this aspect of economic activity, and debate about them, have contributed importantly to culture.

Some colleagues, in disciplines other than those the book mainly refers to (sociology, anthropology, psychology), found the first edition useful for their work on special topics (for example, management strategies and economic cycles). In rewriting, I have tried to increase its usefulness for this purpose, without straying into territory they know much better than I do. If the new edition remains useful to economists and historians it will be because it makes material from outside their fields accessible to them.

Two other decisions guiding revision ought to be recorded here. Where changes were needed, there was no hesitation in making them. At least one alteration, and usually several, has been made to each page kept from the first edition. Some original chapters have been cut down, others greatly extended or heavily revised. The old introduction and conclusion, victims of the advance of knowledge and other rapid changes, were completely replaced. Upwards of two hundred pages of new material have been written. To this extent, this is substantially a new book.

Selection and treatment of material forming the completely new final part raised some hard decisions. Since the early 1970s, the work domain has been struck by a cyclone of change – the collapse of old industries, the long-predicted arrival of automation, the feminization of the labour-force, a revolt against work followed by attempts to restore the work ethic. There has been a bonanza in research into these changes; there have been sharp disagreements over what they amount to.

The water behind this New Wave of economic sociology is still choppy. Earlier approaches have been blown out of sight, but it is not clear how lasting those which have taken their place will turn out to be. I have some doubts, and try to show that a greater degree of continuity with the past than is commonly supposed has been maintained. Indeed, a striking feature of some New Wave work is a revival of problems and styles of analysis that first appeared fifty years ago. Simple repetition can be avoided by greater awareness of what was done earlier.

Another problem was how to handle criticism of ideas put forward in the first edition. Where disagreements seemed relevant to readers' needs, or simply in order to put the record straight, they have been pointed out. But I have tried to avoid polemics. Some people disliked the first edition because it disagreed with their world-view. I have not set out to woo them over. (Some of them apparently made use of the text none the less. I hope they will find this edition useful too – unacknowledged influence is the kind to take seriously.)

There is one dissimilarity with the first edition that ought to be noted. In this edition, definite forecasts about priorities for research, and about trends in interpretation, over the next ten or so years are made in the concluding chapter. If these forecasts turn out to be right, this may give a little pleasure. But I am aware that should they turn out to be wrong, this may still give pleasure – quite rightly so: *schadenfreude* is justified when confident predictions turn into banana skins. But we shall see.

1

Introduction: The Fifth Dimension of Control

There are many valid ways of building up an understanding of work behaviour, but by looking at how people have explained work behaviour over the last hundred years we are led to consider the dynamic relationship between economic conditions, events in workplaces (their politics), and powerful ideas. This method gives valuable insight into an aspect of our economic and social past that most historians overlook. It also highlights the danger of assuming that there may be any simple explanation, good for all times and all places, to apply to social behaviour.

The relationship between the politics of the workplace and theories about them is intricate and far from being understood fully, but whatever we can learn about that relationship is useful and interesting. Anyone concerned with economic life wants to know how far we can trust the accounts of work behaviour that observers have put forward over the years. We cannot begin to do so unless we see how circumstances may affect what the observers say – and even what some observers *see* in the first place.

This difficulty with perspective surrounds the terms we use when we talk about work. 'Work' is an ambiguous term. It often denotes paid employment, though a massive amount of work is done unpaid, in the home or in voluntary activities. While it still conjures up the idea of physical effort that is either tedious or exhausting, the term work can be used just as easily to describe mental exertion that is exciting and creative. Yet all these meanings, and many subsidiary ones, belong on the same family tree. They all grow from a single central fact: that work has been, and remains, an inescapable or 'organic' feature of human life. For most of us, from a practical point of view, work is the single most important *fact* of life.

Unlike animals, human beings *know* that to feed, clothe, and shelter themselves they must expend effort. They also *know* when they are expending such effort. The painting of hunting scenes on the walls of caves marks the point at which early human beings began to develop some conscious understanding of this part of the human predicament. Attempts to handle it in an intelligent, creative way, both through magical means and through the invention of tools, mark the transition from a savage state to civilization. In this way, work, more than any other single influence, has shaped the human mind as well as improving overall human welfare. It will continue to do so.

But this is to talk of work in a highly abstract way. The economic system within which work is done can modify drastically the aims and meaning of work, and hence the meaning of work behaviour. The way of life, traditions, and economic history of the country in which individuals live further alter people's work behaviour and its meaning. So can a local community, an occupation, domestic arrangements, or many other forces. While these forces operate in ways that are always complicated and frequently puzzling, they do not do so in a random fashion. They are *structured* forces. Because they are structured forces, we may succeed in describing and analysing them with increasing precision.

But observers often plot some of the more obvious of these forces and forget about the underlying ones. When we study our own social world, we all have a tendency to overlook everyday facts about it. Whatever we take as obvious and normal never seems worth scrutinizing. We should be more discerning. For example, the economic system we live in is unlike all economies that existed until two hundred years ago. Historically speaking, it is a curiosity. We should remember this when we talk about work.

Three interrelated features of the economic system which has dominated the world over the last two centuries have stamped themselves on the forms and meaning of work as we know it. Firstly, this system, industrial capitalism, is built on paid employment that is offered and sought in a labour market. Secondly, most paid work is organized consciously and applied on a large scale in line with what the organizers believe to be scientific principles. Finally, the underlying motivation of the organizers is the creation of wealth through the pursuit of profit.

These characteristics have left a mark on the theories of work behaviour that will be dealt with in this book. However, the people putting the theories forward have failed often to consider how they do so. Consequently, at numerous points, the main text will revert to the question of how the economic system affects work behaviour, but some brief comments about it are necessary before going any further.

Some readers may object to the stress on paid employment in profit-making firms. It might make us forget how much valuable work is done unpaid, especially by women in the home. Again, the labour market often works quite unlike most other markets. Instead of being open or 'free', it is managed by employers, rigged by unions, or operates in otherwise 'imperfect' ways, excluding people qualified to do certain jobs because of their sex, race, religion, or age. Finally, of course, many work organizations – schools, hospitals, the police – are not profit-seeking bodies.

All these objections make important points about the complete reality of work in our economic system. I would like to develop and deal with them as fully as they deserve. However, the difficulty may be imaginary: what is assumed here is that the *dominant image* of work, the *dominant model* for organizing work, and the *dominant standard* for evaluating work, are derived none the less from the paid work of industrial capitalism. The extent to which other sorts of gainful effort actually evade the pressure to conform to this model is of the highest importance, but it would call for another book.

In a capitalist economy, output – of manufactured goods, or of personal services – is treated as a set of commodities produced for a cash profit in the market-place. Such production is unconcerned with the intrinsic worth or 'use-value' of what is produced. Whatever the commodity may be, if somebody pays enough to make it profitable to supply it, then it has 'value'; and its value is the price consumers pay for it.

Other economic systems have shared with industrial capitalism its open-mindedness about intrinsic utility when profit is to be made. But capitalist industry seeks profit partly in order to invest its gains in new equipment or other resources, bringing a growth in productive capacity as well as money income. Its logic is continuous *accumulation* of productive capacity and the *appropriation* of profit by privately owned organizations or private individuals. Some employees in these organizations may resent such materialistic aims on principle. Many more employees, while not consciously opposing capitalist aims in general, nevertheless resent them when they are pursued single-mindedly by their own employer. For their part, employers can argue that business prosperity, however it is achieved, increases the rewards and job security of employees; and some workers endorse this view whole-heartedly. But whether it is accepted or rejected by those subject to it, the logic of profit-seeking affects the underlying attitudes and behaviour in the workplace of all economic actors.

Such attitudes usually are affected powerfully by the experience of being managed. Pursuit of profitability obliges managers to behave in certain ways rather than in others. In a profit-seeking economy, work is regarded as a commodity that is bought and sold in the market. A wage is the sum paid for work. In its simplest form, work means manual work, or labour. But how much work the buyer of labour – the employer – thinks he is buying is not clear. Hiring a worker *seems* to involve purchasing a period of time. Yet a period of time is just so many seconds ticking emptily away. What is bought, what employers at least assume they are buying, is not time itself but a *capacity to work* during a period of time, and the right to *organize and control* effort during that period.

Even when it is agreed beforehand (as it is under piece-rate payment systems for example) what quantity of work is to be done, a problem may arise over the quality of the finished articles, or of the degree of care to be put into doing a service task. Quality of work can be important even in labouring jobs. In service tasks such as cleaning, cooking, teaching, or medicine, it is usually more important than quantity. In our 'post-manufacturing' economies such tasks are growing more common every day.

To recapitulate: disagreements between employers and workers over effort are built into any economy with a market for labour; in the capitalist economy, employers build wealth from organizing workers' effort in what employers consider the most effective way for that purpose; realization of this can lead to a particularly keen sense of grievance among workers because they feel that the share in the proceeds of the business that they receive is lower than they deserve; this resentment may be increased by a moral or political objection to profit-making; but most workers do not reject the basic rules of the system, even when they complain that their employer is exploiting them.

How far are employees justified in making the charge of exploitation? I cannot deal with the question satisfactorily here. But a short comment on the notion of exploitation is necessary. Exploitation is a loaded term, conjuring up images of starving medieval peasants handing over tithes to fat priests, or a pimp sending his woman out to work the pavement. Exploitation, in its technical sense, does not necessarily imply 'extortion' or 'exaction', as do these lurid images. These are the popular meanings attributed to the word by many English-speakers. In its original sense, 'to exploit' meant no more than 'to put to productive use'. In this correct sense, planting potatoes in a back garden, rather than planting rose bushes, is a way of exploiting the productiveness of a plot of ground.

Muggers and blackmailers practise extortion on their victims, but they do not exploit them. However paradoxical it may sound, highly paid workers enjoying enviable working conditions, and who are thus evidently not victims of extortion, nevertheless can be thought of as being exploited in the more technical sense, provided their labour is being applied in a productive way. Managers, for obvious reasons, avoid the term. But when they talk of 'effective work performance' or 'optimum labour utilization' they have something more or less equivalent in mind.

Indeed, exploitation in this sense must occur in any dynamic economic system. This is so whether industry is owned by private individuals, the State, or co-operatives. In a non-capitalist economy, producers are still faced with pressures to organize and apply their labour effectively; workers can never receive 'the full fruits of their labour', because over any dynamic economy a surplus of output must be made and saved. Only thus can a part of total production be diverted to renew and develop the productive resources – equipment, machines, roads, railways, trained personnel – on which high levels of income and consumption finally depend. Political arguments about exploitation, then, may be not so much about whether exploitation can be avoided, as about whether it could be managed more justly, or more effectively, than it is under capitalism.

Academic arguments cannot settle such questions. Future social experiments might do so. The alternatives to capitalist exploitation developed in the twentieth century – in the USSR, in Yugoslavia, in Israel – have performed patchily, but it may be possible to discover better alternatives than these in the future.

Whether we use the term exploitation or not, industrial capitalism has a built-in tendency to seek as high a level of effort, whether in terms of quantity or quality, as it can get. In practical terms, this is done through a package of control techniques with which anyone who has worked in a fair-sized organization is familiar. For while it is true, of course, that money-reward ultimately may be the single most important means of controlling work behaviour, the wage-incentive is always backed up by numerous other direct and indirect control devices. Indeed, these devices can alter fundamentally the way an employee views his or her money-rewards.

A vast array of such control devices is available, which can be sorted out into five or six main groups. For example, *terms of employment* lay down what rewards, beyond wages, an employee can expect: their personal degree of job-security, fringe benefits, holidays, opportunities for additional training, pensions. All manner of such entitlements are available and may create a sense of commitment to the employer's business aims, but the growth of such a feeling of shared interests does not produce automatically work that is done effectively.

Work, as a technical operation carried out by an individual, has to fit into an overall set of tasks performed by many people. Any worker's tasks are integrated in an overall *work organization*. This often specifies in detail, for each employee, what task has to be done, how it is done, and how long it should take an operative to do it. These are the engineer's and the production manager's traditional ways of ensuring high output. Though sometimes they give the worker a sense of working purposefully, rigid forms of work organization and closely laid down tasks most often produce boredom and frustration. Experiments with more subtle forms of operational control have been fashionable in the last twenty years, as we shall see.

Often these changes in work organization go along with alterations to the more personal form of control over work behaviour, which is exercised through a *supervision structure*. In essence, this makes workers responsible to foremen, inspectors, or managers who check how well work is done, and who are sometimes skilled in building a sense of 'social integration' in the workplace, for example by getting employees to think of themselves as being 'part of a large, happy family'.

A system of *employee representation* may be developed, either by agreement with a union, or by creating a 'captive' staff association or house union, to allow workers' grievances to reach higher levels of management through persons elected by the workforce. In return for recognition as a grievance handler, the union may help to enforce workplace discipline.

Methods of control may often work to produce among workers a sense of attachment to the workplace. Whether they also can nurture enthusiastic commitment to the wider aims of the employer is more questionable. In the most advanced capitalist countries, some employers make strenuous and often sophisticated efforts to gain the positive consent of workers to the economic system, and to transform their reaction to being managed. But all techniques for controlling work behaviour embody an attempt to shape the experience of paid employment by influencing the meanings, values and sentiments given to work by workers, as well as programming and disciplining their behaviour directly through work organization and supervision.

This 'fifth dimension' of control is of the utmost importance to the theme of this book. The account of work behaviour that any observer provides is a framework of interpretation, a set of concepts and ideas that aim to explain the 'world of work' as it really is behind a worker's immediate reactions to it, or behind an employer's stereotypical economic wisdom. Often, these interpretative frames are put forward as 'purely scientific' ways of looking at what people do at work and what people think about work, but managers can also massage the information they embody to propagate a view of the workplace that is favourable to the employer's purposes and social values.

The message that managers have found most often in such accounts is that the interests of workers coincide, in the end, with those of the employer. In this perspective, any resistance or uncooperativeness by workers to being controlled is not just a danger to efficient production. It is also wrongheaded: the reflection of a poor character ('a bad attitude') on the part of the worker; the outcome of his or her 'stupidity'; or the sign of a 'political' motivation. Even when they say it results from 'poor communication', seemingly criticizing themselves for putting the management message across badly, they may actually be blaming workers for not understanding it.

At times managers certainly do have to contend with workers who gain a degree of satisfaction simply from disrupting the smooth flow of production or deflating managerial egos by any means at their disposal, and a handful of political militants may exist in any large plant. But resistance to control is far too wide ranging to be explained satisfactorily in such terms. The causes of resistance are numerous and sometimes surprising: they will be explored fully later in the text, but one source is worth noting now. Individual workers, and groups of workers sharing similar tasks or skills, often define their economic interests quite differently from the way that managers think employees should define them. Many such workers are not actively hostile to the economic interests of the employer: they just do not care about them – this fact will have to be accepted for the moment by any readers who do not like it. Whether workers are 'right' or 'wrong' to perceive things this way is not the real point. In so far as they actually *do* see things in some other way than managers, they grow more likely to resist methods of controlling their effort and their ways of thinking.

Any account of work behaviour should acknowledge the variety of outlooks present in a workplace. Some observers, especially in the earlier decades of the century, adopted the management view of the work process without realizing that in doing so they were bound to misinterpret workers' behaviour. A few, no doubt, had a more sophisticated outlook yet promoted the managerial viewpoint because it paid them to do so. But it was the supposedly scientific observations of the sincere 'managerialists' that gave them credibility as advisers to bosses, or as experts who taught managers how to manipulate workers' behaviour and thinking.

An exactly comparable 'workerist' bias has sometimes been present too. 'Workerism' flowered in more recent years, with many observers assuming that managers and workers could never have an important overlap of interests, or perceive their interests similarly. 'Workerists', just like the 'managerialists', and with no less sincere goodwill, assumed they knew better than the workers themselves what were the workers' 'real' interests. Like the managerialists, therefore, they were likely to suggest that workers who thought differently had something the matter with their heads – that they suffered from 'false consciousness' or 'one-dimensional thought'.

Facts must be faced. What workers think are their interests may be quite different from those attributed to them by an outsider, however 'scientific' or 'sympathetic'. Without thinking first, a few of the workerist observers poured scorn on the notion of science itself, and never pretended that their work was anything but committed or political. This made the observers popular with some middle-class young people in revolt against science. Yet some politically committed workers believed that the causes they supported were best served by science and the scientific approach towards economic life – or at least an approach that they believed aimed to be scientific. To dismiss the possibility that science had something to offer them was to patronize such workers just as any managerialist might.

We can come back to these questions in due course. They are more complicated than they seem and the answers to them have not yet been found.

Both the managerialist and the workerist biases reflect excessively abstract models of the employment relationship: a gut belief in the 'natural' harmony of interests in the former case, and one assuming a 'chronic' conflict of interests in the latter. The refusal of some worker groups to co-operate with those who seek to control their effort perplexes managerialists. Workerists have just as much difficulty explaining why it is that much of the time workers let controllers control them; or, to put it another way, collaborate in their own exploitation. Both sets of partisans overlook the many-sidedness of control as a notion and as a series of facts about what goes on in workplaces. Above all they overlook how often outlooks different from their own are held by the people they claim to speak for, and the sincerity with which, correctly or mistakenly, those views are held.

We should distrust words like 'correct' and 'mistaken'. We aim to see more clearly what is going on – what people want, and why they do the things they do. But outside observers should keep a modest opinion of their objectivity and neutrality. Patterns of control, we should remember too, are not fixed but shifting. Economic sociologists often talk of the frontier of control in workplaces. Strictly, the term should be in the plural. There is more than one frontier: managers resort to a mass of control devices. Otherwise, the image is a graphic one, because frontiers measure the current balance of power in a struggle in which one side, however strong, lacks crushing supremacy.

I pointed out earlier that the five dimensions of control are best visualized by thinking of an industrial firm. We need to consider briefly once more what the idea of an industry implies. It means something more than manufacturing, or large-scale operations in the old 'smokestack' branches of production. What ultimately creates an industry is the characteristic variety of thought that runs through the organization of industrial production. This thinking is marked by a management preoccupation – sometimes obsession – with making production more logical, more predictable, more effective, more *controllable*.

The social sciences always have been regarded as relevant to the problems of control. Social scientists themselves disagree whether they should intervene to further managerial control, or to produce a new social order, or simply log what events seem to be occurring. These are questions on which readers will make up their own minds after considering the history narrated in the main text. But, at this point, it may help to take note of some philosophical distinctions that have run through social science since its origins. In doing so, I can also define where this book stands in terms of social-science disciplines.

By and large, we are going to examine sociological accounts of work behaviour. Others are primarily economic or psychological, but the following remarks apply almost equally well to the other social sciences as to sociology.

'Sociology' refers to three quite separate sorts of activity. What might be called Sociology Type I is concerned with collecting facts, especially statistical ones, about groups or 'populations'. While often tedious, such *sociography* does at least provide some useful raw information about what groups do and think. Sociology Type II aims to create theories about collective behaviour that will hold good for all times, all people, and all places. This *social theory* often comes over as too other-worldly, too abstract. On the other hand, without theory social facts remain an incoherent jumble. For the purposes of this book, however, by far the most interesting and valuable strand, Sociology Type III, is concerned with pinning down and explaining the process by which industrial society has developed and altered over the last two hundred years. All three forms of sociology can produce valid knowledge. And each of them succeeds best when it draws on the others and at the same time feeds them. As stated, this book is a contribution to the sociology of industrial society. This developmental strand, *economic sociology*, is concerned with all the institutions, practices and social values that bear on economic activity. The sociology of industry, which focuses on economic activity organized according to the 'industrial principle', is its biggest branch – at least so far as the economically advanced countries go.

Industrial sociology is noted for sharp disagreements between its practitioners. These partly stem from the political and ideological divisions between managerialists and workerists, but they also reflect controversies over which factors – for example, money, managerial skill, or technology – best explain patterns of work behaviour. These disagreements will be examined in full in the main text, where we shall see that such disputes often reflect the deeper puzzles faced by observers who see themselves as being independent and objective (and in that sense 'scientific'). A few more words about this are due here.

Any organizer seeks to increase his hold over subordinates by claiming that his right to issue commands rests on his technical competence. Such expertise can include what is claimed to be a 'scientific' knowledge of behaviour. He also may seek to prise from such knowledge a set of impressive and comforting moral ideas – a doctrine that explains and justifies what he thinks and does. (Sometimes such doctrines are called ideologies, but properly speaking, ideologies are just groups of ideas.)

Managerial doctrines provide an organizer with legitimacy by explaining his role favourably to his subordinates and to himself. Some writers claim that the organizer's need to have such a doctrine reveals a sinister quest for power beyond the workplace, yet on the contrary, it often points to the organizer's weakness and exposure. Exercising control creates high stress in many managers. Often, their own role is vaguely prescribed by employers. Their jobs can be less secure than those of workers they (seek to) control. They can doubt their own competence, and the wisdom of decisions they take apparently with confidence. Correspondingly, controllers have an urgent need for *legitimation*, for moral reassurance.

Many of the industrial sociologists who might produce the knowledge necessary for these managerialist purposes refuse to undertake any research that might be utilized by employers, on the grounds that employers have a fundamental advantage over workers in the employment relationship, since the workplace belongs to the employer not to those who work there. One or two, as we have seen, sometimes go further and define their task as that of aiding workers to replace the capitalist, though few workers have such an ambition. This sharply limits the research they can do in the field. In any case, research comes to be looked on by them merely as as a means of documenting conclusions they have arrived at already.

Some social scientists seek a role as interventionists on behalf of management, under contract to employers, reporting on workers' behaviour and advising on how to apply the results; or, in creating a 'social philosophy' of management; or, in putting together a brand-new 'corporate culture'. Such intervention has often – but not always – been based on shallow thinking about the nature of work behaviour and attitudes. This reflects the aims of its practitioners to boost workers' output, or increase their compliance with discipline over the short term. It also may reflect the aim of taking the employer for a fat fee for services as a professional consultant by telling him exactly what he wants to hear. Clients sometimes listen joyfully to the reassuring simplifications offered by these plausible rogues.

But whether in good faith, or as political idealists, or as smooth-talking knaves, interventionists alter the situation that their more academically minded colleagues study – many cases are examined in the main text. It is essential to remember this link; because of it, no observation can ever be undertaken with completely 'innocent' objectivity, and no conclusion can be reached with an impartiality that lies beyond question.

Theories of industrial behaviour are frameworks of ideas for interpreting what groups of people employed on industrial work are really doing. The doctrines and management philosophies utilized as control devices by employers are also frameworks of interpretation. Often they do not show what is really happening so much as what those who propagate such ideas want to have believed is happening. However, all observers, whether they are interventionists or not, have to take account of the way social science itself may alter the reality that they try to define.

The problem is made worse because even the cruder doctrines do not completely distort reality, or portray an entirely phoney world. If they did, nobody would be taken in by them. Rather, they provide an incomplete or biased representation. Yet even the most professional reports of this sort are less reliable than accounts produced by observers whose guiding principle is objectivity: they are less *penetrative* as views of reality. Sometimes they may be sufficiently distorted as to lead to absurd actions on the part of those managers who have let themselves be fooled by them. The same can be said of intervention by people holding workerist doctrines.

Doctrines and legitimating beliefs are crafted to serve the interests of a group. In that sense they have relevance, but it is a restricted and compromised relevance. They are not relevant to the needs of other groups. Objectively formed frameworks of interpretation are intended to be generally relevant, to serve human interests as a whole. Whether they have succeeded already in serving such a general interest, or could do so one day, is one test for their superiority to doctrines and dogmas. Another, and perhaps more important one, is what intention is held by the people who put them forward, as well as the readiness of those people to encourage others to check their conclusions through rigorous tests of verification. Only when they fulfil these conditions do they become scientifically valid knowledge.

Many academic social scientists see their task as the larger one of explaining social development by studying it in the context of industry. They reject 'service of employer power' partly on the grounds that it is intellectually limiting and partly because it is partisan. They may also question their own ability to act as interventionists. They may hope that their work has some practical results, for example by affecting wider political and social debate, rather than through immediate changes in workplaces. But their main ideal remains scientific advance itself.

Is this naïve? We have been often told in recent years that there may exist no absolutely pure and objective scientific knowledge, even in 'hard' sciences like physics, let alone in social inquiry. These claims have to be taken seriously as a philosophical position. But, while we cannot be sure that there is any absolutely pure and true knowledge, it is obvious that some interpretations of the world – whether the physical or social world – are, or seem to be, more convincing and useful. They are penetrating and relevant.

There are several standard methods for testing the penetrativeness of an interpretation – logical coherence, scope, intuitive plausability, and so forth. (Numerous examples of these procedures will be discussed and illustrated in the main text.) Relevance, however, presents a different and somewhat thornier problem. It will be taken up again in the concluding chapter, in the light of the overall exposition.

Just a few remarks about the overall form of the main treatment are necessary here. Firstly, it is not intended to provide a full history of theories in industrial sociology, though the first edition of the book was often used by colleagues and students as such. Many interesting writers have not been examined. This is especially so for the more recent period, in which an explosion of new ideas and inquiries has occurred. I have tried to concentrate on theories that have been instructive and exemplary, and not simply influential.

Secondly, because the treatment is interpretative I have arranged the material to sharpen the interpretation. The resulting division into six broad groups of work, each of which is situated in historical time, should not be regarded as a rigid one. I try to make it clear that while some theories lose their appeal, or some of their respectability, they often survive in a modified form, or partly recur in the guise of quite different types of approach. Recent years provide many examples of people rediscovering the wheel, calling it by a different name, and, in all sincerity, filing a claim to patent rights on it.

But, it is none the less striking how the development of capitalist industrialism leads to a periodic change in the dominant *problematic* – that is, in the issues of fact and theory around which the most vigorous research and argument are centred.

Because it is a socio-economic *system*, the order under which we live gives rise to some patterns of action in the real world whose form changes slowly or even seems to remain more or less constant. Yet this system also evolves over time. Its physical fabric, its institutions, and the values and outlooks of the employed population within every industrial country, are affected by a process of change that sometimes seems slow but by historical standards is rapid. Intellectual life does not follow this change in any mechanical way, but a shift in the dominant *problematic* never occurs without some earlier or predisposing change in the real economic world.

There may exist no pattern, no inner logic to such developments. If there is one, we may never be able to grasp it fully or to predict its outcome. Currently, there is a tendency to exclude such possibilities, but the fashionable thinkers who hold these beliefs state the grounds for doing so dogmatically. In this respect they resemble closely the unfashionable visionaries who once claimed, just as confidently, to be able to predict the future of capitalism and industrialism.

The account begins with the attempt of an engineer, F. W. Taylor, to analyse work systematically, or, as he claimed, scientifically. Taylor also sought to redesign work, altering the worker's experience of being managed, and the manager's idea of his role as a controller. This Scientific Management approach to work provoked a strong reaction. Condemnation of it has continued to the present day. To understand it, however, these understandable feelings have to be kept firmly in check.

PART I

THE GREEDY ROBOT

2

Rational Workmen, Incompetent Managers

It may seem unusual to begin a historical review of theories of work behaviour by examining the contribution of Frederick Winslow Taylor (1856–1915), a former craftsman who qualified as an engineer by going to night school. But a life that includes experience of the shop floor makes whoever has it worth listening to on the subject of workers' behaviour. One of the best-known commentators on Taylor, the late Harry Braverman, was a former craftsman, and his own racy critique of scientific management – the system of ideas based on Taylor's work – set out in his book *Labor and Monopoly Capital*[1] undoubtedly gained added credibility because Braverman could play his own ex-craftsman card.

A problem that arises in talking about Taylor is that whatever aspect of his thought we focus on here is liable to sidetrack us into some of the longest-running and most heated controversies in this area of social science, and there is the obstacle of Taylor the man. Taylor was a notorious neurotic – many would not hesitate to write crank; and there is even a case for upgrading the diagnosis to maniac. Wherever he appeared, 'Speedy' Taylor was liable to set people smirking behind his back and telling the story of how he invented an outsize tennis racquet to make the game more efficient – to repeat, more *efficient*, not more fun – or how he had solemnly studied the work effort of cart-horses with the aid of a scientific chronometer.

Yet behind these anecdotes was a grimmer reality. While Frederick Winslow Taylor was running his stop-watch on cart-horses to find out 'just what they would endure', his imitators were doing much the same with men. Even if Taylor's own record as a slave-driver has been wildly exaggerated, there is no doubt that others used his methods to brutal effect. Getting past this image, which mixes the ludicrous with the sinister, is in some ways the most daunting problem of all. Without trying to ignore the man completely – impossible in any case with a character like his – we must scrutinize his ideas as calmly as possible. Most difficult of all, when we find in his legacy, among so much that is shallow, unhinged or repulsive, the occasional insight that is worth preserving, we should not be afraid to look at it. We also need to bear in mind, very carefully in Taylor's case, that there is indeed a certain 'cunning of history' that can subvert the intentions of human actors over the long term, provoking creative reactions against their originally destructive – or degrading – deeds.[2] Let us forget, at least for now, Taylor the madman, waking sweating from a nightmare just before dawn every day of his life; Taylor the craven agent of Capital, plotting the liquidation of the trade unions; and Taylor the crazy engineer, splitting the conception of work from its execution to degrade the craftsman. All these Taylors can be brought to life. A different interpretation is possible.

Since Western science and technology began their spectacular advance 300 years ago, there has existed a way of looking at economic life often termed *technocratic* or *productivist*. Its key feature is the belief that the thorniest problems of our material existence – how to produce, with less effort and less waste, enough of what we need, and more of what we want but do not need – should be capable of rational solution through discovery and application of scientific principles. If the engineer can apply the theories of physics to build bigger bridges, to invent more effective gearing systems, or to harness energy in engines, he should be able to provide better practical solutions for a series of problems which are, in essence, merely those of running a household writ large.

Every political tendency has had its productivist supporters, though many productivists tend to prefer absolutist monarchy, military dictatorship, or modern totalitarianism (State socialist or Fascist) because such regimes can impose a plan on the economy, direct labour, and overawe employers. However, the true productivist is a Utopian who dreams of an entirely new political order, where power will rest not on the force of the State but on the force of productivity.

No productivist has ever stated this better than the now forgotten Charles A. Ferguson when he exclaimed: 'There is no legitimate power but the power to deliver goods.'[3] Ferguson saw in syndicalism – mobilized union power – the political means to reach the productivist Utopia. But like his celebrated contemporary the economist Thorstein Veblen – who compared capitalists who gave showy dinner parties with Red Indian chiefs who burned down their wigwams to impress the tribe – Ferguson looked to engineers to create a new society. Technical knowledge was, they believed, free of all social preconceptions, moral prejudices, or social codes, accessible to all who had the intelligence or will to acquire it. It alone could supply the moral frame of a new culture. It was logical that technical experts – an élite by their achievement, but not élitists since they believed in promotion strictly on merit – should govern the new order: only they could do so without being corrupted by greed or distracted by passion.

The ideal-type productivist in our century has advocated technocracy, then. Those who have held this ideology – I use the term here to mean no more than a group of ideas – have done so sincerely, which may have been naïve of them. The value-freedom and political neutrality of technocracy may turn out to be a mirage, but it is wrong to jump to the conclusion that it is a calculated fraud, that all technocrats have been power freaks on the lookout for a short cut to the top, or capitalist stooges, or simply nasties ready to live by deceit.

Taylor provoked the systematic study of industrial behaviour. Scientific management, as a collection of work-design and control techniques, influenced decisively the problems on which work-behaviour professionals were to focus most attention for thirty years after his death. Even today, there is constant debate with Taylor's ghost – or rather remonstration with it – over his methods and the movement he started.

In some ways, this obsession is hard to understand. As a technology of work-design and control, the integral version of Taylor's system failed comprehensively: it was adopted in a few dozen plants at the most. Even partial versions of it made nothing like the inroads casual observers of Taylorism assume. In France, *le taylorisme* is mistakenly equated with any system of sub-divided work, and the habit has been picked up by some English-speakers, but if we let this solecism pass we still find that fragmented work has always met worker opposition, destroyed the motivation of the best workers, and in the recent past been massively challenged to great effect.[4] In all these senses, Taylorism failed.

Yet Taylorism reinforced the prejudices of many production engineers about the right philosophy for designing tasks and rapidly acquired some respectability as a broad managerialist doctrine. How far it did so is difficult to assess, but experience of the type of managerial devices that Taylorism helped encourage, in particular work-measurement and job-fragmentation, and equally, experience of the bossy technician mentality possessed by some production engineers, affected the way large sections of the working class experienced work and their behaviour in it. Taylorism helped produce a change in industrial culture. In this sense, it is important historically.

Its uneven penetration can be partly explained by the limitations of the theory of behaviour it embraces. At the core of any theory of industrial behaviour lies an image of the typical worker. Formal students of industrial behaviour spell this out systematically, and relate it logically to conceptions of management–worker relations and of the enterprise as a social organization. These propositions, ideally, should be linked to explicit assumptions about the total form of socio-economic relations. How far this is done varies enormously. Taylor never systematized the behavioural assumptions in his work, but they can be easily inferred from contrasting his diagnosis of the core problems of American industry at the close of the nineteenth century with his prescriptions for curing them.

Taylor's diagnosis has a monotonously productivist single theme: inefficiency. For him, the waste of resources, especially the waste of time, was morally appalling. Inefficiency stemmed from both labour and management: On the workers' side, the principal vice was 'slacking' and 'soldiering'; on the manager's side, the complementary evil was incompetence. The words vice and evil are appropriate because Taylor looked on idleness from the standpoint of a Puritan workaholic. At the same time, he perceived that slacking sprang in part from the way groups defined their interests: behind his scoutmaster's language there lurks an informal sociological explanation.

Take soldiering. It has two forms: 'First, from the natural instinct and tendency of men to take it easy, which may be called natural soldiering. Second, from more intricate second thought and reasoning caused by their relations with other men, which may be called systematic soldiering.'[5] Taylor regarded this second form, the group control of output, as the more important kind, not because it shows any inherent group instinct towards sociability or solidarity, but because it 'results from careful study on the part of the workmen of what will promote their best interests'.[6] It was a rational strategy – but it is rational thanks only to managerial incompetence.

Lacking objective information about methods used by workers and the time required to perform industrial tasks, managers resorted to guesswork in allocating tasks or standard times for performing them. When this resulted in easy jobs, managers would arbitrarily alter the times – if workers were so foolish as to complete their tasks too quickly. To give him his due, Taylor declared that the workers could scarcely be blamed if they colluded to ensure the maximum economic returns all round without having to exhaust themselves.

Taylor next asked himself why American factory managers were incompetent in the first place. Firstly, he reasoned, the growth in the scale and technical complexity of industry had outmoded traditional control methods. Worse, the traditional entrepreneur was becoming displaced by a new sort of boss, men 'spiritually aloof from the mass', financiers on one side, careerist managers on the other. Taylor revered the captains of earlier nineteenth-century American industry. As his biographer Copley puts it, these folksy pioneers 'jollied their men and joked with them; bawled them out and beat them up in man-to-man fashion; dealt with them, no matter how roughly or savagely, on a plane of simple human relations, of perfect social equality'.[7] In physical terms, Taylor was unimposing. He longed to be a muscular six footer like William Sellers, his boss at the Midvale Company, instilling a 'fearful' loyalty by his mere physical presence, and not afraid to 'joke with the apprentice boy one minute and giving him a spanking the next'. But these halcyon days, when indiscipline or idleness could be settled promptly by manly fisticuffs in the yard, were passing.

Copley probably went over the top in this passage: he often did. What he is trying to say is none the less valid and important. Taylor saw that control of work operations was passing to men lacking a legitimate basis for their authority. His prescriptions for curbing inefficiency therefore called for a trained and competent management equally subject to the 'rule of law' it must impose on workers. The tones in which he promulgated this doctrine make clear the scorn Taylor had for most of the managers with whom his work as an engineering consultant and efficiency expert had brought him into contact. At times, he sounds almost hysterical. Managers are portrayed as ignorant, arbitrary, selfish, and blind to their own real interests. Compared to that of workers, their behaviour is irrational. Late in life he asserted that 'nine-tenths' of the opposition to his system had stemmed from managers resentful of the new obligations it loaded on them. (He meant his system in its *full* version, of course, not just the time-study methods and incentive schemes in it that caught managers' attention.) It could be that this declaration was a public-relations sop to his critics in the labour movement. I doubt it.

Taylor's technical proposals, his system, put forward devices aimed at reinforcing workers' rationality and suppressing what he took to be the irrationality of managers. By eradicating inefficiency and arbitrary managerial prerogatives it would abolish the workers' rebellious response to the experience of being controlled. Eventually, it would create a close industrial partnership – what Alan Fox, in a ringing condemnation of scientific management practice, has called a 'trust relationship'.[8] But why should either managers or workers accept it? Who would form the vanguard that could implant it? Taylor's replies to these questions were exactly those to be expected from a productivist and technocrat. The two parties would accept the system because it was *scientific*: impartial, universal, *lawlike* in the sense both of an act on the statute book and of an axiom of physics. Only an equally impartial and scientific group of agents – a new class of production engineers – could develop the competence, and therefore the authority, to lead to Taylor's technological Utopia.

These answers testify to the strength of the Victorian faith in science as the intellectual register of human progress and to the sudden emergence of engineering as a profession indispensable to technically advanced industry. All engineers knew that their market value reflected the indispensability of science-based expertise as manufacturing technology grew more complex and many products more sophisticated. A few already vaguely sensed that the engineer's interests were not indissolubly linked to the existing form of industrial ownership: capitalism was preferable only in so far as it was the most technically progressive system. It took several decades for capitalism to prove itself on this score.

Taylor's technical prescriptions form a logically consistent package and can be divided into three broad classes.[9] The first group comprises recommendations about organizational structure and routine, which can be dealt with summarily here. The best-known but most curious ones relate to 'functional foremanship', which would make the worker responsible to four first-line supervisors simultaneously – the 'gang', 'speed' and 'repair' bosses, and an inspector. Craig Littler points out that this suggestion becomes comprehensible when we remember that foremen were often semi-independent labour contractors until 1900: Taylor regarded it as vital to break their power.[10] Attempts to apply functional foremanship usually have been unsuccessful because the gains from supervisory specialization are offset by role conflicts and ambiguities of jurisdiction, though Littler provides interesting examples from countries other than the USA.[11]

Taylor also called for a powerful planning or 'thinking' department to collect information on tasks, oversee the routing of materials and sub-assemblies in the factory and the preparation of job-order tickets for operatives, besides taking care of pay calculation, engagements and discipline. This call for a 'thinking department' graphically illustrates the aim that writers like Braverman place at the centre of Taylor's thought, namely the *separation of conception and execution.*[12] It represents a demand for the extension of industrial 'bureaucracy' in the sense of systematic administration, and is a sign that the scale and complexity of operations were outstripping traditional administrative technique. Equally important, it signals the systematization of the employment relationship.

The second set of proposals, calling for the thoroughgoing study and redesign of all tasks, was profoundly influential. Taylor aimed to discover an optimal relationship between the methods adopted, the time taken, the tools used, and the fatigue generated by any task.

The procedures he invented are best described as no more than a pioneering contribution, which took the following broad form: pick 'ten to fifteen' men already skilled in the work whose 'science' is to be discovered; observe them at work and define the elements of the sequence of operations they employ; time each element, for each individual, with a stop-watch; identify the operations that seem to contribute nothing towards the completion of the task and eliminate them; select the quickest methods discovered for each element and fit them into sequence, forbidding any deviation or the introduction of unnecessary operations; add up the times for each element, and include an allowance for resting. The result will be the 'quickest and best' method for the task. Because it is the 'best way', all workers selected to perform the task must adopt it and meet the time allowed.[13]

Further studies determined the length and spacing of rest-pauses, and the design of new tools. In his studies at the Bethlehem Steel Company, Taylor discovered an optimum load in shovelling. Since the materials to be shovelled varied in their density, an entirely new range of shovels and forks was fabricated to ensure that exactly this weight of material was always lifted. Taylor's critics immediately objected that he viewed rest-pauses merely as a way of postponing physical collapse until the end of the shift. He retorted that he ensured that workers were allocated adequate rest, and demanded that men took a break when they were told to do so, while some foremen would drive men to exhaustion early in the day. But he explicitly stated that 'ordinary workmen' were happier in their minds if they went home exhausted, as he was himself.

The final set of prescriptions, for labour selection and motivation, is encapsulated in two formulae. First, a given task should be performed by a 'first-class' man' for that type of work. Second, 'first-class' men should be given a 'fair day's pay for a fair day's work'. A 'first-class' man is both born and made. Taylor never systematized his selection techniques completely, except for pig-iron handling, where they are clear: 'Now one of the first requirements of a man who is fit to handle pig-iron as a regular occupation is that he shall be so stupid and phlegmatic that he more nearly resembles in his mental make-up the ox than any other type.'[14] This specification is often cited as an example of Taylor's low opinion of all manual workers. This is unjust, but he was extremely foolish not to make it clearer that higher abilities would be demanded in tasks like machining. Again, what matters here is not the crudity of the technique, which is obvious, but that he recommended systematic matching of tasks and abilities.[15]

Training a first-class man involved drilling into him a perfect grasp of the routinized movements of a given task. Managers were enjoined to put large resources into this effort. Refresher courses should be provided to eradicate vetoed methods that crept back in, and it was imperative to convince the worker that he could not know better than the scientific manager how a job should be done. As Taylor saw it, many workers should be grateful to be relieved of the responsibility for choosing his methods. He is reported to have told workers that they were not supposed to think, since other people were paid to do that for them. They would earn more if they could switch off their minds.

A 'fair day's work', Taylor insisted, must be laid down by production engineers after work-study. He seems genuinely to have believed this would make it a matter not of opinion but science. A 'fair day's pay' is more elusive, Taylor conceded, but it should be set substantially higher than the going rate for similar kinds of work in the locality. The level of reward should be tied closely to output through the mechanism of the differential piece-rate system. Under this system, a worker who failed to produce a 'fair day's work' should suffer a disproportionate loss of earnings, but if he exceeded the target, he would receive a bonus so adjusted as to reach a ceiling between 30 per cent and 100 per cent above standard earnings. Taylor stated that a ceiling benefited the worker, since if men 'got rich too quick' dissipation, drunkenness and absenteeism would increase.

This was certainly the view of an arrogant Puritan, but it also shows that although Taylor's conception of worker motivation was essentially 'economistic', he did recognize the possibility that workers might be subject to other motivations – such as the hedonistic use of leisure. Moreover, since the ceiling for bonus payments was to vary with different kinds of task, and therefore with different kinds of worker, Taylor seems to have had an instinctive awareness that the labour force was segmented not only in terms of aptitudes for tasks but also in terms of socially and culturally determined aims and expectations.

It hardly needs stressing how woefully flawed are all these ideas. The whole notion of the 'quickest and best way' is wrong, and so is the means for deciding it. A study of operatives who are already able to do the task rapidly – in statistical terms, a purposive sample – cannot guarantee discovery of ways of doing it most effectively. A sample should include people who do the task slowly although they have effective methods. Only a random sample can do this. When a task is redesigned along these lines and imposed on a whole workforce some workers will inevitably be outpaced. Taylor thought such displaced workers could become 'best men' at some other task. In the real world there was, and is, no certainty that this would happen.

There is a more fundamental objection to the procedure. The 'best' way is a compilation of the movements of several workers. It thus ignores the psychology of individual differences, which will be discussed in Part II. A particular movement may be rapid and economical for one person, within the context of his or her total set of methods for performing the task, but there is no guarantee that it will be so for others, or even for the original subject when they are forced to fit it between the other movements foisted on them from the total technical repertoires of other workpeople. Likewise, the removal of 'wasteful' movements can be self-frustrating. Many such movements, although 'useless' when viewed in isolation, are in fact essential to the rhythm of an overall efficient working motion.

True, the psychology of individual differences was only very poorly developed at the time Taylor was devising his system. He undoubtedly made genuine discoveries about the efficient performance of certain tasks, but these were simple labouring operations in which the psyche is not importantly engaged. When one turns to more complex tasks, such as machining, where dexterity and attention are important, the crudity of Taylorian work-study is evident. And there is little doubt about the source of Taylor's fallacies here. Despite his informal recognition of social and psychological factors, he ultimately saw the worker from an engineer's standpoint; that is, as a machine.

How can a 'fair day's pay' be determined scientifically in a market economy? It is a contradiction in terms. Taylor's reasoning seems to have been that a production engineer who studies the capacities of men and machines in a systematic, quantifying way, with a view merely to increasing productivity not profit, is being scientific, and that since science is impartial and objective, when the 'scientific manager' decides on a price for a job this sum must somehow be objectively right. This is a technocrat's wishful thinking. The very use of the term 'fair' introduces notions of social equity. Taylor's introduction of science into his argument was simplistic. Fairness in payment clearly demands some social reference point. But whose reference point should that be? No science can provide an answer to such a question, certainly not in a market economy.

Unlike some of his close followers, Taylor was unable to think beyond such an economy. He adopted, virtually undiluted, the postulates of individual rationalism, hedonism and atomism of Victorian economics. The worker was primarily instrumental in his approach to work. Social rewards in work were of no account beside the wage packet. Yet he was clearly uneasy about the social emptiness of the wages bargain, which is why in describing his system he invoked a future when a genuine partnership would link the worker to the scientific manager in 'willing, hearty collaboration'. Scientific management, then, was also to be an exercise in social engineering, one of its objectives being – just how important to Taylor it was we shall never know – to remove the gulf between management and worker, replacing it with harmony and fellowship. If conflict was to persist, it would divide workers and scientific managers on one side and the financial controllers of industry and the 'outmoded' trade unions on the other. Mainly implicit in Taylor's writings, a possible division of interest between owners and their employees was stressed by some of Taylor's explicitly 'technocratic' followers.[16] Here, the social doctrine behind the system departed from orthodox capitalist ideology. It did so in a second way: in his conviction that practically everyone could excel at some task, given sufficient training and the proper design of work, Taylor repudiated the 'Social Darwinism' popular with American business leaders of the time. This ideology had raised the labour market to the status of a sacred vehicle of collective evolution, by portraying the failures it weeded out, the poor and the unemployed, as the human tribute society must pay to Progress. Taylor's faith in selection and training constituted an oblique attack on the labour market as a natural, and naturally selective, phenomenon with which only rogues or fools would tamper.

In appraising the prospects for the adoption of his system, Taylor concluded it would require a revolution, and to bring about this revolution, the consciousness of the masses must be transformed by a dedicated élite. Yet the last thing that Taylor had in mind was a political revolution: instead, he heralded a process he termed, with uncustomary grandiloquence, the Great Mental Revolution. This was to be signalled by workers and managers abandoning their squabbles over the division of the product of the factory and agreeing to collaborate on boosting its size. Dynamic energies straining at the leash of tradition and mistrust would be released by this shift of mentality. This is pure productivism.

Taylor believed that scientific management – he rejected the term 'Taylor System' on the grounds that he was merely the medium through which abstract laws of production and progress were entering human awareness – could produce such a shift. Fired with a sense of mission he set out to propagate his good news among production engineers. We can further define the Taylorite view of work behaviour by reviewing the story of this effort.

3

Taylor, the Tory Radical Technocrat

The story of Taylor's career cannot explain either his view of the industrial worker, the content of his system or the course of the scientific management movement, but certain incidents throw light on them, and bring out features of American industry and society that shaped his thinking. Taylor's world-view, stripped of idiosyncrasies, was shared by important groups in early twentieth-century America. As Maier has shown, his productivist vision was widely admired for its 'progressive' strand by Europeans as different as Lenin and Mussolini.[1] It is discredited today because of our distrust for all technocrats but could well revive if economic trouble continues.

Taylor's life story illustrates a constant problem with technocratic thought – its persistent oversight of the social context in which it subsists. It claims its own impartiality to any social grouping or political philosophy with particular stridency. It purports to be undoctrinaire, although it is an ideology at least in the sense that it is a viewpoint shared by a given social group, which naïve misconception renders Taylorism doctrinaire. And it can be readily put to use by dominant groups of whatever society to which its adherents belong. Because he believed his ideas were inherently neutral, Taylor never paid due attention to defining his own political beliefs, with the result that he appeared politically devious when he was not appearing politically simple-minded.

Copley, Taylor's biographer, characterized him as a 'Tory radical'. At first, this seems odd: the very notion of Toryism – at least, in its exact sense of romantic conservatism rather than its recent one of greengrocer economics – is foreign to the American context.

I think Copley was trying to pin down one important aspect of Taylor's overall mission. American society, as Taylor saw it – not entirely wrongly – was taking a course that undermined the East Coast Puritan virtues, particularly that of hard work. Taylor's family pedigree was 100 per cent Yankee: he had enjoyed a comfortable upper-middle-class Quaker upbringing in the then elegant Philadelphia. How could he fail to be marked by such a background? But it is too simple to see this as more than one source of his strange energy. The experiences that preceded his system-building better explain the overall features of his thought.

Taylor had to devise a novel managing system at the Midvale Steel Company in the early 1880s. He stamped out 'soldiering' by sacking, blacklisting and victimizing. (The bitterness of this 'mean and contemptible' struggle stayed with him all his life, like the delusion of having committed unpunished murder. It brought him close to nervous collapse at the time and intensified his nightmares.) The men's output doubled and Taylor began to work out a way to achieve such a result more smoothly next time he needed to try.

Originally, Taylor had been set to follow his father in a law career, but instead of going to Harvard he took up apprenticeships in pattern-making and machining. In 1878 he joined the Midvale Steel Company – one of whose owners was a close family friend – as a labourer, refusing to take an office job, and went on to become a pattern-maker and machinist. He soon became a 'gang boss' or foreman, and for three years waged his war to double output. Since he had soldiered before his promotion he knew every variant of prevarication or obstructionism workers could utilize to block his pressure. He also knew which dirty tricks can break down such opposition: so he cut piece rates; he sacked 'slackers', even men he had worked alongside; he brought in blackleg labour. He had warned the men he would stop at nothing and he kept his promise.

Taylor reasoned that such managerial thuggery was wasteful in the short-term, and probably ultimately counter-productive. The arbitrary powers of management, especially to cut piece-rates, were one of the causes of output restriction. If managers knew the true capacities of men and machines, fair piece-rates could be established in the first instance. But they did not. Setting a rate depended on guesswork and bluffing, and workers and managers were equal victims of ignorance. If working capacities, both human and mechanical, could be determined accurately, and production planned and administered rationally, wages could be raised and managerial autocracy thrown on the scrap-heap. Science would replace rule of thumb and industrial authority relations be recast in a mould of legitimacy.

But where and how should he begin? How could he test his hunches? How could he shape them into a proper theory? How could he demonstrate its validity? At this point, Taylor organized what was to become for dedicated technocrats the equivalent of a productivist miracle. He had started a series of experiments with metal-cutting machines, to increase their precision, reliability, and speed. These experiments were to continue for about twenty years, but soon yielded astonishing findings – for example that some steels could be cut 100 times faster than others. C. G. Barth, a mathematician whom Taylor recruited as a research officer, invented a slide rule which any semi-skilled worker could quickly master, enabling him to set and run his machine almost faultlessly for any metal-cutting job.

Shop order cards drawn up by a special department listed precisely what jobs the worker had to do in a shift. On completing the task, the worker returned the card to the office. Managers complained about the growth of red tape and increased clerical costs. But this 'industrial bureaucracy' easily paid for itself, as planners could compute average times and costs for any job. Taylor published his results in 1886, reading his short paper to a conference of the American Society of Mechanical Engineers (ASME).[2] This body had been founded in 1880, and rapidly grew large and influential, reflecting the explosive industrialization of the USA after the Civil War and the increasing technical intricacy of the manufacturing process. Industrial engineers were eager to assert their identity and extend their jurisdiction over new management areas, even accountancy. A paper entitled 'The Engineer as Economist', advocating the involvement of engineers in work-costing and accountancy, interested the meeting even more than his own.[3]

Numerous engineers put forward their pet management schemes in these years, all of which called for payment by results. In 1895, Taylor, as chief engineer at Midvale, and famous professionally for his machining experiments, finalized his own package. He too insisted on payment by results, in the 'differential piece-rate' formula described in the previous chapter, which discriminated against slow work, but this was to be linked with all his other organizational and scientific managerial innovations. He never stopped repeating that the package had to be implemented whole if it was to work. Expect trouble if you break this rule, he warned his admirers.

That it could work in practice still had to be proved. Taylor got what seemed at first a perfect setting to do this when in 1898 he was appointed as a management consultant in the Bethlehem Steel Company. In his contract he insisted on sweeping powers. The directors of the company never expected him to try to exercise them. They were very much mistaken: they had given a prophet a pulpit, and Taylor's belief in his methods – in their moral no less than their technical necessity – had become gratingly messianic. In one of his more extreme passages, Copley puts his finger on it:

> Let us consider what Taylor was contending for. Essentially it was this: that the government of the Bethlehem Steel Company cease to be capricious, arbitrary and despotic; that every man in the establishment, high and low, submit himself to law. A far cry down the centuries since the days of Latimer and Melville and their demand for one law for kings and scullions. A greatly different scene. Yet in Frederick Taylor, the descendant of those Puritans, the same old spirit flaming up anew; as bold as ever, and as stern, as uncompromising, and as imperious as ever.[4]

Tory radical – or technocratic prig? Taylor was to fight, and lose, a bitter campaign against his top-hatted, bespatted bosses – in photographs they look just like the archetypal capitalist swine of old anarchist tracts. The mere sight of these pot-bellied financiers was enough to send Taylor into a productivist tirade. For their part, they viewed Bethlehem Steel less as a testing ground for new administrative techniques than as a counter in a high-level money game of mergers and trust-building.

Unsuspectingly, Taylor had been hired as a publicity gimmick, on account of his reputation as a mechanical innovator. (He continued his experiments there, inventing a process that brought spectacular economies.) Two years later his dismissal was part of a secret deal for the sale of the firm. His proposals were constantly blocked or sabotaged and it is hard not to feel some sympathy for the unfortunate technocrat. He was experiencing capitalist employee relations at their crudest. Nothing could be further from the productivist ideal or the rule of law invoked by Copley. At Bethlehem Taylor was treated as contemptuously as any other employee of such a company. He responded similarly in many ways. He even staged his own one-man strike.

However, his methods of work-study and task-redesign were first implemented in this firm, with staggering results. It had been hard to determine a 'fair day's work' at Midvale owing to the preponderance and variety of machining tasks. At Bethlehem a large section of the workforce was occupied on heavy labouring tasks. Enter Schmidt, a stocky little Dutchman, who has become legendary for increasing his output fourfold. Before being trained by Taylor in the rationalized version of his job of loading large mouldings ('pigs'), Schmidt could load up to twelve tons a day. Afterwards, he could sometimes load fifty tons.

Schmidt was awarded a bonus that increased his pay by 50 per cent. Taylor claimed that Schmidt was delighted with his rise. The firm was inundated with applications for loading jobs, and Taylor seems never to have understood why other people thought Schmidt was letting himself be swindled. When rumour later spread that Schmidt had died early from overwork Taylor went to enormous trouble to have him traced, alive and well. Seven out of eight of Schmidt's fellow loaders, however, were unable to reach the new level of output and although Taylor redeployed them to other tasks in the yard, the local press carried forecasts that eventually three-quarters of the labour force would be thrown on the street. Though Copley writes up the sequel in heavily tragic tones, it has elements of low farce. On the one hand, Bethlehem's directors fret about the fate of the company's heavy investments in housing and stores around the plant if 'Speedy' Taylor goes on 'systematizing' its labour process. On the other, Taylor waves his contract under their noses, and arrives at important meetings an hour late in plus-fours swinging a golf club (he invented a two-shafted putter) and chattering breezily about his handicap. Experiments with new techniques of shovelling and new designs of shovels and forks proceeded, but in early 1901 Taylor was dismissed, announced his retirement from 'money-making', and spent the rest of his life propagating and defending his management system.

It is ironic that he had never actually installed scientific management as a system at Bethlehem Steel. His detestation for the practices of finance capitalism grew deeper, although this aversion never seems to have helped him understand why many labour leaders attacked his own work. And while railing against financial manipulators and rentiers Taylor himself was living off the proceeds of a share portfolio astutely purchased during the economic recession of the early 1890s.

Obsessing him was the memory of his successful 'systematization' of Schmidt. Henceforward he was obstinately convinced that the science of any work could be propounded and workmen motivated to follow it. Inside all workers was a Schmidt ready to make his pact with the technocratic apostle of productivism. Whenever someone objected that most workers were very unlike Schmidt, or that skilled work might defy systematization, Taylor treated them as a religious fanatic treats the ungodly. Sympathy with the refusal of skilled workers to trade their principal asset, their skill, to the scientific manager in return for a specialized task and an uncertain monetary gain was denounced by him as a deadly economic sin. Opposition to scientific management was to betray progress, a sell-out of unscientific managers and their allies the 'irrelevant' trade unions.

From 1903, when his *Shop Management* was published, Taylor became an increasingly public figure.[5] He was elected president of the ASME, and his monograph *On the Art of Cutting Metals* (why not *On the Science . . .* ?) crowned his fame as a mechanical engineer in 1905.[6] But he now led a growing number of disciples. His old protégé, Barth, began introducing the full version of the 'Taylor System': it was a science, he insisted, and therefore distinct from any individual – into the Link Belt and Tabor Manufacturing companies from 1903, and these firms became the showplaces of 'genuine' scientific management.

The qualifier 'genuine' is essential. As public fascination with efficiency grew, so did the corps of 'fakirs and charlatans' who claimed to be followers of the man whom even the public now called Speedy Taylor.[7] Some had read *Shop Management* and concluded that work-study alone could speed up production. Why bother with bonus payments? Certain consultants offered more elaborate systems, which Taylor endorsed with varying approbation. The two most important of these were the flamboyant self-publicist, F. B. Gilbreth, who went on to add motion-study to Taylorian time-study, and Harrington Emerson, founder of an Efficiency Society.

It is hard to disentangle orthodox scientific management from these other strands. The confusion was equally great at the time. Of course there was a radical element in Taylor's thought: the need to reform managerial authority, to base it on competence not on the power to hire and fire. But this idea had to be sold to employers who often owed their own authority to the laws of inheritance and not to any demonstrable productivist ability, or to managers who would not need the Taylor System anyway if they were already competent – Taylor began to soft-pedal this part of his message, which made it harder for third parties to distinguish Taylorism from its competitor systems. Yet, ironically, Taylorism was to succeed precisely as an ideology for engineers who saw themselves as part of a managerial revolution.

Taylor increasingly trained his fire on trade unionists, and particularly after a legal battle in 1910 (the Eastern Rate Case) which transformed him into a national figure and linked all efficiency systems together as scientific management. The Eastern Rate Case was fought to prove that certain railways could absorb a hefty wage claim through greater operating efficiency[8] and attracted enormous publicity. Following it, a deluge of popular expositions of scientific management flooded the press. Taylor's own *Principles of Scientific Management* (1911), with its bold assertions that management was a science based on natural laws, was treated as just another do-it-quicker manual.[9] The efficiency fever was turned against the unions, and two strikes in 1911 roused the gutter press to paroxysms of hatred for organized labour. The first of these was by bricklayers against Gilbreth's methods. The second involved federal munitions workers who set out to block a full-scale Taylorian rationalization exercise.

This Watertown Arsenal strike[10] forced Taylor to define his attitude towards unions and open a dialogue with them. His intellectual heirs were to continue this dialogue along lines that would have horrified him. He was constrained to abandon the claim that 'genuine' scientific management had never produced a strike – a statement that, though unfounded, had often appeared in his propaganda. Taylorism was suddenly a political hot potato and Congress ordered two public investigations of it. General Crozier, the Controller of Ordnance, had shown interest in Taylor's system as early as 1906, but dithered. Surely, he fussed, time-studies would lead to strikes? Why was it necessary to pay bonuses if the new methods reduced job-times? Taylor remonstrated: 'I can assure you that you will meet with absolutely no success if you leave out [the system's] most essential feature.'[11] But eventually, Crozier gave way. The strike (by moulders) was an almost immediate consequence.

A leading unionist, J. P. Frey, succeeded in promoting a call in the House of Representatives for an official investigation of the system. American labour had, in fact, been counter-attacking the efficiency craze for some time. Even Samuel Gompers, the father of business unionism, had strongly criticized the 'intellectuals' (work-study men) who were trying to 'mechanize' the worker. What did Taylor mean in asserting that the natural laws of management could operate only in an 'improved environment'? Did Taylor mean a union-free environment? Unions were free associations of workpeople. Did the Taylor programme require the suppression of the right to free association? Was this the sort of programme to be enacted in a country that prided itself on sheltering huddled masses yearning to be free? A practised politico could carve through Taylor's ideas like a knife through butter.

A special House Committee was called in early 1912 and Taylor was naturally a leading witness. He turned in an impressive performance, which produced almost 300 pages of evidence. (It is also extremely clever propaganda.) In tone it is vigorous and self-assured, and clotted with autobiographical references. Nearly all his substantive remarks about his system and its rationale were largely reiterations, sometimes almost word for word, of what he had written already. After repudiating the term 'Taylor System', he launched into a set-piece tirade against soldiering. It resulted from the denigration of labour by the literary classes, from a mistaken belief that the total sum of money available for distribution as wages was strictly limited. It is significant that Taylor savaged this Victorian myth, once again popular in our own time, of the wages fund theory of labour. He pointed out the massive historical evidence against it. Why he had never done so before is puzzling. It would have gone down better with the unions than his lectures to them on their obstruction to progress.

But output restriction like soldiering, Taylor thundered, resulted above all from the 'faulty system of management in general use'.[12] Managers horrified at the notion of high pay, even when it went along with high productivity, resorted to periodic rate-cutting, to remind the workers who was boss as much as anything. Only scientific management could create an atmosphere of trust in which management and workers would stop worrying about their own share of the pie, and even more about the slice the other side was given, and work together to make the pie bigger.

Meticulous study of the production process would reveal its laws. Was this not science? Workmen should be selected, trained and paid strictly in line with their ability to perform the new task-structures. Was this not science too? The principles of scientific management and workpeople had only to be brought together to solve, once and for all, the problem of production and the problem of social reconciliation. Taylor noted: 'It is unfortunate, however, that this word, "bringing" has a rather disagreeable sound, a rather forceful sound; and, in a way, when it is first heard, it puts one out of touch with what we have come to look on as the modern tendency.'[13]

It was at this point that Taylor made his famous claim that by far the greatest trouble should be expected from 'bringing' managers to accept their own submission to science; that he personally had suffered far more opposition from managers terrified by the prospect of being forced to submit to a set of rules, as well as having to devise them, rather than just go on swaggering around the workplace barking out orders and putting people down. It has always been hard to evaluate this claim. Most commentators assume he made these remarks in bad faith, or naïvely, or because he wanted to believe what he was saying although it might be untrue. Yet Taylor was never a liar. He had been brought up as a Quaker, seeing honesty as the best policy, and simplicity as a powerful weapon in argument. There was his experience at Bethlehem Steel. He was almost certainly telling the truth, as he saw it.

But he misjudged the feelings among members of the Committee. They insisted that rationalization was concerned merely with speeding up work, with discovering how fast it could rather than should be done. Taylor retorted that any work-study resulting in excessive demands simply was not scientific. Workers suffering overwork as a result, he commented recklessly, could always quit. Such wild shooting, and his insistence on the reality of a Mental Revolution, when the very fact of his being called up to testify marked its failure to materialize in practice, show Taylor's startling unfamiliarity with the world in which people he regarded as his tormentors were living, along with the vast majority of others.

The Committee reported in the spring of 1912 that scientific management offered valuable organizational suggestions but could give the production managers excessive power. Controversy abated, and further attempts were set in hand to introduce the full Taylor System, even in non-industrial fields, such as banking.

The underlying hostility of the unions remained. The last few years of Taylor's life were devoted to preventing the rapprochement with labour that many of his followers now believed was essential to ensure the acceptance of the system. A sign of this growing revisionism was the proposal of C. B. Thompson that unions should collaborate in the determination of a fair day's work and a fair day's pay. Thompson, a declared admirer of Taylor, remarked that it was Taylor's autocratic background that was responsible for his hostility to collective bargaining.[14]

Taylor's dealings with union leaders were devious and unhappy. In 1914, he agreed to meet the Wisconsin Federation of Labor. A representative of the state's federal employees read out anti-union passages from *Shop Management* and pictured the Taylorite as obsessed with speed and de-skilling. Taylor subsequently persuaded A. J. Portenar, a veteran leader of the International Typographical Union who had uttered mildly approving noises about the system, to visit fully Taylorized plants, probably hoping to groom him for a propagandist role. Suspecting as much, Portenar made haste after his tour to announce that what he had seen, and what he had read in *Shop Management*, 'depressed him terribly': the system degraded everyone concerned in its installation and working.

In 1914, Washington decided to establish a Commission on Industrial Relations, with terms of reference including the examination of efficiency systems and labour. It was to be chaired by R. F. Hoxie, Professor of Political Economy at Chicago, whose approach to industrial relations was consensual and pluralistic. This was not a good omen. Then R. G. Valentine, after much discussion among Taylor's admirers, was chosen to represent the scientific management viewpoint. Valentine regarded trade unionism as a natural expression of democracy. At a conference of the Society for the Promotion of the Science of Management in December 1914, when the commission had already commenced work, he insisted that system-building in industry must be a group action. Closed shops might be a valid way to further this, he suggested.

After surveying thirty-five plants which claimed to employ Taylorian methods between January and April 1915, Hoxie's commission put in a report stressing the lack of uniformity in the application of the system. The widest variations in practice were over methods of time-study and task-design – matters at the core of Taylorism. Though psychological and sociological awareness of Taylorism would appear to be an essential qualification for time-study work, they noted, few time-study experts possessed them and were habitually regarded as low-grade technicians.

It went on to affirm that craft knowledge was taken from the worker, and that the union's regulatory effect on managerial power was sharply reduced. As a result, new problems were created, which the Taylor System was unable to solve. Only four of the commission's nine members put their names to the full report but there was a general feeling that the Taylor System had been officially condemned. A cynic might say that this could only make it more attractive to Capital as an anti-union package. But there were no signs of such a response. Taylor was correct in saying that his system would always be cold-shouldered by most employers and managers, because they preferred to get on with what they saw as their job in the only way they knew how to do it. They were not interested in making the productivist revolution. They were interested above all in remaining the boss.

The Taylor System supplied no off-the-peg techniques for manipulating employees; to most managers, it seemed a strange compound of common sense and the burblings of a mad professor. Yet many of these managers began to absorb some of the social philosophy behind the techniques. They began to claim that they already qualified as the professional managers apostrophized by the half-broken but still visionary man who went to an early grave in 1915.

4

The Roots of Taylorism

My main purpose has been to characterize Taylorism as a mode of understanding industrial behaviour. Writers like David Montgomery have been updating the story of the industrial politics of Taylorism that Nadworny began in the 1950s.[1] Craig Littler has explored it in relation to such industrial practices as subcontracting – an area that deserves still more attention, I suspect, if we are fully to understand the hostility to Taylorism on the management side.[2] An excursion into the landscape in which Taylorism is situated can therefore be more summary than was once necessary.

Taylor's death and the Hoxie Report in 1915 were a watershed in the history of scientific management. In the next fifteen years, the revisionist Taylorites were able to come to a close understanding with the revisionist leaders of American labour. Taylor's obsessional psyche[3] is not irrelevant to a full explanation of the content of his system, it is true – and his abrasive personality certainly accounts for some of the hostility it aroused – but we shall continue to disregard these personal characteristics. In terms of his message, Taylor can be seen as a man of his times. Nobody would have paid him the slightest attention if the message had not reminded them – irrespective of whether it offered acceptable solutions – of pressing problems confronting economically powerful groups in turn-of-the-century America.[4]

I am not going to deny that it may be possible to interpret Taylorian science simply as a covert politics of justification that simultaneously provided a set of policies to deal effectively with specific topical problems; that it was taken up because the policies could serve the interests of influential groups yet could be readily presented to the less influential as being in the interests of one and all. However, I am suspicious of such accounts, because they are inherently mechanistic, with events neatly unfolding in response to a contemporary socio-economic situation, or the alleged 'needs' of the powerful.

What increasingly strikes me when I look at the history of our economic system is how often capitalists, or whoever is making the effective decisions, have missed opportunities to make the processes of exploitation more effective and to strengthen their authority by promoting the use of novel justificatory doctrines. In such a perspective, the problem with Taylorism becomes that of why it was not more widely applied. There were conditions in early twentieth-century America that provided uniquely fertile ground for a doctrine like Taylor's. Let us examine some.

The main fact, so elementary that one can easily ignore it, is that Taylor's life coincided with the emergence of the USA as an industrialized economy and a major industrial power – in competition with industrialized European powers, first for its own domestic market and then for international markets. Three facts that underline this transformation are, firstly, the fall from 53.5 per cent to 31.6 per cent between 1870 and 1910 of the proportion of the employed population in agricultural and other primary production;[5] secondly, the doubling of American exports in the ten years following the protectionist McKinley tariffs in 1890;[6] and thirdly, the acquisition of colonial territories and occupation of the Panama Canal zone after a deliberately engineered war against Spain at the turn of the century. In less than fifty years, an isolationist agrarian society transformed itself into an internationally aggressive, economically imperialist, industrial nation.

This pattern, similar, though on a more spectacular scale, to the experience of European powers such as Germany and Italy, obscures one difference that for a time delayed the appearance of certain social consequences of the change. This was the gradual completion of the settlement of the West. The disappearance of the Frontier was of more psychological than material importance, but none the less decisive. On the whole, probably few young men (or new immigrants) had ever had an inclination to 'go West' if urban work was available in the East. But the vision of liberation from the ardours of life in the growing industrial cities had been an important safety valve. After 1890, however, it became obvious to everyone that very little West remained to go to. This change is not altogether unconnected with the growth of American trade union membership by almost 500 per cent between 1897 and 1904.[7]

Immigration, in the view of historians like Gutman,[8] helped to postpone this development in two ways: firstly, the flow of new arrivals desperate for work sustained a buyer's market for labour (particularly unskilled labour); secondly, since each new ethnic wave tended to enter the labour force at the lowest levels, native Americans and earlier arrivals were given better jobs. This collective upward mobility helped to confirm social philosophies of personal opportunity, particularly for those who were somehow more 'American' in their attitudes, as those who had been citizens for a considerable time felt themselves to be and to some extent were.

But the growth of vast urban areas and the settlement of the West counteracted these divisive tendencies. So, too, did the very expansion of American industry, again in two ways: firstly, of course, it abated the buyer's power in the labour market; secondly, and rather more importantly, it stimulated the growth of individual organizations and industrial concentration – classic vertical and horizontal integration. The backyard workshop became a factory, and the family firm a public company. The trusts emerged. Workforces were now masses of labour power to be shaped or bullied into becoming human machines that worked. The harsh supervision adopted to solve this problem, the remoteness of the big bosses and their increasing preoccupation with financial manoeuvre and the mechanization and rationalization of work dramatized the separateness of capital and labour. These processes, necessarily simplified here, stimulated the growth of unionism. But the obedience of the labour force was not management's only control problem. Indeed, it could be viewed as an aspect of the more technical problem of co-ordinating the work process itself.

The growth of mechanization and mechanical complexity, coupled with the growth in the size of the typical factory, went hand in hand with the rise of the mechanical engineering profession. As the managing proprietor disappeared into the boardroom, the mechanical engineer naturally stepped into his place in the workshop. Accountants, the only other significant professional group in industry, could not adopt these directly co-ordinative functions for the obvious reason that they lacked technological knowledge. Significantly, however, they, too, were soon to be faced with comparable problems of co-ordination as white-collar workforces grew. When management began to assert its claims to professional identity it drew predominantly from these two occupations.

Here, then, are some of the key features of the industrial situation that any management science would have to cope with appealingly in speaking to those who needed techniques to boost production and a doctrine to subdue a workforce apparently on the verge of moral rebellion: the growth and concentration of industrial production; the intensification of problems of control; the growing power of labour; the withdrawal of the owner-manager; and the professional self-consciousness of engineers. As a solution to these problems, it would have to supply a technical answer to each one. Moreover, it would have to convince the main parties involved that there was something in it for them; and this appeal would be all the more successful if it could draw on popular intellectual wisdom. Taylorism offered all this and more. Notably, it offered optimism.

Nineteenth-century thought is not uniformly cheerful. Economics, the gloomy science, had recurrently injected stern reminders that if material advance could be sustained in the long run, then it must be at the expense of hard toil for the many. Yet again and again there recurs the notion that Progress, whether it means material or moral advance, is a natural tendency in the destiny of mankind. Progress, in this view, had been given a particularly powerful boost by the Industrial Revolution and the rise of science, yet they had merely accelerated a process that could be traced back to pre-history. In the third quarter of the century, however, a far more sombre perspective on Progress began to emerge.

Malthusian visions, of starvation and apocalyptic social breakdown through overpopulation, always lurked in the background. Individuals, of course, might win personal security or even make their fortunes, and it was morally desirable for everyone to set himself such goals but it was unrealistic to expect a general, rapid advance. Bodies such as trade unions which sought to secure this were spitting against the wind, selfishly demanding a greater share from a more or less fixed 'wages fund' at the expense of other sectors.

Darwinian evolutionary theory, transposed to the social level, powerfully reinforced these sinister provisos. The 'struggle for existence' and the 'survival of the fittest' were now utilized to underwrite the institutions of the high-capitalist economy. Powerful industrialists had demonstrated their fitness for survival by their success; many became adherents of the doctrine.[9] They were particularly eager to preserve the labour market: nothing must be allowed to meddle with this social manifestation of natural selection – that would be tampering with nature. Could trade unions be found in nature? No. Does that exemplary animal the beaver have trade unions? No. Do industrious insects like ants or bees have trade unions? Certainly not. Trade unions are a social invention which men have devised in their foolishness. They are a manifest barrier to Progress, as any ant or beaver could tell them. Later, it was pointed out that evolutionary theory allowed for the possibility that groups, not individuals, might be the best vehicles for survival.

One feature of Taylor's thought that has never been sufficiently noted is the break it insists on from Social Darwinism. Against the Malthusian spectre it offers guaranteed material advance. Instead of a struggle for survival it proposes an idyll of collaboration. Big business is not lauded in Taylor's writings, but condemned for its incompetence and waste. Legitimacy is not to be won simply by surviving better as an individual but by facilitating the survival and progress of the productive unit. Individual potentialities may be hidden from the individual, and must often be discovered, through *scientific* not natural selection, and sharpened by training. This is obviously a far more seductive doctrine than Social Darwinism. Would it not serve powerful interests still better, especially as it simultaneously offered solutions to technical needs for co-ordination?

And if he had been a conscious fabricator of social myths Taylor could hardly have done better than to insist that he was founding a science. This instantly appealed to the new middle men of industry, the engineers. More widely, we must remember we are talking about an age when many ordinary workmen took a close interest in scientific discovery and looked on it with a curiosity – and even an affection – that is almost impossible for us to imagine in an age terrified by misapplied science and disgusted by the chilling indifference of the traditional scientific mentality. For a large section of the population, science offered, in some vague way, an alternative to religious salvation, and certainly an alternative to miracles. Why should it not solve the problems of production and the problems of society?

But if Taylor had wished to appeal more strongly to the latter groups he should have tried to show that employers would not be able to implement his technical proposals simply to boost profits quickly. He never did this. When the question of profit arose, the egalitarian productivist Utopia suddenly dissolved into something oddly reminiscent of the status quo. Taylor – unlike some of his politically more astute successors – by no means deprecated the latter: he was fond of lecturing workers that a factory existed 'first, last and foremost' to make profits for its owners.

Of course, this leaves open the possibility, which Lenin hastened to point out to the Bolsheviks, that the owner of the plant might be the State or a worker collective. If Taylor had expanded on this theme it would have greatly reduced the appeal of his doctrine to the big capitalist proprietors. None seems to have been worried by the risk or to have carried out that other logically admissible extension of his doctrine, shifting its field of application from the level of the enterprise to that of the economy, thus pointing towards centralized planning and control, with its troubling choice between State capitalism and bureaucratic socialism. Taylor never risked scaring them off by evoking the potentiality for rationalization on the society-wide scale.

Altogether, then, Taylor's doctrine could offer American capitalism some novel solutions to emerging problems of control and justification. If functional need in fact determined the production of ideology and ensured its rapid uptake, Taylorism would have taken American business by storm. It is intriguing to note that an open alliance of scientific management with organized labour seemed a more realistic final outcome for about two decades.

Taylor's revisionist heir Richard G. Valentine established a plan of campaign for turning the Mental Revolution into a reality.[10] In late 1915, Valentine renewed a call for full union participation in rationalization schemes. His audience, the Taylor Society itself, still received his call cautiously. But the power of labour became evident the next year. A bill was presented in Congress to forbid time-studies in federal plants. Certain prominent Taylorians joined the National Association of Manufacturers in condemning this step. Nevertheless, the committee appointed by Congress to examine the bill was favourable towards it despite the opinion of most expert witnesses. In the lobbies, most senators and representatives tactfully abstained and it was passed.

The American Federation of Labour (AFL) had been encouraged by the Hoxie Report. The arrival of the Wilson Administration of 1917 produced a government sympathetic to collective bargaining. This became evident on American entry to the First World War: an Ordnance Department General Order decreed that war supplies should be purchased only from manufacturers who maintained working conditions that included opportunities for joint consultation. These and other acts heightened the public status of unionists, and prominent leaders were drawn into the war machine as propagandists.

The federal authorities also made wide use of Taylorians as management consultants during the war. This taste of power, and the explosive growth of union membership to 5 million by 1920, encouraged some Taylorians to anticipate an imminent new social order in which they would play a leading part. A short-lived propaganda movement, the New Machine, foretold the approaching collapse of American capitalism unless it could substitute *service* (a favourite term of Henry Ford I) for profit. Only the scientific manager could handle the problems of this transformation.[11]

The AFL was even beginning to demand government-sponsored research into methods of increasing productivity by limited rationalization. The developing accord was marked by the joint editorship of a Taylorian, M. L. Cooke, and Gompers of an issue of the prestigious review *The Annals* on 'Labour, Management and Productivity', which reiterated these themes.[12] Gompers began appearing as star guest speaker at management meetings, where he stressed the humanizing effects of union objections to scientific management, resulting in an acceptable and still effective set of measures. The climax to this phase of entente was the establishment of President Hoover's 'Waste in Industry' inquiry, sponsored by the management societies and backed by the unions.[13] Five of its six reports were prepared by Taylor's followers and showed that American industry was in many respects spectacularly inefficient, but that whereas only a quarter of the waste stemmed from labour, at least half was the responsibility of management.

However, while understanding between unions and Taylorians continued to flourish during the 1920s, labour was on the defensive. The employed made great use of a rising anti-Communist fervour among the American public by reviving what they termed an open shop campaign. Paradoxically, the Wilson Administration's sponsorship of joint consultation in the plant had paved the way for company unionism.[14] Company welfare schemes, aping the model developed by the Ford Company, removed certain grievances on which the unions could play. Such developments, aided first by the severe economic recession of 1920–21, and then by the rising prosperity of the following years, reduced total union membership by a third.

Despite these setbacks, the official union leadership seems by now to have become genuinely converted to the 'positive' elements in Taylorism. William Green, Gompers' successor as leader of the AFL, enthusiastically preached co-operation with management –

to apply the principles of scientific management, reduce waste and provide bigger pickings for all. American industry was gripped with co-operation fever.[15] On retiring from the presidency of the Taylor Society in 1928, Cooke reaffirmed his own approval of collective bargaining and even suggested that Taylorites should urge workers to unionize. And the writer of a Taylor Society publication of this time called on the unions to employ Taylorites in their research departments. In 1930, the *American Federationist* issued 'Labour's Principles of Scientific Management'. Nadworny comments that these differ little from Taylor's own except for the demand that unions should be recognized and consulted in rationalization schemes.[16]

The slump put an end to all this, but this account shows that the unions could be reconciled to a reformed Taylorism, at least at national level. Management never was. Why not? Some Taylorians invested a great effort to gain its acceptance among American employers but largely failed. Did they in fact fear that adoption of the system would have implied a severe dilution of their ownership rights? Such a possibility is hardly ever raised, let alone debated. Yet it should be. It is all too easy to read Taylorism as a straightforward campaign by managers, encouraged by the bosses, to get a firm grip on labour through the deliberate destruction of skill and the craft organization sustaining it. To the extent that it did permit such a strategy the campaign itself was far more restricted than most writers claim. And this obsession with the alleged degradation of labour – what a patronizing and defeatist term! – diverts attention from the productivist strands in the ideology.

But I am determined to avoid controversy on topics that are not central to the questions raised in an examination of cultural history as part of industrial politics. I have already digressed further into the origins and consequences of Taylorism than will be possible with any of the other approaches I shall consider. This is justified by its particular importance as a practical movement which left lasting traces in the consciousness of working people and managers. It has also been worthwhile to gain some understanding of how a doctrine is spread and utilized. Above all, we must beware of functionalist models of these processes, even when they are presented to us in a racy, radical-sounding language. As a workable managing system Taylorism was refuted by the opposition it generated. If somebody says otherwise, ask what they're using for evidence.

I have underlined the system's weaknesses, especially its evasions and logical inconsistencies, but I have treated it as worthy of a serious hearing as a blueprint for action and for the theory of behaviour it projects. It not easy to recompose the latter. Before leaving it, a recapitulation of what I think are its main assumptions about workers' behaviour would be useful, especially as these formed the reference point for the scientific attack on Taylorism that is still occurring as our appalling century draws to its close.

It has often been said that the most striking characteristic of Taylor's thought is its tendency to equate men with machines. This is brought out graphically in his method of work-study and his notion of the *quickest and best way* to do any task. There is no recognition of individual psychological differences, nor any reliable notion of fatigue. The properly trained first-class man is supposed to function as predictably as a piece of clockwork. Yes, the worker must be rested at appropriate moments; but the clock must be wound, batteries need recharging, and the motor must be serviced.

There is no problem in stretching the machine analogy to meet any objection – the speed at which a machine will run depends on the strength of the current, or the grade of the fuel poured into it. Similarly, the worker is made to work harder by appeals to his materialism. The higher the money incentive, the greater his response. Every other influence on his behaviour, social or psychological – the workgroup, a trade union, managerial autocracy or benevolence – is an unnatural interference that must be removed to allow optimal functioning.

It is a bizarre conception. Thus portrayed, Taylor's worker is a monstrosity: a greedy machine indifferent to its own pain and loneliness once given the opportunity to maim and isolate itself. I am reluctant to reiterate this verdict, although it has often been quoted, yet it can be readily documented in Taylor's own writings and public statements. But we are talking of a conception that he had never thought through carefully. Quite clearly, he had never found it necessary to do so. The greedy robot image partly reflects the state of knowledge of his time, and partly the oddly contoured mind that tormented Taylor day and night.

It is also, though, a recurrent feature of technocratic thinking, in which individuals are always subordinate to a grand design, and it was against the psychological emptiness of this mechanistic conception that critical fire was first to be directed. Later its sociological barrenness, and the crude economistic bias of the money-obsessed motivational assumptions, came under attack. The *human factor psychologists*, to whom we now turn, attempted to rectify the first set of misconceptions. In doing so, they almost replaced the greedy robot with an even odder beast.

PART II

HAPPY HUMANS RUN SMOOTHER

5

The Human Factor

Though the American public had instinctively recoiled from the Taylorite image of the worker, scientific rebuttal of its psychological assumptions was led by investigators in Britain, mainly psychologists, who are usually referred to by the name of a journal, *The Human Factor*, which they set up in the early 1920s.

The importance of British human factor industrial psychology has been underestimated. By substituting an image of the worker as a complex organism for Taylor's greedy robot, it opened the way to study of the less tangible influences on worker behaviour. In fact, some human factor investigators, as we shall discover, began to follow up such leads themselves. Human relations theory depended considerably on its achievements. Later still, theories that explained work behaviour as a response to technology took up numerous problems it had raised first.

Despite its historical importance (and considerable intrinsic interest as a scientific orientation) human factor psychology is neglected. To some extent this neglect is understandable: its literature is inaccessible – it must be admitted that much of it makes somewhat heavy reading. The typical human factor research monograph has something of the air of an unwanted museum piece, which makes it rather depressing simply to look at the faded cover of a vintage report from, say, the Industrial Fatigue Research Board (IFRB).

Fatigue, indeed, is quickly induced by the sight of the list of obscure dignitaries inside the cover, the closely argued text, the meticulously drawn graphs and the ample reference to instruments such as kata-thermometers, Edney sling hygrometers and vane anemometers. These first impressions soon change; and at the very least the faith of the writer in the virtues of empiricism arouses a certain admiration.

'Such non-significant results are to be expected in all biological experimentation, but particularly in the psychological sphere, where the overlapping of mental and physical qualities presents such baffling problems,' writes one of these dogged investigators in a discussion of his research methodology.[1] 'The negative results, however,' he adds, 'are of real value in future researches and save others from traversing the same ground again.' Moreover, such painstaking thoroughness, he maintains 'offers practically the only satisfactory way of dealing with some of our greatest social evils'.[2]

These remarks summarize much of the philosophy of the British human factor psychologists, and point to the political values some of them held. There were links with the Fabian Society, and thus with the 'open conspirators' who sought to initiate a 'gradualist' alteration of British society. The precondition of this was to make industry efficient, productive, and less damaging to the health of people who worked in it. There was a strong technocratic element in Fabianism. But the psychologists were far from being tunnel-visioned productivists, as we shall see.

Industrial psychology (of a kind) had emerged before the First World War in the USA and Europe, particularly Germany, and much work in this field continued in these countries during the 1920s. Why should British work at this period be singled out for special notice? In the first place, it was largely isolated from American developments, and this worked to its benefit. It was highly organized and the bulk of its effort was concentrated on the full exploration of a limited range of problems: by establishing the parameters of physical influences on work behaviour it permitted others (notably Mayo) to proceed to other types of problem and theory. Committed, initially, to one type of explanation, the issues raised by its own findings forced it to widen its horizons. And lastly, it supplied irrefutable evidence of the scientific crudity of Taylorism.

It would be incorrect to imply that the thinking of early British industrial psychologists was monolithically solid or was determined uniquely by its leader, the psychologist C. S. Myers. It retained remarkable coherence for a decade and Myers was its most vocal exponent. As founder and Director of the National Institute of Industrial Psychology (NIIP) and a member of the committee on the IFRB, his official influence spanned the two agencies through which by far the greater part of research and consultancy in industrial pyschology, and to a lesser extent, teaching were channelled. As publicist, fund-raiser and fixer he played the key role. For these reasons, as well as the convenience of not having constantly to write 'early British industrial pyschologists', I shall refer to this group as the 'Myersians' – provided it is understood that this term does not imply a 'school' in the sense of a master of a theory and his disciples.

The NIIP was founded in February 1921.[3] Myers, as a Cambridge teacher of psychology with an interest in applied fields, had been invited to give a short course of lectures at the Royal Institution in 1918, in which he advocated the establishment of centres of applied psychology in all major British industrial towns. This proposal caught the eye of the business community. It was well supported by several leading academic psychologists (this is one mark of Myers's wide contacts and personal charm – academics were generally suspicious of applications) and by certain big names in medical research and education. Psychology and biology were still intimately related and we shall return to some of the implications of this link later. Philanthropic Quaker firms were at the head of those promising support, but basic financial assistance was at first secured from the Carnegie and Rockefeller Trusts. Myers left his university post to run the organization.

The Institute grew rapidly in the 1920s. By the 1930s, it had a technical and research staff approaching fifty, had attracted up-and-coming psychologists such as Cyril Burt and Eric Farmer, and counted such scientific celebrities as Sherrington and Rutherford among its supporters. It had provided consultancy services for 250 firms. It was also rapidly becoming insolvent. In its fifth general report, its financially critical state was well advertised and potential benefactors were reminded, hardly with tact, that bequests would not be detrimental to their current incomes.[4]

It had been intended that the NIIP should support itself on its consultancy work; thus, its problems were dictated by the needs of clients. This resulted in a wide spread of interests and an under-investment in basic research. It was forced to live largely from hand to mouth, and many of its findings on behalf of clients could not be published. Its most consistent studies, in fact, deal with vocational selection and guidance, but a few other types of study were carried out, some in association with the IFRB. And Myers was to claim that the confidence of workers was soon secured because 'the National Institute has endeavoured to base its ideals on sound psychology rather than on the superficial analogy with a piece of engineering mechanism'.[5] He seems to have been eager at all times to drive home the sharp difference, as he saw it, between the model of the worker his colleagues were developing and the Taylorite version. Persuading the employer of the value of the work they did was, in consequence, sometimes more difficult: 'He may already have suffered at the hands of some efficiency expert who, after spending a few hours in the works, has written a verbose, relatively useless report and has charged a correspondingly high fee.'[6]

Pure research was conducted elsewhere. The IFRB was founded in 1918 as a direct successor to the Health of Munitions Workers Committee (HMWC) of 1915–17. It subsequently changed its title to Industrial Health Research Board (IHRB) in 1929; this change was related to changes in approach, but the choice of both the words 'Fatigue' and 'Health' reflect the sometimes contradictory influences with which its workers had to contend both within its directorate and among themselves. From 1921 it fell directly under the Medical Research Council, and an examination of its board membership in the 1920s shows a heavy bias towards medicine and academic physiology, although a prominent trade unionist and an industrialist were judiciously co-opted, and Myers came to be given full board membership. But before it was disbanded in 1947, it was to produce ninety reports, and to move far from its early 'physiologism'. Moreover, its existence was relatively secure and it could explore problems in depth. Its main crisis occurred early, in 1921, when the government of the day attempted to axe it as an economy measure. (This move was blocked by the protest of a group of Labour MPs.)

The relations of the IFRB and NIIP were 'intimate and harmonious' according to Myers. There was some interchange of personnel, the IFRB funded some of the NIIP's pure research, and their main thrusts of inquiry were largely complementary.

6

War and Fatigue

Fatigue is an industrial problem of obvious relevance to both workers and managers. Some 'overtime kings' among workers may feel it shows virility to work double shifts, priding themselves in their ability to stumble around 'taking it'. Back-street employers have usually driven the people who have to take the jobs they offer as hard as they can. In a rationally operated plant there should be no place for such attitudes. Apart from obvious humanitarian and social reasons for opposing overwork, exhausted workers cause accidents and damage equipment. In view of this, the concern of the human factor group with the issue of fatigue was supported by their contacts in the Fabian and union movements, as well as by the employers.

There are cogent reasons why men who call themselves psychologists should have devoted themselves to a study of fatigue in the first years of the IFRB. The Myersians had been trained in an academic psychology which was regarded as part of physiology and biology and as such as least a semi-hard science. Fatigue appeared to be a relatively easily conceived and measured physiological condition. This idea was soon proved simplistic. Both scientific management and the First World War had made it a live issue. If techniques for reducing fatigue could be discovered, support for other problems might be easier to come by, but if study of fatigue began, at least in part, as a way of advertising the usefulness of the research the group were engaged in, and thus attracting further financial backing, they soon discovered that fatigue was a far more challenging phenomenon than they had imagined.

Early twentieth century thinking on fatigue today seems quaint, and some of the inferences drawn from it were macabre. When an individual engages in heavy exercise or labour, his or her fatigue is manifested behaviourally in a rapid pulse rate and heavy breathing. It was established that these signs of growing exhaustion are paralleled by chemical changes in the bloodstream. The concentration of lactic acid increases, while that of certain bicarbonate compounds is lowered. Hence, a hard scientific test of whether an individual was 'really tired' was available. This was to be done by measuring the toxins in the blood – stimuli other than physical effort could produce heavy breathing or a rapid pulse. Certain ghoulish enthusiasts of applied science went so far as to suggest that chemical reagents might be discovered which, injected into the exhausted labourer, would neutralize the toxins that 'caused' fatigue. The chemically revived labourer would then presumably be available for work during the hours otherwise wasted in recovery through sleep!

Such an elixir was never discovered. The toxin theory of fatigue rests on a simple, mechanistic conception of fatigue, and an easily applicable test for it. It was one of the first achievements of the Myersians to show the inadequacy of the concept and the elusiveness of a simple test for it, certainly outside the laboratory. By 1924 Myers was to write:

> If we continue to use the term fatigue in industrial conditions, let us remember how complex is its character, how ignorant we are of its full nature, and how impossible it is in the intact organism to distinguish lower from higher fatigue and the fatigue of explosive 'acts' from the fatigue of maintaining 'attitudes', or to eliminate the effects of varying interest, of excitement, suggestion and the like.[1]

Cathcart reiterated these doubts even more forcefully a few years later. Even in the laboratory, 'It is questionable . . . if it will be ever possible to measure fatigue.'[2] When we are considering fatigue in the actual workplace, he acknowledged, 'Probably the best definition, which does not commit us to any explanation of its nature, is that it is a reduced capacity for doing work.'[3]

The first indications of the complexity of fatigue and the falsity of the toxin theory appeared when emergency studies of overwork had to be conducted by the HMWC in the First World War. Growing manpower shortage and increased demand for armaments had resulted in very long working hours. These led to rapidly diminishing returns, for labour productivity declined and absenteeism and accidents rose sharply. Nineteenth-century philanthropic employers had already shown that excessive hours were self-defeating. Robert Owen, for example, had reduced hours in his New Lanark factories to ten and a half hours a day, when fifteen or sixteen were common elsewhere, with no loss of output. At the better end of the century the Salford Quaker magnate Samuel Mather had reduced weekly hours from fifty-three to forty-eight in his engineering factories which had actually resulted in *increased* production. Inquiries from the American Bureau of Labor in 1904, eleven years later, showed that the benefits had been retained.

Although some limitation of hours in British government factories had been introduced before 1914, the prevailing belief was that to work additional hours must obviously increase total output. Yet this was readily shown to be untrue even where the workers' speed was determined by machinery: beyond a certain point accidents, absenteeism, scrap and sabotage resulted in a net reduction over the day or week. This was rapidly established by the wartime studies: any reduction in hours cut the incidents of accidents, absenteeism and scrap; a drop in daily hours from twelve to ten increased net daily output; a further reduction from ten to eight, with a six-day week, produced similar, though less marked results, except for certain tasks which were machine paced; days below eight hours brought a small rise in hourly output but lower total daily output.

Reducing the length of the working day can be viewed as lengthening of the major rest-pause between working spells. Taylor had, of course, shown that rest-pauses could help increase total output, and in so far as he held any kind of systematic view of fatigue, it was a physiological one. It might at first appear that physiology could explain the HMWC results. However, this was precluded by two further findings, which were of crucial importance. Firstly, a gain in productivity did not appear immediately after the reduction in hours, but in a period up to *several months later*. Secondly, a reduction from twelve hours to ten hours (17 per cent) brought a widely disproportionate decrease in accidents – no less than 50 per cent fewer.

Myers and his colleagues supplanted the notion of physiological fatigue with that of industrial fatigue, but with some misgivings. As we have seen from Myers's and Cathcart's remarks, it was regarded as a provisional concept embracing several orders of phenomenon, whose utility was to be judged solely by its results. Two distinctions were, however, pressed home.

The first was conceptual. Myers continually emphasized the difference between clonic and tonus activities. The former comprise sudden intense contractions of muscles leading rapidly to evident signs of physical distress: this is what he called a 'fatigue of explosive acts'. The latter are concerned with maintaining posture and rhythmical, co-ordinated work. With the advance of mechanization, fatigue of the first kind becomes less widespread. That from the second increases and 'fatigue certainly exists in the central nervous system in the sense of diminished excitability consequent on previous excitement'.[4] It is this kind of exhaustion, which is slow and cumulative and can, to some extent, be fought off voluntarily – for example, in pursuit of incentives – which lies at the core of industrial fatigue. Once it has reached pathological proportions, co-ordination and work-rhythm deteriorate. The worker will seize rest-pauses, become ill, or with loss of concentration become prone to accidents. This condition must be warded off by adjusting the length of the working day and instituting official rest-pauses. Their timing depends partly on the work being done, but also on the individual worker: individual psychological differences are even more important in many types of work than physical variations. Hence, the Myersians' interest in vocational selection.

The second distinction which the Myersians soon emphasized was the essential difference between laboratory and factory studies. Laboratory studies were viewed as artificial and concerned mainly with clonic activities. Discussing the interpretation of individual work-curves, which had emerged as the classic method of studying human fatigue, Farmer stated:

A fatigue curve proper is obtained by getting subjects to perform a test calculated to produce fatigue fairly rapidly. Such a test is not the ordinary occupation of the subjects, but is the invention of a psychologist who has very different ends in view from those who invent industrial processes. Such tests cannot possibly have the same meaning for the subjects who perform them as an industrial process has for operatives who have been performing it many hours a day for many years.[5]

In fact, laboratory studies in Europe reached a similar conclusion at this period, and were approved by the Myersians. For example, in Germany, A. Atzler's work on the rationalization of effort was to be modified importantly by W. Ulbricht.[6] Investigating in depth the operation of cranking a handle to determine the minimum effort for maximum output, Atzler proceeded to propound a basic set of rules to guide the design of all work-tasks. This recalls Taylor's work. However, although some of Atzler's prescriptions are reminiscent of Taylorism, for example that muscle must correlate positively with the physical effort demanded, others directly modify it. A minimum use of energy should always be sought, supposedly 'useless' intermediate movements should not be completely eradicated, and the energy needed for body support should be minimized. And, with repetitive work, moments of variety, such as the fetching of materials, should be deliberately introduced.

Ulbricht was able to show that subjective psychological perceptions of effort in fact intervene in a significant way. Operators often believed they were working harder or less hard than they actually were in physiological terms. For example, in cranking, the length of the spoke used for winding, which is subjectively perceived as the optimum one, is actually slightly longer than the physiological optimum, as defined by energy usage. This introduction of the human factor parallels Myersian thinking about fatigue, which posited a distinction between peripheral (biological) and central (or mental) fatigue – exhaustion produced by continuous excitement of the narrow range of muscles activated by a badly designed task. The latter type, it was becoming evident, was partly mediated by individual perception. This realization led naturally towards a study of monotony.

Georges Friedmann – who we shall encounter again in discussing the work of Braverman, and Touraine – once described the whole search for a test of fatigue as a Utopian enterprise.[7] The complexity of the state of fatigue and the impossibility of its direct measurement forced the Myersians to adopt indirect indicators which were themselves unsatisfactory. Lost time, labour turnover, sickness and mortality rates were all potential indicators, but poor record-keeping by firms and the intervention of other factors limited their utility. Attempts to use them did, however, sometimes lead to other worthwhile findings – for example, that some individuals are more liable than others to cause accidents. Output was chosen as the most reliable guide, but even the explanation for the regularities discovered there could be only hypothetical. And, as attention turned to lighter industrial tasks, improvements in output often accompanying the experimental introduction of rest-pauses could not be explained solely in terms of either peripheral or central fatigue. Why, for example, should output rise just before a pause as well as just after?

Their early physiological bias led the Myersians in a second direction. It had long been recognized that adverse environmental conditions could rapidly produce all the behavioural consequences of physical exhaustion. Consequently, a very considerable part of the Myersian effort was devoted to establishing the ideal environment for varying kinds of work, and up to 1930 about 25 per cent of their reports were devoted to this branch of inquiry.[8] Some of these findings have proved a lasting contribution to the ecological study of work. They lie behind the advertising campaigns, such as that once mounted by the Colt Ventilation Company, which suggest to employers that problems of productivity and compliance with industrial discipline are reducible to the physical conditions of the workplace.

There are some ground rules here that have been well established since early in the century: the atmosphere of the workplace should be cool and dry rather than hot and humid; the air should waft gently rather than cling stagnantly or eddy in sudden gusts; temperature should vary between different sectors of the workshop, and in any one sector at different periods during a work shift.

Failure to observe these canons – which were given quantitative optima for different occupations – may result in a loss of production and loss of tempers. Lighting must be carefully adapted to the work in hand, leaving no deep shadows or vivid contrasts, and sited to reduce dazzle and reflection. Noise and vibration were likewise shown to have some effect on the workers' output and emotional condition; continuous rhythmic noise is preferable to abrupt clattering, and 'meaningful' noise to cacophony.

It is worth noting that these environmental factors range from those which are readily measured to those which are perceived largely subjectively. Individual differences become significant in response to noise: the heat felt before an open-hearth furnace gives less room for subjective perception. This is not to say that the realistic measurement even of temperature did not generate substantial problems. The seriousness with which they were tackled is often mind-boggling. In one report, H. M. Vernon ventured to suggest that 'common experience shows that what is true for the kata-thermometer is not necessarily true for the human body' and explains how he has attempted to 'clothe' the instrument like a human being – 'but in vain'.[9]

Even so, in studies of this type we see a broadening of the factors considered by the late 1920s. In a study by Vernon and Bedford of absenteeism in coal mining in 1928, absenteeism was correlated not only with sickness and accidents, which were viewed primarily as the result of environmental factors, but also with 'voluntary causes'.[10] While the approach here remained essentially positivist (for example, absenteeism was linked to variables such as 'distance of workings from pit bottom' and 'distance of homes from colliery'), the investigators came close to proposing sociological explanations for some of their findings. Voluntary absenteeism was more common among workers who lived near large towns. The investigators toyed with the idea that this might reflect a greater availability of jobs for wives in towns, but decided: 'Another and more likely explanation is that in the larger towns there is more distraction to be found in the way of sporting events, excursions and other amusements.'[11] That such an explanation is rather feeble is unimportant. What is interesting is that it should even be offered. It is one indicator of a subtle shift in Myersian thinking towards a softer methodology. This important change is much more evident in studies of monotony in industrial work undertaken throughout the 1920s, a review of which follows in the next chapter.

7

Explorations in Monotony

In view of the subject of this chapter, I will try to keep it as short as possible. However, in it we come across some of the most baffling problems that confront students of work behaviour. And not them alone. The kind of research that will be briefly examined here contributed to important movements in industrial design, which later emerged in the branch of applied science called ergonomics.

Writers like Ronald Stansfield have always stressed the continuing intersection between a sociology of work and design factors in the workplace. The latter, as already noted, may have an important effect on the safety of workers, or their longer-term state of health. Yet the positive contribution of ergonomics is often compromised by the suspicion or hostility of departmental managers.[1]

The Myers group's interest in monotony sprang from their concern with fatigue, and at first the two phenomena were not fully differentiated. This extension of study was significant. Monotony is a subjective psychological condition, though its appearance is related to objective conditions. Individual psychology and individual differences mediate between these conditions and any behavioural consequences. Such consequences are less measurable than those resulting from fatigue, whether the investigator relies on direct or indirect methods. The effects of monotony may be estimated by measuring the worker's rate of output, but this gives little indication of the extent of his boredom as a subjectively experienced condition. Only the subject's own reports can establish its degree. At first the Myersians shied away from the loss of 'rigour' involved. But they were eventually obliged to adopt this course.

The notion that monotony is not simply an aspect of fatigue occurs first in IFRB studies in 1924.[2] In a study of light industrial work, Vernon and Bedford found that rest-pauses were most effective when the worker controlled his own work-pace; and they stimulated the output of low producers more than high producers. The investigators also remarked that workers snatched unofficial rest-pauses and fetched materials themselves whenever they could. Both of these were put down partly to a desire to escape monotony. In an experimental study of rest-pauses, Wyatt concluded that the drop in work-rate in the middle of a work-spell was due primarily to monotony. After the introduction of an official break the work-rate rose just before as well as just after it.

In a more extensive report published the same year, Vernon examined the amount of variety present in a large number of repetitive industrial jobs – the length of the work operations, or cycle-times, were as little as one to four seconds.[3] It became evident that workers attempted to introduce variety whenever they could. Comparing the effect of changes of activity in a factory setting, and a laboratory study, Wyatt and Ogden[4] arrived at inconsistent results. In the laboratory, unvaried spells of work on a single activity resulted in lower output and quality. In the industrial experiment, a large number of changes in work operation throughout the day seriously cut daily output and quality. Reducing changes to every half-hour increased production by up to 20 per cent. Maintaining work on the same task all day increased output even further. However, the operators complained about the monotony of this arrangement.

More extensive studies were set in hand to explore the effects of boredom further.[5] The results of the first of these were fairly predictable: uniformity of task was generally less productive, activities were best changed every one and a half hours, more frequently when the work was physically tiring. Workers always preferred some resemblance between two consecutive tasks.

The second is much more tantalizing.[6] Very little previous IFRB work is similar to this study. Not only was 'introspective evidence', in other words, the comments made by workers in interview, introduced. The design of the research and presentation of the findings took into account previous research and wider psychological theory. Monotony and fatigue were at last decisively separated as concepts: 'Boredom . . . is a psychical state which may exist quite apart from fatigue, and must be separately considered in any industrial inquiry . . .'[7] Referring to the work of Hugo Münsterberg and more recent laboratory studies, the writers pointed to the possible effects of individual differences and the precise nature of the task performed, since monotonous work varied significantly in its propensity to induce boredom. This might be related to the nature of the mental 'set' which was engaged and its compatibility with intruding desires.

Six different kinds of repetitive work were examined – two types of filament-winding, inserting (an operation in making electric lamps), wrapping soap, packing chocolate and weighing tobacco. Each group was observed for a minimum of six weeks. Aware of the 'Hawthorne Effect' (see p. 140ff), which was to cause excitement on its rediscovery in Chicago several years later, the investigators were careful to compare before and after production records 'to eliminate any disturbing effects which the presence of an observer might be thought to produce'.[8] Conversation and behaviour, as well as the rate of working, were carefully recorded. Each worker was also given an intelligence test.

Nearly 75 per cent of the workers reported that they felt moderate or considerable boredom, and this was at its most intense at certain periods of the day, particularly in the middle of the work-spell. Its onset was registered by variations in the rate of working and a measurable drop in output when it was felt most severely. The estimation of the passage of time was seriously impaired during phases of intense monotony. This seemed partly to account for variations in work-rate.

All this might have been expected. But then – and this was a big step for them, although to us it may seem obvious – the investigators attempted to relate boredom to individual characteristics and the work situation. It was shown that the sense of boredom was more likely in the more intelligent operatives, though, contrary to findings of some previous laboratory studies, they also tended to be more efficient workers. Again, operatives varied in their ability to perform work automatically, and 'temperamental tendencies are important determinants of boredom, and need special investigation'.[9] The technical features of the work seemed to operate as follows: where the task was highly automatic, or where it demanded complete concentration, boredom was reduced. The latter was easily explained. In the former, the worker's mind could wander freely or he could engage in distracting conversations with his mates. The most boring tasks were those demanding partial or intermittent attention.

Once again, the evidence indicated that suitably introduced rest-pauses or changes in activity could reduce monotony, and that some individual adaptation to an initially uninteresting task might be achieved. Payment by results might also ward off boredom. But the most intriguing claim of all, totally unsuspected from previous work of this kind, and seized on later by the Mayoites (see chapter 12), was that work in compact social groups kept boredom at bay:

> The amount of boredom seems also to bear some relation to number and proximity of operatives employed. An isolated operative . . . is much more susceptible to monotonous conditions than the individuals composing a large groups of operatives doing the same kind of work, when mass suggestion has a greater play, conversation can be freely indulged and full expression given to intruding thoughts and desires.[10]

Human factor psychological investigation, publicly at least, embodied an essentially behaviourist model of man and a radically empiricist method. Most of its practitioners viewed clinical methods with extreme caution and were much concerned to demonstrate the scientific nature of their work to academic critics. Yet even workers like Vernon and Wyatt were gradually forced towards a more clinical, and even sociological perspective. At least one member of the Myers group, May Smith, seems to have been basically sympathetic to this approach from an early stage.

In an early paper for the IFRB she remarked that most observers' descriptions of the factory 'are like skeleton outlines, or those wire reproductions of the correction movements of motion study, they are quite true, but they lack humanity'.[11] The 'mechanical point of view' – nowadays we would call this behaviourism – in psychology and scientific management was to be deplored, especially as it appeared 'even in discussions of intelligence'. Industrial researchers, she recommended, should recognize the human complexity of industrial milieux, particularly the variety of human personalities present.

Her attempt at a typology of industrial personalities was no more than a first step. On the managerial side, she identified 'explosive', 'over-anxious', 'obsessive' and 'self-controlled' types; on that of labour, 'truculent', 'ultra-weak', 'fantacist' [sic] and the type who 'seeks a position in other fields'. These types were not portrayed merely as accidental products of individual differences, but as resulting also from the clash between the 'instinct of self-assertion' and the authority relations of industry. We can dismiss this typology as over simple and value-laden, but the worker types are at least reminiscent of the conventional sociological patterns of *rebellion, retreatism, ritualism* and *innovation* in response to a situation of stress. Smith was evidently trying to challenge the notion that a given mixture of workshop conditions will produce a unitary, universal response. As she had trained as a rigorous experimental psychologist unconcerned with the more complex aspects of human behaviour, this was a bold and novel step.

Smith's clinical-sociological proclivities reappeared in her study, carried out with Culpin and Farmer, of telegraphist's cramp.[12] This ailment had long been a recognized occupational hazard, with complex symptoms, ranging from generalized muscular weakness to mental blocks about punching a particular character, and an obscure pathology. As early as 1911 a British government investigation had concluded it must be a disease of the central nervous system. No single objective cause had been determined, though it related in a few cases to length of service, the hours worked, the 'style' of the operative or the type of keyboard worked on. Loss of muscular control could be rapid or protracted but in no case could any anatomical correlate be isolated.

The investigators examined and tested large groups of sufferers, non-sufferers and apprentice telegraphists, employing all the standard apparatus or ergographs and similar instruments, and carefully controlled such factors as age and experience. But they added a medical study which included clinical interviews. These showed fairly clearly that cramp was a psychoneurotic complaint. Respondents emphasized the strain of the work and the need to remain calm. Officious supervision sometimes prevented this, and the work was generally subject to social and psychological pressure. Messages had to be encoded rapidly and accurately to 'a rigid objective standard of behaviour' with a potential critic at the other end of the line whose complaints would immediately become public because the work was done in the presence of others. 'Nervy' telegraphists found this upset the delicacy of their touch.

Sufferers were typically fearful of others, and excessively self-critical. They might be social isolates, obsessively concerned with the physical surroundings of their work, and expressed neurotic symptoms. Smith and her co-authors were able to posit an 'ideal typical' cramp-prone subject: he was anxious, solitary and fearful, dependent and worried about his career progress.

Study of a control group from similar occupations like typing showed up equal proportions of cramp-prone subjects. Since the complaint did not derive from the muscular demands of telegraphy, why were analogous symptoms absent in this group? The investigators concluded that the social aspects of the work situation in telegraphy encouraged the onset of cramp in those liable to suffer, in two ways. First, the immediate social pressures of the job raised the emotional temperature. Second, worries about promotion added to the sufferer's general anxiety. Most perceptively, they noted that cramp was rare in the USA, but there, telegraphy did not offer a career, and cramp-prone subjects presumably selected themselves out of the occupation. In Britain, fear that a career might be terminated could bring on the very disability that increased that risk.

A rigidly biopsychological perspective had finally been discarded in this study, though tight research design was maintained. However, it offered pointers to a less salutary future. In her analysis, Smith briefly referred to the work of Janet (see pp.

115–17) on individual neurosis; in the later work with her associate, Culpin, she pursued this clinical line further.[13] Unfortunately, although she managed to avoid Elton Mayo's excesses, this was to reinforce the preoccupation of Mayo and his followers with individual maladjustment in industry to the detriment of other kinds of investigation.

8

The Myers Group in Perspective

The developments I have sketched help to explain the changes of title of the IFRB to the Industrial Health Research Board (IHRB) in 1929, and that of the *Journal of the National Institute of Industrial Psychology* to the *Human Factor* in 1932, finally becoming *Occupational Psychology* in 1938. This does not mean that the IFRB style immediately disappeared. In 1938, for example, Wyatt and Langdon replicated and extended their earlier studies of fatigue and monotony,[1] but in doing so they anticipated the important work of Baldamus in the 1950s on the phenomenon of traction – the sense of being pulled along by the rhythm of work.[2] The influence of American developments, as well as that of their own earlier studies, was shown in their discovery that workers pick 'pleasant working companions' – not money – as the most important attribute of a job.[3]

Yet, as late as 1941, the HMWC studies of hours of work were repeated under wartime conditions. This, however, was necessary to demonstrate to the Minister of Labour, Ernest Bevin, who insisted that output 'obviously' increased with hours, that he was dangerously mistaken.

But from about 1930, an open concern with less quantifiable aspects of behaviour and the forces operating on it became more respectable. In Myers's collection of readings, *Industrial Psychology* of 1929,[4] although the bulk of articles deal with the kind of topics in which the NIIP and IFRB respectively specialized, there are discussions of the social and economic environment of industry. Admittedly, the conceptual frameworks adopted lack sophistication. For example, in his contribution on 'The Human

Factor in Industrial Relations',[5] J. Drever accepted instincts as the essential motivating forces of behaviour. But, he asserted, they express themselves in the form of the pursuit by subjects of perceived interests, probably as a member of the group; and 'a social group is not a mere aggregation of individuals' because 'when an individual is a member of a social group, his impulses, feelings and behaviour may be modified in various ways and degrees, dependent on the group in question'.[6]

Membership of several groups with competing claims on loyalty, Drever continued, is a fact of industrial life: 'The worker is compelled by the necessity of earning a living to face daily the situations presented in the factory' with no escape because 'he is so enmeshed in the net of circumstance – a family to support, no other employment available, and the like'.[7] Because of the uncertainties of a market economy, the organization could not become the primary focus of social life. If workers were given more say in workplace affairs, and perhaps a share in a firm's profits, closer integration might occur for the benefit of all. We see here that an emerging human relations movement in Britain, quite unlike the American one, had a streak of social-democratic politics about it.

Cathcart had expressed similar views in a book on industrial psychology a year earlier.[8] As an academic psychologist, Cathcart was clearly more at home in assessing findings on fatigue and environmental factors. But he clearly acknowledged: 'When man must be one of the determining factors in every fact and hypothesis, economic or other, in connection with industry, no firmly established laws can be deduced';[9] and 'I have dealt with what may be called the strictly workshop conditions which play a part in the great questions of optimum conditions of labour'[10] (though out-plant factors exert a powerful, if obscure, influence. And when, in an early section, he claimed that 'Man is indeed an irrational being', and briefly referred to McDougall's concept of the group mind, he linked this with the emergence of 'huge soulless organizations'. Noting that these factors complicate the study of work behaviour, he avoided any kind of Mayoite conclusion that work behaviour is basically an attempt to combat the soullessness of modern life.[11]

The recognition of such factors of course implied no fundamental change. It was the extension of a basic viewpoint which had been present, though largely suppressed, all along. Appraising the approach of the Myers group as a whole, George Friedmann was to remark: 'Man, with the whole of his personality, is again introduced . . . The abstract worker conceived by the Taylorians – a crude composite of laziness and desire for gain – yields to a complex being, both body and mind, in whom an all-important act such as work involves the whole personality.'[12]

The human factor school deliberately confronted Taylorism. From 1920 Myers consistently attacked the notion of the 'one best way' of doing any task. An early article by him developing this theme brought a rumbustious reply from Taylor's admirers and fellow scientific managers Frank and Lillian Gilbreth.[13] While agreeing that two workers never perform a task in exactly the same manner, the dynamic duo proudly maintained: 'We shall continue to specialize on the best demonstrator of the best method;' because 'the best results can come only when the worker learns first the One Best Way and practises it to the point of automaticity'.[14] They appended a castigation of 'the wasteful methods of even the most intelligent workers, namely, the surgeons, whose time and motion wastes are so great today that more than 10 per cent of the ether-minutes of the patients can be eliminated in any operation'.[15] Myers's objection that the Gilbreths' *therbligs* (a measurement of work – Gilbreth spelt backwards) had 'no psychological or physiological interest or basis whatever' was countered with sarcastic fury. To clinch the argument that they themselves were qualified psychologists they recalled that 'we have written the first book on the Psychology of Management, and we use it daily in our work'.[16]

Myers renewed the attack in his book of 1924[17] – it had first been delivered as a series of lectures at Columbia University, noting that Taylor's procedure of basing time-studies on the expert worker 'would now be regarded as unsound – scientifically, sociologically and psychologically'.[18] (Sociologically, because 'class loyalty and fear of unemployment were potent causes of restriction of output even when the workers were paid by results'.[19] The NIIP had at first been suspected by workers of being an agency of scientific management:

> They could quote passages from Taylor's *Principles of Scientific Management* or from his *Shop Management* such as his remark . . . 'You know just as well as I do that a high-priced man has to do exactly as he's told from morning to night' . . . that the worker must 'bear in mind that each shop exists, first, last and for all time, for the purpose of paying dividends to its owners.'[20]

He praised the intuitive opposition, which has a 'sound psychological basis', of British workmen to the 'one best way'. Such notions, he suggested pointedly, might seem valid only where immigrant labour is cheap and unions weak.

An example of a less direct kind of attack on the underlying articles of Taylorism is Eric Farmer's discussion of incentives.[21] This recalled that rewards have both economic and non-economic aspects; that workers seek both; that the acceptable level of each varies with time and place; and that no hard-and-fast rule can be given as to whether the material rewards should be paid as a piece-rate or as an hourly rate, given that one merely wishes to maximize output.

There is little question that the Myers group's assault on scientific management was produced mainly by disagreement with the psychological assumptions of Taylorism, but part of its vigour derived from genuine humanitarian concern. Yet did it also, at least in Myers's own case, reflect tactical concerns? After all, if industrial psychology was to prosper, the workers' doubts that it might be merely Taylorism in a new guise had to be laid to rest. Similarly, managers had to be shown that it produced better results than they could expect from the Taylorian techniques.

Myers was in a difficult position. To reconcile these needs and to maintain the respect of academic circles for the new field demanded tactful compromise. The Myersians set out to show that they could go one better than the scientific managers; that they could simultaneously make work easier for the operative and lower its costs for the manager, on the basis of carefully accumulated empirical knowledge. This attempt was, granted its limited objectives, highly successful. Yet a compromise is a compromise, and the Myersians paid two severe penalties. The first was that a large proportion of their problems had to be taken over from the scientific managers. The second was a certain fragmentation of effort. Both are reflected most obviously in the work of the NIIP. It had to live by its consultancies. A good number of these were concerned with the organization and design of work. Did these studies aid theoretical generalization? If they did, did they do so in an economical way? Here we meet the difficulties of interventionist work discussed fully in the Introduction (see pp. 17–20).

Again, we might argue that the preoccupation of the IFRB with fatigue and the NIIP with selection techniques, although obviously valuable in demonstrating the complexity of the human factor beside the crude mechanical man of the Taylorians, may have postponed consideration of other variables influencing behaviour, and thus subtly reinforced a harmonic ideology of industrial relations. I find such a charge a little thin. Yet as Friedmann astutely commented: 'Always present is the postulate of an individualist psychology which can be better understood and judged only by the study of other aspects of the "human factor".'[22] Furthermore:

> The question is not raised here of knowing whether this same man works in the same way in the different workshops through which he passes, depending on the relations with his comrades, his foreman, his employers, his union organizations – in a word, whether the method and output of his work are not related to considerations broader than the organism's own psycho-physiological characteristics.[23]

This latter assertion, as it happens, is not entirely true, but it comes close to the mark.

This is not to denigrate the very substantial and important discoveries of the Myers group. To question their good faith with regard to their subjects, the people involved in their research, is wretchedly mistaken. It is a reminder that the products of scientific effort and the direction of inquiry depend on more than gaps in knowledge and available brain power. The problems an investigator chooses, and his method of investigating them, are always influenced by the ideas of the scientific community with which he identifies, by the perspectives of the broad social class to which he belongs, and by the needs of the people who fund his work. It is extremely difficult for the investigator to detect and acknowledge these forces, and even more so to neutralize them. In industrial studies, with their obvious practical and ideological potential, the need for such vigilance is additionally pressing.

9

Human Factors in the USA

In an interesting critique, Steven Cohen notes that the *American Journal of Sociology* ran a series of articles on industrial fatigue by the psychologist Emory Bogardus as early as 1912.[1] The series was based upon the findings of a massive social survey among steel-workers in Pittsburgh. It documented the experience of fatigue to the sufferer, the disruption it caused in family life, and the increased risk of accidents at the workplace that followed over-work.

It was an analysis that showed at the same time social concern, even a touch of radical social concern, and an awareness of the potentially large theoretical importance for sociology of such information. Yet it was never followed up. Clarification of industrial fatigue as a psychological pathology occurred in Britain but industrial psychology in the USA took a very different path. American researchers returned to these issues only later. This unquestionably affected the quality of industrial sociology too.

Early industrial sociology in the USA can be dated from a set of inquiries at the Western Electric Company in the mid 1920s (see Part III). It was once said that their failings resulted from their having adopted the perspectives of British human factor industrial psychology. By failings is meant a neglect of institutional factors in designing and interpreting the experiments and observation studies at Western Electric, and the adoption of a behaviourist model of behaviour reminiscent of that held by Myers and his followers. There may be something in this view. But the investigators really ran into trouble because they came late to the Myersian approach, did not fully understand it, and therefore failed to take full advantage of its achievements, particularly its lessons for anybody designing field studies. I shall analyse this failure in more detail in Part III. Here I shall try to indicate some reasons why they failed to profit fully from the Myersian achievement, for if they had the Western Electric studies might now be much less controversial; and, though less well known, the object of more general respect.

What evidence do we have that the Hawthorne researchers (see pp. 131–154) were not fully acquainted with the Myersian *opus*? Fairly lavish reference to their work is made in the early sections of *Management and the Worker* but this book was not published till 1939. I shall take up this question once more in Chapter 13, asking whether they learned in full about this work only when their own studies were substantially complete. A more general suggestion is that they knew of it but did not appreciate its relevance, especially as a guide to research procedure.[2]

However, we have a more direct piece of evidence. In his *Human Problems of an Industrial Civilization*, Elton Mayo sets his early review of the Western Electric work partly in the context of selected human factor studies. In discussing them, showing most enthusiasm for the clinical work of May Smith, he plainly states that 'industrial enquiries undertaken in the United States have been driven, step by step, to similar methods and assumptions. This is of some interest, because there was at no time during the early development of the inquiries any relation between the investigators here and in England.'[3] What explains this lack of contact? Mayo had reported some of his early work to a conference of the British Association for the Advancement of Science, Psychology Section. He had published papers in the NIIP's journal in the 1920s and for his part, Myers had lectured and published extensively in the USA.[4]

There seems to be no simple explanation for this lag in communication but an indirect answer may be found by considering the origins and organization of industrial psychology in America, its characteristic mode of finance, and its research preoccupations. Examination of these factors, which are closely related, presents a contrast with the situation in Britain. A full account of the development of industrial psychology in America has been provided by

Loren Baritz.[5] I shall concentrate on its most salient features. The essential differences from Britain are as follows: (1) interest in industrial psychology was aroused earlier; (2) its growth and organization had pronounced free-market characteristics; (3) it was obliged, consequently, to live almost entirely on its ability to produce rapid results (and sometimes on its wits); (4) its problems were largely dictated by demand; and (5) it none the less achieved considerable influence. The latter achievement may also have made it somewhat complacent.

Applied psychology in the USA drew its inspiration from two sources: the work of Sir Francis Galton on individual differences, and the painstaking investigative techniques pioneered by Wilhelm Wundt from the opening of his Leipzig laboratory in 1879. It was promoted by two important enthusiasts, James McKeen Cattell and Hugo Münsterberg. The relevance of differences in individuals to industrial problems is evident. If different individuals possess varying aptitudes (thanks to heredity and/or environment) they will perform better in some occupations or tasks than others. The rationality of industry, and the contentment of abilities of its personnel, can be developed by careful pre-selection. But the divination of these variations should proceed by means of careful measurement. Wundt's techniques pointed the way, and both Münsterberg, who arrived at Harvard in the late 1890s, and Cattell had studied under him. Cattell had also sat at the feet of Galton, and become Professor of Psychology at the University of Pennsylvania earlier in the decade.

Although Cattell's was the first chair in psychology to be established in the USA, the subject had been by no means ignored in academic circles. But it was tied closely to philosophy, especially the philosophy of William James. Until well into the twentieth century, in fact, many philosophers claiming an interest in psychology looked askance at the kind of work Cattell and Münsterberg were doing. For a time, real respectability lay with instinctualism, building on the ideas James had put forward. Popular enthusiasm for the instinctualist approach, too, was lively if we go by such indicators as the sales of William McDougall's *Principles of Social Psychology*.[6] And through writers such as Tead, instinctualism was to make its own kind of contribution to the psychological discussion of industrial problems.[7]

Instinctualism rejected the rational man of economic theory, and, in that sense, was indirectly useful for confronting the simplification of the scientific managers. But it faced three increasingly serious criticisms. First, how many instincts were there? James had identified twenty-eight, McDougall telescoped them to eleven, other theorists offered their own taxonomies. The problem of classification led to much inconclusive argument. Second, instinctualists proved consistently better as coroners than forecasters. They could point to the instincts which had allegedly provoked an accomplished act, but could not specify what kind of acts a subject might perform in the future. Third, and encompassing the previous complaints, their approach was not 'hard' enough: they could not make measurements of instincts. In these respects the academic establishment with which the applied psychologists had at first to contend was profoundly different from that which the Myersians faced.

Wundt himself was displeased with the direction his former pupils took. He was not interested in applications. His programme was to determine universal mental structures and processes through measurement and computation. He was searching for the enduring 'psychological man' behind individual differences, and deplored the appropriation of his laboratory methods for a study whose aim was to map and underline the variety of human mental factors.

Until the First World War, progress towards the acceptance of aptitude testing was not rapid, nor did the students of individual differences come out as strongly against Taylorism as one might have expected. In the early 1900s, Münsterberg had polled employers on the traits they looked for in different classes of worker, and his results were to lead him later to condemn the psychological dilettantism of scientific management and advocate the thoroughgoing participation of the psychologists in industry. But a full study of the relationship between individual differences and actual performance would have required greater resources than were available at this time, and neither Cattell nor Münsterberg were eager to become consultants to business at the risk of their own intellectual integrity. Taylorism anyway was no more than a fringe movement in industry until the publicity following the Eastern Rate Case in 1910. As Baritz states: 'The engineers raised most of the problems with which the later psychologists grappled.'[8] But those problems were not yet clearly formulated.

Moreover, managerial enthusiasms for applied psychology before the First World War derived from its imputed potential as a tool for manipulating consumers rather than producers. A growing number of articles on the use of psychology in advertising appeared in the trade press at this period. Less reserved in his concern to meet the immediate requirements of industry than Münsterberg or Cattell, Dill Scott, a professor of Northwestern University, published his *Psychology of Advertising* in 1908.[9] It was quite successful. Scott was also offering a testing service to industry before the outbreak of war. (In 1915 one of his clients was the Western Electric Company.) Another academic psychologist, Walter V. Bingham, by now also believed that the science of the mind was sufficiently developed for legitimate application, and formed a consultancy at the Carnegie Institute of Technology. It was soon successful.

The ground had therefore been well prepared for the widespread acceptance of applied psychology in American industry before the war. American involvement in hostilities rapidly completed the process. The American army quickly established a Committee for Psychology in 1917 to speed up the placing of recruits. Scott, Bingham and J. B. Watson were set to devise tests. Eventually they were administered to almost 2 million men, and were believed to identify successfully both subnormals and officer material. In fact, most of these tests sought to measure intelligence rather than aptitudes. Scott, incidentally, believed not only that ability could be reduced to a simple scale-score but that the scores could be legitimately computed from interviewer judgements. But criticism of such misconceptions appeared only later. At the time it was believed that the army programme had been a signal achievement; and its discovery that a large proportion of recruits were mentally unfit was thought a great public service.

Applied psychology thus achieved much favourable publicity, massive development funds and full respectability. The stress on individual differences also coincided with a period in which unreconstructed Taylorism was coming under attack on other grounds. Aware of the need to gain the confidence of labour, Cattell went out of his way to convince Gompers that psychology could be a genuinely impartial servant of both parties in industry, as scientific management had unsuccessfully claimed to be, and Gompers readily concurred.

The market for psychological expertise in industry expanded explosively immediately after the war. The academics soon put their consultancy activities on a regular business basis: Scott founded a Scott Company in 1919 and Cattell followed with his Psychological Corporation – a kind of psychologists' co-operative – in 1921. Another body through which academic expertise was channelled was the Personnel Research Foundation (1920), though it had broader aims than the application of tests.

Two developments, however, spoiled this general picture of acceptance and success. Firstly, as they had with scientific management, the 'fakirs and charlatans' cashed in. Fringe operators were soon offering off-the-peg tests to companies, at cut prices, and even by mail order. 'Character-analysts', who would judge aptitude after a quick eye over a subject's physical build or racial background, if necessary from a photograph, phrenologists, palmists, and other self-appointed specialists in the science of the mind and its mysterious powers were all able to exploit the businessman's fuzzy demarcation between real and phoney occupational psychology. Secondly, many companies who had employed respectable agencies began to complain that the results were less remarkable than they had been led to expect. The suspicion that the tests were not valid predictive instruments began to spread, increased by the outbreak of controversy among academic psychologists about the merits of various testing instruments and methods of applying them. Criticism of the wartime programme arose also, suggesting that its supposed measurement of intelligence had really been the assessment of educational attainment. These embarrassments, were, however, fought off. After all, few of the critics were prepared to state that there was nothing in testing. Most argument was about technique and inference, not about more fundamental issues of method (or ethics).

From this brief account the climate into which British human factor psychology was imported should be clear. Applied psychology in the USA possessed an intellectual establishment, a fairly clear accepted problematic, a substantial degree of self-confidence and a consultancy tradition that often favoured the short cut to rapid results in a highly competitive market. Perhaps this accounts in part for the lack of awareness of the work done in Britain. Of course, we have no evidence that the human factor researchers made any special effort to get their work known in the USA, but its plodding caution in research and institutionalized scepticism in interpreting findings must have made it seem quite comically old-fashioned to the fast-buck and quick-fix element among their North American colleagues.

In a way, then, it is not surprising that the first main effort to work outside the prevailing fashion was made by a foreigner. Elton Mayo, whose contribution we shall review in more detail in Part III, had arrived in the USA in 1922. His first industrial assignment was in a textile mill, owned by Continental Mills, in Philadelphia. Mayo's various publications about this study are somewhat muddled;[10] they do not make his approach, or even his main conclusions, entirely clear. This, of course, made it much easier for him to reinterpret his findings after the Hawthorne studies.

There was a superficial resemblance to the research style of the Myers group. The 'enlightened and humane' management of the factory had asked Mayo to resolve the problem of a 250 per cent labour turnover in their mule-spinning department (in other workshops it stood at around 6 per cent). At ten hours per day over a five-day week, with forty-five minutes for lunch, the hours were by no means excessive; they were even generous, by the standards of the day. Mayo conjectured none the less that the physical demands of the work created severe postural fatigue and awarded a group of experimental subjects two or three ten-minute rest-pauses spread throughout the day, during which operatives were required to lie down and relax. This is reminiscent of IFRB work. Less so, however, was Mayo's failure to obtain prior output records or to compare the performance of experimental and non-experimental subjects. It was known merely that the shop as a whole had never produced enough to earn a group bonus.

He noted that the experimental subjects were pleased with the change, and the spirit of the shop as a whole was better. Management awarded the rest-pauses to everyone, and output records, which were subsequently kept more carefully, rose above the threshold required to earn the bonus. When the rests were abolished by junior managers, following a rush order, output declined. Mayo complained to the company president, who ordered their reinstitution, and output returned to its high level. Moreover, labour turnover declined to virtually nil and remained at its low level for at least five years. Mayo interpreted these results in his first report of the study in primarily physiological terms. Output supposedly rose mainly due to relief from postural strain.[11] But there is a psychological hedge. Informal interviews had shown the workers' thoughts to be dominated by pessimistic themes. Rest-pauses allegedly permitted a temporary respite from these reveries.

The early lighting experiments at Hawthorne began shortly after this, in the winter of 1924–5. Mayo had nothing to do with this phase of the Hawthorne studies, and the precise source of their scientific rationale, if there was one, is unclear. The first set compared changes in artificial lighting with output in three departments. No result could be deduced. In the next, workers were split into two groups matched for previous output and located in separate buildings. The lighting in the experimental group was varied, but output for both groups showed a more or less identical increase. The tests were repeated excluding all natural light. Again, both groups increased their output, the experimental one even when lighting was reduced to a very low intensity. Further informal experimentation demonstrated that subjective interpretation of the change was an intervening variable.

Thus, the stage was set for the two Relay Assembly Test Room and Mica Splitting Test Room studies. The aim of these was never to test for social influences on output behaviour, but to relate output to physical and physiological variables, and to test the effect of incentives. The experimental design and control of these studies was inadequate and will be discussed in Part III.[12] Two points should be made at this stage, however. The approach adopted in both these and the lighting studies was squarely in the human factor style; but the investigators seem to have been either unfamiliar with the work of the Myers group at this point, or had quite misunderstood it. We shall probably never know which. But it is hard to believe that if the British work had been well known to them, the investigators would have made so many obvious slips in their research design.

When he came to write *Human Problems*, Mayo had read some of the IHRB studies. Through his contacts with Lawrence J. Henderson, a biochemist, he absorbed a good working knowledge of the physiology of work. He seized on the work of May Smith on telegraphist's cramp, and on Wyatt's and Fraser's study on monotony. Armed with this ammunition, he reinterpreted his Philadelphia study in a manner consistent with Myersian findings and his own convictions about the prevalence of neuroses brought on by the conditions of work throughout industry. He projected these ideas on to the Hawthorne data with fateful consequences.

Clearly the human factor approach had its own very pronounced limitations. Equally, Mayo was capable of gifted insight into the wider forces that impinge on workers' attitudes and behaviour. It seems regrettable, therefore, that his introduction to the British approach was not more thorough, prolonged or at first hand. The Hawthorne studies had to be conducted in a climate where sponsors often lacked patience. It is true that Western Electric were more tolerant than most American firms, but it is plain that the company always expected identifiable payoff. They held up publication of the main set of results for several years. (John Smith has examined Mayo's own relations with the Western Electric management.[13])

It seems likely that the Western Electric team could have profited from a study of the Myers group's experience in designing and administering field studies in the workplace. These are full of warnings about 'Hawthorne Effects', for instance.[14] After a brief overall appraisal of this tradition as a whole the Hawthorne work will be examined in greater depth in Part III.

10

In Conclusion

It is easy to be distracted by the problem of why systematic industrial psychology emerged in Britain when it did. The immediate cause had been a threat to the British war effort but that is hardly a full explanation. In theory, it should have been pioneered in the USA, where there was already a stronger reaction against Taylorism, but an underlying commitment on the part of the technocrats of scientific management to improve the techniques they had already developed.

It is quite clear, too, that work in the human factor vein could have been readily absorbed into such a movement – this point will be taken up again below – but in Britain, there had been no diffusion of Taylorism, though there was an awareness of Taylor's work. Nor was there a strong technocratic movement apart from the Fabian Society, which was identified, quite mistakenly, with a specifically socialist programme. In fact, the Fabians favoured State ownership of industry purely on the grounds that it would render central planning easier.

America was far better supplied with academic psychologists; and, as we have seen, industry was more prepared to try out their ideas. But American psychology had prematurely broken its links with biology, and the applied psychologists looked on their theories as a commodity, a packaged product, for sale in a highly competitive market. Aptitude tests sold best, so individual psychological differences became the major scientific problem. Industry too looked for rapid results, and this prevented the lengthy study and cautious generalization which the Myersians later showed to be necessary. The British context was even less hospitable to a Myersian approach before the First World War.

Both of these facts probably reflect Britain's general situation as an increasingly parasitic economy, a centre of international finance dependent on returns from foreign investment whose increasingly archaic industry supplied captive imperial markets. There was no economic motive to innovate through the rational exploitation of scientific knowledge. Psychology and scientific management were neglected for the same underlying reason that chemicals and electrical goods were. Industrialists recognized no need for them. The Fabians, though, may have been saying that the country did need them, and were able to make such points more powerfully once war had broken out. It seems incredible nowadays that for two years Britain had tried simultaneously to fight a major war and maintain *laissez-faire* economic practices. Faced with growing signs of collapse in 1916, the Government had to create a centrally co-ordinated economy.

The HMWC was one rather small but significant outcome of this rationalization of the war machine. It addressed a set of problems which could remain unrecognized, or could be ignored, in the peacetime economy. Taylorism and applied individual psychology – and later, human relations – were essentially concerned with problems of motivation and compliance. Though such problems certainly did exist in Britain during the First World War, they were secondary to objective bio-psychological constraints on worker productivity. These hidden limits on production could become apparent only in such a situation. In peacetime, the elasticity of the general supply of labour could hide the inelasticity (beyond a critical point) of individual effort. War conditions dramatized this fundamental biological – and fundamental economic – truth.

But if war conditions made the biologically grounded psychology of the human factor relevant, peace soon made it seem redundant (except as a humanitarian exercise) to those with power to employ it or to agitate for its use in factories. Once stagnation and unemployment returned, as the government retreated from economic intervention, British businessmen could see little use for applied social science. In view of this, it is perhaps remarkable that the Myers group survived at all. As we saw earlier they led a precarious existence, propped up by very slight and grudging official support, the contributions of Quaker firms, the donations of individual philanthropists and their earnings from the more commercially oriented work of the NIIP.

Myers's faith in science, not only for its own sake and as a material force but as a humanitarian enterprise, was entirely authentic. He seems to have been sure it was shared by a small but increasingly important group. Winning acceptance would have to be a long-term effort, but was likely to succeed eventually – provided he demonstrated the efficacy and independence of industrial psychology – as the target audience grew in influence. This strategy was the most rational he could have adopted.

Myers's propaganda was not aimed so much at business or Government leaders as at the management movement John Child has examined,[1] and at social-democratic politicians. The managerial stratum in Britain was just beginning to acquire self-consciousness in the 1920s. Many of its spokesmen, much more explicitly than their American counterparts, espoused a socialist version of the technocratic credo; the industry of the future would be operated by scientifically trained professional managers sympathetic to organized labour, leading a productivist alliance. This movement did not grow as rapidly as some people had expected. Industrial unrest of the mid 1920s reduced the new managers' enthusiasm for an alliance with organized labour. The leftist technocrats never became a decisive third force in industry yet many of their ideas gained a vague general acceptance. Among them was the notion that scientific study of work was valuable. Human factor psychology was thus assured of a small but growing clientele.

Its achievements now look modest. As far as its contribution to understanding work behaviour goes, the gaps between these modest achievements seem to yawn very wide but that is because we are looking backwards a very long way – when we do look back, we should remember this. In fact, it has left its mark in two ways. The first is the recognition that there are individual and social factors that modify response to a work situation, and that these are structured in a systematic fashion. The second is the stress placed on the environmental factors affecting work behaviour. This was to help promote a movement for better industrial design, as was noted earlier. It also provides one of the starting points for both the *technological implications* approach to work and the *quality of work life* movement of more recent years.

PART III

THE TRIBAL FACTORY

11

The Six Sides of Human Relations

Human relations is back in fashion – as a set of personnel management techniques, as a doctrine, and even as a social-science approach. That, at least, was the message often repeated in one form or another after 1980 by observers as varied as Theo Nichols, Ivar Berg, Andrew Friedman, Paul Goldman, Donald Van Houten, Charles Sabel, and Richard Sennett.[1] The list could be readily extended. So surely there must be something in it?

Maybe. But it does depend very much on what is meant by human relations, which the historical record shows is a term that many people think they understand much better than they do. Rather like scientific management, it is an emblem-term, the family crest for a whole batch of related meanings, and most of these meaning strands slowly alter over time – inevitably, because the real processes they refer to have changed. Some readers are likely to begin the book here, because of the alleged human relations revival. Others may be skipping it because they feel they have already heard enough about it. I regret this, but I sympathize. No other branch of industrial sociology has raised so great and lasting an interest outside academic circles. Massively popularized and violently attacked, it has been the centre of a semi-public controversy for almost fifty years.

Human relations was much criticized from around 1960 until late in the 1970s. Everyone hit on something with which to find fault: economists ridiculed its rejection of money as the central motivator of work behaviour; political liberals attacked its denial of individualism; radicals raged over its assertion that workers are irrational and cling to management as if it were a substitute for a teddy-bear; managers discarded its supposedly powerful manipulatory techniques as either useless or inoperable; social researchers and theorists of all types exhaustively documented the methodological howlers in its research studies, the gaps and contradictions in its theories, and the dreary justificatory propaganda in its ideology.[2]

Sadists may be looking forward to an imaginative staging of the ritual slaughter. But that sweeping hostility – and there is much that is objectionable, as we shall see, in the approach as a movement or as a doctrine that is nauseating – prevents us seeing the internal diversity of human relations as an intellectual product. To come straight to the point: human relations is still too often equated with the work and thought of Elton Mayo but any reasoned rejection of this approach must hit more targets than this – perhaps rather easy – one.

I aim to bring out the variety of human relations. This procedure will also throw some light on the more general issue of how theoretical ideas come to diversify the change in social investigation. The disadvantage of this emphasis is that it will not leave much space to discuss human relations as a practical movement among managers, or as a managerial ideology. Excellent treatments of these themes can be found elsewhere.[3]

Despite its internal diversity, human relations possessed strong unifying features as an approach to industrial behaviour. According to Elton Mayo, whose word has been accepted somewhat uncritically, its originality lay in its sociological conception of industrial events. In fact, for many years human relations and industrial sociology were virtually interchangeable terms. This sociological approach manifested itself at two main levels, though differently at each one. The first was that of a work group in an organization. Here, behaviour, particularly productivity or cooperativeness with management, was thought to be shaped and constrained by the worker's role and status in a group. Other informal sets of relationships might spring up within the formal organization as a whole, modifying or overriding the official social structure of the factory, which was based on purely technical criteria such as the division of labour. The second level was society as a whole. Sometimes explicitly, but more usually as a set of assumptions, industrial society was viewed as a shaky fabric. Its scale, diversity and constant change supposedly frustrated a basic human desire for intimacy, consistency and predictability in social living. Lacking this wider social certainty, workers purportedly would seek to manufacture it at the workplace by means of informal organization.

The foregoing is necessarily oversimplified but it indicates that human relations adopted a restricted definition of the sociological. The study of informal organization advocated might better be termed anthropological – or even ethnographic – since it promotes a view of factories as unique societies in miniature. A genuinely sociological approach would not ignore a factory's group-life (supposing it has one) but would seek to discover from it generalizations about industrial relationships, and thus relate it to the wider social involvements and experiences of the different categories of personnel.

This naturally requires the conscious adoption of some empirically justified image or model of the society as a whole. Successful analysis of particular industrial situations cannot proceed without an explicit framework of this kind. The model employed by human relationists was incomplete and value-laden. Their image of the worker derives automatically from it. He is compulsively social – obsessed, in W. H. Whyte's terminology, with 'belongingness' and 'togetherness'.[4] They assume that he wishes to belong above all to a work-group and experience the 'togetherness' of collaborative work. Nor need he be conscious of these inbred impulses, which supposedly underlie all his actions at work and may be channelled for 'constructive' purposes by socially skilled managers.

These preliminary remarks will be expanded and qualified in due course, but they provide a reference point for assessing the contributions, which will be examined. Inevitably, this discussion will be critical. It would, however, be wrong to suppose that the human relationists made no important contribution to organized knowledge. No one denies that the face-to-face relationships of the workplace, its micropolitics, are interesting objects of study in themselves or relevant to a full understanding of industrial events.

In drawing attention to them, the human relationists served a useful function. Unfortunately, they did more than draw attention to them: they made them the hub of their analysis. Further, by abstracting face-to-face relations on the factory floor from their wider – and objective – social context, they encouraged the misconception that they could be altered ('improved') by purely local intervention.

There are two major obstacles to understanding human relations: the Western Electric studies (the Hawthorne experiments) and Elton Mayo. Critics and enthusiasts of human relations both take the studies as their main empirical source. Mayo is likewise regarded as the grand theorist of human relations. Distortion results from this emphasis.[5] The studies are one group among many, some of which were better executed, more interesting and in some ways more influential. Responsibility for their prominence lies largely with Mayo, whose popularizations of them reached a mass audience. Unfortunately, too, the two definitive reports of the studies are lengthy and sometimes hard going. Synopses of them were often wrecked by compression as well as by partisanship. Again, Mayo's fame as a social scientist reflects a talent for publicity and is not warranted.

But the prominence of the studies and their link with Mayo cannot be ignored. I shall deal with Mayo first. This, however, cannot be done without a brief account of the studies. The synopsis that follows should also be useful for evaluating the work of Roethlisberger and Dickson later, and a background to this part of the book. But readers should bear in mind my comments above about condensation and bias: unclear or apparently tendentious statements should be checked against the text of *Management and the Worker*.

From the mid 1920s to the early 1940s, the Western Electric Company undertook a complex programme of experiments, investigations and action research into Hawthorne Works in an industrial suburb of Chicago. Various outside bodies, the Harvard Business School being one, advised the company on research strategy, the interpretation of results and practical implementations. Western Electric was a large, bureaucratized, technically progressive firm, employing over 40,000 workers at Hawthorne, with a reputation for good company welfare policies.

Four phases are distinguishable in the research programme. The first lasted from November 1924 to roughly the end of 1928 and utilized an approach comparable to British *human factor industrial psychology*. This phase overlaps with the second, or *clinical*, phase, which concentrated on interviewing; between late 1928 and mid 1931, a quarter of the Hawthorne workforce were processed. From November 1931 to mid 1932 the researchers adopted an *anthropological* method; this phase was terminated by the economic depression, but in 1936 interviewing was resumed in the form of personnel counselling. This final, manipulatory or *interventionist* phase continued into the 1940s, and aimed to increase company control over neurotics and troublemakers by giving them therapeutic depth interviews.

1. *The human factor phase*. This consisted of a series of experiments on the relation between output and illumination; and three investigations of a range of mainly biopsychological influences on the output of three small assortments of workers. The lighting experiments have been mentioned already, in Chapter 9. They showed no conclusive link between the quality of illumination and output, and were too poorly designed to demonstrate anything but the need for careful controls in scientific research. The second series aimed to be more systematic and is described below.

(a) First Relay Assembly Group. This experiment began in April 1927 and was halted by the slump in August 1932; but only the results obtained to June 1929, when thirteen experimental periods had been completed, really interested the researchers or are mentioned by commentators on the studies.[6]

Six women operatives were taken from their normal department and placed in a separate test room. Before segregation, their output of relays (switchboard components) had been secretly measured and they continued with this work in the test room. At the first of a regular series of briefing meetings with the research staff, they were allowed to comment on the test-room arrangements and told to work naturally throughout their experiments. They also received initial and periodic medical checks. An observer was placed in the test room. His duties were rather unclear, but he was supposed to ensure that the women's attitude to the test remained 'constant'. How he was to gauge constancy or maintain it was not clearly spelled out.

Over the first two years the women's conditions of work were progressively changed. Early on they were placed on a group bonus incentive scheme; this was followed by experimental exposures to rest-pauses of varying length and duration, free snacks, shorter hours and a shorter working week. Usually, but not always, old privileges were retained when a new one was added. In the twelfth period, all privileges were temporarily removed. In the next, they were restored. During all but one of these periods, the women's hourly output rate rose, even during the deprived twelfth one. By June 1929 it was 30 per cent higher than base. The observer noted increased friendliness among them. They liked the test room. Their former workmates in the department expressed envy for their conditions, and the women were aware of this. At an early stage, two operators (1A and 2A) were replaced for uncooperativeness.

In time, the observer became more friendly with the subjects, assumed more supervisory duties, and shielded them from their nominal supervisors. However, from July 1929 onwards, the situation began slowly to deteriorate. The women expressed less interest in the experiment, replacements had to be made, and from the summer of 1930 they showed anxiety over their security (the slump was beginning) and output began to fall. The last two years were marked by bitterness and hostility. By August 1932 all had been transferred or laid off except operator 2, who was made a temporary clerk.

(b) Second Relay Assembly Group. Before the first Relay Assembly Group study had reached half-way, the investigators began to assess its results. They seem to have been coming to the conclusion that the rise in output was not due entirely either to better materials and methods, lower fatigue, less monotony or the small group incentive; but they decided to retest some of these factors on other groups.

To test incentives, five experienced relay assemblers were selected – but by a *foreman* not one of the investigators. They remained in the normal department but were paid by the same group bonus incentive method as the first group. They received for this a nine-week period, during which their average individual output rose nearly 13 per cent. Before this experiment, these operatives had been envious – so had all the women in the department – of the advantages awarded to the first relay group. They often expressed their rivalry with it during the test – which was discontinued because their higher earnings spread discord in the department.

(c) The Mica Splitting Group. With the Second Relay Assembly Group, no change in the conditions of work had been made. Only the incentive matched the situation of the first relay group. A second test room was therefore established, and another group of five women exposed to changes in working conditions. But their method of payment was not changed (they were already receiving an individual piece-rate bonus). Five changes in working conditions were made over two years. These were not identical to those of the first relay group but were all deemed to be increases in privileges. However, at times they were required by management to work overtime; and in September 1930 the experiment was stopped through shortage of work.

Average hourly output in this group rose 15 per cent in the first year and fell again in the second (as business declined), but individual variations were more marked than in the other groups. The group never cohered properly and the women were temperamentally and socially very dissimilar.

2. *The clinical phase.* Before the foregoing experiments were concluded – indeed, before the second relay group was established – the company began a programme of interviews that became progressively more extensive and sophisticated. Prompted in part by criticisms of management, overheard in the first relay group, it began 'essentially as a plan for improving supervision'.[7]

At first, the interviews were rather formal, relatively structured, and almost crudely to the point – a standard inquiry was: 'Is your boss a slave-driver?' Replies were analysed for the nature and strength of the respondent's attitude towards eighty topics, ranging from 'advancement', 'payment', 'dirt', to the company restaurant, and of course 'supervision'. Male workers emerged as more economically oriented than women; women stressed the desirability of good working conditions. Gradually, however, a more open-ended approach to interviewing emerged. Respondents were allowed to talk about those issues which preoccupied them. It was realized that an individual's replies cohered in a subjectively rational way, that criticism of 'washrooms', for example, might really be directed at the company as a whole, and that systematic variations in attitudes related to function and status in the plant.

Finally, an interviewing technique close to therapeutic counselling was devised to explore these 'social sentiments' in depth. It demonstrated a relationship between attitude to work and the subject's wider social attachments and responsibilities. This is precisely the kind of influence that, with much fanfare, the social action approach (see Part V) was to put much stress on several decades later, but these links were not thought as important as those between an internal work situation and attitudes.

Some of the last interviews to be conducted were among supervisors. These brought out a likely connection between the fears and tensions felt in this group and its marginal position between the workers and 'real' management. They showed the pervasiveness of 'sentiments' among non-manual groups as well as among the ordinary manual workers. As Landsberger has pointed out, these supervisors were also anticipating human relations as a personnel management technique in their views of workers and handling of them.[8]

3. *The anthropological phase.* Depth interviewing had shown the complexity of the factors influencing attitudes and behaviour in the work situation. In November 1932 the investigators adopted a new research strategy, based on observation, which they hoped would illuminate the dynamic relations between these factors. Advised on study design and research methods by the anthropologist W. Lloyd Warner, they established an observation room to

study the ongoing social relations of a group of fourteen male workers.

Engaged on wiring, soldering and inspecting banks of telephone switchgear, these men were segregated in the observation room and set to work at their normal jobs. An observer sat in the room, as inconspicuously as he could, noting the men's interactions. Periodically, the subjects were also called away for interview. The workers rapidly accustomed themselves to the observer's presence. It was soon discovered that although few of the men properly understood their group incentive payment method, all of them held a precise notion of what constituted a fair day's output. Practically all were capable of exceeding this and on frequent occasions did so. However, they would then report a false output figure close to the norm and work more slowly the next day. Individuals who persistently overproduced were castigated by their fellows as 'rate-busters'; consistent underproducers who falsely reported achievement of the norm were disparaged as 'chisellers'.

Technically, it would have been possible for supervisors to check each individual's daily output report, but this would have been a nuisance and, anyway, over the week reported and actual production moved into balance. Moreover, it soon became clear that first-line supervision connived at this, and at more sophisticated breaches of company rules which gave the men a measure of control over their work situation and optimized their economic returns and ease of work.

But the men's economic shrewdness, exercised to its limits as the depression worsened, interested the investigators less than the social mechanisms surrounding their restriction of output. Various rough measures of interaction established the existence of two cliques within the group. Members of one tended to adhere more closely to the output norm and were ascribed high prestige. Conformity to these informal rules was carefully policed by group members. Even physical sanctions ('binging') and social isolation (an inspector who 'squealed' to management about some malpractices was ostracized) backed up the more common checks of abuse and ridicule.

Besides his general status, each member was found to have what might be called a group identity, often conveyed in a nickname – 'Jumbo', 'Cyclone', etc. Certain individuals assumed roles of leader, diplomat or morale-booster. The skills of the latter were in especially high demand as, increasingly towards the end of the seven-month experiment, unemployment loomed.

4. *The manipulatory phase*. In 1936, after the depression and, it is worth noting, a spread of unionization among Western Electric workers, research was restored in the form of personnel counselling. Theoretically, the counsellor was an uncommitted independent outsider who applied the findings from the interview programme, which had been interpreted to show that emotionally troubled individuals could 'talk off' their obsessions. At the same time the interviewer embodied management's need to 'commit itself to the continuous process of studying human situations'.[9] What did this strangely vague expression mean? One thing is certain. Any serious research purpose which may have motivated this scheme initially soon evaporated. Counsellors took a manipulatory and intelligence role which all found socially demanding and the sensitive ethically unacceptable.[10]

In the next chapter, Elton Mayo's connection with these inquiries and their position in his thought will be examined.

12

What Did Mayo Do?

For many people in his own day, Elton Mayo *was* the Human Relations in Industry movement. This confusion is still common, and often runs roughly as follows. The fact that the industrial worker is a Social Man was discovered by accident during the Western Electric experiments at the Hawthorne factory in Chicago some time around 1930; these studies were conducted by an Australian called Elton Mayo; as a result, Mayo started the Human Relations movement to reform personnel management practice by applying his findings; Mayo thus counteracted Taylor's influence.

This distorted reading of the facts makes a good myth. The Social Man of the human-relations movement originated in the theories of the great nineteenth-century sociologists Pareto and Durkheim. He was rediscovered in modern industry thanks largely to the biochemist Lawrence J. Henderson, and the anthropologist W. Lloyd Warner. If much of the evidence used to publicize the new image of the workers was obtained at Hawthorne, to say that Elton Mayo conducted these studies is a shorthand version of the truth. As a movement, human relations was diffuse, and Mayo never led it except in a symbolic sense and from the grave.

John Smith, Mayo's intellectual biographer, has been trying for years to pin down Mayo's exact contribution to the human relations movement, and it is becoming clearer that although Mayo was greatly admired by some of his close colleagues and other Harvard social researchers he was a lonely man, never entirely happy in the American academic world he had landed in almost by accident, tortured by his own impatience, and with a perpetual sense of having missed a vocation.[1] The comfortable Ivy League world he had entered in the 1920s was torn by the Depression and the underlying social conflicts which it both expressed and disguised. Mayo was eager to do whatever he could to lessen these tensions. But he never had any grand scheme for saving the world: he became a Man with a Message, it is true, but unlike Frederick Taylor he was not a fanatic. An apocalyptic tone creeps into some of his later writings, but it is embarrassing rather than offensive.

Mayo's ability to recognize social problems, and to popularize attractive explanations and solutions for them, won him a good deal of publicity during his life, but much of his fame was posthumous. Others, including some who were a great deal less sincere in their intentions, made use of his reputation. We would probably understand the movement much better if we could simply switch off the spotlight. The strength of the Mayo myth prevents this, and it is certainly true that some of Mayo's personal experiences and preoccupations shaped human relations theory and practice.

The formative period of Mayo's life ended in 1919.[2] In this year he published *Democracy and Freedom*[3] which his critics have always seized on as a pointer to the underlying doctrine of human relations. It certainly has passages that seem to portray democratic politics as symptomatic of social ill-health and explain left-wing radicalism as the product of an unhappy childhood. Personally I don't think we should take it very seriously. It is simply a bad book, written by someone who had been experiencing great difficulty in finding himself, and who never showed much more political sense than could be scribbled on a postcard.

Mayo was born in 1880 in Adelaide into a large Victorian middle-class family. His educational progress was erratic. Family tradition, and what sounds like a rather bossy mother, pushed him towards medicine. Two of his six brothers and sisters qualified as doctors but Mayo kept failing his courses, apparently because he had no taste for the work involved. His worried parents had even sent him to take a course in Edinburgh, but he did no better there than he had in Adelaide. For some time afterwards he simply drifted around London with no clear aims for his life. He did some part-time teaching at a working-men's night school, which may have been as significant for his later life as Smith regards it, or on the other hand, it may simply have been a source of income. It only lasted a few months and he made no attempt to take up the work full time.

But unquestionably he possessed unused intellectual energy, and he finally gave it some direction after he returned to Australia in 1905. A family friend, a professor of philosophy, advised him to study psychology. Mayo took to it immediately, and showed so much talent and enthusiasm that he was appointed lecturer at the University of Queensland soon after qualifying. During the First World War, he became very successful in treating soldiers invalided home because of nervous collapse under the stress of constant bombardment. He gained a reputation and in 1919 was made a professor.

Mayo developed a lifelong interest at this time in the ideas of the psychologist Pierre Janet. A feature of Janet's work is a tendency to represent social conflict as the product of individual maladjustment. Focusing on individuals may result in overlooking how the social structure and economic system breed and shape conflict. This does not mean that *only* such factors matter but social conflict cannot be properly explained without considering its possible social causes. Agitators may or may not have more personal unhappiness than other people, but they can only spread discord if there is some wrong or grievance there to spread discord about. Mayo probably realized this. But his clinical achievements with the shell-shocked patients also increased his fascination with individual maladjustment. He was to argue that industrial harmony could be achieved through personal counselling. This is an astoundingly naïve belief.

Mayo had virtually no knowledge of sociology at this time. It was not until 1926, when Lawrence Henderson introduced him to Pareto's theories, that his interest in the subject was fully aroused. and even then, it was a highly selective interest. In 1922 he had left Australia for the USA, disenchanted with what he regarded as its excessively vocational university system. Future leaders of society, he argued, should also be trained in the social sciences.[4] He regarded America as more progressive in this respect. Almost immediately after arrival he was offered a research post at the

Wharton Business School of the University of Pennsylvania, thanks to a public lecture in Philadelphia that impressed one of its administrators.

This led directly to his research and consultancy work for Continental Mills (see p. 93). Mayo's reports at the time of these studies show that he was then either unaware of the work being done by the British industrial psychologists, or chose to disregard it. On the contrary, Mayo drew heavily on psychiatric theories and laid stress on the individual bases for conflict in the workplace, especially 'pessimistic reveries' about childhood traumas. A few sociological remarks did creep in, but they were very informal.[5]

At the time, this application of psychiatric perspectives to industrial problems must have seemed strikingly original. Moreover, the research had benefited the company handsomely. When the Harvard Business School decided to establish an industrial research programme in 1926, its dean, Wallace Donham, recruited Mayo. He immediately struck up a lasting friendship with Henderson, who had an international reputation for his biochemical studies of the blood. The great scientist was to examine the physiological aspects of work through a Fatigue Laboratory which was set up within the new Department of Industrial Research. He introduced Mayo to classical sociology and current social anthropology.

Periodically, the social sciences are deeply influenced by scholars trained in another discipline. As a biochemist, Henderson was struck by the organic analogy – the parallels between society and a living organism. In social thought, this kind of imagery, which always risks slipping into dangerous superficiality, has recurred since Plato. But it had been applied with originality by Emile Durkheim at the turn of the century as a method of distinguishing between the moral frameworks of industrialized and preliterate societies. The British anthropologists, Malinowski and Radcliffe-Brown were then developing Durkheim's ideas into a systematic functionalist theory of society. In simple terms, functionalist theory tells us that a society is structured as a system of institutions and social roles. Each of these 'organs' has a distinctive function that contributes in its own way to the maintenance of the system, as do the brain, heart, lungs, limbs, etc., in biological adaptation and survival. Clearly, though, the analogy is faulty. It suggests, in particular, that it may be as dangerous to tamper with a social institution as it is with the human brain. This has even led some anthropologists to defend head-hunting among primitive peoples simply because its abolition changes the society. It tends to encourage preference for the status quo rather than change, for conservation of the world as it is. By throwing his biochemical prestige behind the organic analogy, Henderson was to encourage functionalist theory in general sociology, pre-eminently through Talcott Parsons, another of his Harvard intimates. Its suggestion that conflict is a necessary sign of social pathology supported conclusions Mayo had already reached by another route.

Henderson's overriding passion, however, was for the theories of Vifredo Pareto, a nineteenth-century Italian engineer turned social theorist. Pareto's ideas are complex, and we now know that Mayo's admiration for them *as a system* fell far short of Henderson's.[6] But he was impressed with Pareto's concept of *non-logical action*. There can be no doubt either that Pareto's theories about leadership and élites, as recounted by Henderson, made a deep impression on Mayo.

Non-logical action allegedly characterizes most of social life and springs from *sentiments* – a more or less unconscious predisposition or state of mind. People impelled to act in a certain way by a sentiment can offer only a rationalization for their behaviour, a plausible account, not an explanation to be compared to a scientific theory. Pareto also believed that rule by an élite was inevitable – though it is important to add that Pareto stressed that élites that become 'élitist' in the sense of closing off entry to outsiders simply to achieve and maintain exclusiveness are signing their own death warrant.

This part of his thought is rather elaborate, and Mayo absorbed a simplified version of it. He came perilously close to concluding that the majority of people are so dominated by sentiments that they are unfit to control anything but their own private lives, and may need numerous counsellors to enable them to do even that. One implication of this is that they would be unfit to rule in the sense of govern. It is not a very big step from such a position to saying that people are not capable even of participating in the choice of their rulers. Thus we can find in Mayo a man who at least toyed with authoritarian philosophies. We might even say there was something about Fascism as an idea that appealed to him; on the other hand, Smith's research shows clearly that Mayo found real-life Fascists sinister or idiotic.[7]

It is much more reasonable to portray Mayo as a paternalist and a patriarchalist. If an ideological label is necessary, those are the ones to tag on him. But the real point to remember is that we are dealing with a political amateur, a dabbler, rather than with the fellow traveller of blackshirts perceived by some critics of human relations. Preoccupation with Mayo's ideas about élites also distracts attention from his fascination with Paretian *sentiments* as the cement of everyday life, operating mainly to sustain stability in face-to-face relations. We should be wary of condemning out of hand his interest in the covert influences on action. They matter.

It took Mayo several years to absorb these new influences. This is apparent in a report of the department's first assignment. Mayo's account of it is brief and anecdotal. Work in a factory in a small midwestern town had been disrupted by ethnic tensions. The company solved the problem by replacing the trade union, which allegedly represented only the native Americans and had links with the Ku Klux Klan, with a company union. According to Mayo this simultaneously reduced the racism of the workers and their former preoccupation with pay levels.[8]

Mayo's description of these events is probably his most sociologically sensitive account of any concrete industrial situation. His ability to trace in the specific links between the developing in-plant situation and the social structure of the community is especially striking, but his theoretical commentary was abysmally confused. The practical study of labour relations, he declared, requires the integration of several approaches: 'These approaches must be physiological and biochemical . . . psychological and social.' He backed up this claim less by argument than by piling up references to Henderson's physiological discoveries, the work of the Myers group, the psychiatric writers he most admired, and the functionalist anthropologists. He even squeezed in Durkheim.

He was already developing an inclination to preach – in the text, passages attacking class-consciousness as a psycho-pathological obsession that lowers production were heavily italicized. Yet here appeared for the first time, in a gratingly raw form, his message, to be repeated increasingly often as time passed, that managers have a duty to society to create the conditions in the workplace that will foster contentment for individual workers and harmony between classes. He gave this appeal a twist that was almost to disappear in his later works. It is a most interesting one, for Mayo recommended changes to the design of work-tasks that he believed would prevent the build-up of the 'reverie', which causes tension.[9]

This is tantalizing. We seem to have here a rough sketch of the philosophy underlying parts of the Quality of Work Life (QWL) movement, which some commentators see as a new version of human relations.[10] In other respects, to come on Mayo defining the task of managers as a technical one, to be seen in terms of their skill as task designers and work organizers, is startling. In its developed form, Mayo's thought almost ignored the question of work organization. There is nothing resembling the notions of alienation or work degradation that lie at the heart of so many debates in the social sciences of work. There was a good reason for this. For a Mayoite, work was regarded not as an economic act, but as a social one. The most fundamental human impulse was to associate collaboratively with fellow human beings. Work provided the best opportunity in modern society for such collaboration. The logic of this action, then, was not primarily that of production. Production was viewed almost as a kind of fortunate by-product of association, not the reverse.

The duties of managers were specified by reference to this curiously unworldly model. Managers were charged with ensuring that association occurred through selecting psychologically well-adjusted workers, providing counselling services for those who became maladjusted, and providing a sense of security through leadership. Hardly surprising, then, that a doubting economist could comment that Mayoites wanted the corporation to provide 'soulfulness' for its members, not goods for the market. True, there is an assumption in Mayo's statement of the management problem that workers who experience association as a spontaneous act will also be high producers. Cruder Mayoite propagandists made this the core of their sales pitch to employers. In Mayo's later works it was played down.

It almost appears that as Mayo became more closely involved with industry, the further he lost sight of what production is *for* in any society, how this aim is affected by the institutions of the capitalist economy, and how pursuing such aims affects the organization of work. This grossly misrepresents many realities of political economy. But though it was certainly deliberate, it was not the result of any conscious deception. Mayo was entirely sincere in creating and propagating the perspective. That is one reason for his own popularity with managers. Mayo's approach to the Western Electric material was increasingly determined by this perspective.

At this point I had better declare an interest. Professor John Smith has criticized views attributed to me in the first edition of this book, which, as Smith puts it, 'presented Mayo as an essentially lightweight but attractive figure' whose involvement at Hawthorne was merely that of 'the out-of-town uncle who dropped in on the Studies and knew he was on to a good thing'.[11] I like the way Professor Smith puts it. I am flattered too by his suggestion that I have made my view the most commonly held one, at least in Britain and Australia. I have never wished to suggest that Mayo's involvement was just a dilettante or opportunist one; though, as my critic himself shows, well-documented aspects of Mayo's behaviour do leave room for doubt on both those counts.

The view put forward here takes account of the interesting new evidence Smith has made available. This demolishes the idea that Mayo was a fan of Pareto in the same sense as Lawrence Henderson. But while it further discredits the free-loading out-of-town-uncle image it hardly adds to Mayo's reputation as a dedicated fieldworker. Smith shows that between 1928 and 1943, a period of fifteen years, Mayo made a 'grand total of some nineteen visits' to Chicago. Twelve of these visits occurred between 1929 and 1932, making an average of four per year during the busiest part of the fieldwork – and when the project was coming under severe threat because of the Depression.[12] Smith gives the duration of each visit as 'ten to fourteen days', presumably inclusive of weekends. I leave it to readers to do their own arithmetic. Any active researcher will tell you how closely this time allocation would allow Mayo to be involved in a major programme in a distant locality.

I therefore persist in the view that it is wrong to visualize Mayo, clipboard in hand, personally conducting the Hawthorne studies. It seems we shall never know exactly what happened at Western Electric, though we now know a little more than we did: sadly, all the people who might have been able to tell us have been dying off. The books which gave the most factual detail (Roethlisberger and Dickson's *Management and the Worker*, and Whitehead's *The Industrial Worker*, see chapter 13) appeared long after the main experiments finished – they were awaiting company clearance. Meanwhile, Mayo's own *Human Problems* had appeared. It may be that his treatment of the studies, which made them and him celebrated, affected the later works. Again, we lack evidence on this but, as Smith points out, Roethlisberger is on record as saying that 'he saw the writing of *Management and the Worker* as a means of repaying his debt to Mayo for his stimulation and guidance'.[13]

From the beginning the studies were a company-based operation controlled by G. A. Pennock, a Western Electric engineer concerned with modernizing personnel work; though, thanks to Mayo, Industrial Relations Counsellors, a non-profit-making body based in New York City, took a close interest in the programme. Aided by W. J. Dickson, another Western Electric executive, Pennock established a division of industrial research in February 1929. The Harvard Business School had been providing advice from 1927, when Pennock approached Mayo about the puzzling illumination experiments – after the first relay assembly experiment had started. I know of no evidence that during those brief visits he made to Chicago Mayo did any leg-work in the factory.

With Donham and Henderson, Mayo certainly liaised with Western Electric's highest managers (C. G. Stoll and W. F. Hosford). Some of this work was done in the company's offices in New York, not at the plant in Chicago. Mayo showed great interest in the progress of work and suggested new lines of inquiry. But why is Mayo's help with research design or methodology not acknowledged in *Management and the Worker* until the Interview Programme is discussed? It was the anthropologist W. Lloyd Warner who most influenced the design of the bank-wiring room experiment – at a distance, also: he visited the plant only once.[14] As noted already, the researchers eventually adopted non-directive depth-interviewing techniques reminiscent of those favoured by the psychopathologists Mayo had admired for fifteen years. But this substitution was made only after their extraordinarily crude directive methods had failed. One can scarcely believe that Mayo, an expert psychotherapeutic interviewer, would have sanctioned these primitive techniques if he had been more fully briefed before the programme began.

At no time in his life did Mayo show either the patience or scepticism which most social research demands. He was a natural communicator with a flair for propaganda and at this time he was busily writing. In 1930, for example, he produced six publications, including one of the first brief accounts of the early work at Hawthorne. It appeared, interestingly enough, in *The Human Factor*.[15] His main role in the Western Electric research programme, apart from that of fund-raiser and scientific diplomat, seems clear to me: he appointed himself as its publicity officer.

His *Human Problems of an Industrial Civilization* (first published in 1932) confirmed his position. In many respects, and even taking a loose interpretation of the term, this book is unscientific, though Mayo obviously believed its policy recommendations were scientifically grounded. But his choice of evidence was selective. Its least tendentious section is a review of the human factor approach, where he concludes, quite correctly, that biological influences on work behaviour are important only in extreme situations. His treatment of the Hawthorne material, however, was thoroughly uncritical. Here are a few instances of this credulousness.

The output improvement of the first relay assembly group was attributed by Mayo not to financial incentives but to a 'complete reconstruction' of the group's industrial situation, by which Mayo meant merely that its supervisors became more friendly and understanding. This ignores the facts that: (1) members were deliberately selected for their co-operativeness; (2) two uncooperative members were soon replaced (3) one of their replacements urged her associates to make high bonuses because she had heavy family responsibilities; and (4) the second relay assembly group responded to financial incentives.[16]

This conclusion allegedly led directly to the Interview Programme, which aimed to improve supervision. The one finding that Mayo could never stop repeating was that while statements critical of material conditions were fairly reliable, statements critical of supervisors were not. Mayo states that foremen would not be harsh or dictatorial in 'an industry of the highest standing'. Worker reports to the contrary must betray the informant's 'obsession' or some other neurosis. The possibility that they might be objectively correct was ruled out on principle.

But as noted the first interviews had kicked off with the inquiry: 'Is your boss a slave-driver?'! There must have been some worries on this score. In fact, Roethlisberger and Dickson were later to provide evidence that many Hawthorne supervisors were indeed autocratic.[17] Moreover, Mayo himself cites only two cases of workers judged to be 'obsessively overthinking' their situation – and one possible victim of a 'clash of cultures' – among the first several hundred workers interviewed.[18] None the less, he declared that these findings could be regarded as firm evidence of a wider societal breakdown.

Mayo's use of the Durkheimian concept of *anomie* in this context was certainly interesting, though it might not be one that many modern sociologists would feel happy with. Citing the work of the Chicago ecological school of sociologists, an immense body of factual documentation, he argued that the Hawthorne factory was situated in a particularly anomic community, which Mayo contrasted with the traditionalism and stability of the 'Yankee City' that Warner, his Harvard colleague, was then investigating. This small industrial town (Newburyport) in New England certainly seemed at that time to support Mayo's view of the link between community and industrial harmony. A year later, however, this tranquillity was shattered by a massive strike (see chapter 13).

Mayo could not have foreseen this, but it underlines the bias in a distinction he drew between irrational and non-logical behaviour. His 'irrational' behaviour supposedly derives from social maladjustment and manifests itself, for example, in the Hawthorne workers' supposedly unfounded criticism of supervisors. Its source of inspiration is Janet. Non-logical behaviour, on the other hand, fits into a Paretian paradigm, characterizing the apparently unselfconscious co-operativeness and personal contentment attributed to work-groups like those of the Yankee City shoe factories.

Unlike Pareto, then, Mayo treated non-logical behaviour as an evaluative concept. To suppress such behaviour was dangerous. Once an individual begins to reflect on his social relationships, he courts personal unhappiness and threatens 'human collaboration in work, which, in primitive and developed societies, has always depended for its perpetuation upon the evolution of a non-logical social code . . .'.[19] Because he equated such reflectiveness with individualism and economic acquisitiveness, Mayo felt justified in relating social disintegration to the ideas of liberal pluralist democracy.

Yet, in the USA especially, where democracy and a free-enterprise economy have always been so strongly linked in public ideology and the folk wisdom of ordinary people, should not this anti-individualism logically have led him to condemn capitalism? Mayo seems to have been unaware that his political position was not simply consistent with economic collectivism but even pointed towards its desirability. Turning the famous phrase of the socialist historian R. H. Tawney on its head, Mayo complained bitterly that we should stop fretting about the 'sickness of an acquisitive society' and address what he regarded as the real problem, the acquisitiveness of a sick society.[20] This sounds good when you first hear it. But consider it more closely. What does it mean? I am unsure that it means very much at all. It also has a petulantly moralizing ring to it of the kind to be expected of someone who thought of himself as one of the last Victorians.

The political observations of *Human Problems* degenerate into some rum stuff indeed. I used to regard these passages as radically right-wing ideology, a plea for corporate Fascism with a human relations face.

It sounds much less sinister to me now than it used to, although it still seems as dotty as ever. According to Mayo, liberalism has fostered anomie by stressing individualism; and liberal political institutions cannot cope with the resulting social disorder and industrial strife. Indeed, these democratic institutions only aggravate the misery of our dislocated lives. Salvation lies in discovering a socially skilled administrative élite who will treat the problem at what Mayo regarded as its source, in the workplace, by nurturing vital non-logical impulses. Not for Mayo, then, the solution to social breakdown via the rediscovery of Victorian values and the stimulation of an enterprise culture, with full citizenship reserved for those who have the pecuniary mentality of small-business people. He violently attacked the 'atomization' of the *petit-bourgeois* Utopia. Mayo would have detested Thatcherism.

In these passages, Mayo oscillated between verbal fireworks and grotesque political naïveté. Socialism, Communism and Marxism, he protested, 'seem to be irrelevant to the industrial events of the twentieth century', except that they 'probably express the workers' desire to recapture something of the lost human solidarity'.[21] In such declarations as this he seems to be applauding the ambition of collectivism to deliver a sense of security while simultaneously vilifying it on the grounds that is outdated. This shows a confusion, a self-contradiction that we need not dwell on much further. At times his documentation verged on unconscious comic genius, as when he quoted from Brooks Adams to seal his case for a new caste of corporation executives, or Guardians: 'I take it to be an axiom,' Adams had assured his readers, 'that perfection of administration must be commensurate to the bulk and the momentum of the mass to be administered, otherwise the centrifugal will overcome the centripetal force, and the mass will disintegrate. In other words, civilization would dissolve.'[22] This sounds impressive but means very little.

His dismissal of economic bases of motivation was breathtaking. Militant trade unionism in Britain, according to Mayo, was an unconscious attempt to perpetuate stable social relations. That it might aim to win or protect economic advantages was not simply overlooked. Such manifest demands, he maintained, should not fool us: the latent quest for psychic security was what counted. The British case also allowed him to drive home his rather simplified version of Pareto's theory of the circulation of élites. British management had failed to realize that its workers were going on strike for something much more fundamental than pay or job security. What better proof of this élite's obsolescence? But he stated that all countries, including the USSR, needed to establish a new caste of guardians of social health: 'Better methods for the discovery of an administrative élite, better methods for maintaining working morale. The country that first solves these problems will infallibly outstrip the others in the race for stability, security and development.'[23]

The countries that have come closest in this century to espousing the logic of non-logic and the forced circulation of élites were Fascist Italy and Nazi Germany. We know where those paths led, and towards the end of the Second World War Mayo published his *Social Problems of an Industrial Civilization.*[24] Mayo insisted, however, that the war overwhelmingly proved his case.

'*If our social skills had advanced step by step with our technical skills, there would not have been another European war*: this is my recurrent theme,' he argued.[25] *Social Problems* itemized and discussed these skills carefully. The crucial arts were group leadership and personal counselling. In the 1920s, Mayo had stated firmly that clinical interviewing should be left to experts, and he had hedged on its efficacy as a tool in the workplace. Now he declared baldly: 'This is a very simple skill, but it can have the most astonishing effects in industrial situations.'[26] Mayo was impressed with the idea that 'after a few such interviews', uncooperative workers 'return to work with the declaration that they have "talked it off"'. He rewrote the account of his first investigation at Continental Mills in Philadelphia to throw emphasis on the role of the nurse as a counselling interviewer, and that of the company president as a leader. His chapter on Hawthorne concentrated almost exclusively on the Interview Programme.

Effective counselling should make for strong leadership and

each could be seen as crucial aspects of communication. Through skilful communication, the manager would build teamwork by expanding the worker's 'desire and capacity to work better with management'. Higher education should be redesigned to develop communication skills, especially therapeutic interviewing, among recruits to the élite.[27] Teamwork had not been mentioned in *Human Problems* but two studies of labour absenteeism in America in which Mayo had been involved during the Second World War convinced him of its potentialities as a way of promoting social integration.[28] For Mayo, the only valid form of team was one that 'comes into being only when someone in authority definitely works to create it'.[29] (This automatically ruled out the collaboration of the bank-wiring group members at Hawthorne as socially valuable teamwork – not on the grounds that it limited output, but because it resulted from spontaneous action by the men themselves.) Detailed study of such a group had shown that the supervisor and leading hand devoted the bulk of their time to communication.

It is true that such units, especially when they have a definite common project, can result in a high sense of involvement and purposefulness for all the people who make them up. Nobody at all concerned with economic performance and the quality of working life would deny that they are infinitely more desirable forms of organizing work than those usually adopted. Clearly, too, they are consistent with different kinds of political regime and economic system. But employers, managers, trade unions, and many workers themselves, each have very good reasons for opposing such changes. Once again, the problem was not so much the undesirability of the proposals, but the extreme political disingenuousness with which they were presented.

Most of the evidence produced by Mayo was subsidiary to the social philosophy it purportedly underpinned. The philosophy itself was more or less a reiteration of what he had written a dozen years previously. He denounced what he called the 'rabble hypothesis' of economics and scientific management, which pictures people as lonely self-seekers. This tawdry paradigm should be replaced with a vision built on the presumption that money means less to people than the gratification of their non-logical sociability. Critics, as we shall see, were to dismiss this as a 'tribal hypothesis'. A managerial élite capable of fashioning an adaptive society must be created. Manipulation by them of people's inner needs and feelings should be viewed as an historic duty not as an unwarrantable intrusion. Mayo certainly mentioned the possibly tonic effect on productivity of these changes but he left the impression that management is closer to social work than to money-making.

Mayo died soon after *Social Problems* appeared. But his ideas enjoyed a great vogue, among personnel managers especially, for twenty years after his death. His former academic associates and his heirs within the human relations orbit acknowledged his inspiration; many of them shared some at least of his broader theories. Yet to understand human relations it is vital to separate his work from theirs. Several points to emerge from this sketch of his career and thought may clarify the distinctions we shall be making in the next few chapters.

Firstly, Mayo should be thought of primarily as a psychotherapist. He loved this work and did it brilliantly until shortly before he died. He made a speciality of handling the psychological crises of Harvard students or faculty who were on the point of breakdown; the young Roethlisberger was one of his clients. His basic concern was with individual neurosis and maladjustment. Once Henderson had introduced him to sociology, he picked from it those theories that seemed to him most relevant to reducing individual stress. Social medicine on the grand scale was necessary to remedy the endemic 'obsession' of industrialism. But Mayo never grasped how social structure, economic interest, and political institutions complicate social relations and add to the challenge of providing workable solutions to our problems.

Mayo's impatience to help people made him a very incautious scientist. Examples of his shaky command of research technique and of his willingness to accept the poorly researched conclusions of others have been given. They could be multiplied many times. Even his readiness to reinterpret his own work and revise his explanations, an otherwise praiseworthy ability, reflects a growing dogmatism rather than healthy self-criticism. Again, his personal charm and gifts as a publicist seem to have protected him from the discipline and criticism that might have made his work more thorough and his pronouncements better grounded. The *Problems* books[30] had suggested novel solutions to managers faced with recalcitrant workers. But even more important, they designated management as an élite corps of paternally benevolent administrators. This sealed Mayo's fate. To adapt Voltaire, Mayo fashioned the manager in his own image and the manager returned the compliment.

It was, of course, a fate many would covet. Once Mayo's face had appeared on the cover of *Time*, a year or two before his death, together with a covering story in the magazine's pseudo-Homeric style, his thought emerged rapidly as the twentieth century's most seductive managerial ideology. What, after all, could be more appealing than to be told that one's subordinates are non-logical; that their uncooperativeness shields a frustrated urge to collaborate; that their demands for cash mask a need for personal approval; and that you have a historic destiny as a broker of social harmony? We should not underestimate the appeal of such a doctrine. Some social scientists carelessly assimilate managers with employers. Certainly managers are hired to ensure that employees are organized and motivated to serve the employer's interests but the strains on managers that arise in doing this can be considerable. Managerialist doctrine like Mayo's provides those managers who accept it with an exceptionally attractive explanation of what the role of the manager means. It gives that role a social meaning that offsets the distracting idea that the organizer of the collaborative act of production is concerned with wringing the maximum effort from employees. On the contrary, economic collaboration is portrayed by it as the fundamental bonding action of human social life, indispensable as much for survival and continuity as the production of utilities. Those responsible for securing collaboration must be allocated the highest standing. They are the most important experts society possesses.

Some of this might be true, other parts may be utter nonsense but most of it can be neither verified nor disproved. It is not knowledge, but a world-view constructed to justify certain policies. It is not even much use, in itself, for the kind of interventionist purposes discussed in the Introduction. But it is of the utmost value to anybody who wishes to justify such action. To those concerned with plotting the development of industrialism it is also of exceptional interest. I have tried to show why this is so.

It is vital to remember that human relations was not a unitary phenomenon. The distinction between Mayo's contribution and the others we will consider is of fundamental importance. We shall find several that are far more impressive as social science but others that verge on a cynical or mean-minded readiness to exploit such knowledge for the manipulation of employees as producers. Whatever its failings, Mayo's research was undertaken with sincerity. His doctrine, however ill-grounded or otherwise unacceptable some of us may find it, was inspired by a certain vision, and by a generous sympathy for his fellow men and women, characteristic of those thinkers whose politics are equally honest and simple-minded.

13

The Harvard Group

In this chapter I shall examine the work of writers whom I regard as representative of what is sometimes called the Harvard Group. In fact, there never existed any Harvard Group in the sense of a self-consciously organized school of thought, with closely policed orthodoxies and unmentionable heresies. But it is true that in the 1930s Harvard produced a collection of investigators interested closely in questions of industrial behaviour. They encouraged each other, exchanged advice on methods of inquiry, debated unpublished findings, and exerted a degree of mutual influence. The best-known were Lawrence J. Henderson, T. N. Whitehead, Fritz Roethlisberger, W. Lloyd Warner, George Homans, Eliot Chapple, and Conrad Arensberg.

And yes, there was Elton Mayo. But to identify the Harvard Group with Mayo can lead to serious confusion. Perhaps the best-known recent account of the early development of industrial sociology in the USA[1] is weakened by its failure to make this distinction, whose importance was first pointed out by Henry Landsberger.[2]

The investigators listed above were attached either to the Harvard Business School or the Department of Anthropology, and contributed mainly to one of two major research projects; the Hawthorne studies at the Western Electric Company in Chicago (Business School) or the Yankee City studies in Newburyport, New England (Department of Anthropology). Although the latter project was not concerned primarily with industrial behaviour it did lead to a classic industrial monograph, *The Social System of the Modern Factory*,[3] which will be examined later in this chapter.

Furthermore, most of its personnel were later to form the nucleus of the Chicago, or 'interactionist' branch of human relations. And its leader, Warner, provided expertise for the anthropological phase at the Hawthorne plant.

To simplify matters, the writers I shall deal will be those who contributed to the Hawthorne project. By concentrating on them I hope to show that the Harvard Group was a relatively heterogeneous assemblage, and that some of its members' work deserves to be more highly valued.

We must begin with Roethlisberger and Dickson. Earlier I suggested that Mayo's selective use of the Hawthorne data distorted understanding of the studies. What, then, is their true value? Because the studies remain an important source of ideas and inspiration, this is a live question. But it must be taken jointly with another: what is the value of *Management and the Worker?*

Roethlisberger's and Dickson's monograph was the definitive report of the studies. How far was it affected by Mayo's advance publicity? Though we cannot determine this exactly, there are certainly signs in the book that ideas which supposedly guided the design and interpretation of the research were fully applied to data only some time after their collection. Accounts of the painstaking elimination of unproductive methods and hypotheses, which form so much of the text, therefore have at times a decidedly enigmatic flavour. More than fifty years after the studies were undertaken, and over forty since *Management and the Worker* was published, there is no way of finally establishing the book's completeness or reliability as a record. The most sensible procedure is to accept it – initially – as it stands. This certainly permits a useful evaluation of the studies as a research programme. Subsequently, this can be modified by an examination of the book as a document and theoretical essay.

The studies have certainly been oversold as a classic research programme but much about them is thoroughly creditable. The sheer doggedness of the investigators, eagerly collecting masses of data over several years, is impressive. The administration of so many thousands of interviews has rarely been matched. Likewise, the willingness of the investigators to accept advice and attempt novel methods compares well with the rigidity of many other investigators. This relative open-mindedness and caution must at times have annoyed the company's higher management, who obviously never viewed the programme as a purely scientific enterprise. There must have been times when justifying the sheer cost of the growing Pennock–Dickson research empire required diplomacy, and conviction that the final outcome would justify the expense and effort. Again, it appears that the investigators developed a real sympathy for their subjects, comparing favourably with the rather stiff-lipped paternalism of the company towards its employees. A capacity for imaginative projection into the lives of subjects is an asset to any social researcher. (The investigators seem to have been most sympathetic towards junior supervisors, rather less so towards manual workers, and perhaps tactfully evasive about their views on senior managers.)

It is true that handling of subjects – those of the first relay assembly group in particular – was sometimes patronizing, even heavy-handed. Feminist colleagues complain that this reflects inveterate sexism on the part of the investigators – the relay workers were, after all, women. Maybe. An examination of sexism in the studies would be historically instructive. (But note that no distinction is made in the title of the book: indeed the implication is that men and women workers are interchangeable – which of course may indicate another type of bias still.) I think the handling of the first relay group reflected inexperience rather than any prejudiced image of workpeople as irrational members of a preliterate tribe who needed firm treatment. No image of the worker, or of the organization, seems to have crystallized until a fairly late stage. One result of this, as Landsberger has stressed, is that data which support a variety of such images were generated and reported. However questionable the interpretations finally favoured, the rejection of the radical behaviourism marking the earliest experiments – paralleling the advance of British human factor studies – constituted a breakthrough. Again, whatever the defects of the final images imposed on the data, they do not rely on a Mayoite contrast between an anomic wider society and blissful social harmony in the plant.

During the central investigations, in fact, human relations skills were considered feeble, even rather pathetic, *ad hoc* measures adopted by hard-pressed supervisors caught, like other categories of employee, between inescapable pressures whose source lay in structures of authority, company rules, and the technological apparatus. The manipulative phase did not consist of experiments to test leadership skills. If the team had concluded that such skills were powerful influences they certainly could have tested them systematically. Finally, though I would not press this point, the investigators were somewhat unlucky that the Depression occurred when it did. It undoubtedly distorted behaviour and results; though they could have done so more searchingly, they did try to assess its effects on the studies but the drastic effects of the change hopelessly complicated their already daunting problems of analysis.

In all, then, the studies embodied a diligent, relatively open-minded and generally ethical search for valid knowledge about industrial behaviour and (in the event) the business organization as a structured entity. In view of the intra-company control, these achievements are remarkable. Yet these properties are ambiguous. Open-mindedness as to method and interpretation, for example, can lead to lack of focus and direction, and there is a danger of accepting poor advice. To resist only partially pressure from a sponsor is to fall short of adequate independence. The Hawthorne team were far too eclectic in their use of methods. Their research technique was often slapdash even by the standards of the day. It seems more instructive to concentrate criticism of the programme on these grounds. Failures in judgement on the theoretical, practical and ideological dimensions are admittedly related to them. The development of the team's theories certainly did proceed alongside the investigations, but in *Management and the Worker* they are reported in a finalized form. What actually occurred during the investigations could not simply be rewritten, and there is no sign of any such misreporting. Let us treat this research project as a source of useful lessons, for what we can still learn from the many blunders the investigators undeniably made, and not in the gloatingly negative spirit of too many of their critics.

The human factor phase adopted the experimental method. This demands the controlled exposure of subjects to experimental stimuli and the careful measurement of any ensuing effects. Achieving satisfactory control and measuring effects with human subjects is always extraordinarily difficult. Several elementary precautions do, however, reduce the likelihood of spurious or inconclusive results. For example, individual experimental subjects or groups, and a matching control group, should be selected by identical (preferably statistically random) sampling methods from the overall population; if the experiment demands isolation, both groups should be isolated under identical conditions; then the experimental stimuli should be imposed singly on the experimental subjects; and the results of any one exposure should be assessed before introducing a further one.

Such elementary precautions were not observed in the two Relay Assembly and the Mica Splitting experiments. The failure to establish the control group is especially surprising, because controls had been used in the previous illumination studies. The investigators did regard the second relay and the Mica groups as controls but neither were matched satisfactorily to the first relay group; nor were their exposures (to the small-group incentive and improved conditions respectively, but not to both) managed identically.

Moreover – and this is crucial with social experimentation – all these experiments occurred at different times: in the case of the Mica group, the onset of the Depression demonstrated the importance of this time factor – or should have done. The investigators should have foreseen such problems. But, apart from that, they had all been discussed and handled by the Myersians in Britain. Were the investigators ignorant of this literature? Not so. The work of Myersians is mentioned in *Management and the Worker* – but, significantly, only with regard to problems of interpretation. Did the sponsor refuse to foot the bill for proper controls? We shall never know. It remains a puzzling failure. Alex Carey, in his unremittingly critical review of these experiments, has exposed many further eccentricities of design and concluded that the results equally plausibly suggest the finding that the investigators rejected, i.e. the force of incentives.[4] This calls for an observation about the celebrated Hawthorne Effect in social science experiments.

Actually, at least *three* Hawthorne Effects have been distinguished. The first and best known is that discovered in the lighting experiments, where the knowledge that they were experimental subjects modified the behaviour of the subjects so drastically as to wreck the experiment. The Myersians had dealt with this kind of problem in the 1920s. In designing the first Relay experiment the Hawthorne investigators, contrary to most impressions, took careful account of it. What they failed to do was to hit on a method of limiting this I'm-a-guinea-pig reaction. The observer was placed in the test room to neutralize the effect by ensuring that the women's attitude to the experiment remained constant.[5]

But how was he to achieve such a feat? This was never spelled out, and the observer became a kind of friendly supervisor. From their different viewpoints, George Homans and Henry Landsberger both stress the significance of this change in the pattern of supervision.[6] When the investigators claimed later that production rose because the experiment transformed the subjects' total industrial situation, they had his change of role very much in mind. This, then, was a second Hawthorne Effect, which was to fire the imagination of a generation of management theorists about the potency of democratic supervision. But it also illustrates a serious degree of fumbling over experimental control.

We can even define a variant of this second Hawthorne Effect. Whitehead's account of the first relay group makes it abundantly plain that, at least initially, the observer's credentials as a good-pal supervisor were not all that they might have been.[7] What is more, after the two uncooperative subjects were replaced, one of the newcomers, a mettlesome Italian immigrant, assumed a leadership style more reminiscent of the driving, production-oriented variety than any other. The observer did little to check this rather different upset to 'constancy'. If the experiment were not subject to so many other contaminating influences one might even conclude that the real Hawthorne Effect centres on driving leadership.

The third Hawthorne Effect was defined by H. M. Parsons, and is a rather technical one, resulting from a process of *operant conditioning.*[8] This refers to a process whereby a novel pattern of behaviour is implanted by rewarding certain actions and not others. The subjects were informed of their output rates, Parsons points out, and their performance was reinforced by a money reward. The implications of this simple fact were overlooked for thirty years. It should be noted that the effect assumes the power of money as a motivator. This was not the sort of effect that the investigators were going out of their way to discover.

Before these investigations were terminated, interviewing superseded experimentation as the main research method. This apparently accidental change of course was actually to yield the most sociologically interesting and probably most reliable data. At the time of the switch this could hardly have been predicted. Logically, the investigators should have refined their experimental techniques. Quite possibly this would have led to valuable results. We are pushed towards the judgement that they had done no more than flirt with the experimental method, and were later to flirt with an anthropological method. At first, they certainly flirted with interviewing. Subsequently, however, under Mayo's clinical spell, it became their consuming passion and they became very good indeed at it.

Rightly, the semi-clinical depth-interviewing techniques finally evolved are still held in high esteem among teachers of research methods.[9] This is no place to debate the finer methodological problems of the interview method as a whole;[10] likewise, any ethical objections to the interviewing in this clinical phase seem to me poorly gounded – as Landsberger has noted, the company used some of the material to improve conditions, and the programme may have benefited employees indirectly through relaxation of some harsher supervisory practices.

What remains bewildering is the saturation coverage of the programme. A substantial minority of employees were polled. Why some sampling scheme was not adopted remains mysterious. Even a crudely structured sample would have maintained acceptable representativeness. It might also have increased the reliability of data through reducing exhaustion in the interviewers and concentrating the programme in a shorter time period.

The anthropological phase grew more naturally from the clinical phase than the latter did from human factor experimentation. The bank wiring group study, however, hardly deserves its perplexingly widespread and durable reputation as a model of industrial ethnography. Certainly, the investigators exercised ingenuity in its design and execution.[11] Commentators likewise point out that the investigators seem to have realized that rich behavioural data could be obtained only by researching less actively.[12]

But even this commendation would be challenged by many research theorists. Except in very superficial ways the observer was not a participant. Thus, while his description of personnel, practices and relationships is kindly in tone, it is also patronizing. If the observer had truly shared the life of 'his people', or had been capable of a truly sympathetic identification with them, surely the bank wiring men would not have passed into the folklore of the social sciences as a wacky bunch of industrial Keystone Cops? Rather, they would have been portrayed as a group of very worried men faced increasingly with the deprivation and stigma of unemployment: less ethnic, but altogether more authentic. For the Hawthorne team to have planted a secret participant observer in a shop-floor group would have been ethically outrageous. But even disregarding this moral barrier, operational and methodological complexities would have undermined such a manoeuvre. I see no way in which the company itself could have undertaken research of this kind acceptably. Thus the utility of the bank wiring study as actually undertaken is problematic.

It is noteworthy too, that the strategy of segregating the group in a special area derived from a revived interest in factors affecting output.[13] Data gathering was linked to this aim. The researchers' judgement seems to have been that in-plant factors overwhelmingly determined work attitudes and behaviour – by which is meant above all *output* behaviour. Yet interviewing had indicated the potential influence of out-plant social factors on in-plant phenomena. The whole thrust of the bank wiring study systematically suppressed these discoveries. Examination of the group members' external attachments was superficial.

In fact, superficiality and selectivity devalue all those data that were collected. The observer kept a daily record of 'significant happenings', which eventually amounted to 400 typed pages. A 'significant happening' was presumably one which, in the observer's judgement, related to social control of production. Can a record that averages just over one page of 'significant' observations per day convey anything like a full account of developing interpersonal relationships? Anyone who has attempted observation of social situations would find the idea ludicrous. A similar criticism can be made of the observation data on the first relay group.

As a research programme, then, the Hawthorne investigation provides a disturbing number of instances of methodological and technical inexperience, even by the pioneering standards of the day. Commentators like Madge[14] would disagree, pointing out correctly that all social investigators must adapt standard methods, and improvise on occasion. But there is little evidence that the investigators familiarized themselves fully with contemporary research technology. Even their use of the Harvard Business School's expertise seems to have been either casual or belated.

There is no single explanation for these failures. To be just to the investigators, it is worth remembering that the sheer administrative burdens of a major investigation can interfere with methodological self-discipline. Again, though Western Electric was a uniquely patient sponsor for those days, one may presume that there were pressures on the investigators, or that they felt some obligation, to earn their keep. Mayo's preface to the book is laden with generalities about the march of knowledge. Compare this with the authors' own candid statement that 'Management regarded these experiments primarily as attempts to build up a sound body of knowledge upon which to base executive policy and action.'[15]

Maybe an additional explanation lies in the theoretical proclivities of the researchers themselves. Were they, from quite an early date, trying to prove some point, specifically, the weakness of economic influences on workers' behaviour? If *Management and the Worker* is at all reliable as a report of the evolution of the investigators' thought, it supports this hypothesis strongly. Many commentators have noted that Roethlisberger and Dickson protest far too much their perplexity over surprise findings and their diligence in checking them. The variability of this scepticism is demonstrated most strikingly in the denial that the first relay group's output increase could be attributed to its incentive alone, or that the bank wiring group's restriction of output mainly reflected fear of unemployment. Quite against their own evidence, they singled out changed supervision and fear of technical change respectively as the key variables.[16]

An underlying predisposition to devalue, though not to dismiss, monetary and economic influences goes far to explain the form and course of these studies. Subsidiary to this is an inclination to locate the crucial variables within the plant. To recapitulate: though the interview programme amply demonstrated the vital importance of workers' out-plant affiliations it was followed by a study presuming the primacy of the in-plant situation. Whether such biases affected the running of the studies themselves, they certainly stamp themselves on *Management and the Worker* as an interpretative essay. H. A. Landsberger's *Hawthorne Revisited* provided the first and still the only extended assessment of Roethlisberger's and Dickson's work.[17] It is strongly recommended to readers who wish to pursue this question in greater depth. Here I shall merely summarize Landsberger's main points, before adding one or two of my own and briefly commenting on Landsberger's own critique.

The very least to be said for *Management and the Worker*, Landsberger argues, is that its plodding documentation compares well with Mayo's excited tracts. Readers are provided with enough information to challenge its conclusions. It acknowledges some force in economic incentives and conditions. It describes the design of investigations in some detail. Hawthorne Effects are discussed. Supervisors and managers are often portrayed unflatteringly, both in their treatment of workers and of the research team. Little faith is expressed in standard human relations techniques. Again, the authors eschew any image of workers as entirely irrational or non-logical tribesmen in overalls. 'Sentiments' may govern *some* of their actions, and *some* of the actions of managers too, including the formation of informal groups. But much of their action embodies a subjectively and even objectively rational component – their response to incentives and resistance to technical change, for example.

Nor is it true that out-plant affiliations are ignored. Certainly, the effects of union membership on work behaviour are omitted. But during the main investigations, Hawthorne was a non-union plant. Actually, Landsberger seems to have overlooked the fact that some interviews suggest that union officials were trying to recruit members in Hawthorne – the company's known anti-union policy could have affected the attitudes to their work of potential (or secret) recruits – but he is correct in claiming that the authors express no hostility to unions as such.

Managers and supervisors, too, typically cut a poor figure. The first relay group experiment is reported largely as a tale of escape from arbitrary supervision. The interviewing programme aimed to improve supervision. Interviews with junior supervisors showed that they had been constantly bullied by higher managers. Invariably harassed, frequently petty, and sometimes ineffectual, the Hawthorne managers seem poor candidates for the Mayoite élite. Implicitly at least, the book suggests that the structural requirements of efficient production impede the formation of such an élite.

Finally, Roethlisberger and Dickson have very little to say about the effects of some supposed anomie in the wider society on the deportment of workers. Stressful familial situations are often referred to in discussing the attitudes and behaviour of individual workers, particularly when these impose heavy financial responsibilities or check the 'Americanizing' influence of plant experiences on social activities. But Hawthorne is not conceived, or proposed, as an actual or potential community for uprooted obsessives.

Against this, some very serious faults must be recognized (curiously, Landsberger does not include the eclectic methodology and blundering research technique). One of the gravest faults is a highly selective conception of industrial conflict and its sources. While several varieties of intra-plant conflict are examined, their causes are located within the organization. Output restriction supposedly stems from resistance to technological change, not from any wider hostility to management, from the experience of being managed or – here they are least perceptive – from economic self-protection.

Because the book was published in the late 1930s, after the slump and substantial unionization of Hawthorne workers, Landsberger rightly stressed that the authors 'committed a well-nigh incredible sin of omission' in failing to notice that the conditions they had observed a decade before, might have some bearing on this surfacing of open conflict.[18] In the later, more theoretical chapters the authors also introduce a concept, the human organization of the plant, that apparently embodies 'the collective purpose of the whole organization'. Thus, while the social system of the factory is not naturally harmonious, its human organization is – or, presumably, should be.[19] Further, the collaboration of the first relay group is regarded as of a higher order than that of the bank wiring group – because the former did not split into cliques, or because it was more manageable?

Moreover, in the two final chapters, which briefly outline the 'counselling programme', the authors endorse managerial manipulation. Landsberger emphasizes that these 'how-to-do-it' chapters are vague and contradictory. The first relay group's co-operativeness allegedly arose from a distinct battery of supervisory practices. Yet co-operativeness was a chief criterion of selection into it, two operators were dismissed for uncooperativeness, and a replacement, as we noted earlier, became an informal production-centred supervisor.

Finally, the authors do not mention that the Hawthorne counsellors were expected to adopt an active role. Subsequently, the Wilenskys were able to report from first-hand experience that a counsellor did not need to be contacted by a troubled worker before adjustment services were applied.[20]

Landsberger makes several more contentious claims for the studies and the book that require comment. He suggests, for example, that the studies were impeded by the 'radically behaviourist direction' of industrial research when they began.[21] He is presumably referring to the British human factor work. Yet by 1927 the Myersians were modifying their approach. Despite the frequent reference to the work of the Myersians in *Management and the Worker*, there is no sign that the studies benefited at the design stage from the British work.

He claims also that delayed publication promoted misunderstanding of the book. It was misinterpreted even by human relations enthusiasts. If they had examined it more carefully, they would have modified their theories and practical proposals. There is something in this. But if the authors themselves believed their colleagues were making such misinterpretations why did they not disabuse them? They had ample opportunity for doing so, both informally and in print.

Landsberger's reassessment is summarized in the following passage:

> *Management and the Worker* presents a very sensitive picture of the forces which today draw classes together and pull them apart. Differences in levels of income; the worker's economic status and security; his subordination in a large impersonal organization; differences in past background and present interests; new barriers to social mobility in the form of educational requirements for promotion – they all tend to produce a clearer differentiation between workers and management, and they are all described in greater or lesser extent in *Management and the Worker*.[22]

I recognize that this reading can be made, but I would put the stresses in a different place, more or less as follows.

The organization is a social system performing two functions, the production of goods and the supply of individual satisfactions. This social system possesses two chief aspects, which interact: the technical organization and the human organization. The former consists of 'all those physical items related to the task of technical production', i.e. technology in its hardware sense. The latter includes what might be called technology as software, i.e. the division of labour into work-roles, but it also comprises a social organization, which, when analysed, itself splits into formal organization and information organization (this might be termed 'liveware').

The formal aspect of the social organization is constituted by hierarchical and functional categories of personnel – the authors distinguish between managers, technologists, supervisors, office workers and manual workers. It operates to secure both economic objectives and formal co-operation between personnel. By itself, however, it does not necessarily secure a sufficient level of co-operation. Informal organization arises more or less spontaneously to satisfy individual social needs. In so doing, it may supplement formal organization beneficially from the point of view of output, at any rate: this occurred in the first relay group. Or it may conflict with formal organization, to the detriment of both the informal group and the organization: this occurred with the bank wiring group.

Clearly, the authors regard informal organization as inevitable, but not necessarily dysfunctional. Potentially, it can be utilized by managers for their own purposes. Further, all company personnel are involved in it to some extent. Likewise, all personnel are motivated by the logics of cost (values for judging organizational profitability), of efficiency (values about organized co-operation) and of 'sentiments' (values about gratifying face-to-face relationships). However, managers and workers espouse these logics in varying degrees. This results from varying familial and professional socialization and from experiences at work. The balance between the forcefulness of the logics can vary in any individual or group. Rapid change in particular may increase the force of sentiments, thus reinforcing informal structures. The equilibrium necessary for organizational effectiveness demands managerial intervention, because 'the limits of human collaboration are determined far more by the informal than by the formal organization of the plant'.[23]

Evidently, a Mayoite manager could read into this a Mayoite message. But, as already noted, the implied trust in human relations conflicts with the authors' other statements, and, in fact, it appears almost as an afterthought – is this a shred of comfort to the sponsor? Such an interpretation is by no means preposterous if one takes this chapter, which is often unclear, as a whole. In my view a thoroughly plausible interpretation of this passage would characterize it less as an essay in human-relations theory than as a precocious contribution to the technological implications approach. Consider this statement:

> The two aspects into which an industrial plant can be roughly divided – the technical organization and the human organization – are interrelated and inter-dependent. The human organization is constantly moulding and re-creating the technical organization either to achieve more effectively the common economic purpose or to secure more satisfaction for its members. Likewise, changes in the technical organization require an adaptation on the part of the human organization.[24]

Without anticipating the fuller examination of the technological implications approach in the next part of the book, several properties of it may be noted now. One, the organization tends to be viewed as a system embodying a supposed common purpose. Two, a technology (both as equipment and as a set of work-roles – hardware and software) realizes this common purpose. Three, technology is thought to mould worker behaviour and relationships (liveware).

All of these assumptions underlie the quoted passage. Roethlisberger's and Dickson's theory, then, possesses the chief advantages and limitations of the later approach. In its favour is a recognition that the technical apparatus severely limits human relations manipulation of the workpeople and their informal organization. Against this, it underplays the influence of factors which operate from outside the workplace, and it is somewhat behaviourist.

Nothing could be more ironic than that Roethlisberger and Dickson, the chief empirical authorities of the human relations movement, apparently ascribed to the structural properties of the organization a non-human power to determine human action. The behaviourism of the human factor school, whose perspectives they supposedly rejected, was unconsciously resurrected in their new guise.

The distinction between Mayo and his main Harvard associates can be further clarified by brief reference to T. N. Whitehead. I once called Whitehead 'Mayo's Mayo'. This is too glib by far, and John Smith's historical work in the Mayo archive[25] shows that Mayo found Whitehead personally unsympathetic. All the same, Whitehead undoubtedly saw some things as he seems to have thought Mayo would see them.

Anyone who wants to establish some sort of link between human relations and Fascism should start with Whitehead. He is known as the author of a strongly worded tract *Leadership in a Free Society*, published in the mid 1930s.[26] It exaggerates the viewpoint and tone of Mayo's *Problems* books – though Smith tells us that Mayo came close to detesting Whitehead, who was one of those many arrogant, supercilious not quite upper-class Englishmen which the country loosed on the world in the days of Empire. It is full of breast-beating over social breakdown and, in effect, invites industrial managers to step in to restore order. But his real claim to attention here rests on his *The Industrial Worker: A Statistical Study of Human Relations in a Group of Manual Workers*.[27]

Whitehead had an academic training in natural science, and had worked for the British Admiralty. He became involved in the Western Electric studies as a statistical adviser. His father was the celebrated scientific philosopher Alfred North Whitehead. He was an associate professor of the Harvard Business School when he published *The Industrial Worker* in 1938.

The first thing to notice about the book is its title. For a competent statistician it was a audacious one indeed: generalization was to be based largely on one case, the first relay assembly group at Hawthorne. Secondly, it is an analysis of the statistical and observation material for the whole five years of this experiment collected by the company researchers: these data were handed over to Whitehead as an independent expert. His assignment was that of chief data-dredger and number-cruncher: to seek out any correlation between output and hard objective factors – fatigue, health and weather, etc.

No such correlations of any significance were discovered, whereupon Whitehead proceeded to analyse the group as a small society undergoing continuous change. The first volume of the study presents the tabulated statistics as a whole, and as such, is a *tour de force*. The sociological volume is long, boring and opinionated, and it made much less impact than *Management and the Worker*. Of course, it covered only a fraction of the studies, but Whitehead's treatment of the relay group attempted to repeat Roethlisberger's and Dickson's treatment of the bank wiring group, focusing on its developing social relations. Its two main points of interest are its revelation, sometimes unconscious, of facts about the first relay group which Roethlisberger and Dickson played down or omitted, and its highly confused recognition of the role of microscopic change, of the 'processual' element in social life.

These virtues were often combined. The example I shall mention here is Whitehead's examination of the leadership role assumed by operator 2, who replaced the 'uncooperative' operator 2A, after she joined the group in January 1928. He noted: 'From now on the history of the Test Room revolves around the personality of Operator 2,' giving as an illustration of her normal leadership style her reaction to a poor set of output figures: 'Oh! What's the matter with those other girls? I'll kill them.'[28]

Whitehead also provides much evidence suggesting that supervision in the main department was autocratic, that the group were, in effect, deceived when the investigators told them to 'work normally', and that the onset of the Depression seriously undermined morale. There is much other information, intriguing because Whitehead mentions it so offhandedly. For instance, when the first relay group was disbanded in 1932, its members were briefly replaced by a team of substitutes. This was thought to be broadly acceptable from a methodological point of view!

But his portrayal of the relay group as a 'small society' whose members' behaviour was governed by Paretian sentiments reaches the heights of absurdity. 'Obviously,' he states, in analysing the social personality of operator 2, 'the instinct for combination was strong compared with the persistence of her aggregates.'[29] This makes her sound like a bad mix of concrete. Dealing with the anomie of Chicago, he wrote as if he bore the city and its inhabitants a personal grudge. (Wasn't it an Irish mayor of Chicago who declared in the 1930s that he would punch the King of England on the nose personally if he set foot there?) Hawthorne, with its immense workforce and national connections, was one of the few stabilizing social forces. (This can be compared with Roethlisberger's observations about 'large, impersonal organizations', and overlooked the enormous contrast between the sprawling patchwork of the Windy City as an urban area and the warmth and intimacy of its individual ethnic communities.)

For Whitehead, Hawthorne executives already constituted the Mayoite élite. These executives 'acquire an attitude towards their work which is most easily compared with that of civil servants in a few European countries':[30] no mean compliment, presumably, since Whitehead as a former Admiralty bureaucrat himself fitted the model perfectly. The British public, however, has usually regarded its higher civil servants as distant, condescending, out of touch and secretive. Perhaps they know no better than the Western Electric workers what is good for them.

I had better stop. I could never be objective about Whitehead as a person, which I regret. Nor is there any point in expanding on Whitehead's misinterpretation of his material or his flagrantly pro-management biases. Let's just say that his showing as an analyst was disappointing beside that of Roethlisberger and Dickson. *The Industrial Worker* is nowadays of little more than antiquarian interest as a theoretical essay. As an illustration of élitist propaganda masquerading as science it should remain prized as a document of the utmost value. That said, I am happy to leave it to specialists and turn to a case that always mystifies me.

According to the admirers of Harry Braverman, 'bourgeois sociology' avoided the whole question of the de-skilling of craft labour, and in so far as it addressed the question at all before *Labor and Monopoly Capital*[31] put us all right in 1974, it did so from a narrow and evasive viewpoint. I am going to present some evidence to the contrary. This evidence seems to provide an impressive case of scientific anticipation. For although I shall argue that many of the claims that were to be made by Braverman had already been made by Warner thirty years earlier, and copiously documented, Braverman himself apparently knew nothing of this work,[32] though it would have supplied him with some excellent case material, albeit at some cost to his own strictures about sociology.

Though critics of human relations like W. H. Whyte (no relation of W. F. Whyte) regarded Warner as a typical member of the 'school',[33] and I have always found Warner's work on class structure unhelpful, I discovered his other work with growing admiration. *The Social System of the Modern Factory*, which he co-authored with J. O. Low, surely is one of the most insightful and sensitive monographs the school produced,[34] for its period uncannily penetrative and relevant, a work to set beside Chinoy's *Automobile Workers and the American Dream*. (Chinoy will be discussed in chapters 22 and 26.) Its sociological observations are often dazzling; but, better still, they were linked to an historical and economic analysis of considerable insight. Regrettably – infuriatingly – these qualities were offset by a persistent, almost wilful, bias: yet I shall argue also that it is not dissimilar to one of the most persistent biases in Braverman. But if the book had appeared ten years earlier it could have substantially altered the development of industrial sociology.

Since its field material was collected nearly fifteen years before the book's publication in 1947, the delay in its appearance is striking. Administrative overload and theoretical disagreements with associates probably account partly for this procrastination. This statement will be explained later. The delay mainly reflects priorities. The book was the fourth volume of the Yankee City series, which reported the mammoth investigation Warner led in Newburyport in the early 1930s. Warner was primarily interested in Yankee City as a community, especially in its class, status and ethnic ranking systems. These topics were covered in the first three reports.[35] The report on the workplace had to wait its turn.

This decision demonstrates more than a methodological choice, for although the community reports emphasize the existence of many underlying disunities in the town, they leave an overall impression of relatively harmonious integration. Yet the focal point of *The Social System of the Modern Factory* is a strike in early 1933 that shattered community relations. The reported data, and indeed, much of the analysis, make it apparent that, to adopt the Marxist terminology which seems so appropriate here, the uneven development of the Yankee City workers' class consciousness was suddenly redressed: a proletarianized local working class was transformed by the trauma of the Depression and the strike from a class *in* itself into a class *for* itself.

Warner had to recognize that the community had lost something of the surface of harmony that had previously characterized its social relations. In fact, his explanation of the strike relies partly on emphasizing that, before this storm, these relations had been becoming more brittle. The strike had to be interpreted, he finally claimed, as breakdown of community: when they embraced the unionism they had formerly shunned, the workers were really displaying their quest for community, for *Gemeinschaft*.

This bias is also reflected, I think, in the timing of the appearance of *The Social System of the Modern Factory*. In the book, it surfaces in a much more arbitrary form: arbitrary, because we are repeatedly told that material which not only speaks for itself but is deliberately amplified by the authors really means something quite different from what it is obviously saying.[36]

A brief examination of what the book actually says is worth setting beside what the authors intermittently protest it says. The immediate cause of the strike was unemployment in the shoe industry, on which Yankee City had depended for over a century, which came to a peak in late 1932. In March 1933, the previously deferential, 'unorganizable' shoe workers began to strike, spontaneously, against further wage cuts and redundancies. Their solidarity was virtually complete, crossing previously wide ethnic, religious, sex and skill divisions. Within a month the strikers had joined an industrial union, become the most active group in it, and won their demands. This explosive change, Warner and Low concluded, had to be viewed against a backcloth of long-run economic and technological change. In the chapters that trace this change they often sound like 'Bravermaniacs'. Economically, shoemaking had progressed from a local cottage industry to a strand in the fabric of nationwide finance capitalism. Ownership and control of tools and products had gradually fallen from the hands of the immediate producer. Various stages of capitalist organization succeeded one another, until a period when 'full capitalism has been achieved; the manufacturer is now the owner of the tools, the machines and the industrial plant; he controls the market'.[37] Under 'super-capitalism', the local economy had become subject to global forces beyond its workers' control or comprehension. (The term had not yet been invented, but the authors then launched into an analysis of the transnational enterprise.)

In parallel, shoemaking was transformed from a skilled handicraft to a mass-production process. Mechanization and rationalization slowly replaced a division of labour based on a craft specialization and seniority to one of fragmentary, machine-paced job functions uniformly low in status. Opportunities for promotion decreased, and contacts with superiors were rendered increasingly distant and formal, as the scale of operations grew and employers recruited professional managers to plan and oversee production. All these changes were made because they increased efficiency and therefore profitability. Warner and Low sought to hit exactly that note of moral outrage at this destruction of the skill community by capital that was to characterize Braverman's treatment.

The concentration of workers in large units, subordinate to machines, performing broadly similar semi-skilled routine tasks, with broadly similar pay and conditions, with little chance of promotion, subject to the decisions of distant bosses in line with the uncontrollable fluctuations of a mysterious economy, produced an industrial proletariat in which the Depression triggered a final awareness of a common situation and common interests.

There is no need for more description. Social and labour history provides many examples of such accounts. For the moment, too, I shall set aside the question of whether Warner's and Low's handling of this historical material amounts to a 'Marxist' approach. What I find bewildering is that having provided a perfectly coherent explanation of events, the authors then proceeded to 'explain' it. The class consciousness and class action of the workers were certainly affected by objective socio-economic conditions, they agreed, but these masked the workers' 'real' concerns, which were to do with their status in the plant and in the community, and with pursuit of the success ethic of the American Dream – there is another parallel here with Chinoy. The disappearance of a skill hierarchy in shoemaking robbed the worker of the opportunity for achievement in his occupation. He could no longer acquire prestige among his workmates, and sank into the anonymity of an undifferentiated mass.[38] Simultaneously, he lost the status in the community, whose own coherence and identity was imperilled by the advance of mass society.

In their final chapter the authors foresee catastrophe, for workers and capital alike, unless better provision can be made for the individual's search for status, by which they partly mean rank, and community – which is necessarily a stratified, or ranked, collectivity, albeit an egalitarian one in terms of face-to-face contact.[39] Governments might encourage greater social mobility, but they do not place much faith in this solution. For workers, an alternative – though a highly limited one – might lie in trade unions. But their final solution was stupefying enough to be worth quoting in full:

> Great international capitalistic enterprises, often monopolistic in character, have succeeded in crossing national boundaries and have developed methods of organizing some of the diverse economic units of the world. Opponents of such systems continue to fight what the authors believe to be no more than rearguard battles which only delay advance. Such capitalistic enterprises are the enemies of nationalism, and, as citadels of capitalistic power, they are the foes of labour and of the remnant forces of nineteenth-century liberalism. The cartel, one of the most powerful forms of international capitalism, must be recognized as a new social structure, developed by us in our desperate efforts to reorganize human behaviour to function on an international basis. At the present time, such economic institutions may or may not be evil in their effect, but international institutions of some kind are absolutely necessary if the world is to evolve a reliable international order.[40]

The authors hastened to add that these monoliths should be 'complemented by church, associational and political hierarchies' in the 'new social order'. But in that new order 'the social principles characteristic of hierarchies will be stressed more than at present, since the peoples who compose it will be more diverse and more difficult to organize, and the need for lines of authority and responsibility will be greater than in any other time in the history of man'.[41] This outdoes Weber for 'metaphysical pathos' over inevitable bureaucratization; and even Mayo was rarely so apocalyptic.

IBM save the world? Even IBM doesn't think quite that big. Did Warner mean what he set his hand to here? This bizarre peroration, which rides so uncomfortably with so much of the foregoing analysis, seems attached too artificially to the main text to take very seriously as a practical proposal.

Such questions are nowadays less interesting perhaps than the extraordinary overlap to be found with the work of Braverman in the examination of the historical fate of the skilled worker. the most obvious differences from Braverman is that Warn Low's de-skilled craftspeople actually turned to fight Braverman's craftsmen lack the will and capacity to resist.) As noted, the heart of the similarity is an emotional and ethical attitude towards skill; or, more exactly, towards the craft – the craft as a social system and moral community. For Warner, the craft supplied a moral framework based on a rank that measured skill and experience. We can shrug this off as the ideology of any suburban masonic lodge, rounded out with a crust of academic hype, but on the other hand, the craft has supplied the core image for many social Utopias – notably that of Ruskin and William Morris in the English-speaking world, and, among the French and other continental Europeans, that of Pierre-Joseph Proudhon.

This puts us in a position to answer a question raised some paragraphs earlier. Is there a Marxist element in Warner's and Low's analysis? No, though to split hairs, I think there is in many places something resembling a Marxian one, that is, an element which utilizes Marx's most penetrative concepts but does not commit the user to a Marxist political conclusion, though it would of course permit one. Yet the values of the craft are foreign to both Marx and classical Marxism. Warner was a Proudhonian in this respect. So too was Braverman.

I hope to be able to present a better case for the latter claim in chapter 30. Maybe this chapter has helped to demonstrate the heterogeneity of the Harvard branch of human relations. It was by no means composed mainly of managerial apologists and scientific incompetents. I have not hidden what seem their faults. A limited and selective rehabilitation is due – in the sense both of timely and justly owed.

14

Storytellers of Chicago

By the mid 1930s, latent differences between the Business School coterie and the Department of Anthropology at Harvard were coming into the open. These tensions partly account for the later migration of Warner and a large proportion of his research staff to Chicago. Some of the Yankee City workers were beginning to find Mayo's influence irksome. The source of disagreement was methodological – about how investigations should be organized and results interpreted, not over what the results should be used for.

There was a split between clinical work, which was grounded in psychiatry, and sociological grand theory in Mayo's approach to results. It was not this bifurcation so much as what the Yankee City researchers saw as his lack of interest in living social relationships and social processes that concerned the anthropologists. There was a further consideration. The Hawthorne research had moved from the 'hard' human factor, statistics-based methods to the 'soft' observational techniques of the anthropological phase. It appeared that each had produced valuable results. What if the two methods could be combined to get the best of both worlds, a kind of 'anthropology with numbers'?

This renewed interest in measurement was stimulated by the methodological doctrines of a Harvard physicist, P. Bridgman.[1] Central to Bridgman's thought was *operationalism*. To simplify, operationalism insists that no branch of empirical study qualifies as true science unless its concepts translate into corresponding 'operations'. These operations consist of explicit, replicable measuring procedures. If this translation is impossible, the concept is vacuous. Conversely, if *some* measurement operations are feasible, then these measurements *define* the concept. Consequently, a sociological concept like 'integration' possesses meaning only in so far as we can specify objective and measurable indicators of it. Subjective, unquantifiable impressions of the level of social integration in a group – including those of the group's members – are inadmissible.

The question how far, in the social sciences, operationalism can be made to work, or is a desirable method for them, will be taken up later. Two members of the Yankee City team, in particular, Conrad Arensberg and Eliot Chapple, were convinced it was. George Homans, who was appointed a junior fellow at Harvard in the same year (1934) as Arensberg, portrays him as a keen theoretician and lively debater who never passed up an opportunity to share his ideas.[2] Warner had entrusted him with devising a general theory to explain the Yankee City material, and Arensberg invented what came to be known as *interactionism*. The Yankee City series certainly shows its imprint, but it is most marked in the industrial studies undertaken after the group had arrived in Chicago. In the meantime, Arensberg had conducted an anthropological study in rural Ireland.[3] Whether his absence impeded or expedited the write-up of the 'Yankee City' material would be worth knowing.

Arensberg issued the first systematic specification for his brand of interactionism in association with Eliot Chapple (Arensberg's Arensberg: he resisted his mentor's later modifications) in 1940.[4] Group life, they argued, is created by contacts, or interactions, between organisms ('including men'). Group life is amenable to rigorous scientific study because: (1) the participants are readily identifiable; (2) the frequencies of different contacts can be computed; (3) the sequence of interactions, and of the acts composing them, is evident (because time is unlinear). Furthermore, the observer who adopts the technique is freed from personal or scientific preconceptions about the forms of social life. The observations, being restricted severely to the behaviour of the persons observed, would allegedly detect, more or less automatically, any regularities in conduct which are 'really there'.

This was, they declared grandly, 'the method of natural science and the discovery of natural law'.[5] Maybe, but it is certainly operationalist. By implication, any subjective feelings or meanings a person associates with his interactions can be treated only as dependent variables. Consequently, as Homans laconically dismissed the method: 'To put the matter crudely, whether a man liked another or not depended on the timing of the interactions between them,but the interaction did not depend on the liking.'[6]

The practical inferences are evident. To put the matter even more crudely – and why not, as we are dealing with preposterous assumptions – if a foreman wanted to become liked by a worker, he had merely to adjust the timing of his encounters with him. Arensberg and Chapple, in fact, believed they had discovered the key to reliable social engineering, and its potential sales appeal did not escape them.

Soon they had founded a Society for Applied Anthropology, Inc., which published the first issue of its house journal, *Applied Anthropology*, in late 1941. Chapple, as editor, could hardly have been franker about its objectives. It was to be 'devoted to the solution of practical problems of human relations', particularly 'how to increase our human adjustment and at the same time . . . increase our technological efficiency'; and it addressed itself to 'those concerned with putting plans into operation, administrators'.[7] Administrators were left in no doubt that members of the Society for Applied Anthropology, Inc., claimed to be able to supply manipulatory expertise. Many early editorials read like material from a job-placement bureau. It is a sweeping understatement to say that the applied anthropologists had confidence in their product. One writer went so far as to claim that its human engineering experts could have averted the unrest of the Depression period. Strikes and what they referred to delicately as 'political unpopularity' were simply problems that could be solved in precisely the same way as any other engineering problem.[8]

But this aggressive self-confidence was relatively short-lived. From an early date, a tension became obvious between the editorial sales patter and the articles actually published in the periodical. Descriptions of changed eating habits on Pacific islands and similar esoterica outnumbered industrial reports in the first five years. Moreover, the latter show that strict operationalism was soon discarded in the field. Chapple and Arensberg were, little by little, forced to climb down.

In the later 1940s, a distinct shift in the appraisal of industrial situations occurred, acknowledging a more complex world. As early as 1946, one article conceded that 'while the development of a code of restriction of output is in one sense an attempt at protection for the group, at the same time it expresses a feeling that workers are different from management-oriented employees'.[9] The whole approach and tone of what was to become a celebrated piece – 'The Industrial Rate-Buster', by M. Dalton published in 1948 – is poles apart from the original philosophy.[10] A year later, the journal changes its name to *Human Organization*.

The retreat was moral no less than methodological. The Mayoites justified managerial manipulation as a social mission. The applied anthropologists were more frankly technocratic: manipulation was industrial social engineering to boost industrial efficiency. This stress, aggravated by the hard-selling tone of the journal and Chapple's and Arensberg's combative self-confidence, rapidly brought them into worse odour than the Mayoites themselves. It is amusing to note that Arensberg contended that this reaction resulted largely from a Mayoite failure of communications. 'We are often asked', he wrote on becoming the editor of *Applied Anthropology* in 1947, 'and more often scrutinized, for our "values" . . . It is possibly our interest in the concrete which is strange or repellent to many persons.' Purposes had been misconstrued merely by the 'historical accident' of the choice of title for the journal. The Society for Applied Anthropology, Inc. recognized that outsiders might mistake consultants for manipulators. To banish such a risk it was preparing a professional code of ethics.[11]

But the switch of policy was not caused by intellectual remorse. Whatever its wider methodological failings, the pure interactionist research techniques proved mechanically inoperable. Even under laboratory conditions, with a team of carefully trained observers, the obstacles to distinguishing and recording interpersonal acts in full are well nigh insurmountable. The work of Bales was to prove that conclusively.[12] Distinguishing the sequence of acts, which Arensberg believed was straightforward, is actually one of the thorniest problems. To be fair to him, he eventually conceded this; Chapple did so more reluctantly and less graciously.[13]

Yet, this episode had at least one positive effect. Because it demanded meticulous attention to interpersonal activities, and the inclusion of all relevant interactions, it encouraged investigators to steep themselves in the ongoing life of workplaces as a whole. Observations had to extend beyond the work-group, to workers' interactions with managers, work-study men and union officials. Observation thus became more inclusive than that undertaken among the bank wiring group.

Thus it could lead in two interesting directions. A sensitive observer could not long overlook the fact that interactions are influenced by the *ecology* of the workplace, for example by the layout of machinery. Further, he would perceive that their form is affected too by the organization of tasks, whether productive or managerial. These properties vary somewhat from one plant to another, since different products require different manufacturing processes and control systems. In sum, the interactionist method led researchers to grapple with the question of how technology and human action were related. The implicit theory of *Management and the Worker*, as noted before, also pointed in this direction but *en route* lay a serious pitfall, which *Management and the Worker*, with its stress on the uniqueness of the human organization, and interactionism, with its even stronger emphasis on the ramifications of relations throughout the plant and their complex, interdependent development, heavily camouflaged.

The trap lay in viewing the plant as a unique network of evolving personal contacts. Of course, all workplaces are 'special'. Good research brings this out. At the same time, the social investigator is concerned with generalization. A means must always be devised to combine the description of plant particularism with broader theorization. A comparable problem at a higher level occurs with culturalist explanations of national peculiarities in work behaviour, as we shall see in the final chapter. The great danger is that of circularity.

This particularizing risk was, paradoxically enough, amplified by the evident need to rectify one of the glaring methodological lunacies of operationalist interactionism, that is, its deliberate neglect of personal feelings and motivations as possible determinants of patterns of association. By reintroducing personal meaning as a crucial analytical reference point, the student of plant life might take a profoundly anti-sociological course. Like that of the later enthusiasts of subjective sociology, which we shall look at in chapter 27, his analysis would deteriorate into a series of anecdotes about colourful personalities and their strange deeds. At the same time, it had a stimulating effect on some observers at the time, and it is interesting that a New Wave investigator like Michael Burawoy (see Chapter 35) has taken a great interest in the applied anthropologists.[14]

The work of W. F. Whyte illustrates all these dangers and possibilities, and is the crucial link between this Part of the book and Part IV. Because I shall discuss only that area of his work which facilitated the transition between the human relations and technological implications approaches, my treatment of Whyte will seem imbalanced to those who know his later work as an organizational writer of great distinction.[15]

Whyte is the only major figure of the human relations period to survive it with his credibility intact. No doubt this is partly due to his celebrated charm and sincerity. Again, many people know of him only as the author of *Street Corner Society*, a classic community study and source-book on participant observer method.[16] It is hard to portray this former inhabitant of Cornerville, and, as such, an accessory to electoral malpractice, as any sinister servant of power, but Whyte was undeniably a manipulator during his Chicago years. If he survived, it is partly because his brand of human relations accepted unions as partners in man-management. Even more, it is because he constantly revised his ideas. Between the late 1930s and early 1950s, Whyte revised Arensberg's interactionism, fell into the story-telling trap, struggled out again, and cleared the group of integrating technological factors into explanations of workplace behaviour. He also helped to rehabilitate economic incentives as important influences on worker behaviour.

Whyte's transfer from community to industrial studies was logical enough.[17] He graduated as an economist and embarked on his study of Cornerville in 1936 with an interest in racketeering. At Harvard he encountered the Yankee City anthropologists who were later to move, almost *en bloc*, to Chicago and concentrate largely on industrial research. Arensberg coached him in research methods. Whyte also seems to have had a certain rather woolly do-gooding streak. Industrial problems probably seemed to offer better opportunities to 'help'.

He arrived in Chicago in the early 1940s and for a brief period collaborated with Burleigh B. Gardner. Gardner was a former Yankee City investigator and had connections with the counselling programme at Hawthorne. Not surprisingly, then, the flavour of their joint reports might be characterized as Mayoite interactionism. Reviewing the growth of unionism and strikes among American foremen in the war years, for example, they portrayed the foreman as a *marginal man* caught between contacts with, and loyalties to, both managers and workers.[18]

They lavishly prescribed solutions. Managers must be nicer to foremen because 'the first-line supervisor largely may determine the extent of co-operation or friction between workers and management'; he secures co-operation by fostering teamwork through communications. All the muddle, wishful thinking, and contradictions of Mayoism and interactionism, in fact, were combined in this piece. They are neatly stated in the following: 'he [the foreman] does good turns for them [the workers], unobtrusively, as a natural part of his behaviour, and they reciprocate':[19] in other words, the foreman manipulates the workers without really being a manipulator, and his action, which we must not call manipulation, will be effective. But strict operationalism had been abandoned in this analysis. Whyte's own brand is demonstrated in his reviews of two cases of industrial conflict resolution. In one, an entrepreneur, Buchsbaum, had refused to recognize his workers' union. Touched by the restraint of a strike leader who prevented his enraged followers from attacking blacklegs, however, Buchsbaum suddenly invited a delegation to his office. He and the leader took to one another. As the relationship developed, the workers began to suggest economies in work-planning, and Buchsbaum recognized the union.[20]

In the second, the story covers a longer period (twelve years), during which a factory's human relations passed through the phases of unorganized conflict, organized conflict and organized co-operation.[21] Again, the turning point was the transformation of the relationship between a nasty reactionary boss, one Gossett, and a 'bolshy' union leader Whyte calls Love. In both cases, management and union learned to trust one another and be 'good listeners'. But *rapprochement* occurred only after certain critical encounters that changed the whole course of communications.

But why were communications misdirected beforehand, and how could they run properly after these key events? Whyte's explanation is in terms of four central concepts: *interactions*, *sentiments*, *symbols* and *activities*. I do not propose to discuss these here. Suffice it to say that they are all mutually influential. Thus, a sentiment could govern an activity, and an interaction generate a symbol – vice versa and *mutatis mutandis*. Whyte imposed them after the fact to explain why the story developed as it did. For example, when Gossett first met Love, he refused to shake his hand. This, understandably, intensified their dislike of one another. In Whyte's language, the initially hostile sentiments resulted in an interaction that symbolized this hostility and aggravated the hostile sentiments. But is the application of this conceptual apparatus *worthwhile*? Is it justifiable? Indeed, the jargon becomes positively embarrassing when Whyte tells us that Love seriously misconstrued the 'symbol' of Gossett's snub because Love was black.

To go straight to the heart of the matter, Whyte's interactionist scheme (as used here) systematically eliminates any sociological or other generalizing explanation of events. Everything – even the power play between groups – is particularized. When we ask, 'Why did human relations change?' the only real answer is, 'Because the relations between *these* humans changed.' That this unsatisfactory reply is couched in a scientific-sounding jargon is all the more grating.

Finally, it is worth noting that it was not only the characters in the story who were stripped of any wider social identities or attachments. If we had only internal evidence to go on we would also conclude that the plant was sealed off from major political and economic events, for example, the Second World War and the Taft-Hartley Act, which greatly affected industrial relations. Even a six-month industry-wide strike in 1946 was treated as a kind of interlude or close season after which the *dramatic personae* returned to the serious business of life by interacting in the plant.

Whyte is indeed an enigmatic figure, for the book reporting this second case appeared several years after he first remarked that he was 'interested in observing the impact of technology on the social system' of the factory.[22] He first followed up this interest in his book, *Human Relations in the Restaurant Industry*,[23] a popularly written work, with much advice to restaurant managers on keeping employees happy, containing little systematic theorizing. In an accompanying scholarly paper, however, Whyte showed how an interactionist approach could be fortified by linking it with an examination of formal structure and layout and equipment.[24]

In a large restaurant the formal structure of work-roles such as manager, waitress, chef, dishwasher, etc., is complex and hierarchical. Role incumbents must communicate constantly. In most formal structures, initiations – orders or instructions – flow from high- to low-status positions. But because customers' orders ('initiations') in a large restaurant can be injected at several levels, a low-status worker often initiates for a superior. Resenting this, a high-status worker can retaliate successfully by delaying response to the initiation. Demands for quick service for a hurried customer relayed by a waitress to a counterhand, for example, would result in his slowing down. This increases the pressure on the waitress.

Whyte suggests that while an acceptable or optimum pattern of initiations can be conceived abstractly, the business of measuring the requisite interactions is too complex. None the less, a reduction in interaction often improves attitudes, especially when the initiator is of low status. But how was interaction to be pruned in restaurants, where constant communication is vital? Whyte's reply was: by exploiting layout and equipment or technology. He then suggested various devices which permit communication but exclude face-to-face contact. In restaurants, telephones and public-address systems may help; but personal symbolic contact, by means of the voice, remains. High counters, however, and impersonal spindles on which orders are spiked sever all face-to-face contact and therefore the presentation of inhibitory symbols.[25]

Shortly afterwards, Whyte developed his insights into technology as hardware, or layout and equipment, and software or formal structure.[26] Already, before Joan Woodward (see chapter 21), Whyte had begun to throw doubt on the generality of classical principles of organization and was even suggesting that human relations skills were a less valid method than organization restructuring for improving co-operation and performance.

Only two crucial elements of human relations remained to be rejected: its neglect of out-plant influences on workplace behaviour; and its unconcern for financial incentives as motivators. In *Money and Motivation*[27] Whyte faced up squarely to these tasks. In many ways this book is still the best general treatment of the whole issue of incentives as they operate in factory situations. Unfortunately, however, there was still rather too much interactionist conceptual clutter, a degree of managerial bias, and a tendency to view factories as social and economic islands.

Incentives are pictured as symbolic stimuli. But the connection between stimulus and response is complex. Pavlovian psychology, for example, shows that the conditioned reflex becomes less rapid and dependable as time passes, and confusion over the meaning of a stimulus produces individual disorientation and lethargy. In industry we find a similar phenomenon.

Rate-setting was pictured as usually haphazard activity:

> As we examine the rate-setting process and the economic results of increased production, we are forced to conclude that the connections between the symbols and the promised rewards are neither simple nor consistent. This does not mean that the piece-rate symbol will evoke no response. It does mean that the response will be importantly influenced by the context of human relations within which the symbol is offered.[28]

The context of human relations has many dimensions: the relations of individual workers to the work-group, the relations of the group to other groups and their relation to management. Acquisitiveness is a socially acquired trait and even in the USA varies between groups. Incentives therefore appeal strongly only to a small minority of 'rate-busters', are regarded with indifference by 'restricters' (who prize the social bonds of working life), and between them is a heterogeneous category of workers torn between group loyalty and cash.[29]

The work-groups in a plant make up a social system that can reach equilibrium. Disturbances to this are created by group earnings discrepant with the status of its members, or by changes in the flow of work affecting group prestige. Once social and economic status become discrepant, the affronted groups will seek to resolve the dissonance. In terms of interactionist theory, the symbol of changed status provokes a change in sentiments (hostile attitudes), which in turn change activities, for instance a production slow-down in an adjacent department, and hence change interactions by producing hostile encounters, or dissociation.

Where a work-group is in conflict with management, a 'loose rate' will result in quota restriction, a 'borderline rate' will be defined as impossible, but workers will perhaps make out, and a 'tight rate' will produce the 'goldbricking' described by Donald Roy in his study of the Geer plant.[30] (Quota restriction aims to avoid spoiling a loose rate by overproduction; goldbricking involves ignoring the incentive and falling back on the basic hourly rate.) Where co-operation prevails, the loose rate still evokes a quota, but at a higher level, the borderline rate will be given a fair trial, and the tight rate will be submitted for renegotiation. Note that these activities largely define conflict or co-operation, and the continuance of quota restriction under co-operation deserves more comment.

To maintain harmony between work-groups, which is constantly threatened by the changes following in-built technological advance, the manager needs to plan with regard to social as well as technical and short-run financial criteria. Co-operation was to be built by the manipulation of sentiments and activities.

How do we change sentiments and activities? How do we build sentiments of co-operation when conflict existed before? . . . The general answer to these questions is simple: we change sentiments and activities through changing interaction. And we change interaction through changing the symbols that are presented to the people in question or through changing the work-flow or the organizational structure.[31]

Symbols such as the work-study man with his threatening aura, Whyte acknowledged, could not be changed by propaganda, by counselling or by any other form of communications. Experience proved that 'sentiments are not changed through such a direct approach'.[32] But the symbol could be changed by changing the man – too often the time-study man was a failed engineer unfitted for his key role – and by restricting his freedom of action. Changing the work-flow and the structure were alternative lines of attack. The first is clearly a production engineering task, and the acquisition of greater social-scientific knowledge by engineers should be a matter of urgency. The second depends partly on liberating 'originations' in the plant. Workers at the bottom of the organization power pyramid do not initiate for anyone. Their appetite for a share in control is thus diverted into production restriction. Legitimate originations from them could, however, be fostered by grievance procedures and by suggestion schemes.

Studies of situations where co-operation prevailed, Whyte concluded, showed that originations from management to union, and vice versa, from workers to union, and so on, were all highly developed. Later research, Whyte argued, might enable organizational theorists actually to quantify the optimum frequencies and content of all such origination channels. This was a very backward-looking Arensbergian touch. Meanwhile, management ought to accept unions as legitimate bargaining and consultation partners and forge with them the structures which could facilitate collaboration. Such claims, it is true, begged the question of whether multilateral 'originations' and 'initiations' can procure collaboration, or merely express it, and that of how – since some originations, and some originators, are more important than others – the realities of power were to be handled. What was to happen when workers' originations were deemed inadmissible?

Whyte himself recognized that his prescriptions were very general. The last chapter was to outline 'a practical programme of action'. His main suggestion was adoption of the Scanlon Plan, named after Joseph Scanlon, a former leader of the United Steelworkers of America. The main feature of schemes like this was the award to workers of a bonus equivalent to savings gained through implementing suggestions submitted by them on a collective basis. Normal suggestion schemes are based on the brainwaves of individuals, and usually have to be submitted in writing. They fail because inventive workers fear reprisals from their workmates – or foremen, who are made to look incompetent for not spotting the chance for improvement themselves. Employers often do not reward them properly. Many suggestions, anyway, are discounted as hare-brained without further examination because the isolated worker cannot appreciate technical complexities or express his ideas in the correct jargon. Under the Scanlon system suggestions were worked out in group sessions. This certainly can reduce resistance to change, promote teamwork and permit the refinement of ideas thanks to the pooling of expertise, where adequate levels of trust already exist. Some writers of the time called the scheme revolutionary since when it worked as intended managers were obliged to participate more fully and workers could insist on managers implementing jointly agreed changes.

Whyte acknowledged that the Scanlon system had sometimes failed badly. He ascribed this to 'semantic confusions' among managers. By this Japanese-sounding euphemism, Whyte meant ideological prejudices about the worker. These had to be discarded, he announced as sternly as he could. For their part, unions must recognize that participatory schemes demand a change of their activities. Both sides must abandon their winner-takes-all or 'zero-sum' notions of power. Power, Whyte affirmed, was just 'an ability to get things done'.[33] Management usually *appeared* to be the dominant industrial partner but this was simply because managers are able to get things done. Once the participative philosophy was embraced by accepting originations from the union and the workers, the relationship would become reciprocal and the workers share power – he really meant *share in* power, I think. This 'revolution' would oblige managers to become true leaders. Maybe – it would certainly be much harder work for them.

One feature of this analysis is obvious. It shows far more

awareness of what actually goes on in workplaces than does the work of Mayo or the applied anthropologists. In that sense, in its descriptive richness and accuracy, it is far more like the work done much more recently by anthropologists in industry. In this connection, Michael Burawoy comes immediately to mind. We shall be looking more closely at Burawoy's work in chapter 35. Although he is known as a neo-Marxist investigator, there is something very reminiscent of the Chicago approach in his work. A further way in which Whyte's procedures are called to mind is by the subjectivist approach to organizational behaviour, typified in the work of David Silverman, with its strong bias towards a 'story-telling', situation-grounded analysis (see chapter 27).

Whyte's work is notable too for some extremely sophisticated advocacy of the role of the interventionist. It bears comparison, in this respect, with the thinking of an interventionist like Trist (see chapter 23). In fact, Whyte can be seen as one of the main influences behind the later Organizational Design (OD) movement, which also drew on the ideas to be discussed in the next chapter. His impact on the organizational theorists (reviewed in chapter 19) was considerable too, thanks to his exploration of the interdependence of work behaviour, technology, and formal organization.

I have no doubt that Whyte was personally committed to greater employee participation as an end in itself. One of the virtues of the 'story-telling' approach to work behaviour and organizational life is that it shows how people can come alive once they gain opportunities to influence the way they do their jobs and the way they are supervised. What is one to make of methods of participation along the lines of the Scanlon Plan? It has to be said that it is not only the opponents of the capitalist system that regard them with a flinty eye. Employers and managers themselves took up the Plan largely as a gimmick or as a cosmetic during the vogue for them in the early 1950s.[34] But to operate as intended they demanded more effort from managers, and more backing from employers, than was forthcoming.

Commentators of the 1960s were in substantial agreement among themselves that such techniques failed even to produce economically interesting results, and that talk of using them to cut costs, increase worker motivation, improve the design of products, or make products work more reliably and look nicer, was just management consultancy hype. The Japanese imported the Scanlon idea thirty years ago, took to it enthusiastically, adapted it, made it work better as a management tool, and have been re-exporting it to the West in the form of the Quality Circle concept on a massive scale since 1980.

15

The Psychological Puppeteers

Psychologists had been more excited by *Management and the Worker* than were sociologists, largely because in the later 1930s industrial psychology was already coming to take as its chief problem the effect of leadership on work behaviour. There are two major reasons for this. The Hawthorne studies had begun within a psychological framework, and had shown the limitations of the human factor approach. 'Changed supervision' had allegedly overridden economic and workplace-environment variables on the attitudes and behaviour of the relay assemblers. Informal leadership among the bank wiring group had appeared to play a critical part in integrating their workplace micro-society. We saw how incorrect it is to equate human relations with Mayo. If the term 'Mayoite' ever meant more than a vague term of abuse, it designated a psychologist.

The second reason was the personal influence of Kurt Lewin. Lewin, a refugee from Nazi Germany, was a passionate believer in democracy. Clearly, the idea that less authoritarian supervision could simultaneously boost both the morale and productivity of workers was something to excite him. But Lewin was also a powerful theorist whose ideas spread rapidly during the late 1930s. His *field theory* derived from his admiration for hard science, particularly physics. It viewed an individual's behaviour as the product of forces operating on him; and, in a social situation, he himself was a force exerting reciprocal influences.

Although this kind of imagery has its uses, it can easily lead to absurdity or mystification. Lewinians tend to take it over-seriously, talking of 'vectors' and 'force-fields' and other pseudo-physical – and totally hypothetical – phenomena. (A Lewinian subject does not move: he 'locomotes'.) Clearly, it tends to suppress the idea that human action can be calculated and voluntary. Lewinians deny this; but voluntarism can be fitted into their scheme only with difficulty.

Field theory can be viewed as the psychological equivalent of Arensberg's interactionism. It has the same concern with operationalization (though the borrowing of concepts from physics prejudges the nature of human activities). Everyday terms like 'leadership' obviously carry numerous and often vague connotations. Lewinians overcome this problem by talking of 'initiations'. For example, if A is observed to issue suggestions or orders to B, C and D, and they respond to these initiations more often than A responds to their initiations, A may be called their leader. Similarly, 'participation' may be operationalized and measured by noting how often A invites their comments or suggestions on a proposed course of joint action.

This precision had to be matched by methodical examination of variables. Ideally, this demands laboratory conditions where all variables other than that being tested are rigorously controlled. If one were testing the relation between participation and 'performance' (the Lewinian term for output), for example, one would recruit experimental and control groups carefully matched for age, sex, skill, etc. The field theorists, however, were eager to work in real-life situations whenever they could, conducting experiments on actual work-groups. Unconsciously, the Hawthorne team had indulged in action research of this kind. The loss of control implied in abandoning laboratory conditions was regarded as adequately compensated by the verisimilitude of experiments with real work-groups.

Research by Feldman in the 1930s had shown that the productivity of industrial work-groups varied with the supervisors, but no attempt had been made then to specify what characteristics of the supervisor might account for this.[1] The first major experimental work to suggest some clear relationship between the nature of leadership and group performance was in fact a study of boys'-club hobby groups by Lippitt and White, the first report of which appeared in 1940.[2] It was regarded by some investi scientific proof of the superiority of democracy and anti-Nazi propaganda.

This study indicated that while autocratic leadership might sometimes ensure as high a productivity as democratic, the latter kind was generally superior in this respect; furthermore, it produced much less tension and frustration in the group. An extension of the studies to test the impact of *laissez-faire* leadership style was to give little comfort to anarchists: such groups were both tense and unproductive. The latter study is important, not just for the lead it gave but as an example of action research. Patterns of conduct appropriate to the various styles of leadership were calculated beforehand and acted out by trained assistants in a concrete field setting. The ethics of this may be controversial, but the artificiality of a laboratory setting was avoided. This increased confidence in the results.

A further set of experiments which prepared the way for the entry of Lewinian psychology into the human relations orbit was conducted in the war by Lewin himself. Although concerned with dietary habits, not with work behaviour, they seemed to show that producing a change in behaviour desired by an administrator is simplified if a group of persons can be first led to agree among themselves on the need for change, and are brought together afterwards to review adherence to the new pattern.[3] The Lewinians were thus beginning to realize the Mayoite aim: *leaders* (managers), they believed could manipulate *participation* (informal organization) through *communications* (social skill) to produce a superior *group climate* (morale) thus enhancing *satisfaction* (integration) with the *group life* (social system) and improving *performance* (output). There is a fascinating parallelism between the concepts used by the Mayoite psychologists and the terminology of Roethlisberger and Dickson.

Application of these notions in an industrial milieu was achieved first in a series of experiments carried out in the Harwood Manufacturing Company just after the Second World War. The findings seemed to be saying clearly that if managers involved difficult employees in the planning and execution of technical changes, the employees' antagonism to change would be overcome. The title of the best-known report of the study, 'Overcoming Resistance to Change',[4] suggests optimism and practicality, and it announces its management bias with almost disarming frankness. However, there seem to me to have been serious methodological flaws in the best-known study; and its findings were not altogether consistent with those of the less well-reported study.[5] For more information on this and similar organizational experiments at the time I strongly recommend Malcolm Warner's *Organizations and Experiments*.[6]

The trouble with *action research* (interventions that also aim to generate scientifically valid data and conclusions) is that it tends to be based on a single case and many variables are not controlled. Local factors may also complicate interpretation; and, by definition, most field experiments cannot be adequately replicated, if only because of the time variable. The Harwood findings seem plausible enough. However, we are certainly not given sufficient information about the local context. Shortly after the group-decision experiments, the workers struck over a unionization dispute with management. The successfully 'changed' groups were as pro-union as their colleagues. To explore the suggestive Harwood findings fully, work of a systematically comparative nature was needed.

In the years after 1947, this was carried out on the grand scale, funded initially by the Office of Naval Research, by the Survey Research Center (SRC) of the Institute of Social Research at the University of Michigan. It was here that Lewin transferred from his Research Center for Group Dynamics at the Massachusetts Institute of Technology (MIT), which had collaborated on the Harwood studies. The aim of the SRC was to integrate the efforts of psychologists, sociologists and anthropologists involved in the study of groups – an aim almost identical to that of the Tavistock Institute of Human Relations founded in Britain at the same time and with which it maintained close links. Neither foundation completely succeeded in achieving this integration of social scientific research, but each attempt was instructive.

The SRC's first major study examined clerical workers in the office of the Prudential Insurance Company in Newark, New Jersey. The productivity and morale of a large number of working groups were checked against the personal characteristics of their supervisors. Important differences were detected: supervisors in charge of high-production groups were found to be rather less arbitrary and authoritarian.[7] This finding was soon supported by a study of railway maintenance gangs.[8] Though broadly confirming the earlier results, however, a worrying finding was that those railwaymen who were most satisfied with their work were members of *low*-production gangs. This called for a more careful formulation of the relationships between high morale, teamwork and productivity. Perhaps prematurely, this material was taken to show that the attitude and behaviour of supervisors were more significant for production than were the attitudes of the worker. A similar negative relationship between productivity and close supervision was established in a study of work-teams in the Caterpillar Tractor Company.[9]

Studies such as these enabled the construction of a broad profile of the successful supervisor, and hence the design of practical supervisory training courses to impart or nurture the desirable personal qualities – abandonment of close supervision of work for which men can be trusted to supervise themselves; care not to nag about the need to get work finished; willingness to help out in rush periods; readiness to take a sympathetic interest in the operative's personal worries; concern with explaining instructions instead of simply giving them; and maintaining discipline, for instance over time-keeping, by persuasive rather than punitive means. In the late 1940s there was a mushrooming of courses claiming to teach these leadership practices.

Unfortunately, they had a less solid experimental backing than the reports pouring from the SRC at this time suggested. Critics were quick to point out, for example, that a finding that high productivity is associated with relaxed supervision is ambiguous. It is risky to assume any straightforward cause–effect chain here, in any case. But even if we do, relaxed supervision could be viewed as an *effect* of high production rather than its cause. Similarly, high morale among workers may be the precondition, if not the precise cause, of a democratization of leadership. Studies of the 1960s provided considerable evidence for these alternative interpretations. In fact, old-fashioned autocratic supervision maximizes production more often than the enthusiasts of the democratic style care to admit.[10]

The main SRC researchers soon began to have such doubts themselves. In the railway-grants study, too, it was postulated that the kind of leadership behaviour any supervisor can adopt may depend on his relations with his own superior. A study by F. C. Mann of an electrical utility drove this point home: the degree to which supervisors implemented good human relations practices was ultimately dependent on the attitudes of higher management.[11]

Findings like this one do not invalidate all human relations ideas but they do suggest that studies of the work-group and its leader in microcosm must be supplemented. And they indicate the democratization must spread to all leadership levels in the organization. This line of reasoning was to be adopted by the neo-human relations theorists of organization (see chapter 19).

By the early 1950s, however, doubts were beginning to creep in about the desirability, from a management point of view, of cohesive groups. For example, the interactionists Arensberg and Horsfall, in a study of four seven-man teams in a shoe factory, had shown that the employees had adopted a method of equalizing production between fast and slow teams, thus frustrating the management's incentive scheme; the more cohesive teams were also the more restrictive.[12] Cohesiveness came to be seen increasingly as a somewhat ambiguous property, though some studies continued to provide evidence that the involvement of cohesive groups in minor decision-making could increase production, cut turnover and weaken the power of a trade union.[13] But in 1954, an SRC investigator was exclaiming: 'We emerge from this study with some new ideas, but mainly with considerably increased respect for some old ones . . . The popular admonition to supervisors that they should develop a cohesive team, if carried out indiscriminately, may merely lend force to the divisive influences within the larger organization.'[14]

It is surprising that critics of human relations as a management movement have not paid more attention to this psychological wing. The most frankly manipulationist textbooks on human relations were produced by industrial psychologists, not sociologists, in the post-1945 period.[15] Although these manuals paid considerable, often critical attention to Hawthorne and the work of the Chicago school, they paid even more to the early Lewinian and SRC studies. A whole brood of managerially oriented organization theorists followed in their footsteps but, as we shall see, these 'organization psychotechnologists' reintroduced the problem of formal organization, and adopted a rather different psychological methodology.

These developments occurred at a time when Mayo's thought in particular was coming under severe attack. How could the psychological Mayoites and their psycho-technological successors have ignored this onslaught? The answer is that they did not ignore it, but believed that their work was innocent of the charges levelled at human relations and Mayo. They protested that they had been the last people to portray managers as an élite, with the sort of mission Mayo had envisaged. On the contrary, had they not been preoccupied with democratic leadership, almost to a fault? They favoured participatory democracy as an end in itself. The workers they dealt with were not regarded as blue-collar, non-rational tribesmen but responsible adults. No managerial élite was called for in their scheme of things. On the other hand, they had called for training and re-education for managers who might, before undergoing it, have an élitist, autocratic streak.

It is possible to view such a defence as an ingenious way of seeming to square the circle. On the other hand, much of it is justifiable: like so many of the people who were attacked for their involvement with human relations, their real fault had been lack of foresight, a certain naïveté, in not seeing how they might be open to criticism. Like most well-meaning people who feel themselves unjustly accused, they protested more in hurt puzzlement than anger. Or, at least, most of them did. Arensberg, whose own record (as we saw in chapter 14) was rather more blotchy, was astute enough, when he took up the cudgels to defend human relations against the gibe that it was an ideological plant sociology – a set of parables about an élite (managers) and aborigines (workers) – to base his defence largely on the work of the Mayoite psychologists. (He was replying to a classic attack by Clark Kerr and Lloyd Fisher on human relations.)[16] 'What irony', he thundered, 'it may well be when we finally learn, with empirical proofs rather than moral homilies, that the best way to manipulate man to organizational goals is the very representative democracy these economists think they are defending.'[17]

The irony of *this* reply will not be lost on those who have read the passage on *Applied Anthropology* in chapter 14. Arensberg overlooked a major problem with the work of the psychological Mayoites, which stems from their methodology as much as anything. As we noted at the outset, Lewinian psychology, so powerfully influenced by physics, overlooks the *voluntarism* of human action – the sometimes small, but genuine scope for free choice in action. People do not just respond to 'forces'. Managerial social skill cannot be thought of as an electric current operating to shape the workers' behaviour. The idea of a plant physics, with workers standing for pins, and managers as magnets, is a little cranky. This core image of industrial relationships had to be abandoned.

If the ideal of democratic supervision was to be implemented, it would have knock-on effects throughout the work organization. It would be far more costly in time and training than had at first seemed likely. Democracy always carries a price tag. This might have been realized earlier but it is scarcely possible to complain about the call for greater democracy itself. Here, I have some sympathy with the defence put up by the psychological Mayoites. Their propaganda for easier relations between people in work organizations undoubtedly increased the conviction of the teachers who were putting across this idea in the management schools. It had a similar effect on the other people who wrote articles in the management press extolling these practices, and the researchers, such as those we shall consider in chapters 19 and 23, whose own research and writing was to be inspired by it.

This, too, can probably be taken as an instance of what people who talk of a *dialectic* in social life probably mean. Because ideas seem to serve only one set of interests when they first appear does not mean that persons having those interests will accept them. They may fail to do so. The ideas may then be utilized to justify pursuit of quite other interests. The history of interpretative frameworks in the sociology of work is very largely made up of such curious paradoxes and unforeseen contradictions.

16

Overview

Human relations was in many ways a surprisingly diverse approach – certainly more so than either Taylorism or human factor psychology. But this diversity – this elasticity, even – becomes apparent only when the equation between Mayo and the movement is discarded. Once this has been done, even the meaning of the Western Electric studies becomes open to surprisingly diverse interpretations. Although I disagree with some of his claims, I think that Stephen Ackroyd's suggestion that it may be worth looking more carefully at some of the broader ideas of the school is valid.[1] But I disagree about that word 'school' – it is like saying a couple of whales, a half-dozen tuna fish, a porpoise or two, and the odd basking shark, makes a school of fish. The whales and porpoises aren't even fish.

The closer one looks at the work of the personalities and research groups that allegedly made up the school or the movement, the less it seems to belong in the same basket. This relative fluidity complicates assessment of the approach overall. When its ideological and practical dimensions are also scrutinized, the task becomes almost unmanageable. Reaction against human relations became counterproductive once it became uncompromising, but that was in the late 1940s. Several decades later, those of us who deplore so much about it surely have more self-confidence? Warner's, Whyte's and even Roethlisberger's and Dickson's writings still repay a critical reading. As an ideology – I use the term to mean a set of concepts knitted together, a structure of thought, without any necessarily pejorative overtones – so does Mayo's.

Detailed arguments already given for such individual rehabilitations will not be repeated here; nor will specific complaints against value-bias, and similar lapses, or technical failures in method and explanation.

Human relations interpretations of work behaviour were adopted in the mid 1930s in America because the human factor psychology of the Myers group was incapable of handling 'social man', because Mayo was a gifted publicist, because Harvard had become a leading sociological centre, and because American management faced novel problems of social control and legitimation. Although the Myersians were sensing the significance of the social factor by the late 1920s, their trained incapacities and lack of resources prevented them exploring it. Unrestricted by disciplinary boundaries, in fact, by normal scientific prudence, Mayo eagerly propagated 'helpful' new ideas. These drew on the work of Henderson and Parsons at Harvard, which was rediscovering in nineteenth-century sociology and contemporary anthropology an image of man and society that stressed irreducible elements in collective life. The Depression had unveiled social antagonism, stimulated unionism, promoted government intervention in industry and generally rendered workforces less tolerant and respectful of managerial authority.

All these factors were of importance. Yet we do know that there was a strong concern in the sociology that was coming into favour at Harvard for tackling problems of the economic depression of the 1930s – especially the political problems created by the slump. We have the testimony of a particularly frank and well-placed witness that Harvard sociology was designed to renew faith in American institutions, especially in American capitalism, among the generally upper-crust student body. 'As a Republican Bostonian, who had not rejected his comparatively wealthy family,' George Homans has explained, 'I felt during the thirties that I was under attack, above all from the Marxists.'[2] Homans later went on to collaborate with members of the Harvard Group. He became a sociologist, in effect, because he saw in it a powerful weapon for conservatism!

Political bias, and a 'sociologistic' *reductionism* – the tendency to represent all collective phenomena, especially problems that are essentially economic ones, as essentially social – was written into their message to youth of Harvard's functionalist social thinkers. They were phenomenally successful too: Henderson's course on Pareto was a sell-out year after year. He was better known among undergraduates as a sociologist than as a biochemist.

But human relations inherited empirical and practical concerns from industrial psychology, which most early functionalists, as grand theorists of the Type II described in the Introduction (see p. 15), tended to regard as a task for the data-gathering peasants rather than the social-thinker barons. These concerns, reinforced by Mayo's clinical bent, produced one of its sustained methodological faults, its preoccupation with the plant. Its treatment of industrial conflict as a local, or plant, problem stems from this obsession with cases as much as from anything.

Changing socio-economic conditions, disagreements about theory, and adverse reactions all partly account for its diversification from the late 1930s onwards. However, the concern with supervisory skill and communications in the early 1940s, and acceptance of unions as legitimate partners with management around this time, show keen awareness of new realities in economic life, though probably not very keen approval of them. Such changes resulted directly from the stresses of wartime production and the growth of organized labour. The two developments coincided, and that was not an accident.

Arensberg's case demonstrates that theoretical controversy within human relations could be lively. In his hands, social man almost disintegrated. His technocratic justification for research and intervention, his enthusiasm for a hard methodology, and his eagerness to vend the presumed skill of applied anthropologists as social engineers were likewise barely consistent with Mayo's own thinking. Promising so much to managers, apparently better able to deliver it thanks to interactionist social engineering, and like other early industrial sociologists rising rapidly to professorial power, Arensberg's role in provoking the reaction against human relations has been underestimated.

A full account of this reaction would be interesting but only a few points can be made here. It began earlier than is often supposed, in the mid 1930s, and the first critical fire was brisk and accurate.[3] After a relative lull during the Second World War, it began in earnest. Between 1946 and 1950, nearly all the conventional charges against the school were systematically pressed: neglect of unions; managerial bias; acceptance of manipulation; inadequate treatment of industrial conflict; failure to relate the factory to the wider social structure; and fear of anomie.[4]

Surprisingly, however, no very careful examination was made of the empirical reliability of key human relations investigations. Not until the 1960s did Carey claim that the Hawthorne studies, on which so much human relations theory depended, were too incompetently executed to demonstrate very much at all.[5] As noted in several places already, this autopsy on the methods and research techniques has turned into something to rival the *Mousetrap* as a long-running show, with important contributions – John Madge (1963), Alex Carey (1967), H. M. Parsons (1974) Franke and Kaul (1978), Steven Cohen (1983), John Smith (1987) – every few years, regular as clockwork: Smith also examines the growing specialist literature on Mayo.[6]

The edge of earlier criticisms was often blunted by the critics' failure to discriminate between the various branches of human relations, and their frequent resort to guilt by association. Any target which had a remote association with Mayo was subjected to a kind of intellectual carpet-bombing.[7]

Some of the venom – it is the right word – in some of these attacks reflected revulsion against the political bias of human relations. But there is a surprise here. The most violent of the reasoned attacks did not come from left-leaning critics. It is worth remembering that there are aspects of the Mayoite ideal society that are reminiscent of a certain kind of socialist Utopia – that envisaged by William Morris in particular. I shall be arguing later that I see a 'Proudhonian' veneration of skill in the thought of writers like Georges Friedmann or Harry Braverman. Did this result in Mayo being criticized less harshly than he might have been by these craft romantics? The myth of a pre-industrial social world, stable, ordered, calm, is one they share with Mayo at least. What is certain, however surprising, is that leftist critics such as

C. W. Mills, with only one or two exceptions, have been relatively measured in their observations.[8]

The definitive assaults on human relations were to come in the 1950s, that is, when industrial sociologists had already adopted a new paradigm of behaviour, and in the wake of the widespread failure of human-relations training schemes. The senior author of the first of these was an economic liberal, Clark Kerr; the second came from a business commentator, W. H. Whyte, editor of *Fortune*.[9] By the standards of the day, these were somewhat right of centre. The rage and sarcasm of these attacks is remarkable: they fix on what they regard as the inconsistency of human relations with traditional American values – market values such as the legitimacy of high monetary incentives, individualism, career-mindedness, and competitiveness. Whyte accuses Mayo and Warner of plotting to destroy the Protestant work ethic and substitute a social ethic in its stead.

Few of the people attacked answered any of these complaints directly. When they did so, their replies tended to be feeble or intemperate.[10] Their readiness to accept the rational element in the criticism is difficult to judge. W. F. Whyte's openness to a broader view is shown by his willingness to consider technological explanations, and his re-examination of economic incentives. But perhaps he is an exception. Writers of influential textbooks on human relations in the 1950s continued to chirp away about supervisory skill and the potency of communications as if very little had changed.[11]

In some senses, very little had. Industrial sociologists turned their attention to technology and formal organization as influences on workers' behaviour. But their eyes remained fixed on the plant, or the work organization, as the main unit of analysis. Similarly, manipulatory intervention could still be advocated, through an adjustment of the technological setting rather than through a reform of supervision. These concerns of the human relations approach were retained. But it is maybe noteworthy also that the fullest elaboration of the new approach was to be made outside the USA, where human relations lacked an academic infrastructure.

PART IV

IMPERATIVES OF THE MACHINE

17

Credo for an Age of Growth

Winding up the review of the work of Roethlisberger and Dickson in chapter 13, I showed that these writers came close to formulating a view of work behaviour that lays stress on a presumed capacity of technology to mould attitudes, relationships, and group loyalties. What exactly is meant by technology is important for the kind of claims and explanations put forward by any theory referring to *technological implications*. We have seen, too, that the anthropologist Bill Whyte began to weave technical factors into his study of stressful work situations and shop-floor conflict relationships in the early 1940s.

On close inspection, one finds that the industrial sociology of the 1940–55 period makes repeated use of the idea that behaviour is shaped by specific technical arrangements or actual machines. In this sense the idea was already very current before anyone took the decisive step and suggested that technology was not just a relevant factor for fully explaining work behaviour – indeed, social behaviour more widely – but that it was the critical explanatory variable.

Most social scientists would agree unhesitatingly with the first part of this proposition, though they would be very unsure about how to fit technology into an explanation, or how much weight to give it. Almost all – no, I will go further, literally all – would nowadays reject the idea that technology alone can explain behaviour, though a few would give it prominence in particular circumstances. Single-factor 'necessitarian' theories are out of fashion, and anything smacking of *technological determinism* is regarded with intense suspicion or even hostility. This is something, moreover, on which Marxist sociologists see eye to eye with their orthodox colleagues.

If we are to come to a sensible view of what a technological explanation can and cannot do we need to appreciate some of the factors that may have influenced the onset of the fashion for this approach. The beginning of the great vogue for technological explanations can be dated very precisely, to within a year or two either side of 1955. It collapsed equally abruptly fifteen years later, though minor variants have remained influential into the present and seem likely to do so for the foreseeable future.

One set of factors is institutional. In Britain, for example, the foundation of the Tavistock Institute of Human Relations shortly after the Second World War was of decisive importance, as we shall see shortly. But we need to take note of some less obvious, predisposing circumstances.

Intellectually, the attack on human relations, building up explosively around 1950, discredited explanations centring on the unique relationships within a work-group, a workplace, or a firm: they have only revived very recently, with the growth in fascination with *corporate cultures* in the 1980s. When this was combined with a reaction against the openly manipulative and managerialist doctrines of true Mayoites, the approach lost respectability, though training programmes based on the applied theories continued to be popular. But there was a more important change in the offing.

Here, we must brutally condense a complex and intriguing story to a few lines. In the 1950s, a number of social scientists who had been Communists or Trotskyites, active or fellow-travelling, in the radical 1930s, finally rejected Marxism. But they did not reject the *dialectical materialism* of interwar Marxism – the notion that the movement of history is almost exclusively shaped by economic factors, of which the most important is the level of technological development forming the base of an economy. As Seymour Martin Lipset was to argue, history had 'proved Marxist methodology right, at the expense of Marxist politics'.[1]

Capitalism had not collapsed, as the radicals had once expected, but was now in spectacular expansion, thanks ostensibly to its ability to apply technology. There rapidly developed a general theory of *convergent industrialism*,[2] which predicted growing similarity between all social and political regimes thanks to their common drive to exploit modern technology. This doctrine hung everywhere in the late 1950s intellectual and political atmosphere.

Explaining how technological advance could become so seductive an idea is especially difficult at the present time, when technology is seen so often as a multiple *threat* – to employment, to the environment, to sane ways of thinking, and to life itself. But the scale of this aversion reflects the depth of the immediate post-Second World War love affair with technology: it arose partly in direct reaction against it. We must try to imagine, or remember, how it was to be living in a world of rapid economic growth, full employment, and low inflation; which was democratizing car ownership and jet travel; had already given almost everyone a television set; and was about to stage on television the ultimate spectacle of a manned flight to the moon.

In this growth era, when so many parts of life were suddenly being altered directly by new inventions and processes, there arose a natural predisposition to resort to the technological variable. To put things a little crudely, why go for any other explanation if a technological explanation could be made to fit?

Thus, technology supplanted the human relations climate as the favourite variable for explaining industrial behaviour. In the USA, this change was associated with an institutional one, as industrial sociology – the most distinct, developed and coherent branch of inquiry on work behaviour – was all but wound up, in name, anyway. Increasingly, investigators took the title of *organization theorists*. Combined with applied psychology, the sociology of organizations formed the core of a newly popular and heavily promoted academic area, organizational behaviour. Its greatest ambition was to define universal laws of organization. When applied, they would guarantee success. It became especially urgent for these theorists to pin down the influence of technological factors. (We shall examine this project in chapter 21.) Let us look more closely at the nature of the approach.

The core of the technological implications approach lies in an assumption that technology and work behaviour are ultimately related. Writers have varied in their views of this relation, and this is best shown by examining their contributions. In doing so, it is instructive to note their varying treatment of the following questions: (1) what is the nature of the technology-behaviour link – is this direct, or does it operate via the organization of work?; (2) to what extent is behaviour a sheer response, a reflex, to a given technical or organizational milieu; is some individual interpretation of the milieu allowed for?; (3) what is meant by the term 'technology'? Does it refer to plant, equipment and other elements of the production apparatus, or is work organization itself included?

Because they were one of the first examples of a technological approach, led to the long-time research effort, and generated a theoretical concept – the *socio-technical* system – which many people have found compelling, it is important to examine first the studies of coal mining undertaken by the Tavistock Institute of Human Relations in the late 1940s. The title of a paper of 1951 by Trist and Bamforth, 'Some Social and Psychological Consequences of the Longwall Method of Coal-Getting', clearly indicates the chosen orientation.[3] It was to be pursued in a research programme in British coal mines lasting almost ten years – which finally came to grief for reasons that have still never been made clear.[4] It lies behind the quality of work life movement that became internationally influential in the 1970s.

A thorough examination of the Tavistock's other early industrial studies and research philosophy written by Richard Brown has been available for some time.[5] Only a few points from it can be noted here. The Institute was founded in 1947 as an agency for psychologists with interdisciplinary inclinations to make available to industry the expertise they had accumulated on personnel and other problems during the Second World War. An important early study was of joint consultation in the Glacier Metal Company, whose managing director, Wilfred Brown, was something of a management thinker and enthusiastic supporter of applied social science. The mining studies, also commencing in the late 1940s, were initially concerned with 'the conditions likely to increase the effectiveness of the "dissemination of information" about new social techniques'.[6] Fortunately, the researchers seem to have interpreted this brief liberally.

Bitter conflict had marked the industrial relations of British coal mines between the wars. Nationalization had been expected to reduce this conflict, both in its overt forms and in absenteeism, labour wastage and low productivity. This did not happen. Medical observers of the mines, however, had for twenty years been noting an increase in morbidity and psychosomatic illness among colliers, which one at least related to growing anomie as confidently as any Mayoite.[7] This period, however, had also seen the displacement of traditional 'hand-got' mining organization by the Longwall method. Older miners often expressed a nostalgia for the former system that did not seem compatible with the great difficulties of the work methods they had experienced.

Aware of these paradoxes, and that tentative modifications of the normal Longwall organization since nationalization had sometimes been 'accompanied by impressive changes in the social quality of the work-life',[8] Trist and Bamforth set out to identify those technical features in the traditional, and the conventional longwall, systems which might produce different human consequences. (Bamforth had spent eighteen years at the coal face himself.)

Whatever the technology employed, certain features of coal mining as a productive operation make it distinctive. First, the underground situation is dirty, dangerous and dark. Second, geological variations constantly threaten the smooth flow of operations. Third, operations logically divide into an endlessly repeated three-phase cycle, namely: (1) *preparation*, or cutting the fresh coal in the seam; (2) *getting*, or removing the cut coal from the seam and the coal face; (3) *advancing*, or moving forward machinery and the pitprops supporting the roof, into the gulf created by extraction, to prepare for the next cut.

In the days of 'hand-getting', the technology available at the face was rudimentary, consisting of little more than hand tools such as picks, shovels and, later, pneumatic drills; metal tubs were used to remove the won coal and feed it into the haulage system. Work was organized in the so-called *single-place* form on a *bord and pillar* layout. Briefly, this consisted of creating square pillars of uncut coal by driving tunnels into the seam at intervals of about 40 yds; *places* of 6 to 11 yds in length were then allocated on each set of pillars to small teams of miners.

The team of about six miners was *self-selecting*, that is to say, new members had to be chosen unanimously by its existing members. Because of the general use of a three-shift system, two of its members would be at work on any one shift. Each member was a composite workman; that is, he had to acquire all skills required at the face before he stood a chance of selection into one of these small groups of *marrows* (mates). Each marrow group of six colliers was paid a lump sum related directly to output, and could divide the proceeds as it agreed, taking account of internal variations in experience or effort. Its relation to wider management was almost that of a sub-contractor, and in matters of discipline and output it was virtually self-regulating.

It could be claimed that this form of organization was well fitted to the technology available and the unique features of the underground situation. Within limits, each team could set its own pace. This was satisfying to its members and convenient to management from many points of view: for example, the flow of coal from the face was fairly even throughout the shift, thus avoiding jams in the haulage system to the surface. Again, if geological difficulties were encountered, each collier possessed the full experience to meet them both technically and psychologically. When the cycle of operations was delayed on one shift, the oncoming pair of marrows could take up where the foregoing pair had been forced to halt. The deputy (first-line supervisor) stood largely in the service relationship to the group, which accorded well with the colliers' independent, egalitarian spirit.

Longwall layout was introduced into the mines from about 1900 onwards. It seemed necessary for the exploitation of the new moving conveyor belt. Pillars and places were abolished and continuous faces of up to several hundred yards attacked. This was accompanied by a mass-production factory philosophy: 'the work is broken down into a standard series of component operations that follow each other in rigid succession over three shifts . . . so that a total coal-getting cycle may be completed once in each twenty-four working hours.'[9] The production engineering logic of an elaborate division of labour thus eradicated the tiny marrow group of all-round craftsmen and installed task groups of specialized workers tied to particular operations on a particular shift.

Such changes were at odds with the miner's belief both in general equality, since they created a new status system tied to job gradings and tasks, and in a status reflecting his composite skill, which disappeared. Management were faced with new and severe problems of supervision and co-ordination. The cycle and shift groups were no longer self-regulating. They bitterly resented efforts to regulate them from outside. But unless the general task of a given group was completed in its given shift, control was lost because the oncoming shift was specialized in different operations and was neither willing nor able to tackle unfinished work. Given the unpredictability of underground conditions the pattern of operations became a bad-tempered struggle from crisis to crisis with frequent stoppages.

Almost invariably longwall faces yielded an average output far below their theoretical potential. Absenteeism and sickness rates climbed. These effects were masked by the general conflict between workers and management, and the powerful economic weapons that management possessed, in the bitter 1920s and hungry 1930s. The post-Second World War situation made them more apparent.

In 1951, the Tavistock workers were not yet ready to formulate a detailed model to account for this contrast between traditional and longwall methods, nor to propound organizational solutions. 'As regards the longwall system,' they note, 'the first need is for systematic study and evaluation of the changes so far tried. It seems to the present writers, however, that a qualitative change will have to be effected in the general character of the method so that a social as well as a technological whole can come into existence.'[10]

I shall touch on the later stages of the studies in a later chapter. For the moment, two features of Trist's and Bamforth's approach are worth noting. Firstly, they undoubtedly distinguished varying social and psychological concomitants of the two technical systems. Secondly, they saw these as mediated by the organization of work.

They did not claim that the technical apparatus necessarily produced certain human effects directly, nor that it entailed a specific form of organization. In this respect their outlook, unlike that of many other technology theorists, was not rigidly determinist or behaviouristic. The writers to be considered in the next chapter were less cautious.

18

The Technological Countryside

Almost simultaneously with the first stages of the Tavistock coal-mining studies the fieldwork for what was to become an equally important contribution to the exploration of technological factors as influences on work was being undertaken by Walker and Guest in the USA. This was to be written up as *The Man on the Assembly Line*,[1] and Walker's and Guest's monograph of 1952, soon followed by a companion, *The Foreman on the Assembly Line*,[2] rapidly became, and remained for many years, a key point of departure in discussions of the relation between technology and the worker's experience of his job situation in the large mass-production factory. Even today it makes instructive reading.

It soon becomes clear that the authors were conscious of breaking new ground but were not altogether sure how to tie in their findings with previous work, or in what tradition of industrial studies they were working. There is an amazing scarcity of reference, even critical, to the work of the human relations researchers, though the results of the study plainly indicated that the human relations theory needed revision. They had, however, evidently studied critiques of what the French writer Georges Friedmann called *technicism*.[3] Friedmann was a growing source of inspiration to English-speaking industrial sociologists at this period, as translation made them more widely accessible: I shall be saying more about it in chapters 28 and 30. At this point, we merely need to note that concern with *fragmented* work grew steadily from this point until the so-called revolt against work in the 1968–73 period (see chapter 29).

But it is noteworthy that the most lavishly referenced previous work was that of the Myers group psychologists, Wyatt and Fraser. However, Walker's and Guest's theoretical discussion was very low-keyed. They seem to have hoped that their results would speak for themselves.

They offered no ambitious theoretical scheme. For this, they were duly apologetic, commenting that 'the new geography of man-at-work has received so little scientific study'.[4] Note the term 'geography': it is very revealing. We are to be taken into a countryside of machines. In the geography of the mass-production workshop, the machine is the commanding feature. 'The machine will be surveyed less as a tool of production than as a part of the topography of a man's workplace, and mass production not as an engineering method but as a code of law governing his behaviour and way of life in the factory.'[5] A code of *law*, it should be noted. The machine is boss. It is also worth noting at this point that adjustment of worker feelings was viewed by the researchers as an 'elementary problem area', and leads to the question, 'To what degree can – or should – men be "adjusted" to the new environment of machines, and to what degree is it possible to adjust or rebuild that environment to fit the needs and personalities of men?'[6] Only idealists had ever asked such questions up till then.

The research results were derived from interviews with 180 autoworkers from 'Plant X'. The vast bulk of this sample were assemblers of one kind or another, and nearly two-thirds were in machine-paced operations. Plant X was a newly built plant in a previously non-industrialized area. Only one in ten of the respondents had previous experience of machine-paced repetitive work. Walker and Guest recognized that these facts might affect their findings, but in a psychological rather than sociological manner. (They talk of their population being possibly less 'conditioned' to mass-production than workers in, say, Detroit.) Indeed, although some of the best-known sections of the monograph became those where they outlined the impact of technology on social relations in the plant, the investigation was essentially a study of attitudes towards mass-production work, of responses to its salient features.

This bias is not immediately apparent. After arguing that the three key features of assembly-line work – programming of production, mechanized handling and fragmentation of work operations – yield a job which typically is machine-paced, repetitive, unskilled, fractionalized, unchallenging and monotonous, they picture the worker's total job situation of consisting not merely of the work itself (and its pay, physical surroundings and promotion opportunities) but also of relations with workmates, with supervision, and with the union. Thus social factors were certainly considered, but not fully investigated. Only about a quarter of the report was devoted to them. The chapter dealing with the behavioural consequences of the working system is a bare eight pages long. The authors note that 'Technological factors of automobile assembly work affect the worker, both directly and indirectly. They affect him directly through the immediate job, and indirectly by modifying the basic organizational and social structure of the plant.'[7] But it should be understood that they are mainly considering the psychological effects on the worker.

The findings can be briefly summarized. Machine-paced work was found to be thoroughly disliked, ranking first of the three most disliked features of the work mentioned spontaneously. These other features, repetitiveness and lack of challenge, however, are clearly related closely to machine-pacing. Evaluations of a particular type of operation correlated highly with its objective mass-production characteristics.

Hardly surprising, the work itself was the least-liked aspect of the total job situation and money was the best-liked feature. Three-quarters of the sample claimed to work at Plant X solely for its high pay, which was sometimes a 50 per cent increase on their pay in previous work. The work was regarded as steady, and was also liked for this reason particularly by the men's wives. However, the variation in reward between different jobs was small. This reflected company and union policy, but also the homogenizing effects of the production system. A further consequence of this sameness of the work was the relatively poor opportunity for promotion. Yet many workers felt their chances for promotion were in fact higher in Plant X than in their previous jobs, and only a fifth expressed any frustration over their hopes of promotion. Most respondents aspired to transfer to jobs 'off-line', that is, away from the main assembly-line. These were sought not for higher status or earnings but as an escape from pressure and monotony. But chances of making such transfers were generally low.

The findings on the social side indicated, in brief, that less than half of the sample experienced frequent social interaction on the job. It was prevented not only by environmental interferences such as noise but by the layout of the line. Since this varied from one shop to another to some extent, opportunities occurred to talk with a few workmates quite often, and in rare instances men could be said to belong to teams whose functionally interrelated tasks permitted some social cohesion. But few respondents were conscious of belonging to any identifiable work-group, and some were cut off from any contacts at all. The investigators emphasized that lack of social contact represented a serious form of deprivation, while 'those who were members of true teams spoke of their group interaction in positive cheerful terms'.[8]

The findings about relations with management figures could be described as bimodal, or split two ways. Contacts with foremen, or other first-line supervisors, were generally frequent. An unfavourable assessment of the job did not generally lead automatically to bad relations with foremen. Three-quarters of respondents claimed to get on well with their supervisors, and remarks about them were generally favourable. Thus the technology did not preclude a kind of 'compensatory' relationship with the foremen.

As for other managers, contacts were typically rare, superficial or non-existent. Walker and Guest obviously feel that this was undesirable. They were to comment:

> in so far as the technology of the line keeps the work groups weak and non-functional, it tends to weaken the individual's sense of belonging to a bona fide industrial community. There is a close personal work bond between the individual and his immediate boss, but all other bonds either with supervision or with local management are non-personal or impersonal.[9]

Yet their data on workers' assessment of the value of worker-foreman interaction suggest that such relations were not of primary importance. It was thought important to have a good foreman, but factors like pay or the job itself were relatively much more highly valued. This shows that human relations doctrine – the belief that workers *ought to want* a close relationship with supervisors – was still influential. Reference to other industrial research was sparse. Even Mayo was mentioned once only. But this reference suggests that they accepted unquestioningly the Mayoite assumption that membership in a tightly knit work-group is of absolute importance to workers.[10]

Yet this appears in an analysis of the workers' relation with the trade union – the plant had been rapidly organized by the United Automobile Workers, and relations between it and management were reasonably cordial. Although often 'green' unionists, two-thirds of the workers were favourably disposed to the union. The authors comment:

> The nature of the workers' comments together with other evidence suggests that, in addition to its usual bargaining functions, the union met a psychological need by counterbalancing in part the sense of impersonality and anonymity men felt in their work.[11]

By now the pattern of thinking underlying this study should be clearer. The lie of the mechanical countryside has had, at times, determinate influence on the social and psychological experience of work. Technology can prevent the formation of true work-groups and this frustrates the worker's natural urge for social attachments. He becomes maladjusted and tense:

> Causes of poor adjustment to the group situation are manifold . . . but too often overlooked is the fact that technology in any given operational unit may be the crucial factor in determining the character of the social relationships for any individual or for a group of individuals.[12]

But unlike Sayles (see chapter 20), a researcher with an otherwise comparable view of the deterministic nature of technology, Walker and Guest seem to have been relatively uninterested in its effects on workers' *behaviour*. Their brief chapter on this topic amounted to little more than a discussion of quit-rates (or turnover) and absenteeism: these were generally high in the automobile industry, and in Plant X quit-rates correlated with the number of mass-production features in the job. Despite their respondents' statements that machine-pacing was the most disliked feature of the work, and the men's suggestions for improving the work by introducing rest-pauses and the chance to vary their work-pace (by building 'banks', or 'working up the line'), Walker and Guest saw the main problem as one of overcoming some kind of psychological starvation:

We suggest that the sense of becoming de-personalized, of becoming anonymous as against remaining oneself, is for those who feel it a psychologically more disturbing result of the work environment than either the boredom or the tension that arise from repetitive and machine-paced work.[13]

Certainly, they were correct in claiming that one of the interesting results of the study was 'a fairly clear picture of the kind of social interaction a moving-belt technology permits and also the kind it denies'.[14] Yet those contacts within the workplace constitute only one part of work behaviour as a whole. The most important aspect of that behaviour was surely the initial *decision* of the workers to take work that was so highly deprivatory. This was to be a question taken up systematically in studies of automobile plants in the 1960s (see chapter 25).

At the same time, it is interesting to discover that they recommend *job-rotation* and *job-enlargement* for countering the monotony of assembly-line work. These are still perhaps the most widely used techniques for enriching work and would allegedly alleviate deprivation by increasing the extent of social interaction – contacts with other workers as an operative moved from one work-task to another. They might also reduce boredom and monotony, but that was not the main aim in introducing them. Their call for experiments to determine how far jobs can be redesigned to permit more social contact, and their recommendation of group incentive pay schemes – a direct echo from Wyatt and Fraser, and Mayo – also show a value commitment to the idea of teamwork. But such remedies ignore the possible implications of the orientation of workers to the job. This had already been sketched by Dalton,[15] though it is to be explored more thoroughly elsewhere.[16]

But in focusing on the question of how workplace phenomena

might be influenced by the technical apparatus of production, this study amounted to – a geographical pun cannot be avoided – a watershed in studies of work. The impulse behind the call for job-rotation and job-enlargement was laudably humanitarian. Neither set of devices have quite lived up to expectations, which were never very high in any case, but they have certainly led to minor alleviations in the monotony of mass-production work.[17] The limited nature of their impact has also led to a search for more radical ways of rearranging the mechanical landscape. The study helped to sow the idea that it is not fixed once and for all time.

19

Organizational Engineering and the Self

One important school of writers whose work in a number of respects accords with the technological implications approach became influential, especially in the USA, in the later 1950s. They are variously labelled the *neo-human relations* school, or as *organizational psychologists*, or the *organizational design* (OD) theorists.[1] Much in their work certainly justifies the first title. The second embraces a more heterogeneous group of contributors than those whose work will be examined here. I prefer another term, *organizational psychotechnologists*, on three counts: (1) they view 'conventional' formal organization as a set of techniques embodying specific psychological assumptions held by its designers; (2) they assert that this form of organization generates individual psychological distress; (3) they offer technical prescriptions to improve organizational design.

The original psycho-technologists were greatly inspired by the ideas of a psychological guru, A. H. Maslow, and they propagated them zealously. Sometimes they seem to me to have done so in a rather wide-eyed way, as if they had suddenly 'got religion'. But the longer-term results of this have been worthwhile, even if the short-term effect of the doctrine leaves some people a little queasy. Why it should have this effect I have never quite made out. In many ways it seems entirely commonsensical, and it can be reconciled with some far weightier theoretical ideas. Let us have a look at it.

Maslow suggested that human behaviour is driven by distinct sets of needs or motivations.[2] In order of importance, these are: *physiological* need, *safety*, *love*, *esteem*, and *self-actualization*. A kind of ratchet mechanism governs the quest for fulfilment of these needs. To simplify, when a man is hungry his overriding obsession is physiological, for food; but once this need has been satisfied his behaviour will be governed by a search for safety. Failure to gratify the next set of needs results in frustration, and eventually in pathological symptoms. If, however, the objects of the class are attainable, they become powerful motivators, and the appetites of those fortunate enough to obtain them will graduate to a higher set still. A lucky minority will even succeed in satisfying their needs of self-actualization. The latter signifies a sense of personal worth and achievement, a realization of one's human potential.[3] Maslow was careful to qualify this general theory of behaviour by noting the need to investigate modifying factors, including 'the role of association, habit and conditioning' and 'the relation between needs and cultural patterns'.[4] Enthusiastic followers have sometimes been less guarded.

Douglas McGregor is a case in point. His views were conveyed, with almost embarrassing sincerity, in his book *The Human Side of the Enterprise*.[5] Acknowledging his debt to Maslow, McGregor distinguished three major classes of need: physiological, social needs, and self-fulfilment. Self-fulfilment was especially important, but McGregor argued that conventional organizational structure and practices totally ignore it. The 'theory' lying behind this form of organization is called Theory X, and is pernicious. Its assumptions are that workers are passive, indolent, unambitious, self-centred, resistant to change and gullible, and therefore the manager's task is to coerce and manipulate them by any means at his disposal. Practically the only acceptable assumption of Theory X, McGregor seemed to be saying, was that management has a basic right to organize the enterprise to pursue economic goals.

It reappeared as the very first term of Theory Y, which is healthy, and otherwise directly opposed to Theory X in all its assumptions. This tells us that employees are unconcerned with organizational goals only because experience teaches them to be so; that all employees are capable of at least some personal psychic development; that managers ought to structure the organization so that employees' private goals come to coincide with the needs of the organization. Theory Y, in fact, is more of a programme than a theory. McGregor used it very effectively to argue against conventional forms of organization, pleading the case for the spread of job-enlargement, participative leadership and the decentralization of organizational power in general. In the 1950s, it should be said, such objectives were regarded as very distant ones. But twenty years later, after the great cultural upheavals of the protest-peak period (see chapter 29), they were to become all the rage.

Rensis Likert, a more empirically minded writer, likewise viewed prevailing organizational structures as self-defeating and unacceptable. Higher management apply a militaristic logic of line of command organization and job specification. Such neat organizational geometry is characterized by upward flows of information and advice, each in its private channel, from a number of subordinates to a single boss; reverse flows of orders and instructions are handed down from the superior to each subordinate. Group activity within each such organizational segment is thus prevented, reducing collaboration and delaying the transmission of information.

Likert claimed that research had demonstrated a link between high production and the practice of general, delegating, considerate supervision. Successful organizations are, he asserted, always staffed by personnel with attitudes favourable to one another. They do not rely merely on financial incentives, but tap such powerful motivators as desire for status, recognition, approval, security and new experience. They thus become 'tightly knit, effectively functioning social systems' where there is good communication, participation in decisions and sensitivity to others.[6] Such findings, he stated, became comprehensible in terms of the Maslovian needs hierarchy mentioned at the outset. They suggested desirable changes in organizational structure. Organizations should be restructured as a series of interlinked collaborative groups. Likert highlighted the critical role of group leaders by designating them the *link-pins* (note the engineering flavour of the term) of organizations. But they can only act as link-pins when their own bosses accept and operate a sincere participative philosophy. Subordinates will do so only when their own superiors do so. Thus participation should be practised throughout the organization, from top to bottom. Likert promised that this change would improve performance because a cohesive group is superior to the individual as the basic work unit – an obvious human relations idea – but it will enable organization members to perceive the importance of the organizational mission, that is to say, its overriding task. To get this message across, the manager must relate it to the individual aims and views of his subordinates. Participative groups would enable him to appraise these aims quickly.

Since both of the foregoing writers were highly prescriptive, and over-selective in their use of evidence, I shall not discuss their ideas in any detail. It is fairer to assess the school as a whole by looking more closely at the work of Chris Argyris, its most interesting member from the point of view of this book.[7]

Argyris's starting point was 'an assumption that human beings are need fulfilling, goal achieving unities. They create various types of strategies to fulfil their needs and to achieve their goals'.[8] An organization usually takes the form of a pyramid. Yet these structures conflict directly with the individual needs of their members. Individual and organization are strongly opposed. This conflict is usually severe, because in 'our culture' – and Argyris's partial escape from the imputed universalism of the Maslovian scheme should be noted – we acquire certain expectations. As we grow up we are encouraged to proceed from a state of dependence to independence, from passivity to activity, from narrow to a broad choice in our behaviour, from casual to sustained interests and amusements, from a short to a long time perspective, from indifference towards social rank to positive status-striving, and from sanctions on our behaviour which are imposed by some external agency to internal self-regulation. In short, we progress from irresponsible childhood to responsible adulthood, and learn to associate lack of responsibility with childishness, and its possession with maturity.

Yet a person's condition in most work situations is one of dependence and constraint. Several factors that create this condition can be distinguished. 'The formal organization-structure is the first variable and it includes technology,'[9] Argyris stated.

Usually associated with this are directive leadership, and managerial control measures such as budgets, quality control, time-and-motion study and rate-setting. As we descend the organizational hierarchy the more severe the constraints stemming from these sources become. As a more sociological writer – John Scott or a Graham Salaman – would put things, organizations reproduce social class distinctions.[10]

As a psychologist, Argyris was worried that dependence produces frustration and tension. These might only be resolved through absenteeism, quitting, apathy, defensiveness, the creation of informal adversary groups or claims for higher wages. Moreover, the organization is directly responsible for many other social ills, since people come to 'accept these ways of behaving as being proper for their life outside the organization'.[11] For its part, the organization seeks to repress these responses, especially formation of informal organization, by tightening the formal structures. This closes a circuit of positive feedback, a vicious circle.

As an example of the process in action Argyris referred to the case of the XYZ Plant. Manual recruits to this organization were carefully screened by the personnel department to detect any disposition to rock the organizational boat. Those passing were assigned to either highly skilled or low-skilled working categories. In terms of supervision and economic rewards, the situations of both categories in the plant were more or less comparable. But the highly skilled group worked on more challenging and absorbing jobs. In interview, distinct differences in predisposition between the two become apparent. The highly skilled showed themselves much more concerned over the quality of their work, more interested in it and more conscious of their 'self-worth'. But they were far less concerned with money. Argyris asserts that these predispositions were generated after entry to the organization; they were a response to the conditioning effects of the work situation. But his evidence for this claim is indirect, and in my opinion inconclusive. As we shall see in chapter 34, Argyris is describing here the operation of an *internal labour market*: the theoretical importance of these for labour economists was only recognized by them many years later.

Where the nature of the work situation bars self-actualization, Argyris claimed, a strong informal organization comes into play. This can undermine the authority of supervisors, who become passive. Although they acknowledged that production performance was good, the XYZ management disliked this style of supervision adopted in dealing with ordinary workers. It was too easy-going, they complained. It might be taken as a sign of weak character. They therefore put pressure on foremen to be more 'go-getting' and constantly to inspect the workshops. Strangely enough, workers did not object to this extra attention, and some actually welcomed it.

But the foremen resented having to act in this fashion. Argyris asserts that their dissatisfaction was shown in agitation for more money, status and control, and an increased tendency to contract out of active leadership. This intensified managerial pressure on foremen and the frequency of their own visits to the shop floor. Management, however, were generally pleased with workers' behaviour, which they attributed to their own carefully selective hiring policy. Thus, Argyris proposes, the managing system, like technology, 'coerces psychologically different employees to behave in a similar manner'.[12]

Five observations on the work of the organizational psychotechnologists are worth making. Firstly, the status of the *needs hierarchy* concept is uncertain. If we assume that needs are real how can their existence be proved? As with all such psychological constructs, no direct method of doing so is available. We are obliged to resort to indirect methods. We can say, for example, that if a man is observed to pursue status, that suggests he has a need for status. But this is unsatisfactory: to say status is sought because of a status-seeking propensity reminds us of Voltaire's joke-explanation that opium makes us sleepy by virtue of its 'dormative properties'. We can argue just as well that if status is sought, it is not necessarily as an end in itself, but as a means to other ends, such as more wealth and power. How many needs are there, in fact? None of these writers seems able to agree. These difficulties recall the arid disputes between instinctual psychologists. Again, are the needs, and their imputed ordering, universal and innate? Comparative data suggest emphatically that they are not. And if we accept some cultural variation, as Argyris does, we must still be careful. The expectations that he suggests are implanted in 'our culture' are perhaps those which guide child rearing mainly in suburban America.

How sound are the assumptions that there is evidence on which much of this work rests? It is true that there is evidence of an association between repetitive work and high absenteeism, quit-rates and comparable indices;[13] and even between low occupational status and poor mental health.[14] But an explanation of this in terms of frustrated needs or expectations – particularly non-financial ones – is far from being the only plausible one available.[15] If widespread frustration and dissatisfaction exist – and some writers question their alleged extent – they may be as much the product of conflicting social value systems as a sum of individual responses to deprivatory work situations.[16]

A recurring theme of the psychotechnologists which this and the previous objection throws into question is that frustrated higher needs breed an obsession with cash rewards. This doctrine is obviously attractive to employers but its research foundations are shaky. There seem to be many people who want both more money and more higher-need fulfilment, and, when they get more of each, want more still. Our socio-economic system encourages both high materialistic and emotional expectations at least in many people if not in everyone.

These writers are highly selective in their use of evidence, especially of that which bears on their proposals for organizational reform. Much of it derives from the studies of work-groups undertaken by the Survey Research Center, especially its early studies. We saw earlier that SRC workers had modified their earlier conclusions drastically by the mid 1950s (see chapter 15). Moreover, all of this work has serious methodological defects. It was hazardous to base sweeping generalizations on it.

But I am glad that they did so. These writers may have repeatedly muddled their interventionist aims and their scientific obligations, but they were always people whose goodwill you could pick up on your radar while they were still at the railway station. They were genuinely concerned with the well-being of all groups in the organization, and eager to remove destructive stresses. It is appropriate also to endorse here a point made some time ago about them by David Silverman: unlike many organizational theorists they do not view the worker as a being who merely *responds* to a technological setting or formal organizational structure; he or she brings to the workplace certain needs and expectations which also affect behaviour in the workplace. In other words, their position is implicitly anti-behaviourist.[17]

This is important. There is an aspect of the technological approach reminiscent of the human factor school's treatment of environmental conditions in the workplace, which they pictured as shaping behaviour in fairly predictable ways. The constant temptation they had to contend with was to regard technology as a determinant force on behaviour – as *the* determinant force on behaviour. The followers of the organization engineers in the 1970s placed an even bigger stress on individual autonomy, and the employee's presumed entitlement to self-actualization. Here, they both drew on, and in turn amplified, the strong *post-bourgeois* cultural movement of the times.[18] An alliance was also struck with the Tavistock-derived movements for industrial democracy and autonomous work-groups, to form the Quality of Working Life or QWL movement. This important effect on the work-culture of their times may have been based, all along, as much on normative as on scientific grounds. There is an irony in this which repays further thought.

20

Designing Aggravation Out

Robert Sayles gave no space at all in his report *The Behaviour of Industrial Work Groups* to structural prescriptions for good organization or formulas for producing self-actualization.[1] Sayles reintroduced an industrial actor who seeks group membership not because he is driven by an inner need to associate but because collective action is a more rational way of pursuing economic aims. This was the first empirical study of the workplace to have capitalized on W. F. Whyte's many throwaway remarks on work-group behaviour. Sayles gave Whyte and Chapple generous credit in his preface.

The report was based on an ambitious comparative study of data on 300 work-groups in thirty manufacturing plants, collected over a four-year period. Sayles set out to examine and explain behaviour, actual patterns of activity. He had little interest in the attitudes towards work that people in his survey may have had. And the behaviour that he found most instructive was *grievance activity*, that is to say, involvement in workplace conflicts which arise from a sense of inequity – or which may be partly justified on such grounds. High grievance activity certainly marks off those sections of a work organization where tension and conflict have become marked, whether spontaneously or as a result of some foreplanning. In any case, Sayles's starting point is that certain plants or workshops, or sections of them, have a reputation for being troublesome either to managers or to union officials, while others are noted for being trouble-free.

What Sayles set out to show was that 'troublesomeness' was related to the organization of work – the labour process – which in turn was largely a product of the technology.[2] He defined four basic kinds of group in terms of patterns of grievance activity: this could be *apathetic*, *erratic*, *strategic*, or *conservative*. Sayles was to cause considerable confusion by adopting the term 'group' here. He was classifying patterns of grievance behaviour, exaggerating and formalizing them into an ideal type set of dominant features. The behaviour of people working together – sometimes they were no more than loose aggregates – in a workplace was fitted into one of these categories. Sayles made it very clear what he was doing,[3] but it would have been better to have found another term, such as 'pattern'.

There is no problem about the patterns as such. They are almost self-explanatory. The *apathetic* pattern was marked by quiescence, disunity, suppressed discontent, lack of leadership; aggregates showing it were poorly led, low-paid, and low producers. The *erratic* pattern was characterized by inflammability, inconsistent grievance pressure and sudden switches in loyalties. Departments falling into this category had a single strong leader; their output fluctuated wildly, and so did their grievance activity. Managers loathed them. The *strategic* pattern was one of continuous pressure on management, backed up by carefully planned grievance activity. There was high internal unity, but also high productivity. The *conservative* pattern was one of restrained pressure to achieve concrete objectives. It followed a regular, cyclical path that managers could readily predict. It was associated with high-status or skilled work. Workers in these aggregates had a good reputation as producers.

Actual departments or shop segments approaching a given pattern, Sayles stated, show 'a striking similarity in technological characteristics'.[4] For example, aggregates with a conservative pattern often turned out to be highly paid craftsmen, who were trusted to get on with their work without constant inspection. Often, too, they worked in a place considered to be 'their' building, or might have such a base but work out of it much of the time, with only the most general supervision – for example, undertaking maintenance duties. Sayles says, such groups are noted for their capacity to 'scatter'.

Each pattern was associated with a certain kind of technical milieu. Sayles denied that it was possible to jump to the conclusion that technology caused each pattern: after all, groups did have genuine grievances as well as ones that might be fabricated to start a campaign or maintain or build solidarity. There is a more subtle, indirect kind of influence that technical factors can exert, as a set of background conditions which facilitate or restrict the emergence and continuation of a pattern. 'We believe that a group's behaviour in the plant is a product of its *inherent ability to function in a certain way*,' Sayles stated.[5] Ways of functioning depended on the *enabling* conditions set by technical arrangements.

He went on to examine two major sets of technically related factors. The first were those which set a group off, or segregated it physically, or in some other way distinguished it from other aggregates. The second were those which affected the internal structuring of the aggregate, which limited the extent to which it could become a tightly integrated group. Under the first heading, Sayles listed nine factors: the labour segment's status in the plant; its size; homogeneity; discretion in work; compactness; sex-composition; hours and work-schedule; the degree of repetitiveness in its work-functions; and how essential these functions were to the plant as a whole. This showed that activity is influenced most by the segment's status, the indispensability of its work, and its size and homogeneity.

Taken together, size and homogeneity appeared to be particularly important. The larger the group and the more homogeneous the tasks of its members, the greater the likelihood of its mobilizing to press grievances. Sayles here introduced an interesting concept which he called 'resonance'. This is how he described it:

> What seemed essential for verbalizing complaints and uniting people to 'right them' was some reinforcement or *resonance* factor. Where this reverberation was provided by people having identical experiences, each one could hear his own grievances repeated and magnified.[6]

The kind of process Sayles was trying to define here is similar to those that other people, such as David Lockwood, were pointing to as conditioning factors in the readiness of workers to join a union.[7]

They are well known to theorists of social class, especially those who adopt a Marxist perspective on the question, stressing the importance of class members being able to communicate a sense of awareness of their common circumstances the one with the other. As for factors affecting the internal organization of an aggregate – internal task-differentiation, promotion chances, frequency of interaction, the work-flow – Sayles found that: 'Technology also shapes the relationships within the work group, and thus the structure of the group itself.'[8] For example, where job skills were very mixed, status and sectional interest prevented concerted action. Again, in an otherwise homogeneous department, technical arrangements might create 'islands' of workers whose highly interlocking task-structure encouraged separatism and cliques.

Taking both inter-group and intra-group factors together, some clear associations emerged. A high degree of grievance activity was present among workers with fairly high jobs, high indispensability, and wide control over their own effort; a low degree of activity and unpremeditated action occurred among crews or assembly-groups with interdependent work-operations; and deliberate, predictable activity was a feature of segments with individual and independent jobs – though the pattern sometimes appeared also in very homogeneous teams and crews, or groups on short assembly lines.

Sayles commented:

> Upon reflection it appears as though all four relevant variables are related to the technological system designed by the company to organize the work process . . . We recognize that many persistent industrial relations problems have their *roots in the technology* of the plant. We are in the habit of attributing these to individual worker or manager characteristics . . . However, this study also suggests that the social system *erected by the technological process* is also a basic and continuing *determinant* of work group attitudes and actions.[9]

Was this a technologically determinist explanation or not? I have italicized the phrases in the above passage which suggest this. Yet in fact Sayles recognized that although technology may influence the patterns of conflict within workplaces, it could not initiate it. He went on to say 'these technological factors are really *enabling* conditions. They do not explain what sets off a spate of aggressive activity, what brings it to a halt, and what are the personal motivations involved'[10] (Sayles's own italics here). The motivations Sayles regarded as most important were economic: he seems to have had little time for any Mayoite idea that aggregates would seek to become integrated groups in order to fulfil a longing for sociability *per se*. A scheme for interpreting how individual economic aims might coalesce into a group-based form was provided in a diagram on page 105 of *The Behaviour of Industrial Work Groups*. This is very reminiscent of Whyte's scheme in *Money and Motivation* (see pp. 163f). Sayles also recognized that leadership may be necessary to articulate grievances effectively, but did not press this point. The groups he had investigated constantly compared their status and earnings with those of other workers, to the extent that Sayles exclaimed: 'In a sense the groups we have been talking about resemble the purely selfish economic men of classical theory.'[11] This was the fuel that fired the motors of grievance.

Launching into a general discussion of research and theory on groups in industry, Sayles emphasized the limitations of Mayoite thinking about the link between teamwork and productivity. The hypothetical quest for social equilibrium of Mayo's social man ignored simple economic interest as a group unifier and motivator. Investigators ought to focus on intra-plant interest aggregates: 'To repeat, this is not the traditional concept of the informal group seeking conformity with established norms of conduct. These are much more free enterprise units, interacting in a struggle for maximization of utility.'[12]

The interest aggregate was thus often involved in a triple disloyalty – to management, to a union, and to fellow workers. Sayles looked on himself as a reformer within the human relations tradition – that, anyhow, is what his other comments, and the subtitle of the book, suggest. But managers had to learn a more sophisticated way of limiting grievance activity than improving their leadership skills. And if technology causes conflict, it is futile to blame it on hotheads or agitators, or hope to eradicate it by 'better communications' or participative management, however desirable each of them might be in their own right.

Sayles pointed out that his report ought to be studied carefully by industrial engineers and production managers, as well as personnel people.[13] Many of them already had accurate ideas of where trouble was likely to break out. His research had helped systematize the study of technical factors in workplace industrial relations. At the least, managers and engineers could pinpoint likely trouble spots and devote extra attention to designing trouble out of the system. He also addressed this message to trade-union officials, since they also could be caused a great deal of what they regarded as unnecessary trouble in dealing with chronically aggrieved groups. They could urge engineers and job-designers to cut out this kind of aggravation at the drawing-board stage.

From several points of view, this is an interesting message, wide open to the complaint that it reveals an outrageous readiness to intervene on the 'wrong side'. But I see no point in harping on this. What is far more striking, in view of the spread of New Wave analyses of the workplace, especially of those that focus on the *internal labour market* (see chapter 34), is the striking way in which the industrial sociology of the 1950s anticipated – maybe that is not quite the right word – the political economy of the 1970s. Sayles even used the term *labour segment* to describe his interest aggregates. Much of his analysis was concerned with a segment's 'politics' – its own ability to cohere around a strategic plan to pressurize management into altering the internal labour market.

Otherwise, his work is inconsistent with much of New Wave thinking. Instead of an all-powerful employer deliberately using technology to divide and rule the workforce, we glimpse a world where managers seem to have lost a degree of control precisely because technology has been designed without thinking of its social consequences. Many of the workplace situations described by Sayles present a picture of a workforce already deeply divided by the layout of equipment, machines, and an associated work organization. He urged managers and engineers to *reduce* the factors sustaining sectionalist politics among labour segments, not to find new ways of creating such divisions. According to New Wave theory, he must have got things very wrong. But at least agreement would be reached that there is a real possibility for organizational choice at the design stage.

21

Organization, Technology and National Culture

Joan Woodward will always be remembered on at least two counts. She was the first woman professor of industrial sociology in Britain. As she gained her chair in the very male surroundings of Imperial College in South Kensington long before the advance of feminism, this was a remarkable achievement. (She was succeeded by the even more formidable Dorothy Wedderburn.) She was best known internationally, however, for her pioneering research in the late 1950s on the link between management organization, the tone of workplace human relations and technology.[1]

This path-breaking work challenged conventional human relations thinking and, in part, the theories of the psychotechnologists. But it also threw doubt on the universalism of the standard classic works of administrative theory; that is to say, it questioned whether laws of organization existed that were correct in all places at all times. Her early findings shocked some teachers of administration, especially in Britain, where management studies was taking off as a respectable subject for universities to teach and for aspiring executives to study. To these people, her report *Management and Technology*[2] seemed a tactless way of contributing to the academic and industrial credibility of administrative science. If they had thought more carefully about it, however, they would have realized that Woodward's ideas point to a more subtle form of universalism. I will come back to this. First, though, some more scene-setting. Woodward's conclusions have been superseded or modified but they altered the whole course of the debate on *organizational universalism* – the notion that building given structures or forms into an organization will always produce a predictable effect on behaviour. Something more needs to be said about this discredited theory.

For the first half of the twentieth century, administrative and management writers, and many university sociologists, believed there must be a determinable *one best way* to organize any set of operations. Here, they often muddled the ideas of F. W. Taylor on work redesign with Max Weber's discussion of bureaucracy. Weber had predicted the spread of bureaucracy, they assumed, because he believed it was a more 'scientific', more 'efficient' form of organization. This was mistaken. Weber explicitly denied such a link and habitually wrote the word between inverted commas. He believed bureaucracy produced *predictable* outcomes, but not necessarily efficient ones. We cannot say more on this here, but it is important to note it in passing.[3] But even when administrative writers doubted whether anybody had yet found universal principles of organization, they never doubted they could and would be found one day.

Accounts of Woodward's work in South Essex are easy to obtain, so I shall provide only an outline here. A survey of 100 firms, virtually a full census of industrial plants with over 100 employees in this area of Britain, conducted mainly in 1954–5, showed up wide variations in their formal organization. The latter was not be related straightforwardly to size, industry or effectiveness. Half of the firms followed accepted principles of administration – recipes specifying so many workers to each foreman, so many levels for the management hierarchy, and so on – but their profitability, their growth, or their industrial relations was, overall, no better than those firms who ignored the accepted principles.

But when the firms were grouped according to their technology, distinct patterns began to emerge. Woodward's definition of technology at this time was not rigorous. Sometimes it merely stands for tools and equipment, i.e. hardware. At other times, it seems to refer mainly to working methods and managerial control systems, i.e. software. But generally it appears to denote a mixture of the two, which Woodward also called the 'production system' or the 'system of techniques'.

Eleven categories of *production system* were specified and

firms allocated to the one they fitted best. Adjacent categories were then telescoped into three major classes: (1) *unit* and small batch; (2) large batch and *mass-production*; and (3) *process* production. Both the detailed and the general production groups, however, were subsequently used for a more ambitious analysis. In fact, they always embodied a developmental theory of industry, whose logic Woodward explains as follows:

> It will be seen that the systems of production given [above] form a scale; they are listed in order of chronological development, and technical complexity; the production of unit articles to customers' individual requirement being the oldest and simplest form of manufacture, and continuous-flow production of dimensional products, the most advanced and most complicated. Moving along the scale . . . it becomes increasingly possible to exercise control over manufacturing operations, the physical limitations of production being better known and understood.[4]

Distinct association between certain broad features of formal organization and technology, that is, the type of production system, were detected (e.g. a lengthening of lines of command, an increase in the ratios of managers and clerical workers to production personnel, a narrowing of the chief executive's span of control) as technical complexity increased: 'Therefore the main conclusion reached through this research project was that the existence of the link between technology and social structure . . . can be demonstrated empirically.'[5] Furthermore, the most 'successful' firms in each major production category possessed structural features approximating to the median values for each dimension of organization which could be put into figures. For instance, in process production the median value for the number of levels in the management hierarchy was six; those process firms which had six levels were much more likely to be successful than those with four or eight.

Woodward commented: 'While at first sight there seemed to be no link between organization and success, and no one best way of organizing a factory, it subsequently became apparent that there was a particular form of organization most appropriate to each technical situation.'[6] This appears to put paid to traditional administrative theory. However: 'Within a limited range of technology this was also the form of organization most closely in line with the principles and ideas of management theory.'[7] This might be because many of the classical management theorists were themselves once practising managers in this branch of production – in fact, it is mass-production – and have generalized their experience, sincerely convinced that what was good for General Motors must be good for all industry.[8]

How these findings undermine human relations and psychotechnological views about the springs of work behaviour is clear. They indicate that the effectiveness of a firm relates to the fit between its production system and its formal organization, and not to the leadership style of supervisors or to participative, interlocking teams. Why they upset complacent teachers of administrative science is even easier to see. But in themselves the South Essex data do not take us much further. Woodward usually described her studies as a contribution to industrial sociology. Yet they provide relatively little behavioural or attitudinal data about groups of people staffing these organizations. Nor did she explore the fact that these firms were *British* organizations. This is important in the light of subsequent research into work organizations, as we shall see shortly. Woodward herself admitted that she could not explain the association established between technology, organizational form and performance in casual terms, sociological or not.

To be just, the initial assignment was to verify the 'laws' of administration, not to study and explain industrial behaviour. Therefore the data collected, which derived from broad indicators of formal organization, related almost entirely to formal organizational properties. Only the most superficial behavioural information – for instance, on industrial relations climates – was gathered in every one of the firms. Then again, no fixed definition of technology was adopted. Woodward regretted her 'lack of a satisfactory instrument for measuring technology', going on to wonder whether 'the control system [is] a further dimension of technology?'[9] There is a case to be made out for this, though I find it more logical to think of technology as an aspect of the control system. What matters is to treat it consistently. In the South Essex studies it sometimes squeezes in, at least implicitly. At other times it is treated either as an aspect of formal organization or as a separate variable. Anybody who wants to split hairs could of course complain that this wrecks the Woodward thesis: in so far as technology equals organization, the finding that organization varies with technology is less than surprising. But to reason this is too negative by half.

Some of Woodward's critics also bewail her failure to follow up her numerous *aperçus* about the relation between product-types and production systems. Her scale of technical complexity (or 'advance') is equally a scale of the standardization of the article produced, and of the predictability of the process by which it is produced. Will the control system become more highly structured and specific as a result? Or will it have to adopt a less rigid form, one calling for more worker autonomy? Such a conjecture raises many questions. But, at the time at which she was writing, automation was still rare, though it was already much discussed. Concepts such as the *flexible manufacturing system*, which would allow production of short runs of highly specialized products, existed in the pages of futurological engineering manuals. They have become reality only in the last decade. Their social and human implications are only now becoming fully researchable.[10]

Woodward was aware of such possibilities, and the problems they would raise for the conceptualization of technology. She was developing more sophisticated measures of production systems at the time of her premature and tragic death.[11] She would have been keenly interested in some of the research recently undertaken in this area. It is probable she would have regarded the debate over organizational structures were *culture-free*, that is to say, the her findings suggested that universal principles might exist *within* certain limits set by technical factors. Has this question yet been settled?

The first attempt to extend Woodward's work by defining more extensive sets of organizational variables and measuring their interplay rigorously was undertaken by a British team with strong international links based at the University of Aston in Birmingham. Derek Pugh and his associates began with a sample of fifty-two organizations. Further samples gradually added to their data-base, which grew to be an impressive one. While finding more organizational profiles or 'shapes' than Woodward (they also sampled non-industrial businesses and administrations) their conclusions followed what they took to be hers in claiming that organizational structures were *culture-free*, that is to say, the same the world over when allowance is made for whatever product or service an organization is providing.[12]

But anomalies appeared when investigators in other countries applied the Aston measures. The Aston researches were also treated with great reserve by many of the team's British colleagues on philosophical grounds. One of these arose from the apparent fixation of the Aston team with the interdependence of structural dimensions, as if the world of these abstractions – for a span of control, or a degree of task formalization, is certainly an abstract notion – was more real than that of the human beings who actually staffed the organizations in which they were measured. Inevitably, they caused the greatest affront to those investigators who had turned against surveys, scales and statistics, following the fashion of the day for subjectivist styles of inquiry, some of which led to the denial that social actors were influenced by anything but their own mind-pictures. (A favourite heresy among a generation that had discovered LSD.) This aspect of the matter will be taken up again in chapter 26.

Objection to organizational universalism does not need such elaborate philosophical underpinning as the subjectivists gave it. The well-travelled layman's observation that performance of identical tasks is often organized in strikingly different ways from one society to another already had the backing of scattered items in the research literature. One of the most entertaining was Richardson's contrast between crew organization on American and British merchant ships, which he experienced as a participant observer.[13] An identical organizational mission led to quite dissimilar organizational properties.

One way to interpret such differences is to put them down to the effects of different core values between nations, leading to different types of work motivation. A similar sort of explanation is more psychological, starting from the assumption that different countries produce a different average human type, or, to put it technically, varying modal personality structures. Actors, in this view, influence structure because they have learned ('internalized') a national culture. In organization studies, the most effective use of these ideas was first made by the Frenchman Michel Crozier.[14] But Crozier also pointed out that the 'Frenchness' of the values and perspectives that affected the French State employees in his inquiry were sustained by the character of certain institutions that could be remodelled, given sufficient political will, to encourage different values and therefore different behaviour.

This culturalist approach appeals to common sense, and we shall need to examine it again in another context. But there are risks and penalties in adopting it. Obviously we can define sets of values, traditions, and preferred ways of looking at the world, that are linked to nationhood. But not all members of a given society share this abstractly defined national culture. Even when they do, factors like class membership, age or gender are more potent influences on behaviour in many situations: indeed, we can usually observe an impressive underlying similarity from one country to another in the behaviour of people in such strata.

Again, the internal cultural diversity of many advanced countries has been growing for several decades. Populist politicians have been trying to revive coarse kinds of nationalism to distract attention from other problems. Their success has so far been mainly confined to the 'boot boy' section of society, and those journalists and other opinion leaders who share its mentality. The attempts, and their restricted success, point to the growing internal diversity of these societies. Transnationally powerful values and perspectives have always operated strongly on certain groups – practising Christians, capitalists, trade-union activists – and even set them apart in the society in which they hold citizenship.

For such reasons, it seems prudent for sociologists to hold culturalist explanations in reserve, until they have examined the possible influence of material, institutional, class, or demographic variables, factors which are by their nature transcultural and transnational. When, however, they have exhausted explanations in these objective terms, without being able to account for differences between societies, it is perverse to refuse to look at cultural influences.

But there may exist an explanatory middle way. In the early 1970s, French investigators at the Laboratoire d'Économie et de Sociologie du Travail (LEST) at the University of Aix-en-Provence began studying matched samples of French and German manufacturing firms. The main purpose was to find out how skills and qualifications were spread in each pair of firms of similar size, and how closely pay levels related to these patterns in each country. Already, they were finding sharp differences between firms of exactly the same size producing exactly the same product in the two countries.[15] (In France, pay differentials were far steeper, non-works white-collar workers were paid much more than their German counterparts, and lines of command were much longer, especially in the factory.)

Follow-up studies, which were to include comparisons with British firms,[16] further documented the reality of a strong *societal* effect on organizational structure. This does *not* mean that effects of the type pointed to in Woodward's work do not exist cross-nationally. They do: a large car plant in country A will resemble a large car plant in country B in ways that matter and set them both apart from large chemical plants in any country. The point is that such effects seem to matter less than do societal ones.

The explanation for this put forward by the Aix investigators (Maurice, Sellier and Silvestre) has important implications for any theory of industrial behaviour, and seems likely to gain greater currency in the years ahead.[17] For this reason, I shall say nothing more about it here but come back to it in the last chapter of the book.

22

Automating for Harmony – or Revolution?

We noted in the last chapter that the debate on the consequences of automation began a long time before there were any consequences to observe. The reason for this was the obvious one: there was no automation. Perhaps we ought to be careful and say there was not *much* automation: automatic transfer machines for milling, grinding and boring engine-blocks have been used in the motor industry since the 1930s. But if by automation we mean such a high level of integrated manufacture as free of human intervention as this, then there has been little automation until recently: electronic control equipment was too bulky and expensive, human labour too cheap and compliant, to make it worthwhile.

When office computing began to get cheaper, in the early 1960s, it was unhesitatingly dubbed 'office automation' though most schemes merely used computers to do faster – sometimes faster – what had been done for years using Hollerith-card counter-sorter equipment, desk-top electric tabulators, or other standard office machines.[1] Some employers began to aim at introducing integrated management information systems (MIS). Many of these, having been foisted on the customer by fast-talking computer salesmen, amply deserved the inauspicious MIS label. Far from bringing about 'automated management', whatever that might mean, they nearly always brought about chaos, and occasionally bankruptcy.

Anyone who was involved, as the writer then was, in studying the farcical bumbling of British firms supposedly 'automating management' could be excused for treating the whole concept of automation, whether in the factory, the office, or the executive suite, as nine-tenths hype and one-tenth hope. Only more recently has it seemed warranted to agree with those colleagues who claimed there was no shortage of production automation in industries like steel-making, oil-refining, paper-making, electricity generation, or chemicals. They might add water-catchment or, to be sure, sewage-treatment. (The latter provide excellent examples of automated process industry.)

At the same time, it is surely desirable to automate many tasks, the sooner the better, provided displaced workers are fully indemnified and retrained. Many of us are impatient to know what the effects of automation will be but these are still very unclear. Some parts of process industry are highly automated in a fairly strict sense. Yet whether they can be said to be prototypical in their technical characteristics or their effects on workers is to be doubted. Maybe there will be no single, clear set of such effects to point to. It is reasonable to guess that the consequences of automation will be many-sided.

But automation has always brought out the prophetic side in some social scientists. Let us look at two memorable cases.

Robert Blauner's *Alienation and Freedom*,[2] an ambitious comparison between certain objective features of work in various industries, has never been surpassed as a study of automation that is empirical and speculative in equal measure. The market strength of firms, the division of labour, and social composition all shape an industry, Blauner agreed; but, he went on, the 'most important single factor that gives an industry a distinctive character is its *technology*'.[3] An element of choice arises in the design of work-roles and relationships, Blauner conceded, but it is of minor importance. His main interest, anyway, was in the implications of technology for the *alienation* experienced by workers. This in turn has implications, he claimed, for workers' readiness to collaborate with management.

Writers have taken whole books to define alienation, disagreeing with other writers, making copious use of polysyllabic words, and then ending up without a definite verdict.[4] Blauner was well aware of this risk. His definition was arbitrary, but not unreasonable. Alienation for him meant 'a general syndrome made up of a number of different objective conditions and subjective feelings-states'.[5] These conditions and states refer to four kinds of satisfaction or deprivation that a work-situation can create. He labelled them *powerlessness*, *meaninglessness*, *isolation* and *self-estrangement*. Each of these can be researched successfully, Blauner went on, only once they have been *operationalized*. Operationalization involves choosing easily identifiable features, usually termed indicators, of a social situation that can be objectively appraised, and ideally, counted up. For example, we can assess workers' power position by asking which of their conditions of employment they can affect, by listing what opportunities they have to regulate the work process and trim their own work effort, and by studying how far they can select their own working methods. These are in fact the areas of control on which Blauner focused. He could also have examined how far workers could contribute to or check managerial policies, or determine which products are made and how they are sold. But he disregarded them on the – highly contentious – grounds that American workers express no interest in such aspects of power.

Meaninglessness refers to the immediate significance a work operation or product has for the worker. Some products, such as shoes, are intrinsically meaningful. Others, such as computer memory-banks, need setting in a technical context which must be learned. *Isolation* refers to 'absence of a sense of membership in an industrial community',[6] most obviously one based on the plant, but possibly on an occupation or a union. *Self-estrangement* is perhaps the hardest dimension to assess. Blauner tells us it is maximized when work denies a sense of wholeness and identity. This could be just a product of the three other dimensions. But it also arises when work is not 'highly integrated into the totality of an individual's social commitments';[7] that is, when it is not a central personal, social or religious value, but merely a resented means to other ends.

Using various measures, some rather rough and ready, for each dimension, Blauner went on to assess the typical level of alienation in four industrial environments – printing, cotton-spinning, automobile-making and petrochemicals. Each of these industries employs a characteristic technology; in turn, craft, machine-tending, mass- and process-production. (They are reminiscent of Woodward's broad types of production-system.)

Printing – traditional printing using hot metal – emerges with a low score for alienation. The printer set his own pace, escaped management pressure, chose his own techniques and was supported by a powerful union. He exercised a complex skill, enjoyed rewarding social contact during work, and had a high job-status. He identified closely with his work. Until the later 1970s, automobile workers suffered extreme alienation. Mass-production denied control, minimized meaning, increased social isolation and prevented any sense of self-actualization.

Process-production was and is less alienating to the worker. Petrochemical industries are generally prosperous and their equipment is technically advanced and often automated. Except during crises when pipes fracture or reactions go critical, process workers control their pace of work and are free to move around talking to workmates or – highly important for Blauner's conclusions about industrial relations – to managers trained in science or technical specialists possessing a professional, and social, cachet. Organized in teams responsible for the safety of the process and quality of the product, process workers can attain considerable understanding of the chemical reactions whose progress they monitor. This, Blauner insisted, inculcates a sense of belonging, achievement and responsibility, which their highly educated and modern-minded managers reinforce.

The foregoing industries allowed Blauner to state a strong case for the technological determination of alienation. Objective features of the various work environments do seem to match up with workers' subjective feelings, at least, as they are reported in attitude-polls – we shall come back to this point. However, Blauner's fourth group, machine-minding textile workers, presented a problem. Their control over their highly repetitive, monotonous and gruelling work was minimal. They had to bow to autocratic supervision. Social contact during work was impossible. This added up to a high degree of objectively measured alienation. The machine-minders should thus have experienced considerable self-estrangement.

Not so at all. Statements by these people and other subjective indicators showed a relatively contented workforce. Blauner explained this by pointing to out-plant attachments. His evidence was based on mills in small, tightly knit rural communities in the southern states of America. Observers have often suggested that southern mill-workers form a kind of industrial caste in which notions of submissiveness and fatalism dominate the subject's world-view. In this deviant group, subjective alienation is held at bay by community loyalties and values. Is this patronizing towards 'rednecks'? Maybe, but these people are not best known for their psychological maturity, the sophistication of their social thinking, or the subtlety of their political attitudes: country-and-western songs perhaps give us a stereotype, but life in these states is lived differently than in northern suburban areas.

But if alienating tasks can be neutralized by out-plant self-actualization in the community, where does this leave a theory anchored in technological determination? Anybody wishing to say that subjective and objective experiences form a unity, must talk his way round this glaring counter-instance. Alternatively, we must set aside the idea that alienation is a property of industrial environments rather than being a *systemic feature* of the socio-economic formation.

Actually, Blauner's indicators for *self-estrangement* (subjective alienation) were less than convincing. Such a complex state of mind and feeling might be mapped out in lengthy, heart-to-heart depth-interviews, or measured with elaborate attitude-scaling devices. Blauner, however, relied too much on data from a job-attitude poll conducted *over a dozen years* before he wrote his book. The pollsters asked workers standard do-you-like-your-job questions and about how much their work interested them, whether they would pick the same job again, and so on. Their answers had to fit into 'Likert-type' response-scales, which have just five points. (For example: strongly agree, agree, unsure, disagree, strongly disagree.)

Such questioning methods produce acceptable results when we need to establish the level of people's liking for wholemeal bread, breakfast television, or the Prime Minister. To use data produced by such techniques as valid evidence for or against a sense of self-estrangement is, quite simply, reckless. But not only did Blauner use these findings, he used them *selectively*. Some of the poll findings, if they could validly do the job he forced them to do, seem to weaken his thesis. For example, the job-satisfaction poll shows that no less than 49 per cent of printers – for Blauner, the model occupation for a sense of self-actualization through their work – were either unsure that they would, or said they definitely would not, choose the same occupation again.[8] Surely that is a bit high? But we can relax: all this poll really demonstrated for certain is that workers in different industries expressed varying amounts of satisfaction with their work when questioned by pollsters.

Blauner's procedure undoubtedly distinguished important substantive variations between industrial environments and his confusion over subjective alienation could be disregarded if he had left things there. But his mapping of the objective levels of deprivation in work was intended to serve a much more grandiose purpose. This was to show that the historic trend in production technology would lead inexorably towards greater social harmony and political consensus: by removing alienation, automation ought to abolish an enduring source of serious industrial conflict and of the political dynamic of the labour movement.

Blauner reasoned that since industrialization commenced, alienation had followed the path of an 'inverted-U curve': non-alienating pre-industrial craft work was superseded by alienating machine-minding and mass-production, which in turn is being superseded by automated industry of tomorrow's world, process work offering an advance example of this. The process, he maintained, had a clearly perceptible outcome. Whether such a conclusion is warranted by the technical and economic realities remains unclear, though anyone looking at his evidence as a whole would have to agree that Blauner put his case as well as it could be put. Most of us follow him in expecting automated industry to remove a significant number of the deprivations of contemporary mass-production work.

But will automation remove alienation? Will automation

produce harmony and consensus? To answer the first question, we must agree on what alienation signifies. As suggested earlier, the chances of gaining any general agreement about that are remote. Nevertheless, we can make several points bearing on Blauner's use of the term that are uncontentious, or fairly so.

Point one: Blauner's use of the alienation concept owes as much to the fashion of his day as to his understanding of its historic meaning. The alienation concept originated in Protestant theology, where it indicated a sense of abandonment by and severance from the Holy Spirit. In the philosophy of Hegel, it signified a similar sense of exclusion, but, in this case, an exclusion from awareness of the inner logic of the World Spirit. It was next appropriated by the young Marx, who also began by conceiving it as a property of individual human existence. But, for this young Marx, the central 'alienating predicament' was not only spiritual in nature but material too: man, to survive, had always been obliged to struggle against a hostile nature – in a word, to labour.[9]

Point two: in the 1950s, English-speaking social scientists were rediscovering Marx's early works. They came across passages of vivid writing in which the ardent young Rhinelander began asking how the invention of powered machinery might alter mankind's experience of labour. In these essays Marx also began to explore how the need to labour gave rise to social relations, especially those of domination and subordination. But what struck Marx's new admirers of the 1950s was his stirring condemnations of machinery and repetitive work. They did not realize that in describing such work as alienating Marx was thinking of it as an expression of social relations, of domination and subordination, as well as a series of technical operations.

Point three: Marx put the notion of capitalist exploitation at the core of his later works on political economy, but the notion of alienation did not disappear in his mature thought. His liberal admirers of the 1950s wrote off these works, *Capital* especially, as ideological or political. Marx certainly stated a point of view in them, and did so with vigour, but it is wrong to say he lost interest in humanist questions like alienation. In fact, the reverse is true. Marx's examination of political economy was a stage in his uncompleted *philosophical* programme. That is why he repeatedly complained to friends about the time he had to waste 'wading through all this economic shit', as he once delicately put it. His work as a whole can be viewed as an exploration of, and search for a solution to, the problem of human alienation.

Point four: true enough, the reality of alienation in Marx's later thought is linked to those of exploitation and domination. In brief, Marx believed it was impossible to overcome alienation without abandoning production based on exploitation and the system of political domination he associated with it. Now we may decide that the political implications that seem to derive from this analysis are unacceptable to us, or that we are prepared to persevere with an economy based on exploitation because such an economy functions effectively. Yet it is clear that it is possible to accept much of the analysis for its own sake, that is, as one possible vision of reality. That may render us intellectually Marxian without rendering us politically Marxist. Alternatively, we may decide to reject the analysis, in substance, or out of hand, because it is unilluminating – as well as being warped by values we reject.

But in either case, we must be consistent in our handling of the alienation concept. If we are Marxians we must remember that to use it commits us to many other ideas, some of them rather shaky. If we take the second option, then we must forgo use of the concept at all, except when we are talking about Marx's work as a system of ideas – one that we explicitly reject. In each case we must bear carefully in mind that it is a violation of Marx's work, of the Hegelian philosophical tradition against which he reacted, of the profound Christian theology which preceded Hegel, and of logic itself to represent alienation merely as a technical aspect of production: of the length of task-cycles, degree of choice of working methods, opportunity for creativity, or freedom from close supervision.

We can go further. The problem is not simply that such a concept cannot be lifted from one intellectual context and transplanted into another that is quite different. Hijacking a concept like alienation in such a way brings a risk of seeming to reason over-ingeniously. Let me say quickly that I do not think Blauner *is* at such fault. Carelessness, not deliberate legerdemain, produced his conclusion that automation will remove human alienation. But this conclusion was misleading because Blauner's operationalization of it had stripped away its true meaning. Deprivations suffered at work are a *facet* of a worker's alienation. But the conquest of alienation would require something more than the elimination of the production-line and autocratic supervision, because it is a *systemic* property. It would thus require the prior abolition of exploitation and domination, whether by capitalist or by State socialist methods of extracting surplus value, and the inauguration of an economic system based on freely contributed effort, unrelated to money reward or personal authority, in an egalitarian republic of producers.

If that seems a tall order, it is. Perhaps we must conclude that such a socio-economic order cannot yet be placed on a serious *political* agenda. But that does not mean it makes no sense to try to visualize such a society. On the contrary, it is a sign of intellectual health to make such efforts, rather than to resign oneself to the world as it seems to be. For such exercises, we cannot dispense with concepts like alienation. That is why we must always prevent them being misused and distorted.

Before leaving this question, it is worth noting how differently the alienation concept was handled in an almost unflawed study of mass-production workers by Eli Chinoy.[10] Chinoy certainly brought out the deprivatory grind of assembly-line work. But this analysis was linked with an exploration of how the workers attempted to reconcile their real situation – doing a dreary job and having little hope of rising to anything better – with the ideals spelled out in the American Dream ideology of achievement. These men knew that a lifetime of hard work was unlikely to bring them much more than a small house and rough hands, but they struggled to square the cultural circle,[11] in which objective reality clashed directly with deep commitment to the values of achievement. Chinoy portrayed their alienation with a moving simplicity that it is instructive to set beside the bold claims that recur throughout Blauner's text. But sadly, this book has always been less well known than *Alienation and Freedom*.

Let us turn now to the less philosophical question of whether automation will reduce friction on the shop-floor between managers and workers, and, more widely, promote harmony between capital and labour. It is convenient to approach this by what will seem a rather odd route, which involves a review of a theory that reaches the very opposite conclusion: namely, that automation will regenerate a revolutionary working class. In fact, this apparent digression turns out to be a short cut.

Until very recently, many commentators believed there existed a serious possibility that a proletarian revolution could occur in France. The Partie Communiste Français (PCF) regularly gained around a quarter of the votes cast in general elections and was noted for the toughness of its political line. But the PCF could never quite bring about revolution. It could not even stop the takeover of power by the traditionalist and conservative General Charles de Gaulle in 1958 during a government crisis. This was hardly the moment to expect anyone to produce a theory arguing that a left-wing revolution was likely to occur in the foreseeable future. The workers had been far too busy polishing their new cars to take to the streets to block de Gaulle's takeover.

The author of this amazing prediction, Serge Mallet, had been forced to leave the PCF on account of his unconventional political ideas. In his provocative book *The New Working Class*,[12] Mallet based his prediction on four main steps of reasoning. First, he argued that the working class was split between its old section (the traditional proletariat, working in dying smokestack industries) and a new section based on sunrise industries using advanced technology. According to Mallet, the old working class was blinkered by faded visions of what kind of society should follow capitalism. Burned out by its past struggles, blinded by the deprivations of 'archaic' work-tasks, yet increasingly consumer-minded, it could not envisage the alternative society that would rekindle the idealism of people for a socialist experiment. Only the *new working class* was capable of such a task.

It was not just capable of it. It was *destined* to achieve it. The main reason for this lay in the circumstances of its members' daily working lives. These were shaped by the glamour of advanced technology, with its great humming plants monitored by white-coated technicians sitting at computer terminals in immaculate control rooms, a world away from the grimy squalor of the smokestacks. This modern industry characterized by automation, Mallet exclaimed, is 'the veritable dialectical negation of the fragmentation of work', rendering the human operator a 'distant demiurge' as human intervention moves away from the point of production.[13] Automation thus forces a new consciousness on the human 'demiurges', who interact with it as equals. The operator-technicians thereby gain in confidence, rapidly developing an ambition to participate more closely in setting the objectives of their department, their firm, their industry . . . and – why not? – the economy as a whole.

Their vehicle for doing so would be a new brand of unionism – or rather, an updated traditional brand of unionism, *syndicalism*, aimed at gaining control over management prerogatives and winning the right to set objectives and to check up on their achievement. Ironically, management itself would encourage such intervention. Workers will need extensive training to operate equipment, Mallet argued. This will heighten their sense of importance to the organization. Managers will seek to integrate workers in a tight plant community to cut turnover, which will be additionally costly as competence becomes specific to the firm. This will create workers' solidarity, and 'the more the modern worker reconquers *at the collective level* the occupational autonomy he lost during the mechanization phase of work, the more trends develop towards a demand for control'.[14] The demand for workers' self-management (in French, *autogestion*), repeated in hundreds, then thousands, of installations would produce a 'revolution from below', rather than on the top-down pattern favoured by the old working class which required the prior seizure of State power. In sum, automation will incur a revolution – a clean, sanitized revolution, unlike the revolution that has been evoked in traditional Marxist literature.

Mallet's theory shares a great deal of ground with Blauner's. Obviously, both cannot be right in their predictions: harmony and social reconciliation on one side; conflict and revolution on the other. However, both can be wrong. And if both are wrong that is because so many of their ideas about automation are wrong. Note how both theories rest on technological determinism, the assumption that a given technology must produce predictable effects on attitudes and behaviour. Note also how vague each is in its handling of the concept of automation – Mallet uses the catch-all term 'modern industry' interchangeably with it; Blauner assumes process industry can represent all forms of production automation satisfactorily. Even before these theories are confronted with empirical data, we lose confidence in how securely they are put together. Structures that at first look firm begin to seem flimsy. If you give them a good logical shake there is no mistaking the noise: they rattle.

But what does the evidence say? Until the mid 1970s, some industrial relations experience seemed to support the Mallet thesis. For example, in Western European countries higher-grade workers like technicians in 'modern' industries like aeronautics or electronics began joining unions and going on strike. On closer inspection, however, it became clear that these developments mainly reflected a drive to protect occupational advantages; they were only rarely linked, and then very loosely, to the aim of intervening in management policy.[15] These were 'reluctantly militant' actions stemming from economic self-defence, not an assertive quest for self-management. The pattern holds for all three Western European countries – Britain, France, and Italy – with the strongest or most militant unions at this period.[16] Of course, it can be retorted, quite justifiably, that an increase in industrial conflict in such industries also counts against Blauner's prophecy of growing workplace harmony.

By far the most stringent test of the theories to have been undertaken involved a study by the British sociologist Duncan Gallie of four oil-refineries fitting Blauner's definition of automation.[17] In no way do these findings, based on over a thousand interviews, on observational studies of the plants, and on close inspection of records detailing their industrial relations history, bear out either theory. One source of their weakness is that both prophets have a picture of process industry that is factually wrong at key points. Most process workers do not wear white coats: they wear blue overalls and orange helmets. They do not lounge in futuristic control rooms: they do messy jobs, some of them outside in all weathers. In other words, many of them are doing tasks that are no different from semi-skilled smokestack work. Again, cost pressures sour the relationship between supervisors and workers much as they do in traditional plants. It is just not true that the industry is prosperous enough for management to pay over the odds and hand out easy task-assignments – and Gallie's research was done before the recession and current oil-glut, which must have increased cost pressures dramatically.

Now for the sting in the tail. Two of Gallie's oil-refineries were located in France, and two in Britain. If technology is a determinant influence on attitudes and behaviour it should operate with equal force irrespective of cultural context. Yet in neither country was there much serious support for the abolition of capitalism and the institution of self-management, though there was more among the French sample than the British.

But nor were there any aspirations for a much closer relationship with the plant management or any expectation that it could be developed. The French hoped to develop greater influence over plant-management action but this can be readily traced to a lower level of management legitimacy in France and the weakness of unions as bargaining agents. The British workers resented their managers as social types far less – though they were less impressed with their technical prowess. Their unions had easy access to managers and were taken seriously as bargaining partners.

What this study showed, in other words, is that the technical milieu had no readily demonstrable effects of the sort predicted by either theory: indeed, it had no significant effects of any sort that could be attributed to it alone. This does not mean it had none whatsoever, but any it may have had were not registered. If such a careful study as Gallie's could not find any, the chances of there being any are very small. On the contrary, workers interpreted their experience of work in line with expectations and frameworks of interpretation possessing a distinct pattern in each country. These patterns in turn reflected real circumstances, especially the relative degree of influence each pair of workforces actually possessed, as well as varying traditions in politics and industrial relations.

This is another example of the importance of the *societal* effect discussed in the previous chapter. It further discredits the notion of technology as the determinant influence of workers' behaviour. But are we to say that technology has no influence on behaviour worth bothering about? As we shall see, such a view is unacceptable to many organizational practitioners.

23

Socio-Technical Visionaries

None of the writers examined in the last half-dozen chapters should be thought of as a technological determinist in the strict sense of claiming that technology uniquely determines behaviour. Yet they adopted technology as their main explanatory variable in accounting for psychological deprivation, levels of workplace conflict, management effectiveness, or the shape of organizations. Technological 'exigencies' (a term that is next-door neighbour to 'demands') would permit only marginal adjustments to the system of work-roles created to exploit the equipment, through *job-enlargement* (giving workers more tasks to do, or a more challenging task) or through *job-rotation* (switching workers regularly between a set of tasks). These conclusions were gloomy indeed.

Hence, the development of the concept of a *socio-technical system* by investigators of the Tavistock Institute twenty years ago caused a considerable stir because it was intended not just as a device for explaining how people interact with machines but also as a means of getting across the message that: 'Unlike mechanical and other inanimate systems they possess the property of "equi-finality"; they may achieve a steady state from differing initial conditions and in differing ways.'[1] The language used in this claim is not very simple to follow, but what it amounts to is this: organization can be significantly varied without a change of technology, resulting in greater worker satisfaction and involvement, and this may well be accompanied by a growth in productivity.

This is a claim that has always been treated with great suspicion, though we should all want it to be true even if, like many of its critics, we would prefer a different socio-economic order from the one we have. Whether it can deliver all that it seems to promise still remains unproven. At the same time it has been utilized by certain social scientists to attack the trained incapacities of production engineers. It has always functioned too as a rallying-point (and as an advertisement) for social-scientific industrial consultants: around it, some very ingenious justifications of interventionist activity of the kind discussed in the Introduction have been put forward. Even critics of intervention, who complain that such concepts are misleading or even mystifying, will sometimes acknowledge that they are sometimes interestingly misleading. Again, it has usually been misapplied or oversold by other parties than its original proponents.

The *socio-technical system* was first aired at length in *Organizational Choice*, a full report of the research undertaken by Tavistock investigators in the British coal mines.[2] I began by reviewing its early phase and the tendency of the researchers' thought (see chapter 17). It is instructive to end by examining their thinking in its highly influential mature form, before noting how the Tavistock investigators modified their ideas later.

The empirical core of the book consists of the comparative studies of what the authors term *conventionally* and *compositely* organized mining teams working on longwall coal faces. Conventionally organized mining teams had been replaced, in informal experiments, with some kind of composite organization here and there, and word of this had been coming to the researchers' ears since the pilot work in 1950. Such Longwall organization was composite in four senses: the miner acquired a wider range of face skills; work groups were self-selected and shared out preferred and disliked tasks equitably; they received a bonus to be divided as they decided in addition to their flat-rate pay; and they proceeded to the next phase of the cycle of operations when they reached the end of the task they were doing, not merely when a shift changed over. These arrangements built on aspects of the traditional organization described earlier and depended on its associated values.

To test the notion that composite working might be at least as productive as conventional organization, and probably more harmonious than it, two depth studies were made, the first involving a composite and a conventional team and the second, two composite teams, one being 'more composite' than the other. The measures used to test the consequences were rather simple, and clearly environmental factors could not be fully controlled. This was especially true of the geological one; allowance was, however, made with expert advice.

In the sum, the composite group produced more, had lower absenteeism, maintained their cycle-targets, sometimes even forging ahead of them, and their members expressed higher work satisfaction. These results were repeated among the variably composite teams: the 'more composite' had narrowly better records for output and absenteeism. Moreover, the relations between the composite groups and the management altered significantly: the manager was treated more like a specialist adviser and problem-fixer to the groups.

To explain these results the authors reason along the following lines – or at least, I *think* they do: these theorists often write an infectiously obscure 'social-science-speak', examples of which I shall shortly provide. Any productive system consists of a given kind of equipment, that is laid out in characteristic ways, and a work-organization designed to exploit the technology. The technology sets *limits* on the design of the work-organization, but it is usually possible to make *choices* in how tasks are designed; the work-organization, once designed, takes on a life of its own, with certain social and psychological properties independent of the technology. For example, within the limits set by the longwall technology in mining, it was possible to choose between conventional and composite work-organization: and the socio-psychological consequences to the two were shown to vary importantly.

They push the reasoning further. Though one can examine the socio-psychological properties of systems at a multitude of levels, from that of the individual worker to, in this case, that of British Coal, certain convenient boundaries can be distinguished: here, the boundary surrounding the primary work-group was chosen. But that boundary is not sealed fast: on the social dimension, the primary work-group is a component of what the authors term *seam society*, and its relationship with this larger collectivity is likely to affect work-group behaviour.

Nor does the enterprise live in isolation, so constraints other than technology and wider socio-psychological attachments must be taken into account. As one of them put it: 'A socio-technical system must also satisfy the financial conditions of the industry of which it is a part. It must have economic validity.'[3] Thus the productive system has three key dimensions which are all interdependent: the *technological*, the *social* and the *economic*. Yet each of these possesses its own scale of independent values. To pursue one set of these and ignore the others is to invite trouble, if not disaster; more formally, maximizing along one dimension does not produce optimal results for the system as a whole. Overall system optimization usually implies sub-optimizing along each dimension.

In more concrete terms this means, for example, that if you set out exclusively to maximize profits the workers will resent it and/or your equipment will become outdated; that if you introduce technical change too quickly you will generate resistance to change within the enterprise and probably go broke into the bargain; the latter will also happen if you pay the workers too much and permit lax forms of social organization. Were the team trying to say very much more than this? These are facts of life, after all, well known to people who run firms in a free-market economy. Is the whole exercise, as the harsher critics have concluded, merely one of getting workers to accept the logic with which the employer operates?

Such a conclusion has to be accepted, but only in part – and there is a case, under any economic regime, for explaining to employees the logic with which the employer operates. My own complaint with the package is a different one. It is claimed by its proponents that the socio-technical systems approach is entirely objective and impartial, and that its logic does permit significant choice, by those with decision-making power, on at least two distinct levels: that of the whole organization and that of the work-group. Impartial? I am far from sure. At the first level, in theory, managers could favour profits and ignore technological innovation and the workers' socio-psychological well-being. But because of the interrelation of dimensions this would only work where competing organizations were equally non-innovating and where worker dissatisfaction was contained by, say, a high level of unemployment.

Alternatively, they could ignore economic considerations and concentrate on maximizing worker satisfaction. The policy, however, would require external subsidy. Given a market economy it is clear that there is little choice at this level: the organization would need to make at least a normal profit to continue. Granted such an assumption, the model can be made to look awkwardly like a device for defending capitalism, but not doing so openly and candidly but by subterfuge. They might reply that the model is sufficiently abstract to be applied to most imaginable economic systems, and could be applied readily to existing ones. If they do believe this, why have they never met criticism by saying so in plain language? The least one can say is that their public relations have been appallingly mismanaged in this respect.

Their own predilection has always been for small-scale intervention, affecting work-group behaviour. As they put it in *Organizational Choice*: 'It is the socio-psychological system which affords the greatest opportunity for either formal or informal change at the level of the cycle-group – in such matters as altering the pattern of work-group organization.'[4] As we have seen, such change proved possible, and promoted further socio-psychological optimization. It also increased output. It is likely that the durable sub-culture and the dangers of mining make socio-psychological factors exceptionally important in that industry. In other industries a change of organizational form might result in an increase in output but a reduction in worker satisfaction. How would the Tavistock group view such a result?

It is fair to point out that they have always been concerned to some extent with what they call 'social health' as an end in itself. Their leader, Eric Trist, was to become still more so in later life. But in the 1960s the team were far too eager to promote themselves as consultants who could produce 'economically valid' results. The closing chapters of *Organizational Choice*, as I read them, show a growing preoccupation with the priority of economic and technical objectives; tend to patronize the miners as irrationally resistant to change because of 'the unanimous character of local rationalizations' (this sounds like Mayo paraphrasing Pareto); and can be viewed as a soft-sell for Tavistock manipulatory skill in changing organizations.

Now for the good news. Eric Trist and his followers have subsequently made an impact beyond their own consultancy sphere in three main respects. Firstly, they gained enormously in their awareness of the wider political circumstances that affect the situations they examine, and this makes aspects of their approach much more acceptable to some of their former critics. In the mid 1960s, a Tavistock team led by Trist was invited by Einar Thorsrud, the leading interventionist in Norway, to examine the functioning of a worker director scheme in Norwegian industry, which was then being hit by bankruptcies, industrial militancy, and multinational company takeovers.

The visiting British interventionists devised an alternative scheme of industrial democracy – or as Trist prefers to call it *organizational democracy* – based on workplace groups.[5] They believed that the system would rapidly spread throughout Norwegian workplaces. This view was based on an appraisal of the overall society – Norway, they had concluded, was notable for the homogeneity and egalitarianism of values and social behaviour; direct democracy in the workplace would fit the culture well.

In fact, it was to be the neighbouring Swedes who grabbed at the idea. Over the next ten years they adapted the methods used in the Norwegian experiments, orientating them more towards ensuring an input from involved workers on job redesign. Thus in Sweden a very direct link was made between the *quality of work life* (QWL) and *worker participation*. This was a period that saw the climax of the post Second World War boom, and the emergence of large-scale social and cultural rebelliousness which will be examined at greater length in the next chapter.

Scandinavian employers began to conclude that they must concede more to labour in the area of control over work operations and get rid of as many repetitive jobs as they could afford to. (This was to lead to some pioneering experiments in work reform in the Saab and Volvo car-plants.[6] For their part, Scandinavian trade unionists have always looked on social science in a very different way from their counterparts in, say, Britain or France, where even sympathetic social scientists are still often kept at arm's length as 'academics'. What matters here is that the *socio-technical* concept was no longer regarded as an idea that belonged to bosses, but one of which labour, too, could make use. This idea was also to make some headway in countries like Germany and Italy.

The British socio-technical researchers had been increasing their contacts at the personal level in the USA ever since the 1950s, and many American academics who doubled as industrial consultants had grown to admire the work they did. The most influential of these was Louis Davis of the University of California at Los Angeles (UCLA). Thus there came into being an extensive international network of people of varied experience, background and motivation, all of whom were linked by their interest in the notion of socio-technical systems. (These links extended into Eastern bloc countries.)

To some observers, such developments can look suspicious, if not sinister. I would have no trouble in depicting the international socio-technical network as a tool of capital, wittingly or otherwise deploying its expertise to impose more subtle forms of control and exploitation. I think it would be equally plausible to draw a picture of the international socio-technical network that makes it appear bumbling, naïve and boy-scoutish: some of the things its leaders *say* are almost unbelievable. I expect that among its several thousand hangers-on there must be some villains, just as there are unquestionably some clowns.

But they remind me most of the 'open conspirators', some of them principled technocrats, some honest social democrats, and some of them power-hunting cynics, who formed up behind the Webbs in the Fabian movement of early twentieth-century Britain. I also think there is a more accurate, and more interesting, way of looking at it and evaluating their work. A concept that also grew out of the Tavistock studies was that of the *autonomous work-group*. These are groups of employees which take decisions about their work, rather than being told what to do by a supervisor. Now, of course, unless the group also happens to own the workplace, no work-group can be fully autonomous. There must always be limits on its decision-making authority, and, in the world that we have, this scope is likely to be very narrow. In that sense, the notion of autonomous groups is deceptive or ideological. We could also say that whoever seriously proposes to spread a philosophy stressing autonomy for work-groups, in the face of managers who are generally jealous of their own authority, is extraordinarily, even ludicrously optimistic.

But this is clearly a concept that may set workers' minds thinking, when they come across it, about the situation that they actually experience at work. The autonomous groups message, which has been preached with an almost religious zeal by some socio-technical theorists, is based not only on a belief in face-to-face democratic participation but on idealistic principles of job-design: work-tasks should offer plenty of variety and challenge; the opportunity for continuous learning; the recognition of individual effort and support from higher-ups in the organization; the prospect of some future advancement; and a sense of meaning from performing the tasks that are performed. What is more, in the 1970s these objectives were advocated more as ends in themselves than as ways of leading to higher output. The reason for that may have been pragmatic – to avoid criticism from trade unionists and sceptical academics of the real motive behind the movement.

Now that unemployment has removed some of the expressions of labour indiscipline associated with the growth era, we might expect, perhaps, a reversion to a stress on the material and economic gains to employers from adopting these philosophies. But it is hard for the advocates to change tune so abruptly. Often being academics, or, if not, being expected to imitate academics by putting their ideas and achievements down on paper, the advocates are mortgaged to their past declarations. In any case, their statements can be cited or otherwise utilized by those people in the labour movement who seek an alteration of work and its logic on entirely different philosophical grounds.

Accompanying the socio-technical movement, and making use of the ideas that came out of the Tavistock mining experiments, in the 1960s there had also been growing up a powerful parallel movement based solidly in American business schools and their European imitators. The main inspiration of this Organizational Design (OD) movement had been the socio-psychological work examined in chapters 15 and 19 and described fully by writers such as Warner.[7] But it took note of the growing discussion of alienation and work-deprivation among the sociologists and began to take an increasing interest in the debate on employee participation. Its exponents began to voice ringing endorsements to the more convoluted calls for change in work organization and the forms of management authority that the socio-technical theorists proper had been making.

Trist has gone on record as stating that the late 1960s and early 1970s were not just a period of unusual turmoil in industry but also saw the emergence of a work reform movement built on a coalescence of the aims of socio-technical theory, OD, and theories of post-industrial society, which involved acceptance among its supporters of a New Paradigm of organized work whose most prominent features were: (1) denial of any imperatives of technology; (2) demotion of the machine to a role complementary to that of its operator; (3) a view of workers as a resource to be developed not plundered; (4) replacement of control imposed from outside with control exercised from within; (5) preference for flat and participative organizational hierarchies to 'alpine' and bossy ones; (6) demands for collaboration or 'collegiality' to replace gamesmanship and competition; (7) convergence between organizational and societal purposes.[7] Application of such design principles will lead, Trist has affirmed, to commitment and a will to innovate.

One of the more interesting facts about this almost Utopian specification is the time when it was made. It has all the appearances of being made in the early 1970s, when the revolt against work (see chapter 24) was at its height. Actually, it was made ten years later, during a period of widespread economic gloom and chilly reaction against the political and cultural turmoil of ten years earlier. Was Trist preaching a message that had by then lost its disciples and its clientele? I think Trist would go on preaching his message in the wilderness, though he is hardly cut out personally to be a prophet. But he has no need to. The followers and the clients are still there. The message has become institutionalized and so has the movement. This is a remarkable achievement.

One of the ways this institutionalization has been expressed since the early 1970s is in the quality of work life (QWL) movement, which was initiated at a conference at Arden House in New York state in 1972 involving only a few dozen academics. Ten years later a similar gathering in Toronto attracted several thousand participants, including many trade union officials, as well as academics, personnel managers, and interventionist social scientists. I have undertaken a more extended analysis of the QWL movement elsewhere,[8] concluding that it ought not to be dismissed simply as a new version of human relations, as observers like Goldmann and Van Houten[9] have argued – though they are absolutely right in saying that it can be utilized for such a purpose. Nor is Ivar Berg pinning down the full truth, though he, too, is making a valid point, when he characterizes QWL as a gimmick used by cynical managerial gamesmen to authenticate their right to manage by showing they are ready to use all the latest smart ideas.[10]

Here we should remember that even when they consist mainly of ideology, management movements – and let us be clear, the QWL movement is nothing unless it has support among managers – may well have what a functionalist sociologist would call unintended consequences, and a Marxist, contradictions. Let us take the case of human relations. We can write off human relations as sheer manipulative ideology or trashy justificatory doctrine. At the same time, some of its ideas – considerate supervision, a trained corps of managers, work as the expression of sociability – are in themselves either justifiable or appealing whatever our political preferences. Moreover, the spread of those ideas did have an impact on the expectations of workers, on standards adopted in personnel management, and on acceptable supervisory practice.

There is a broader inference to be drawn here, if the point I am making has anything in it. The process of change to be perceived in our system is not the cyclical one discerned by so many self-styled Marxists, but a *dialectical* one. My own view of QWL, then, is that it will modestly reinforce attitudes consistent with its core ideology and continue to have some influence on work-design despite economic change and stress. Whether this outcome is 'what capital really wants' or not, this is what the outcome will be.

Where, however, does this leave the scientific investigation of industrial behaviour? The technological implications approach, in its earlier forms, pictures behaviour essentially as a response moulded by immediate experience of a technical environment, or as a response to the experience of filling some work-role that a designer has created to exploit a machine or technical process. This response may become deeply imprinted, and justified by reference to social standards. In other words, it becomes institutionalized, socially entrenched, and therefore of interest to sociologists. Yet the approach depends on an original characterization of the relationship between people and machines that is *behaviourist* – a stimulus implants a learned response – in the strict psychological sense. In this respect, some early socio-technical theory is strangely reminiscent of the 'happy moo-cow' simplifications of the human factor approach, while the 'technological topographics' of Walker and Guest explicitly adopted these behaviourist assumptions: these authors saw its behaviourism as its strong point.

By the 1980s this similarity had almost vanished. Rummage through the heaps of literature produced by veteran socio-technical theorists, by ageing O D pundits, by Q W L enthusiasts, and by commentators on all this effort, and you will not detect or distinguish any definite *scientific* assumptions about behaviour. This does not mean there are no such assumptions. I merely report that any scientific ones that may be held are extremely difficult to detect and identify. On the other hand, there are a number of vehemently held assumptions about what *should* constitute superior forms of work-design and what *should* be the responses of the kind of person who *should* occupy such posts.

In other words, the assumptions held are about what people and situations should be, or should become, not what they are – *normative* assumptions. Moreover, in many respects they are the normative assumptions associated particularly strongly with the admirers of the young Marx, the humanistic rebel against mechanization. To put it another way, a universal worker, victim of technical rationalization, is projected, not *varieties* of worker whose distinct patterns of behaviour, perspectives and values are shaped by the structural circumstances in which they find themselves. We may find the QWL model worker appealing as a doctrine. But it does not say much about what we should expect to find in the real world. But then, why should it? Its rationale is to rally the followers and heighten the appeal of the message.

Thus the interventionist aims of the QWL movement, with which most of us have some sympathy, seem to be compromising its scientific contribution. No better illustration of the difficulties even of 'desirable' intervention discussed in the Introduction could be found. For me they are compounded by several others. For example, I wish the work reformers would deal more fully with the issue of *technological choice* as opposed to organizational choice.

The strong form of the technological choice thesis, put forward by writers like Stephen Marglin or David Noble,[11] claiming that engineers are commissioned by capitalist bosses to devise equipment or technical systems with a clear idea of how they will perform to control workers, is unproven. It is probably mistaken to credit technologists with so much skill and capitalist employers with so much foresight. But the work reformers are in a very strong position, as consultants, to report more extensively on this question. Certainly, Trist and others have been arguing for thirty years that production engineers have applied, indiscriminately and uncritically, a specific design paradigm for over a century – and, as we shall see in chapter 36, the more aware New Wave economists like Piore and Sabel have been spreading this idea among their colleagues. But to evaluate the technological choice thesis we need much more informed opinion.

It is disagreeable to end on a sour note, so I will not follow through one original intention, which was to document the extraordinary verbiage and gobbledegook that crops up in some – no! lots – of the literature put out by the socio-technical movement. It can be maddening, and raises the suspicion that writers either don't have much to say or want to dissemble what they are actually saying. The Tavistock group in particular were abominable communicators. I am sure some of the hostility towards them, which has been expressed in theoretical terms or on ideological grounds, sprang in part from the exasperation of people who had to struggle hard to find out what they were saying and often, understandably enough, gave up before the pay-off.

PART V

ACTION THAT MEANS SOMETHING

24

Work as Social Action

Human factor psychology and technology theory viewed the worker as a passive being who responded to the physical or technical surroundings. This is reminiscent of behaviourism in psychology. Taylorism and human relations attributed paramount drives to him – universal economism and universal sociability respectively. But all these approaches neglected or dismissed the influence on behaviour within the workplace or in other contexts relevant to work, such as union involvement, of socially patterned motivations which derive from the worker's experiences and attachments *beyond* the workplace. Obviously, though, work and community involvements interact, even when workers, some of whom understandably often wish to forget about work the moment they leave the workplace, themselves deny any connection between the two spheres.

The *actor-centred approach* (ACA) to industrial behaviour (also called the action approach or even actionalism) attempts to explore the work-community nexus and to show how socially generated and distributed aims, attitudes, and values can account for work behaviour.

By the late 1960s, the ACA was being assiduously promoted by a number of British and French investigators. They were hoping, of course, to correct the biases of the technological implications approach. They also wished to counteract the assumptions of *organization theory*, which, following the growth of business schools, was then becoming widely taught, and, when it was taught uncritically, promoted the view that all members of any work organization share the aims of organizational leaders. (How far they do so is an empirical question.) The recommendations of these Western European industrial sociologists were sometimes made rather stridently, reflecting their enthusiastic conviction that industrial studies must be given a solid sociological foundation before they could usefully proceed further. An added complication, which we cannot go into here, had to do with the rapid growth of social science in Western Europe at this time, and signs of the influence of neo-Marxist ideas, which are discussed in chapter 29.

What an ACA entails requires further explanation. Only certain points will be made here. Fuller accounts can be found in standard texts.[1] In general sociology it derives from the methodological recommendations of Max Weber.[2] Societies tend to be studied by theorists either as abstract systems of institutions and role-patterns, along the lines of what I referred to in the Introduction as sociology Type II, or as the collective artifacts of purposeful human action, which in turn inject meaning and value into specified activities, usually with the Type III aim of determining a pattern of development in them.[3] The first represents society as something independent of man, the second as man's product. Both modes of inquiry tend also to presume that the social element in collective life is not only distinguishable but logically separable from others, such as the economic sphere, although Type II theorists are much more given to this than the developmental theorists of Type III.

To be tactful, we would state that neither image should claim absolute validity; and that, ideally, study of society should integrate system and action perspectives. However, the magnitude of this latter task is discouraging. Followers of both Max Weber and Karl Marx sink their differences in agreeing that the second approach is more interesting or more relevant, though there they usually part company. The Weberian strategy of inquiry demands an attempt not only to distinguish *typical* social actors and *typical* patterns of action, but also the *meanings* actors typically attribute to their actions. The notion of 'meaning' here is often obscured by ambitious attempts to clarify it. To simplify, we could call them *social values*; or interpretative frameworks; or socially distributed subjective motivations. What matters is that the investigator assumes *social* action is produced partly by reference to a set of meanings – some observers might call it the consciousness – the actor shares with others.

Many people confuse this with a psychological approach. But in so far as the approach involves a study of *motivation*, then it is a motivation shared with others. This clearly need not exclude, though it precedes, an examination of the individual psychology of the motivations of particular persons. Another point concerns *rationality*, an important notion for Weberians, which they are expert at rendering confusing. Generally, actions are presumed to be *rational*, at least as far as the *typical subject* is concerned.

This does not mean they will always seem 'reasonable' to an outsider. Rather, it means that the typical social actor of a specified group acts in accord with a logic that at least seems reasonable to him or her. A sympathetic outsider might not find the reasons persuasive or attractive – 'This man is eating his dead enemy because that will make his spirit stronger' – but they do provide a consistent account. The purpose, or goal, of the action may seem irrational in the observer's eyes, and the means adopted to achieve it equally so. Actors act, however, in accordance with their own interpretations or definitions of the situation. The observer must therefore try to project himself into the actor's situation; if he succeeds, he will achieve a sympathetic understanding of observed acts, not merely a group of statistics about their relative frequencies and causal connection with other acts or social properties.

Achievement of such an identification with subjects is seldom straightforward, but its implications for industrial inquiry are obvious. Consider the bank wiring men in the Hawthorne studies. Roethlisberger and Dickson interpreted their restriction of output as a means of resisting technical changes that would upset group stability. But little effort was made to view the situation through bank wiring men's eyes – at least not in the published accounts of it: off-stage, as it were, these investigators were much more sympathetic to their subjects than they appear in the cold tracts of print of the published monograph. But, a Weberian would say, that is just the point: if they had been more conscious of this methodological issue, leading them to a study of the men's backgrounds and current attachments outside the plant, perhaps they would have adopted the explanation that was finally rejected – that restriction of output served wider social and economic interests.

In other groups of workers, different backgrounds and loyalties might have resulted in different behaviour. This is precisely what is shown in such studies by Melville Dalton of *rate-busters* and *restricters*, where readiness to respond to incentives closely matched varying social backgrounds and values.[4] An ACA, in fact, though it was consciously promulgated in the 1960s in Europe, had existed in American industrial sociology of the period when human relations doctrine was coming under challenge, long before it was promoted in this way. There are even traces of it in *Management and the Worker*. Some of these informal actionalist studies deserve brief mention if only as a reminder that the orthodoxy of previous approaches was not universal.

Without any question the most impressive was Chinoy's research, reported in *Automobile Workers and the American Dream*, which explored the inconsistencies between the harsh realities of the automobile workers' situation and the American success ideology, which I referred to in chapter 22.[5] Chinoy could have been taking words out of the mouth of one of the self-conscious advocates of an actor approach when he stated that 'men need more than the satisfactions derived from predictable patterns of social interaction on the job from working with a "good bunch of guys". They seek in their jobs to satisfy desires derived not only from their co-workers but also from family and friends from their experience as members of the community and wider society.'[6] 'Desires' implanted by the wider society stress ambition, incentiveness, responsibility, leadership, independence and material success. Every aspect of mass-production factory-work denies their realization.

The workers' aspirations, consequently, had either to be redefined in terms of more modest objectives (promotion to a slightly less monotonous task, the purchase – in the indefinite future – of a small business), projected into ambitions for the actor's children, or deflected into the acquisition of showy consumer goods or some similar domestic project. Chinoy suggests that the adoption of specific aspirations follows the life-cycle: by the time the typical worker was nearing retirement, 'success' had diminished to mean little more than ensuring security in old age. The processes involved repeated redefinition by the subject of his situation and his objectives, as desires clashed dynamically – and depressingly – with reality.

Chinoy's portrait of motivations, values and perspectives held by the *typical* worker in this automobile factory could hardly be less like that drawn by the Mayoites. Workers suffered less from failing to discover a quasi-tribal intimacy in the workplace than from the fear of being, or feeling, stigmatized as social failures: failures in terms of general cultural values like success. Their redefinition of the success and the work ethic resulted in what has been called a *subordinate value system* of the wider society – a *negotiated* version of the dominant value system.[7] Chinoy noted that this could be viewed as an aspect of, and an attempt to escape from, their alienation in a society with highly structured inequalities and a pervasive dominant ideology which denied the existence of deep inequalities, while covertly justifying them – we have already noted how his use of the alienation concept antedates Blauner's by several years and is much more faithful to the classic sources.

Gouldner's studies of industrial conflict in a gypsum mine also represented a major anticipation of the ACA.[8] In explaining the origins of a wild-cat strike, and the functioning of various *patterns of bureaucracy* (organizational control systems), Gouldner constantly contrasted the varying orientations towards work of managers and workers generally, and the different kinds of aim and perspective among managers, and sought to account for these differences in terms of varying social origins, community ties, and group outlooks. While shaping certain managerial practices and the workers' reaction to being managed, the ongoing train of events provided experiences that modified the outlooks and expectations of actors, and in turn caused them to revise their conflict strategies. The result is a subtle analysis of processes of conflict and co-operation in the plant which, unlike those of interactionists like Whyte, he did not uncouple from their wider social context.

Gouldner undertook another study in the mid 1950s in which varying orientations towards work even more explicitly guided his interpretation.[9] This showed how differing *latent social roles* (or *actor orientations* – that is to say, those outlooks and identities which actually most influenced actors' behaviour) underlie the attitudes and actions of personnel occupying similar roles in an organization. Though the group studied, the staff of a small American university, was non-industrial, Gouldner's primary distinction between cosmopolitans and locals provided a fruitful comparative tool for the examination of the managing and professional cadres of organizations in general. Similar kinds of distinction were being toyed with by other organizational sociologists at the time, but they did not link varying orientations with individuals' non-organizational attributes as carefully as did Gouldner. (Another study by Melvin Dalton, of industrial managers, is an outstanding example of one that did.[10]

None the less, by the end of the 1950s a very substantial body of work had accumulated which recognized, in one way or another, that work behaviour could not be accounted for adequately without paying attention to factors outside the organization – whether these were community affiliations, social origins, position on the life-cycle, or national culture.[11] But it remains rather mysterious that nobody in the USA, with the partial exception of the economic sociologist Amitai Etzioni,[12] attempted a systematic formulation of an action perspective; one that spelt out its methodological assumptions and delineated its potentialities as an instrument for industrial investigation and theorizing. In the next chapter the first and perhaps most influential effort to do so will be examined.

What I hope has been made clear in this chapter is this: although some of the methodological and theoretical discussion that an ACA has aroused is extremely heated and abstruse, there is nothing very mysterious about the approach in itself. Its appeal to common sense is direct, and it has been used in recent years to provide some of the best empirical studies to be found in industrial sociology. Yet some of these were to show a weakness absent from the early American prototypes: timidity in tackling the broader value systems and institutional complexes of society as a factor affecting localized behaviour. Again, sociological investigators became aware that their analyses were omitting structural economic factors that might have a decisive influence on behaviour. This issue will be taken up in Part V.

For example, was the post-1945 economic growth permanently altering the old social landscape, replacing traditional working-class values, world-views and behaviour with novel patterns? In European countries the answer seemed to have extensive implications for class structures and politics, not merely for economic life. Even a modest attempt to provide a properly researched answer was found to be controversial. The Luton Study of newly *affluent workers* illustrates this well.

25

The Money Men of Luton

The Luton studies, which can be characterized as an example of middle-range actor-centred research, were seen as a central contribution to a once rowdy controversy over the question of the possible *embourgeoisement* – a term I will explain shortly – of affluent workers, and have become a subject of controversy themselves.[1] Yet even the sharpest critics of the Luton inquiry have always regarded it as the most important contribution to British industrial sociology of the 1960s, perhaps the most important since 1945. The reasons lie less in the strictly industrial findings than in those bearing on the issue of *embourgeoisement*, a term borrowed from French colleagues who had been engaged in a similar discussion. This revolved around the question of whether, in the prosperous conditions of the growth era, newly 'affluent' workers were becoming 'middle class', not just in patterns of consumption, not just in their attitudes, values, and perspectives, but were actually merging into the middle-class.

A once-heated subsidiary discussion about the industrial material is also still bubbling on gently. The researchers themselves described the monograph reporting the industrial data, *The Affluent Worker: Industrial Attitudes and Behaviour*, as a by-product for the larger investigation – a 'more or less unforeseen' one at that.[2] But the contribution of the Luton studies rests as much as anything on the linkage of research in the workplace and the community to investigate the sort of problem that lies at the heart of empirical sociology – or should do. In the late 1950s many commentators were concluding that affluence in Western countries was leading to the incorporation of prosperous manual workers into middle-class society.[3] In Britain, the Conservative victory in the general election of 1959 seemed to confirm this *embourgeoisement* hypothesis.

In 1963, however, before the survey results were available, Lockwood and Goldthorpe had shown up the astonishingly shaky logic to which many parties to the debate resorted. Several forms of the thesis could be rejected, they argued, on logical grounds alone.[4]

Lockwood and Goldthorpe had been attracted to Cambridge University, where the economics faculty was making a less than enthusiastic attempt to meet suggestions that sociology should be added to the syllabus and research promoted. Both had researched in the sociology of work previously. Lockwood was author of a well-known monograph (*The Black-Coated Worker*) dealing with the class-consciousness of office workers. Goldthorpe had studied friction between supervisors and coal-face workers in British mines.[5] It is noteworthy that both studies embodied historical perspective, particularly an awareness of changing socio-economic conditions and organizational structures. When their 1963 article appeared the work of testing the *embourgeoisement* hypothesis empirically was already well in hand in Luton.

Luton, an English town lying forty miles west of Cambridge, was painstakingly targeted as a testing ground for the theory. In brief, if affluent workers in Luton were not moving into the middle class it seemed improbable that *embourgeoisement* could be occurring elsewhere on any scale. The project was designed very carefully to test not only the central hypothesis but subsidiary aspects of it. The nature of the industrial data collected illustrates this well. To test technological-cause theories, workers from varying socio-technical settings – mass-production, batch-production and process-production – and with varying skill levels were deliberately sampled. As we saw in chapters 21 and 22, technological implications theory indicated that some settings facilitate *embourgeoisement*. Process plants, in particular, had been widely portrayed as places where, relieved of an 'alienating' environment, workers who were so disposed might assimilate the values of the technologists and managers in whose company much of their work was done. In some process plants nearly everyone seemed to wear a white coat. It is easy to read too much into this.

In fact, the collected data suggested hardly any significant differences attributable to socio-technical settings, and relatively few related to levels of skill. Patterns of attitude and behaviour showed remarkable consistency between the three workforces sampled, but the prevailing syndrome was especially pronounced among the mass-production workers of Vauxhall Motors, the British subsidiary of General Motors of the US. Much of the material on these assemblers is directly comparable with the findings of previous studies of automobile workers, and some of it was reported before *The Affluent Worker* was published.[6] Particular attention has therefore been devoted to it. At this stage, exposition will be simplified by following this practice.

The Vauxhall assemblers nearly always described their fragmentary, machine-paced tasks as boring and monotonous. They had little opportunity for in-plant sociability, except of a very superficial nature. Thus, objectively speaking, the assemblers were clearly suffering considerable deprivation of intrinsic satisfaction from their work. But this deprivation, though it was keenly felt, did not lead to any marked dissatisfaction with their *jobs*. Some deep inner need for self-actualization may have been frustrated by production pressures but if it was it did not provoke any general desire to seek other work or any deep, brooding hostility towards management. On the contrary, the assemblers expressed broad satisfaction with their jobs as a whole. Indirect indicators of dissatisfaction, such as absenteeism and turnover, were low and consistent with these subjective appraisals. Two additional facts are relevant to these findings. First, most of the sample had held jobs at least equivalent, and sometimes substantially higher, in skill and responsibility before joining Vauxhall and alternative work was readily available in Luton when they were polled. Second, open industrial conflict was virtually absent: unlike other British motor firms Vauxhall was then celebrated for its freedom from strikes. Some local union activists dismissed it – half jokingly, half in exasperation, but meaningfully – as a 'cabbage-patch'. Indeed, a substantial minority of workers did have rural origins.

What explains the apparently paradoxical coexistence of objectively visible, and subjectively registered, deprivation with objectively measurable, and subjectively claimed, satisfaction? 'Satisfaction' evidently did not mean contentment. Nor should it necessarily be construed as resignation. In the Luton team's view its nearest everyday equivalent would be *practicality*. Asked what kept them at Vauxhall the vast majority replied, unprompted in any way, 'The money.' The only ones that did not do so without hesitation were those who stared briefly at the interviewer, almost in disbelief that anybody could not know the answer they were about to give. They had been sampled precisely because their earnings were above the British industrial average of the time – though these earnings were hardly spectacular by motor-industry standards in towns like Oxford or Coventry.

Lockwood and his associates supposedly came to regard the Luton workers as the classic *economic men* of economics textbooks, whose dissatisfactions were crudely bought off by an open-handed employer. This is not so. After all, other British car-workers appeared to be equally, or even more money-orientated, yet were far more adversarial in their view of management and readier to make use of the strike weapon to maintain control over methods and output. All industrial workers – indeed, practically anyone who works – is by definition economistic in greater or lesser degree, in a market economy especially. To claim that money lay at the heart of the Luton workers' industrial motivations would have been true but trivial. The Luton team, rather, suggested that the assemblers' *economism* was one aspect of a broader *instrumental orientation* towards work which was linked with a *privatized* community existence. They had made an elaborate, but calculated plan which resulted in their acting *like* economic men for certain purposes or in given contexts. This syndrome possessed specific features. The Vauxhall assemblers in particular were thought to display an unusually intense instrumental-privatized orientation to work. In fact, Goldthorpe personally initially characterized the Vauxhall sample as a 'deviant' one in this respect. Later, and more contentiously, this verdict was revised. The Luton workers were finally put forward as *prototypical*, pointers to the likely future characteristics of most workers in manufacturing.[7]

The intensity of the assemblers' instrumental-privatized orientation is suggested by much interview and observational evidence. Technical factors, but managerial policy more so, debarred tightly knit work-groups, the assemblers expressed no hankering for solidaristic attachments at work of any kind. Jovial familiarity was expected of everybody at work but they had a revealing maxim: 'Mates are not friends.' This held true for out-plant life also. Similarly, foremen who left them alone were strongly preferred. Meddlesome, friendly, human relations supervisory styles, no less than the autocratic varieties, seem to have received adverse reactions. Work, then, was not a place where social intimacy was either expected or sought. It formed no part of the workers' *effort-bargain.*[8] As was noted in discussion of the effort-bargain in the Introduction, parties to it may sometimes have relatively clear sets of expectations, which renders the employment relationship relatively stable – at least, for a time. This is a good illustration of the point.

This calculating dissociation recurred in their more general image of the firm. Somewhat ritualistically, the majority affirmed that the organization was comparable to a football team; and, rather more alertly, that it was a better employer than most others they knew. Belief in teamwork, however, did not imply any positive emotional or moral identification with management. It merely acknowledged an overlap of economic interests. Some members of the team (work-study men in particular) were portrayed as less than consistently sporting players. Most workers kept a well-trained eye on the profitability of the firm. Their reason for doing so was not to cheer when the team scored but to judge the opportunity for pay bargaining. The bargain acknowledged management's right to manage, but it excluded extortion and profiteering. Industrial peace was strictly conditional.

Unionism, too, was apparently regarded in calculative terms. One or two assemblers viewed the unions as an expression of working-class power and social solidarity, as a means of worker-participation in management, and even as an avenue to eventual workers' control. But most were unconcerned with union affairs beyond the workplace, or even beyond their own department. The shop steward was regarded as a combined auctioneer, news-bearer and solicitor. Joining the union was seen as a method of increasing one's personal security and bargaining power mainly at this very local level.

Early reports of these findings stressed that they could not be understood as *responses* to the socio-technical setting of work or to supervisory practices. Nor did it make any sense whatsoever to portray them as the product of partly satisfied and partly frustrated universal human needs. To solve this explanatory puzzle it was necessary to assume that the calculativeness which apparently marked the assemblers' attitudes and behaviour at work governed their entry to that kind of work in the first place. They could be viewed as a highly *self-selected* group.[9]

The notion of self-selection is an extremely important one in all modern societies, where persons can move geographically and socially in ways that the rigidity of pre-industrial societies often excludes. Clearly, it becomes all the more important in a capitalist society, and not just in the obvious sense that the job-market results in considerable movement between employers, but also in a more general one: people may take the market as a *pattern* for other life-decisions, making deliberate choices to associate, or to try to associate, with certain groups rather than with others.

The Luton researchers argued that entry to an occupation is rarely random. Even in semi-skilled work considerable choice exists under conditions of full employment. Workers will shop around for a job which provides a mixture of rewards that matches most closely an ordered set of personal priorities. Some types of worker will demand a good deal of intrinsic interest from their work-task, for example, or numerous opportunities for social interaction on the job, while others will give such rewards a low weighting and earnings a much higher one. As a result, like-minded individuals who also tend to share similar domestic and other circumstances will concentrate in the work-forces of certain organizations. The Luton team's methodological conclusion was 'that in any attempt at explaining and understanding attitudes and behaviour within modern industry . . . orientations to work which employees hold in common will need to be treated as an important *independent* variable relative to the in-plant situation'.[10] In other words, if we want to understand what goes on inside factories we must look outside them.

Very detailed research by Blackburn and Mann several years later but when the job-market was still buoyant in the English town of Peterborough was to question or substantially qualify some of these conclusions, and some of the assumptions behind this version of self-selection.[11] For example, it is not correct that there are such great differences between semi-skilled jobs as Goldthrope suggests, though there are some. What is important, none the less, is that workers often *perceive* their range of choices as much greater than it is, objectively speaking. Then again, while some workers systematically scan all current jobs that they believe may be open to them, most others are not involved in any such search. Once they have found a job they like, they will stick in it: in this sense there is a considerable amount of random placement in jobs. Blackburn and Mann also have some very interesting things to say about worker orientations, but let us first see how the Luton team handled a very tricky problem that arises in explaining behaviour in such terms.

The question must arise of where we look outside, and what we look at. Where, to put it bluntly, do orientations come from? At this point the Luton team were faced with considerable difficulties in locating the sources of instrumentalism as they candidly acknowledged in a frequently overlooked disclaimer:

> What accounts for the fact that . . . our affluent workers reveal such a markedly instrumental approach to their work-tasks, their work associates and their work organizations? Answers to questions of this kind are, in any circumstances, hard to establish; and moreover, it is at this juncture that the difficulties which stem from our study being a more or less unforeseen by-product of a larger investigation become particularly acute. In a number of respects we lack what would be the most useful and relevant material.[12]

Very tentatively, they distinguished several factors apparently associated with heightened instrumentality: position on the life-

and family-cycles; the character of Luton as a community – or rather, a level of skill. Crudely stated, an argument which arranges these factors logically might run as follows: young married men of lower skill who have experienced average financial commitments and feel a need to compensate for their loss of standing with relations. This need to compensate for their loss of standing with relations requires that they carry out unpleasant but highly paid work for long hours and restrict their non-work activities to the family circle. Instrumentalism at work and privatization outside it may have been reinforced (or at least, not weakened) by the character of the community – in the case of Luton a 'town of migrants' in which persons of their own type predominated. Reinforcement may also have occurred in the workplace. Insufficient attention given in the study to workplace, or in-plant social processes, and the probability of its occurring on an important scale was not examined in any depth, as Bechhofer, a team member, has acknowledged.[13]

The Luton researchers could hardly have made plainer the conjectural nature of this explanation.[14] It was merely consistent with their available data and is not the product of irresistible statistical reasoning or backed by systematic observation. Whether or not it is a valid conclusion is not a point that can be usefully discussed here. The same goes for most of the other empirical findings, especially about *embourgeoisement*. Some shifts in activities and values towards a possibly more middle-class pattern were detected. These changes aside, the Luton workers remained decidedly working class – though it would be quite misleading to characterize them as proletarian, as some have gone on to do: most were buying their own homes, and their leisure patterns could not have been more different from the proletarian, cloth-capped Andy Capp stereotype.

But the fact is major investigations are often misunderstood. This is true of the Luton studies. The main misunderstanding they have promoted derives from the use of the action frame of reference to make some sense of the industrial data. The nature of this misunderstanding revolves around the concept of orientations towards work and the manner of their explanation. From an uncritical reading of *The Affluent Worker* it might easily be supposed that the task of the industrial sociologist reduces to delineating the orientations which predominate in a particular workforce and correlating them with a number of other easily measured social characteristics. Some critics have made such a reading and then assumed that any differences in work-attitudes and -behaviour would then be explained in terms of varying out-plant characteristics of workers. The result they conjure up is a proliferation of 'sociologistic' *middle-range theories*, which abstracted real industrial situations from their wider socio-economic context, and ignored their internally dynamic aspects.[15]

It is ironic that the Luton studies, which were concerned very much with an aspect of the wider socio-economic structure and with social process, should be thought to encourage such a tendency. I do not think the authors realized how their treatment, which relied predominantly on the interpretation of survey techniques, would encourage this view of them. Survey questionnaires have several serious weaknesses. The range of richness of the data collected depends on the questions put to the respondent as well as on his honesty, memory and verbal skill. They also project a static image of social reality. We cannot, therefore, be sure that *The Affluent Worker* sufficiently reports the attitudes and behaviour of the respondents. The investigators acknowledged this, but maybe did not pay sufficient attention to the second problem. They linked high instrumentalism – albeit cautiously – to position on the family-cycle, so by implication its intensity is variable. But the implication here seems to be that orientations change, if at all, only in line with out-plant factors, not through experience at work.[16]

It may be empirically true that the orientations of the Luton workers were highly stable, and were formed and modified exclusively by out-plant factors. What is unwarranted is any suggestion that this applies to all workers. W. W. Daniel made haste to point to the very real danger that actionalists risk suspending their analysis at the factory entrance just as previous researchers have done at its exit.[17]

But the Luton studies certainly encouraged no such tendency. Nichols and Armstrong, in a well-known study undertaken a little later in a process plant very probably located on the Severn estuary between Wales and England, were to take an almost aggressively anti-Luton line in their insistence upon the importance of in-plant processes.[18] This reaction was, if anything, the typical one of the time. We have also mentioned the Blackburn and Mann study of Peterborough, which modified so many of the Luton conclusions about orientations and self-selection. Another of its findings was the scarcity of orientations in the 'strong' sense adopted in the Luton study.[19]

It would have been astonishing if it had persuaded researchers that they need consider nothing but orientations, and that all workers possessed such 'strong' ones as the Vauxhall assemblers. Many studies of strikes especially have long shown how quite dramatic changes of orientation stem from in-plant experiences.[20] Further, when orientations are changed externally there is a very real risk of 'sociologistic' reduction in identifying the origin and agency of the change. Warner and Low, whose study of the Yankee City strike was reviewed in an earlier chapter, finally decided that the workers' loss of social status in the community was a crucial out-plant determinant of their unionization. In fact, however, much of their own analysis demonstrates that any such cause was a mediating factor at most: the real origins of the change lay in general socio-economic change and immediate economic crisis.

This excellent but perverse study linked the out-plant change with in-plant change. The two were inseparable modes of the wider socio-economic transformation of which the situation in Yankee City was a purely local, precise instance. Readers can be left to decide for themselves exactly how far treatment of the Luton workplace data, and the method recommended for industrial sociology, actually fell prey to the risks earlier sketched. Some further, more general, comment is, however, in order.

The Luton researchers contrasted the instrumentalism of the Vauxhall assemblers with a *solidaristic* manual worker orientation ascribed to *traditional* workers.[21] The traditional worker, like the instrumentalist, is an *ideal type* – an artificial construct to aid analysis. But such a construct must depend ultimately on a sound empirical reference. Though they treated the evidence then available cautiously, the Luton team had no doubt that the traditional worker had existed historically in large numbers and could still be found, here and there, nowadays. But historical and other evidence has seriously questioned the extent of the solidarism ascribed to traditional workers, and even their existence.[22] Pronounced instrumentalism is by no means a recent syndrome; and workers in traditional industries such as shipbuilding, as Richard Brown and Peter Brannen were to show, appear to have been far less collectively minded than sociological folklore once had it.[23]

This throws great doubt on the speculation that the Luton workers were prototypical in their degree of instrumentalist-privatization. Although they undoubtedly differed in some respects from other groups of British workers, both historical and contemporary, it now seems dangerous to ascribe their difference to their high concern for money rewards. When sociologists indulge in such predictions they should offer a model of society as a whole, or at least set out their main assumptions about it. The Luton team did so. In the final volume of the 'affluent worker' series, *The Affluent Worker in the Class Structure*, they contrasted the liberal-pluralist and neo-Marxist conceptions of industrial society and its evolution, but refused to accept either. They envisaged a 'relatively open' future.[24] The problem with such a model is its vagueness. Yet they had made one prediction about this open future. The money-minded men of Luton could be regarded as prototypical. This claim was always hostage to economic fortune.

From the first, they had acknowledged that their predictions were conditional on the continuance of the stable growth of Western economies. In the Britain of the 1960s such a continuation seemed probable. Changes since then suggest that the economic dimension should be given more attention. Any prototypicality would nowadays be argued on other grounds perhaps; for example, in terms of the Vauxhall workers' situation as employees of a large transnational organization in an industry whose future has become very cloudy. It seems absurd to me that the Luton team should be faulted for having failed to predict the specific dislocations recently evident in British capitalism in particular, and Western capitalism generally.[25] None the less there seems to be a lesson here: if sociologists are to make predictions – and a relatively 'open' future is a prediction – about major social processes, such forecasts should be better grounded in contemporary economics.

It is noteworthy that Goldthorpe has more recently been situating his work on social class and mobility within a political economy framework: one that lays stress on structural change in Western economies and the role of government in determining the response to crisis.[26] A second feature of this approach is that it obliges the investigator to situate – or, to use the right technical term, to *locate* – his analysis within specific socio-economic wholes, typically the nation-state. This change is very much in line with other developments, which can be attributed to an effort to synthesize the insights of the ACA with the work discussed in Part VI. But this statement must immediately be qualified. Some versions of the ACA are much more valuable for this purpose than others. The next chapter will illustrate the problem.

26

Talking of Situations

It is very difficult to avoid what may seem a rather philosophical preliminary discussion.

The radicalism of the 1960s was *cultural* before it became political. That is to say, conventional ways of behaving, of seeing the world, of judging right from wrong – even of judging whether there was a right and a wrong to distinguish – were being vociferously questioned long before some of those people who had been challenging the existing order as a set of cultural facts concluded that if there was to occur any permanent change in everyday life, in everyday behaviour and everyday attitudes, it could be brought about only by transforming institutions through political action.

Politicization occurred only after a massive but vague counter-cultural mobilization. Indeed, the 'politicos' were never followed by more than a small number of the many who felt themselves in some way embattled against cultural reactionaries. This was never grasped by some of the political radicals in social science, because on the campus, or at least in the social-science wing of the campus, politicized radicalism was the main force. Nevertheless, there did arise in social science, above all in social psychology and sociology, a form of opposition to the orthodox professors that was quite different from that of the authentic Marxists. There is still no convincing label for this movement, but I will call it *subjectivism*. Other commentators might follow Mark Poster[1] perhaps in terming it existentialism, while maintaining that it, too, had a strong Marxized element.

Certainly, the subjectivists were apt to talk about the great

French existentialist writer, Jean-Paul Sartre, as some Christians might talk of St Paul. And 'St' Jean-Paul had been declaring himself a Marxist for several years – while anathematizing the French communists. His newspaper, *Libération*, which his English-speaking followers greatly admired, besides blasting the Boss and the State, and the Stalinist PCF, supported avant-garde views on sex, drugs, and popular culture. (It became an up-market yuppy paper around 1980.) But the subjectivists also venerated such diverse figures as Michel Foucault, Marshall McLuhan, and Timothy Leary. Their sociological heroes were Irvine Goffman, Harold Garfinkel, Alfred Schutz, and George Herbert Mead.

If there is any formula expression for getting close to the heart of subjectivism in one step it is W. I. Thomas's declaration: if men define their situation as real, it is real in its consequences. Intuitively, this is such a persuasive maxim that some people never recognize how incomplete it is as a guide to understanding the social world. But let us note this gap now.

Stress on the actor's own, on his *subjective*, definition of a situation, may lead us to play down unduly, or even ignore, the *objective* properties of the situation in which action occurs. These objective features *condition* action. This does *not* mean that objective features determine the subject's action: it *does* mean they can facilitate some forms of action while excluding others, and encourage some while discouraging others. To note the reality of the objective world is not to see it as deterministic or necessitarian, but to see how it shapes action. Of course the subject's perceptions of it can mediate his action. But subjects cannot choose to perceive what is not there, or to ignore what is there – at least, they cannot do this without suffering a penalty.

Subjectivists do not like the tone of warnings like this one. They complain that to stress the constraint of the objective world shows a methodological bias which is also an ideological and political one, against personal freedom. Untrue. To be free is to recognize the real constraints on freedom: liberation comes from trying to reduce constraints, not from looking the other way or from saying a wall is a doorway. Alternatively, subjectivists argue that, unless we adopt the subject's point of view, his or her actions may appear inexplicable, irrational to us. In their opinion, the belief of orthodox social scientists in the need for the observer to remain objective results in a patronizing attitude towards subjects. Untrue again. Because actors are not sovereign in defining and acting in accordance with their definitions of the situation their action can go amiss in terms of its own aims, through miscalculation or some similar human failure. Thus action that is subjectively rational may well take a form that an observer has every right to call objectively irrational.

It is not arrogant or patronizing for investigators to acknowledge this, at least in principle. Unless they do so, social inquiry could offer no important generalizations. Men are never completely free to define their situations independently of structural constraints, to identify their objective interests fully, or to act completely rationally as a result. Marx expressed this as well as anybody when he exclaimed: 'Men make their own history, but they do not make it just as they please; they do not make it under circumstances chosen by themselves, but under circumstances directly encountered, given and transmitted from the past.'[2] People may struggle to attain genuine liberation and the ultimate value of social science lies precisely in assisting these efforts. But misplaced empathy for subjects may result in a sentimental exaggeration of their freedom to act rationally, and thus indirectly assist their continued suppression.

What, though, has this to do with industrial work? To begin with, methodological assumptions about the nature of social action and the characteristics of social actors must be of general importance for understanding what is, in one mode, the aboriginal human social act – the Rationalized Hunt of the Introduction. But there are immediate, basic reasons, too. Our assumptions about the rationality of the actor and the role of objective constraint lead us straight back to the issue of technological determination, for example. In the work we are going to consider in detail, they are deployed with great fluency in a critique of organizational structure as a determinant of behaviour. Examining this still remarkable work will bring these questions alive.

The vogue for radically subjectivist styles of inquiry – variously labelled *symbolic interactionism*, *ethnomethodology* and *phenomenology*[3] – reached its high-point in sociology in the early 1970s, and was then taken up enthusiastically by teachers of business studies and even accountancy: an unexpected but quite logical destination! Exponents of these styles seek a philosophical grounding for their methods in the phenomenological social thought of Alfred Schutz. Whether Schutz's philosophy is truly phenomenological is always being disputed, but his admirers suppose it is and we can characterize the radically subjectivist approach accordingly.[4]

Its advantages for studying work behaviour first put, with great skill and clarity, by David Silverman, its leading British exponent, in his book *The Theory of Organizations* – a slightly misleading title since Silverman never offered any comprehensive theory of organizations. His objective of seeking 'to draw out the implications for study and theory building of a view of social reality as socially constructed, socially sustained and socially changed'[5] was essentially a methodological one, and it involved an extensive critical appraisal of the assumptions of conventional organization theories.

Silverman's critique of three variants of the prevailing image of organizations as *systems* underscored the tendency of a systems approach to produce *reification*, that is to say, the portrayal of organizations as 'living' entities with pseudo-biological needs for survival, stability or growth. Organizations can have no such needs, nor can they take action independently of their human members.[6] To ascribe such properties to them results partly from an unwarranted extension of everyday speech, and partly from a disguised value-judgement: namely, that the most important 'needs' of organizations as entities are either simply those of organizational leaders, or those that a business consultant believes will improve efficiency. In sum, Silverman concluded, the systems image depends on logical confusion, unwarranted practical convenience and ideological thinking.

Conventional definitions of organizations were therefore not to be trusted. The claim that organizations are social units possessing goals obscures the variety of aims that their members, including their leaders, pursue in practice.[7] Likewise the hierarchical, formal nature of organizational relationships is easily overstated. Actual working arrangements are much more fluid than organizational charts or manuals suggest; and, anyway, other social units can be hierarchical and formal.

Silverman, however, maintained that though such definitions are inadequate we cannot ignore the common-sense division between organizations and other collectivities or social networks. Moreover, founders of organizations characteristically set down objectives, rules and formal structures. Their successors constantly reassert or replan these in a deliberate manner. The controllers of an organization at least do not take its everyday life for granted.[8] Because of this conscious drive from the top to organize and reorganize, which may be resisted from below or have other undesired or unforeseen consequences, the study of organizations can be a specialized area of sociological investigation. So far so good.

The method for investigating the life of organizations advocated by Silverman, an actor-centred approach, was identical to the one he believed sociology should adopt. Citing many weighty methodological writings Silverman argued strongly for recognizing a radical distinction between natural and social science.[9] Social science, he pleaded, should concern itself with patterned human action whose meaning is derived from the social context in which it occurs, but is changed by experience of interaction with others. This formulation, he suggested, brings out the paradoxical aspect of social living, for while the social world is a human *creation*, or product, it is nevertheless *experienced as given*. We live in a world that we create, but we do so as if it were created for us by others. Society creates the subject by giving him identity and his actions meaning, the subject concurrently creates society through his actions and, less directly, through changed perceptions of his social circumstances. Still nothing wrong.

Perceptions and meanings are socially distributed. Some are shared by all members of a given society at one historical moment, but many vary from group to group. In studying organizations, attention should be fixed on typical patterns of member-involvement, typical actions and the consequences of such actions, both intended and unintended.[10] These will depend on members' varying social values and definitions of their situations may engender changes in involvement, aims, and definitions of the situation.

The stress that began to creep in here was quite clearly on the desirability of charting social processes and explaining them in terms of subjective – though typically subjective – actions and definitions of the situation. Reworking some standard material, Silverman suggested the possibility of classifying organizations in terms of their *predominant meaning-structures*; the *sectional aims* of varying groups of members; and *power* – or rather, the 'relative ability of different actors to impose their definition of the situation on others.'[11] This last statement is unusual enough to come back to it in due course.

The emphasis here on how meaning-structures originate, operate and change was significant. It reappeared in later sections of the book in an increasingly emphatic form. Because 'the special role of the sociologist is to understand the subjective logic of social situations', Silverman argued, theorists should be wary of imposing *their own* definitions on the situations they study. Supervision, which has the appearance to an observer – a soft-hearted liberal sociologist for example – of being autocratic, might be construed and experienced by workers subjected to it merely as 'interference' or even as leadership.[12] Still more provocatively, Silverman asserted that 'when the definitions of a relationship change even where the original physical behaviour patterns remain, the relationship has in a very real sense changed'.[13] From here onwards it becomes harder to stay with the approach.

Assuredly these more contentious ideas intermingled with many valuable reminders about the limitations of conventional research techniques and instruments; and about the risks for social-scientific theory when theorists simple-mindedly ape what they take for natural-science procedures.

But there are serious shortcomings in Silverman's treatment of power; society; and the role of the investigator.

Organizations are created to marshal, express and apply power: in work organizations, the labour-power of individuals, once combined, is not only greater than the sum of separate contributions but is different in *kind*. Organized *quantity* transmutes *quality*. The internal structure of organizations embodies differences in power and is related to systematic variations of power in society, in ways that writers like John Scott or Graeme Salaman have explored.[14] Silverman recognized this. But his conception of power was bizarre: or perhaps I ought to say, the relative emphasis he placed on different sources of power was bizarre. His recommendation seems to be that we pay less attention to how much power organizational actors *actually* possess than to how much they *believe* they possess. We should concentrate on *their* definition of their own power position, and *their* definition of the power-position of adversaries.[15] Moreover, actual power should apparently be considered as a resource which enables a group to impose its definition of the situation, not its *will*, on its less powerful adversaries – or, as Silverman would presumably have to say, on those who 'underestimate' their power.

Perceptions of power have to be taken into account by investigators of course, because actors often misestimate their power resources, sometimes with the result that their bluff is called, sometimes with the result that they are conned. Likewise, organizational factions habitually engage in propaganda wars to impose their viewpoints on adversaries and the public. But they hold in reserve coercive weapons such as strikes, sackings, slow-downs, black-listings, and physical violence. To use the language of another organizational writer, Amitai Etzioni, the normative, or *symbolic*, power of ideas and definitions is usually matched by the *material* power of incentives and often with the *coercive* power of force.[16] To view the exercise of power exclusively, or even primarily, through the medium of definitions of the situation is incomplete and misdirecting.

Silverman himself stated: 'He who has the bigger stick has a better chance of imposing his definitions.'[17] But many power-holders do not need to modify a subordinate's perceptions to have their own way: faced with difficult underlings, they simply threaten to cut their pay, demote them, sack them, send them to a psychiatric hospital, put them in prison, or shoot them, as the case may be. In most industries, no strike occurs without bosses pleading that higher pay will bankrupt the firm. Workers will counterpose their own view. The *Financial Times* will comment on the situation. So will the *Sun*. The government may also weigh in, on behalf of 'public opinion'. At such moments social observers should be alert: behind this battle of definitions lie realities of power like balance sheets, order books, pension funds, seniority rankings – it is these that will finally determine the outcome of such struggles. Or they will in nine cases out of ten. Silverman's procedure will be useful for that residual case. But it is the first nine that for practical purposes are the ones that matter.

Let us look first at the sticks: to decide who has the bigger stick requires empirical observations of a reality that may be confused by the noise of a propaganda war, but is there for us to penetrate to. Ability to impose definitions of a situation is part of that situation. Penetrative investigation proceeds by examining such situations *first*. Examinations of actor-definitions of them is important – no, give Silverman his due, indispensable – but secondary.

Critics of subjectivist sociology correctly point out that it is one thing to take the actor's definition of the situation into account, but quite another merely to take it.[18] The latter procedure leads directly into a relativistic social world of disembodied perceptions and actions. In this world, no system of meaning extends beyond a single individual. From a collective point of view, no meanings exist. It is meaningless, it is absurd, it is mad, this solipsist world of human islands. Less floridly, may I point out a clear danger for the study of industrial behaviour by drawing an analogy with the interactionist wing of human relations examined in chapter 14. Interactionists like Whyte produced a series of *stories* or anecdotes explicated by such concepts as 'sentiments', 'activities' and so on. A language of definitions can be utilized to produce stories and anecdotes too, with people talking about situations and defining them, with the investigator summing it all up by referring to a *logic of definitions* instead of the Mayoite logic of sentiments.

Silverman raised the question of where orientations, definitions and meanings originate. 'One valid answer,' he claimed, 'would be that meanings are given to men by their society and the past societies that precede it', with social reality '"pre-defined" in the very language in which we are socialized'.[19] (*One* valid answer? Could there be two *valid* answers to such a question? Silverman here subjects his own analysis to the logic of definitions.) But his answer suggests a somewhat mechanical view of collective life much at odds with the dynamic perspectives otherwise advocated by him.

To resolve the contradiction, he argued that social reality is *empirically* stable but intrinsically 'precarious'. Unless they are constantly reinforced by the words and deeds of others, taken-for-granted assumptions about the social world are discarded or transformed. Since there is an element of discretion in our performance of a role, patterns of interaction can mutate; in their struggle to make sense of these innovations people generate new meanings.

This is plausible, but leaves several unanswered questions. If discretion exists in role-performance, do variations occur purely randomly, or are they produced by other factors which operate systematically? If some action is meaningful only *after* the event, as a result of retrospective rationalization, being otherwise based on unquestioned assumptions, has Silverman exaggerated the rational component in action generally? The inference to be drawn in such passages recalls Vilfredo Pareto's idea of non-logical action, which was discussed in relation to Mayo's thought.

Silverman also came close to endorsing a quasi-Mayoite image of the actor in such statements as: 'The fact that the stock of knowledge upon which action is based tends to change rather slowly, reflects the vested interest we all have in avoiding anomie by maintaining a system of meanings which daily confirms the non-problematic nature of our definitions of ourselves.'[20] This passage suggests social actors *choose* conformity. Obviously, some do, consciously, after struggling against it. Others choose conformity 'consciously' too, but as a *screen* for their evil deeds and scandalous lifestyle. But most people do not get such a choice because there are other people with a vested interest in stopping them doing so. The clash of *interests* results in objective restrictions on human freedom and human rationality. These constraints are not the side-effects of a great collective game with consciousness and definitions of the situation. They reflect a systematic structure of economic inequality, political advantage, and cultural competence. Seeking to establish an image of the actor as liberated from these constraints, social phenomenology can only explain the fact of social order in terms of some hypothetical drive towards conventionalism.

A compulsive 'Marxizer' could rephrase the passage quoted several lines above as follows: 'The fact that exploited social actors fail to perceive and act on their objective interests reflects the success of dominant class members in perpetuating their privileges, thanks to their socio-economic power and their allies in government, the State apparatus, political parties, trade unions, the mass media and education.' This sounds raw and unpolished. But is it any less plausible than Silverman's more subtly worded formulation?

The extreme relativism permeating this methodology leaves even its exponents unsure finally whether it has anything special to say. Summing up different theories of work behaviour, Silverman went so far as to comment that 'it would be foolish to suggest that any view is better than any other or that each person ought necessarily to be interested in the conclusions of the others'.[21] This agnosticism is logical enough within a phenomenological value-framework. Scientific theories are presumably higher-level definitions of the situation, and must therefore be respected for their subjective rationality. This leaves us in a relativist never-never land. Nobody wins the race, but everyone gets a prize. In the night, all cats are black.

Schutz's thought, which underlies a phenomenological ACA was once aptly summarized as follows:

> There is no social structure of history beyond those determined by the interests of some social scientists or historian or other. In particular, Schutz's 'phenomenological' sociology and history are the only social sciences: they do not depend on some other structural science. The effect of Schutz's humanism is a speculative empiricism of the surface phenomena of social formations in which social structures and historical events are reduced to givens which govern but do not appear in the analysis.[22]

Throughout this book I have stressed the importance of the fifth dimension of control in workplaces, that concerning frameworks of interpretation. At the outset I suggested that social theories of industrial behaviour can be created, or utilized, simultaneously as ways of penetrating closer to the core of objective reality and as instruments of legitimation and for shaping thought along lines favoured by established controllers. I want to make it clear that we should have the highest regard for the potentialities of subjectivist theory as a tool for identifying, penetrating, and deconstructing the interpretative frameworks utilized in organizational struggles for control. It also provides a valuable reminder of the importance of face-to-face social relations and the micropolitics of workplaces.

The more technical disputes that arise in subjectivist organizational research have been discussed by a number of notable commentators, such as Burrell and Morgan, or Michael Read.[23] Likewise, some years ago Clegg and Dunkerley made one of the most interesting attempts to locate the approach in a broader historical perspective on organization, which, like the present one, views actual organizational practices, and formal theories about those practices, as two sides of a complex reality subject to constant alteration.[24] Such treatments still differ sharply from those of the true subjectivists by insisting that, however difficult it may be to define its impact, there is a real material basis for both the structures and for theories that try to account for them.

But that material basis has been changing drastically. In the coming period of history, will not society *as a whole* need to redefine its situation, especially its relationship to production, as economic life becomes less and less affected by manufacturing industry? Are new groups of cultural agitators and radical communicators already spreading a *post-industrial* definition of work, thus displacing old change-making alliances such as the *labour movement*? The final version of action-centred approach to be considered, for its admirers 'tomorrow's social history', to its critics yesterday's futurology, suggests the best reply is an unhesitating 'maybe'.

27

The Ultimate Artisan

Anyone who believes that the nature of work is dictated by all-powerful capitalist employers, or, for that matter, anybody who believes that the automated tomorrow of the post-industrial society will displace work as a source of meaning for human beings, will not enjoy what they are about to read.

I am going to review here a variation of the actor-centred approach originally proposed by Alain Touraine in his book *Sociologie de l'action.*[1] This work attempted to link work phenomena with a complex theory of social development. Regrettably, it has never been translated into English. To gain the most from it, it is necessary to consider the context in which it was produced and some of Touraine's other theories. These can only be sketched in here, but longer examinations are available in *Servants of Post-Industrial Power.*[2]

Nothing could differ more from Silverman's approach. For the subjectivists, *only* individual meaning matters for understanding social action. For Touraine, there can be no meaning for *individual* actors – or, at least, none that matter for understanding historic social change. On the other hand, Touraine placed an enormous stress on an entity he called the *historic subject*, a kind of *collective social actor*. The historic subject would generate new values for society as a whole through its action. There is a sense, then, in which this historic subject would define the situation for us all, or attempt to do so.

Of course, the historic subject, as Touraine often made clear, is a convenient fiction, much like many other models or ideal types – social man, the authoritarian personality, the proletariat – that social scientists have patiently stitched together in order to communicate complex ideas economically. But it is true that such entities can suddenly take on a life of their own – sometimes it takes no more than one flash of lightning to galvanize the Being which then begins to wreak havoc. Some English-speaking observers always feared there was a particularly high risk that given half a chance the historic subject would get loose and go on the rampage.

But it seems logical that a social theory should attempt to work with collective entities rather than via individual experience. We ought to be sympathetic with this *holist* element in Touraine's work. Studies of a particular social sphere should relate to an image of society as a whole. A subject's experience of work, in any case, is inseparable from his total situation in society. Experiences of work, the challenges and frustrations it supplies, may or may not develop a subjective sense of identity in an individual, but they do help to form an objective social identity. Such identities are not randomly but systematically distributed throughout society and are one – and possibly the most important – embodiment of social structure.

To repeat a statement from the Introduction: analysis of work as a social practice requires some conception of society which penetrates beneath the surface properties of social behaviour but can none the less deal with those properties adequately. These two requirements are inseparable: functionalist approaches to the problem, either in orthodox sociology or in *marxisant* doctrines, portray any given social structure as a set of abstract arrangements which permits the continuance of that society just as it is, clockwork obedience to shared values in one case, craven acceptance of domination in the other. Each variant certainly pursues generalization – with a vengeance. So do structuralist perspectives, which portray societies as abstract systems of signs and meanings. These Type II varieties of sociology, despite their passion for the abstract, of course derive from, and are applied to, the study of actual societies, but their logic demands that concrete social forms should be treated as *instances* of a set of universal principles, not as the material from which generalization is built.

Because these principles purportedly apply to every society, no society is necessarily more advanced than any other, though it may be more complex. Likewise, Type II theories underestimate internal tensions, because a society which was not relatively well integrated would by definition not exist. No major element of structure governs the form of other elements, nor is that form produced by economic forces. Neither perspective, then, can convincingly explain social change. Functionalists mutter about inherent impulses to adapt or integrate better; structuralists conjecture a gigantic human game with innovation – society changes because it's fun to be different; the Marxizing functionalists often talk about struggle but they do not always give the impression they mean what they are saying.

Investigators who deplore the submersion of the concrete in an abstract scheme, who hold that structural elements are ordered in importance and that conflict is a critical social fact, and who insist that social analysis must embody historical perspective, consideration of economic factors and some notion of human progress, could once embrace deterministic Marxism, the 'dialectical materialism' confected by Moscow court theoreticians. Such perspectives never offered any advantages over their orthodox or Marxizing competitors, except the sense of being on the winning side and being able to parrot out ready-made formulas and believe them. Adoption of crude images of economically determined class conflict historically evolving in a unlinear direction merely leads to the same dreary old terminus: scrutiny of particular societies for evidence that upholds the basic thesis.

We have already remarked, in accounting for the popularity of the approaches examined in Part IV, the change to an optimistic mood in the late 1950s. Earlier in that decade, a few adherents of each perspective began to modify their approaches, however cautiously. Functionalists began examining conflict, the economic basis of society and social change. Marxists paid more attention to what historical materialists called the *superstructure* – meaning everyday social relations, attitudes, beliefs, values – and even began to express doubts about the necessary evolution of capitalism into socialism as a result. Lonely and despised revisionists in each camp repudiated their abstract Type II schemata in favour of more factual analyses of contemporary industrialized societies. Consequently, two major kinds of substantive theory of socio-historical development were gradually pieced together, for which *industrial society* and *technological society* are convenient descriptive terms.[3]

Broadly, the theories of industrial society claimed that a *logic of industrialism* overrides societal differences stemming from national traditions or formal political systems, producing a structural convergence of all advanced societies in the long term. While these societies might promote more people to their élites on merit, advanced industrialism would demand a continuing measure of social inequality as the price of this higher social mobility. Ideologies that contested this, whether from principled egalitarianism or principled élitism, would have to be discarded for the sake of efficiency.

Adherents of the technological society theories accepted much of this. Capitalism was no longer visualized by them as a self-destructive economic shambles. Class domination would be perpetuated because the bourgeoisie had learned to exploit the power of the State more rationally for their own purposes, through economic planning and welfare, while technological innovation would guarantee prosperity for the masses and social peace. Manipulation through advertising and the mass media would tickle up 'false needs' in consumers, which could then be gratified to produce false satisfactions and false loyalties to the system but very tangible profits. Domination would be perpetuated on the pretext of technological necessity. This analysis was extended to cover what the doctrine-makers called the 'state-capitalist' Eastern bloc countries: in these sad lands, bureaucrats, technocrats and Party *apparatchiki* constituted a New Class unsympathetic to social democracy. Convergence upon totalitarianism was a global tendency produced by the frenzied drive to exploit technology.

Both theories, we now see clearly, exaggerated the present extent of convergence and the capacity of both capitalism and state socialism to contain their internal problems, though capitalism has done so better.[4] Curiously, the technological society theory, though Marxist in inspiration was less economically determinist than its bourgeois twin. What matters for the present exposition is that each discouraged a view of society as a *humanly created* entity over which a greater measure of human control might be exerted to secure relevant progress. Neither slammed an air-tight lid on opportunities for personal growth or access to a higher quality of life. Rather, they suggested that nobody would be allowed to need such benefits, whose relevance to profit or state power was not evident.

Luckily, they got it wrong. Touraine's work was to offer a corrective to this latter deficiency. Whatever its faults, it still has this virtue of pointing to how people may be able to reappropriate parts at least of everyday life and change them – for the better: why not? – through a kind of cultural guerrilla.

The particular relevance of Touraine's contribution to the theme of this book is that in *Sociologie de l'action* he linked societal analysis – an examination of societies as entities – directly to the study of work. But the latter extended ideas which Touraine had put forward already in a much earlier work, *L'évolution du travail ouvrier aux usines Renault.*[5] It will, then, be helpful to come to *Sociologie de l'action* after a glance at this examination of 'the evolution of manual work' in the Renault plant.

Published over thirty years ago, when Touraine was about to embark on a period of intensive empirical research in French industry, *L'évolution* reported an investigation of varying socio-technical settings in the Renault car factories. Because of this concern with technology, and partly because only badly translated extracts were available in English,[6] it was at first mistaken for a contribution to the theory of technological effects. Taken as such it seemed to back up the claims of Woodward or Blauner that *craft production* (which Touraine calls 'phase A work') and *automation* ('phase C) share agreeable social characteristics, while between them lies a historic stage of dreary and alienating mass-production work ('phase B').

Such interpretations could be read into it, but Touraine had been the student of one of the most trenchant critics of the scientific management movement, Georges Friedmann, who from the early 1930s had been mounting a barrage against work-fragmentation and the destruction of craft work – and therefore of what he saw as the *moral* superiority of craft skill and the craft community.[7] In chapter 30, we shall need to come back to Friedmann in examining the contribution of Harry Braverman, whose critique of *work degradation* forty years later is incorrectly supposed to be the first Marxist analysis of the question after Marx's own. By 1950, Friedmann had long since discarded the language of historical materialism, but his mind was, in certain respects, rather set in its ways and some of Touraine's speculations in what was supposed to be just a research student's report made his supervisor uneasy enough to mutter in his foreword that he found them 'a bit on the daring side'. What haunts the treatment is the image and lore of craft undergoing an astonishing historical transformation.

Touraine certainly argued that work as a whole is evolving from phase A (craft organization) to phase C (automation). But the social characteristics of these two systems present a sharp contrast. The phase A worker was incorporated into a tightly knit craft group which jealously policed its internal status distinctions and prerogatives with respect to other groups, thus maintaining sectionalism throughout the plant. Phase C *integrates* work processes throughout the entire plant, with instrument monitoring and information-recording operations supplanting direct handling of the product. Individual *polyvalence* (adaptability and availability for a range of tasks) and flexible group relations, rather than manual skill, become indispensable for the operation of the complex automated work-system.

Unlike craft work, the versatile or polyvalent work of phase C derives meaning neither from its intrinsic interest nor from the exclusiveness of a narrow craft-group membership, but from wider social reference points – the overall social relations of the plant, pursuit of a particular lifestyle outside work, a strategically planned domestic project, or wider social attachments and values.

Strangely enough, phase B (mass-production), far from being the polar opposite of the two other forms, is, Touraine contends, similar in many respects to phase C. It is a contradictory, transitional phase wrongly supposed to be typical of industrialism. Under it, progressive standardization and rationalization of work occurred. These changes might temporarily aggravate its dehumanizing properties but these are the prerequisite of phase C. This was an insight he owed to Pierre Naville – one of the first interpreters of Marx to point out that Marx's 'rough sketch' of *Capital* (the so-called *Grundrisse*) not only allowed but actually encouraged such a view.[8] Touraine further asserted that, in Renault at least, phase B work led to a *lengthening* of the job hierarchy not the cramping of it that most commentators claimed to find. This enhanced overall opportunities for upward plant mobility in the workplace. Though it wrecks some of our romantic illusions about craft production, Touraine observed, we should remember that under that system many labouring mates (*compagnons*) failed ever to attain journeyman status.

By eradicating the rigid task-structures of the craft period, phase B facilitates transition to phase C. Since, in phase B, work ceases to provide the rewarding sense of social involvement of craft work, and becomes a 'purely technical' experience, any other sort of value or meaning has to be projected on to it only by reference to wider social values.

This is a claim that hands us the key for understanding Touraine's wider social philosophy. Though an act is nothing but a learned routine, once we do it in association with other persons we sense a need to attribute a meaning to it. Since it lacks intrinsic meaning, we will impose on it an agreed meaning or value, more or less as a money value is printed by agreement on a piece of paper to make a banknote. We might almost say that Touraine sees an advanced society as one that must, and does, mint meaning.

But the persistence of craft work prevents the emergence of such standards, because beside it phase B work can easily be made to appear meaningless. For the craft romantics, it is a pushover: they keep us forever looking sadly backwards instead of forwards, to the new social world we could fashion around automation. By sentimentalizing craft culture, we are caused to see what is to come as a tragic mirror image of the past, glimpsing mythical deprivations in the automated future that give us a chance to alter the entire meaning of work. Touraine asks us to remember work which '*has no meaning – is sheer inhumanity – derives its one and only significance from the social milieu and the social value system to which it is related, in such a way that there may in fact be nothing in common between two working systems which make an appeal to quite distinct evaluative standards*'.[9]

All this will seem unforgivable to craft romantics, and maybe Touraine is a little hard on them here. But Marx would have had no time for the nostalgia of some Marxist craft romantics or Bravermaniacs. Touraine agrees with him. And that, maybe, is why Touraine was once misidentified as a neo-Marxist thinker.

Until automation is generally applied, Touraine went on, mass-production work should be rationalized to reduce technical pressures by designing jobs which call for minimal attention. This will eventually facilitate the social reintegration of complete workforces after the temporary turning point of mass-production has been passed. The nature of this reintegration would depend on a revision of society's conception of work. How will this be achieved? Touraine's answer was not as clear as it should have been, but he firmly denied that advanced technology ought to evoke any 'natural' or universal emotional or social response. The response we usually *do* have is socially determined. The craft romantics have programmed it into us. And we might even say, he argued, that if ever work experience is technologically determined, it is so under craft production, not under mass-production or automation. As he puts it:

> This study of Renault factories should have indicated that the prevailing form of the technical environment, far from signifying the domination of technical factors and their at least partial autonomy with respect to the social conditions of work supplants that autonomy which on the contrary characterized the craft system of work, and subordinates the meaning of work entirely to its social conditions.[10]

In his preface to *L'évolution*, as we noted, Friedmann rather anxiously described these conclusions as a little daring: a very restrained reaction for a craft romantic. Touraine might have said how a general shift in social attitudes away from craft ideology might be procured. New meaning could not be generated independently of structural innovation. But what kind of structural change? He seems to have seen a link between the content of general social philosophies of work and the properties of the socio-economic whole, but he refrained from spelling it out.

In *Sociologie de l'action* Touraine returned to the problem he addressed in *L'évolution* of linking microstudies of the work situation with macrosociological analysis. Earlier on, I noted that this book is not easy to read, and I can do no more than sketch my own interpretation. Touraine hypothesizes a dynamic link between work and society, along the lines of that sketched in the Introduction. Work is the cradle of novel forms of social action and new values, both for the individual worker and for society. Society can be conceived as a *collective worker*, which through its productive operations may heighten self-awareness and a sense of purpose among its members – an implied historic project – and therefore generate a *historic subject* (*sujet historique*). Neither any one individual, nor even a majority of members of a society, necessarily achieves such awareness, though all members of society unconsciously participate in the historic subject; and in particular epochs it may be closely identified with a particular social formation, such as the working class.

In identifying the historic subject, the analyst's main criterion is its potentiality for promoting human emancipation. Touraine explained: 'The study of the historic subject is, above all, a sociology of *freedom*, it is always a quest for the movement by which, simultaneously, the forms of social life are constituted and contested, organized and then put behind us, sublated [*dépasse*].'[11] Sociology should be concerned with the genesis of social values, and this implies study of the 'orientations of action' which, 'far from imposing a sociology for the "inner life" can and should be studied in action'.[12] Action becomes historic in so far as it results in 'creation, innovation and attribution of meaning'.

New meaning and new action are generated above all through work. Work transforms society, or facilitates transformation, by altering the material basis of existence, and by modifying man's conception of his needs and identity, that is, his human nature. But work entails some system of social relationships; and, for

Touraine, a society, the *collective worker*, can achieve self-consciousness by reflecting on its productive system just as his experience of work may contribute towards the individual worker's self-image. Societies which acquire a *historic consciousness* of their needs, identities, and emancipatory potentialities become true historic subjects.

Note that for Touraine, the *collective worker* means society as a whole, not, as it does for some neo-Marxists, a workforce, or the employed labour-force as a unit. And unless some poetic licence is granted him it is very difficult to grasp what he means by the historic subject. Apparently, it must be apprehended largely through series of paradoxes and exclusions of meaning. 'The historic subject is no more a concrete actor than it is the collective consciousness of God,' he stated. 'It defines a certain relation of a society – a collective worker – with itself, a relation defined by the capacity of the society to comprehend its environment as its product, its artifact.'[13]

Such a capacity is a variable partly dependent on a society's level of economic development. But Touraine rejected any Marxist notion of a determinate relationship between the material base and the social superstructure of a society. His base, so far as he offered any equivalent, seems to have been the extent of a society's self-awareness. Such awareness may be inferred empirically by examining the objectives expressed in undertaking work, and deprivations suffered in performing it, and less directly in the norms of social institutions and content of symbolic systems – language, the arts, and mass communications. Society, Touraine claimed, 'transcribes' the effects of its work into novel institutions and symbols. Consciously or unconsciously, it projects its self-image in so doing.

Touraine seems to have believed that industrialized societies have reached a stage of considerable self-consciousness as historic subjects. Advanced technology was transforming production systems; problems created by the social relations of the workplace overlapped with all others; and the State increasingly intervened to promote technological change, to regulate the economy, and to plan social life. Work had become a totalizing force.

This, he pointed out, was something of a paradox. Work as a sheer economic necessity is becoming less important precisely when the societal element projected into – and social consequences of – work relationships bulk larger. Likewise, the technical rationalism which underlies work organization is becoming increasingly evident throughout the community. A curious but interesting result for social scientists, he alleged, is that a genuinely scientific study of society – which must begin with work – was becoming feasible for the first time in history. 'If the Sociology of Work was born with the industrial revolution,' he claims, 'it could not become scientific until work had become social [i.e. societally encompassing], until the notion of society once more took on a meaning, with the emergence of industrial societies, that is to say, which organize the control of the collectivity and its technical and economic activities.'[14]

To some readers the inferences which might be drawn from these allegations will seem either absurd or sinister. Was Touraine seriously suggesting that industrialized societies have arrived at the threshold of 'authentic' history? Or was he claiming that it is the State nowadays that embodies the emancipatory historic subject in its purest form? I believe Touraine is stating that industrialized societies all possess the *capacity* to become self-liberating historic subjects, and that State power can be used to aid this process. These developments have become possible – even probable – but by no means inevitable. He distinguished between an industrial civilization, a pattern on which societies are converging, and industrial societies. Though the latter were all 'sublations' or *dépassements* of class societies they varied enormously among themselves.

Such variations seem to arise from numerous dialectical processes. I am by no means sure that the nature of these processes can be made clear by me, or by Touraine for that matter, but I will do my best. Work expresses two universal, necessary but opposed principles or motions: one towards *creation*, the other towards *control*. A productive act performed by an isolated producer necessarily implies some drive to create. A completed product breeds a sense of achievement, a 'proud consciousness'. Likewise, the producer normally seeks to control his act of production and his created product. Yet production also involves recognition of the need to produce to survive; and the product must be consumed, or traded for others which will be consumed. The struggle with nature and the inevitability of consumption generate a 'submissive consciousness'.

'Creation' and 'control' are, then, in Touraine's scheme of things, inherently ambiguous activities. Any productive act, whether it is individual or collective, tends to evoke two currents of consciousness in those people who perform it, and these two currents run contrary to one another. It is, as it were, by examining the motions of the sediment swirled along and eddied by these opposing currents that we can infer the *projects* actually pursued by historic subjects. More prosaically, any such examination will always reveal a conflict between a desire for material progress on the one hand and a desire for greater freedom on the other.

In society, submissive consciousness reappears as 'constitutive consciousness' – an emergent central value-system to which persons must subordinate their selfish impulses. Some groups – the 'masters' – identify with the constitutive consciousness more closely. Thus the proud consciousness of workers is repressed and class struggle – or rather, a 'dialectic of social classes' – results. Rejecting soapbox Marxism, Touraine indicated additional complexities. Progressive and reactionary elements coexist in all class formations. Politically radical workers may be social reactionaries, voting Communist one day and abusing blacks the next.[15] 'Masters' likewise may be economically go-ahead but socially repressive as in Nazi Germany, or technically backward but socially easy-going, as in imperial Britain.

Consequently, a *double dialectic* of social classes ensues; and, from this, Touraine deduces that 'all classes, all social groups are at every moment carriers of the historic subject . . .'.[16] Similar double dialectics are detectable in the life of organizations, political parties. All embody the productive embattlement of the forces of creation and control.

When we analyse society at the highest level of abstraction Touraine suggested, the terms 'creation' and 'control' can be replaced by those of 'development' and 'democracy'. Development means more than economic growth and, *a fortiori*, than expansion. It is transformation of society by work. Democracy is not an institutional mechanism . . . it is primarily the awareness, freely formed and expressed, of the legitimacy of ways of utilizing the product of individual and collective work.[17]

The impulse towards democracy is expressed in historic social movements, when, unable to gain the sense of participating effectively in the historic subjects as individuals, people create appropriate organizations. But, Touraine warned, the labour movement, the classic example of such, was coming to the end of its central position, as economic growth removed many of the deprivations against which it had struggled, and internal disagreements sectionalized its components. Any future successor would have to project the same unifying ideals as the labour movement once possessed. Perhaps there would never be such an equivalent. In any case, the societal context was undergoing a decisive transformation as a result of which societies will 'cease to be historical and become historicizing: they are no longer in history, they make history'.[18]

Touraine has modified many of these ideas since the mid 1960s, when he wrote the book, and went through a phase of being written off as yet another glib prophet of the post-industrial society eager to appear on television and the front page of *Time*. This reaction was excessive, but understandable. He had been saying things that elements of the French Left found offensive or ludicrous – he even managed to publish a book called *The End of Socialism* (*La fin du Socialisme*, Paris, Le Seuil, 1981) several months before the French socialists won a landslide majority in 1981. He is reported to have lost long ago his interest in work at a moment when it is changing more dramatically than it has done in two hundred years. This too looks like bad timing to some of his former admirers.

In a critique of soapbox Marxizers, the Marxist scholar Eric Hobsbawm once drew up a very precise list of what he saw as the properties of an adequate sociology of historic change. They ran as follows: it should provide an account of historic change which can explain social order in any given period; demonstrate that change derives from the evolution of production but is not a direct outcome of technical or economic advance; show that change can facilitate genuine human progress ('emancipation'); provide criteria for judging progress; demonstrate how 'the internal contradictions of socio-economic systems provide the mechanism for change which becomes development'.[19]

These are exactly the ones which seem to have actuated Touraine in writing *Sociologie de l'action*. How important are the substantive failings of the book – I have examined them in detail elsewhere[20] – beside its intentions? It seems that one of his errors was to confuse discussions that agitate the Parisian media and intellectual giants with actual movements in behaviour and values in the country itself. Then again, Touraine had a habit of generalizing about all advanced societies on the basis of post Second World War France – where accelerated industrialization and the prominence of state intervention in the economy, together with the rapid collapse of peasant society, growing urbanization, the retreat of the Church, and the erosion of the revolutionary Communist Left in politics, and many other local specificities, undoubtedly affected his analysis.

And even the scepticism directed against the craft romantics has an enigmatic aspect. Friedmann adopted Pierre-Joseph Proudhon's image of the craftsman as a morally and intellectually superior social type. As Touraine pointed out, not all craftsmen may have lived up to this idealized image, and in any case it left masses of less skilled workers, and junior members of the craft, out in the cold. Yet, when we come to examine Touraine's historic subject, that elusive being appears to possess exactly those superior virtues that the romantics attributed to the craft worker as a type. This might be a misreading. Life would seem more interesting if Touraine was correct when he evoked the possibility of a genuinely dialectical jump in our attribution of meaning to work as we move into what appears to be a new stage of economic development. But it is hard to be convinced.

His work still offers a provocative vocabulary for defining some of the more urgent questions that are beginning to confront us. Its main limitation is its level of generality. Many of us neither can nor wish to operate outside the bounds of named societies. It is within such societies that all the most urgent issues will arise for the foreseeable future. The concluding chapter will attempt to outline a *societal* approach which can begin to meet this requirement. First, we need to summarize some of the conclusions reached in this Part and in the text so far.

28

Structure, Action, Consciousness

In the social sciences, a perennial – and so far unsolved – problem arises over the relation between human actions and social structures. The general form of this problem is easily grasped. On the one hand, it is evident that human action is affected by social structures. On the other, such structures do not come into existence unless they are created by repeated patterns of action; and they cannot be thought of as continuing to exist unless they are reaffirmed in action. Let me illustrate this.

One universal feature of social structure is the ranking of social groups in terms of their power, reputation, or prestige. We can get a rough idea of this ranking by asking any member of the society about this scale: many will be able to sketch an answer without trouble. Our informant is describing a mental diagram, a mind picture with a more or less definite form. But it is a model that by its nature is abstract. All the same, that picture has been built up largely on the basis of experience, by observing what others do, as well as what they say. Even as he or she speaks the informant may be recalling real situations or imagining possible ones in which social actors engage in encounters. The informant may give us a summary description of this ladder of status which may seem dead and rigid. But behind it are a thousand shadowy meetings of which even the speaker may be only half aware.

We could not talk about a status ladder unless some people acted 'respectfully' towards the higher-status members and 'graciously' towards those lower-status members who in turn show respect towards them. Showing respect might take any form from simply paying more attention to what an older person says to throwing oneself on one's face in front of an ayatollah. The range of deferential actions tells us exactly what kind of status ladder we have to deal with and what sort of society it is located in. But that is not what is most important here. What is, is the apparent inextricability of action and structure. It is clear that if we ask which is the cause of the other we shall be in trouble.

Certainly when the question is posed at the generalized, philosophical level, we cannot point confidently to a chicken and an egg. But that is because we are loading the dice against ourselves by asking an excessively abstract question. Once we come to examine *real* structures, in real societies, the dilemma is far less acute. For a start, we can stop talking of 'causes' and ask in what ways a structure *influences* action. Similarly we can examine how action *sustains* or *alters* a given structure.

In the workplace we have special circumstances, because, as we saw in the Introduction, the economic transaction of the effort–wages bargain underlies the social structures of the employment relationship. We know that tensions are inherent in this relationship, that they must be handled in the daily actions of the parties. Likewise, managers make an attempt to structure the relationships of the workplace in a deliberate way through creating work-roles and lines of authority. We are dealing, in other words, with formally organized relationships, with organizations deliberately created at a given moment in time for specific purposes.

It may be – it is not a question I can take up here, though readers might like to think it over themselves – that the social sciences of work offer a *unique* opportunity to understand the general links between social action and social structure. But our more immediate concern is the actor-centred approaches (ACA). It is easier to evaluate them in the light of the foregoing remarks.

Despite the enormous international prestige of the Luton study, its industrial analysis never created a theoretical movement comparable in scope and influence to that of the technological implications approach. One reason for this is elementary. We have already seen that many earlier inquiries had incorporated an examination of workers' wider economic attitudes and values as influences on their work behaviour. The Luton study merely did more formally – it is tempting to say more ceremoniously – what had often been done before. Most people, in any case, had never believed that work behaviour really could be determined only, or mainly, by technology or by human relations management techniques. They had no need to be told that how the workers saw things also mattered, and might be the most important factor of all in accounting for some forms of behaviour.

In this regard, there was little resistance to the approach of the Lockwood–Goldthorpe team. The real trouble arose, as we saw, firstly over the way work-orientations were conceived – their stability, coherence, and intensity – and secondly, over the particular issue of instrumentalism in the labour-force.

On the first count, an inquiry by Blackburn and Mann[1] (we shall be examining it in detail in chapter 34) was to show the apparent rarity of firmly fixed orientations to work. This does not mean that where orientations should have been these later researchers just found a large gaping hole. But interpretations of their own economic involvement among their worker sample were often unclear or shifting. On the second count, that of the characterization of the economic perspectives of actors, the typology suggested by the Luton team (*instrumental*, *solidaristic*, *bureaucratic*, and *professional*) has been treated sceptically or ignored: it was always a rather too schematic construct.[2] When it was applied to research findings, it proved feeble. At an early date, for instance, Richard Brown and Peter Brannen failed to discover among the Geordie shipbuilding workers of the British North East the kind of folksy solidarism predicted for them down in Cambridge.[3] More radical New Wave critics of the Luton approach added further objections along these and other lines.[4]

It is worth noting that some influential American theorists of organization of the mid 1960s had begun to stress the importance of types of worker involvement for the control systems ('compliance structures') of the workplace. By far the most impressive of these was the elaborate framework put forward by Amitai Etzioni.[5] As an intellectual structure, it is still interesting but it boils down *involvement* (orientation) to three basic forms – *calculative*, *normative* and *alienative*: a worker complies either because someone pays him to, because he believes it is right to do so, or because someone forces him to. (The *instrumentalism* canvassed by the Luton team is a variety of calculative involvement.) But this reduction invites us to obliterate the finer differences in economic perspective we may find among actual worker groups.

The phenomenological ACA was much more closely attuned to the intellectual radicalism of the protest peak years, to the mind-games of a counter-culture that was tripping on psychedelic drugs, and to the needs of narcissistic proto-Yuppies who devoured manuals about the 'presentation of self in everyday life'. Although an ideological and cultural threat to social traditionalism, the new *post-bourgeois* values and frame of mind emerging among middle-class youth in the wake of the real radicals was perfectly consistent with a maintained capitalist system. Thus the adoption of this approach in the Open University courses on organizations screened by the BBC in the early 1970s was by no means a coup for media Reds, as some right-wing editors muttered. It is perfectly logical that the most vociferously subjectivist sociology department in any British university (at Manchester) should later come to specialize in teaching young accountants. If a balance sheet is not a 'negotiated order', what is it? Nor is it surprising that a graduate business school in the same part of the country has included tuition on deconstruction and post-modernism – notions that most people associate with literary studies or coffee-table books on the cinema – in its organizational curriculum.

Such apparently zany and self-indulgent policies can be explained without difficulty, and justified within the context of business education relevant to current circumstances. The phenomenologists are fascinated by the frameworks of ideas and meanings that people adopt and apply in order to interpret the world, especially the social world, and insight into such matters provides useful weapons to wage commercial war. But one of the problems with their way of doing things is that it tends to individualize and particularize these interpretative frames to such a high degree that we are left with as many ways of seeing the world as there are people – we could almost say they think there are *more* interpretations than people, since some individuals themselves switch from one frame to another.

Of course, the old cliché is true: everyone is an individual. Nevertheless, many interpretative frames are widely shared with other people. We must explore these overlaps, and how they are established within groups and maintained by all the usual techniques of social discipline. For the social analyst, furthermore, it is exactly these shared, overlapping areas of meaning, value and perspective that offer another means whereby the link between social structure and social action can be determined. Action is always influenced by such *social maps*, and sometimes depends largely on them. The consequences of action may result in the accuracy of the map being confirmed or in its being redrafted.

An effort to undertake a survey of varieties of such frames in the British labour-force is reported in Beynon's and Blackburn's *Perceptions of Work* (1972).[6] But depth was sacrificed to breadth here. By far the most insightful study in terms of depth was undertaken some years later by Howard Davis, which showed that certain types of economic perspective *are* shared by worker groups; but there are marked disparities between group outlooks, while the latter are related to occupational and skill differences, rather than to those of class.[7]

Class imagery was intensively studied by several investigators in the 1970s: the social and industrial turmoil of the post 1968 period made it intensely topical. But these inquiries were guided by a theoretical framework, the so-called IOTA framework,[8] that was intended to measure the coherence and intensity of class consciousness, which English-speaking writers like Mann[9] and Gallie[10] had borrowed from Touraine.[11] Such an awareness is only one element in the economically related frames held by social actors, however, and, in any case, class awareness was found to be less intense than many people had assumed.

It was also shown that heightened class awareness is not automatically produced by a person's location in society or by his or her job. One important influence is access to information or to an ideology already shaped by a class-conscious view of social relations. Once again, exposure to the ideas of class politics does not automatically result in adoption of the 'classist' perspective. We are not talking about indoctrination – which is far harder to undertake than usually believed. In the workplace, however, competition often occurs to shape interpretative frames.

Touraine once rightly pointed out that the work organization can thus assume a potentially important role in social change-making.[12] What images of society and the economy are promulgated by unions and the employer respectively? How carefully are they worked out? How forcefully or skilfully are they communicated? These questions were neglected by the industrial sociologists of English-speaking countries, with the exception of Theo Nichols in *Ownership, Control and Ideology*,[13] until the question of 'class and the corporation' was taken up by writers like John Scott and Graeme Salaman.[14] They could receive still more attention in coming years.

But what kind of attention are we talking about? Of the ACAs dealt with here, Touraine's is the most relevant to any reply. This does not mean that the other varieties are uninteresting or misdirecting. On the contrary. But they are incomplete. And indeed, Touraine's version does not offer a readily applicable formula for a more penetrating and more relevant economic sociology, but it has two great assets. First, it directs analysis towards society as a whole. Second, it embodies a sense of *historicity*, that is to say of shifts in social structure or changes in ideology which alter decisively the societal whole.

It seems regrettable that these properties have never been so well appreciated as they should have been. Personal and political factors may partly account for this. But there have always been two other severe obstacles. Even in French, Touraine's writing can be extremely unclear. The imprecision and allusiveness of his style are magnified by translation. Rather he said half as many interesting-sounding things, but said them as intelligibly as he can at his best. Also, he has often muddled the statement of social facts with an interpretative scheme for revealing their logic.

The significance of a fact, in such an approach, is not governed by the numbers of persons it affects, or some such criterion, but by whether the interpretation 'predicts' that it should be important.

There *is* a serious methodological problem here. This is not a wide-eyed plea for empiricism. An empiricist would not mention a writer like Touraine. The real problem is that if a theory says that such-and-such a change will prove historically decisive, then the theorist may trick himself into finding evidence of the change where none of any substance exists – at least not yet.

Perhaps methods can be devised for limiting the dangers that thus arise. It is growing clear the time has come when the sociologist of work can and should take up this question. Some proposals along these lines appear in the Conclusion. Whether these are valid and useful, or otherwise, we have now reached a point in the development of our societies, and in that of the social sciences of economic life, where a historically aware *societal* approach will generate more relevant and more penetrative research than any other. This likelihood has been increased, and facilitated, by the recent, and now rapidly diminishing, impact of the New Wave approaches examined in Part VI.

PART VI

DIVIDING THE LABOURERS

29

Protest Peak and the New Wave

In the 1960s, Western societies seemed to have solved all their essential economic problems. This does not mean that economic issues were unimportant. But the problems in the news were those of success, not failure. Some countries, notably Britain, lagged behind others in maintaining a high rate of economic growth and competitiveness in manufacturing goods for export. But even in Britain most people had been experiencing a steady rise in their real standard of living for two decades, and home-produced goods, if sometimes of poor quality, could still be sold without trouble on the home market to newly affluent and undiscriminating consumers with increasingly easy access to credit. Above all, anybody who wanted paid work could find it.

In all Western countries those districts that had a long-term unemployment problem were viewed as economic curiosities. The notion that large-scale permanent unemployment on the pattern of the early 1930s could return was regarded as alarmist. Politicians, economists and commentators were convinced that Keynesian economic policies, which required active intervention by the State in the economy, could indefinitely maintain full employment and growth. Expansion of the welfare state increased consensus and provided employment openings in numerous semi-professions or office occupations.

In countries like France or Germany, where the rate of growth and prosperity were exceptionally high, the self-confidence of economic managers was almost complete. The liberalization of international trade, the cheapness of raw materials and oil, the general docility of industrial workers and trade unions, and the regular appearance of new products and processes, added to the blithe feeling that underlying economic security was absolute. Even the horrifying reality of Third World poverty was shrugged off as a transitional problem. Development was taken to mean building steelworks and car-plants, and replacing buffaloes with tractors. This would boost even further the advanced economies, who would supply the new plant and equipment. The Third World would then take off into self-sustained economic growth.

When an economist got worried it was usually because he feared that governments might run out of bright ideas for creating budget deficits. Thus the decision of the USA to compete with the USSR in sending man to the moon was greeted by Keynesians with jubilation. A space race, they exclaimed, was the ultimate sump for public spending. It was just what was needed to perpetuate world growth and technological progress. It would make a marvellous television spectacular, too.

Other factors reinforced a belief that a golden age of stability and security was only just beginning. The first Cold War had thawed in the détente of 1963. European countries were rapidly decolonizing their former empires. Consensus politics and centrist parties increasingly dominated their governments. The jackboot Right and the Stalinist Left had been pushed towards the political margin in places where they had only recently been strutting. Conservatives found themselves maintaining a welfare state and public corporations. Socialists preserved free markets and private-monopoly capital.

Social scientists were not slow to theorize the apparently permanent settlement that emerged in the early 1960s. History seemed to have made a decision. As chapter 17 suggested, technological implications theories were encouraged by the optimistic technocratic atmosphere. This was a world of low international tension, of rapid technical change, of consumer prosperity and full employment, of harmony between classes as between bosses and workers; a world unconcerned with political or religious doctrine. It was a world ready made for the pragmatist, the experts proclaimed, a mass society whose high level of internal cohesion and stability was evident in the collapse of doctrinaire thinking – in the *end of ideology*. Other features of these theories have been noted in discussing the work of Touraine (see pp. 284f).

Events were soon to prove the analysis spectacularly wrong. In the *protest peak* period of 1968–73, the post-Second World War social settlement suddenly fell apart. The extent of this collapse became apparent only a decade later, with a revival of the radical Right. It is vital to appreciate this context to follow this Part of the book. The intellectual movements it reviews were products of a historic international cultural upheaval followed abruptly by economic reversal. Work and the division of labour were thrust unceremoniously to the political foreground.

As noted elsewhere, already there had been occurring a largely submerged and now forgotten spread of interest from the earlier 1960s in the issue of *alienation*, especially as it was exmplified in work deprivation. This rediscovery of the young Marx who had analysed the man–machine relationship was even made the subject of a lengthy essay in the very book in which Daniel Bell hailed, without quite saluting, the supposed end of ideology.[1] When writers like Andrew Zimbalast state that there was little interest in such topics in the 1960s, as opposed to the 1950s, it must be supposed he is reporting a personal experience based on the USA.[2] In Western Europe, in which it was becoming possible for purposes such as the present one to include Britain, precursors of the protest peak intellectual stars were certainly debating alienation from 1965 onwards.

What we will all agree on is that the issue of rationalized work revived spectacularly among radical intellectuals early in the protest peak period. Their scathing attacks on the machine-paced work that reflected human alienation in capitalist industry were to be picked up by some labour leaders, or were directly imported into unions by young radical students who had 'gone to the People'. 'Alienated work' was to surface as a grievance in some of the internationally famous strikes of the early 1970s, notably the Lordstown stoppage at General Motors in the USA and the Renault workers' strike at Flins in France. By the end of the period, labour spokespeople were becoming adept at feeding journalists good copy about 'blue-collar blues' resulting from workers reacting against being robotized by Taylorism.

They and the working journalists knew the revolt against Work had become a favourite subject with sub-editors and that the politicians were scared enough by it to demand government inquiries. But there was an entirely genuine resentment against rationalized work welling up in the workforce. It showed up in figures for turnover, absenteeism, timekeeping, as well as a growing disregard for the authority of foremen and managers. Many employers simply ascribed this to the effects of agitation, or, as the *Economist* put it, the 'growth of bad habits' because of persisting high employment levels. Elsewhere I have contended that the erosion of industrial discipline reflected the spread of *post-bourgeois* values which are relatively deeply implanted and now being transmitted to younger people, despite high unemployment.[3] Full employment increased workers' expectations; a simple economic explanation for this surfacing of work as an issue in the politics of everyday life is insufficient. We shall come back to this point. What matters is that work had to be written on to the political agenda.

It is now plain that the end-of-ideology prophets had confused two types of integration long ago defined by David Lockwood.[4] As socio-economic *systems*, that is, as assemblages of social units and economic institutions, these societies manifestly hung together surprisingly firmly given their size; indeed, as systems, they were to continue to do so even into the present troubled period. When we turn from *system* integration to *social* integration, however, the position was startlingly different. Social integration refers to the degree to which typical social actors 'fit into' institutions, the readiness they show to follow through officially approved standards of behaviour, and the extent to which they adopt stereotyped ways of looking at the world in common with others.

In these terms, most advanced countries had never become culturally homogeneous mass societies, but had remained characterized by sharp ethnic, regional, and social-class divisions despite the often vigorous attempts of governments to suppress variation and – less often – reduce inherited disadvantages or social discrimination that stood in the way of any common national culture. Some such variations were exacerbated by the post-Second World War boom, because already favoured groups prospered disproportionately well and because new ethnic groups were sucked in as cheap immigrant labour.

But the greatest mistake was to fail to perceive how this growing internal diversity was magnified by a generational change that was also a historic change.

The simplest way of putting things is as follows: those persons who grew up after the Second World War were individuals for whom peace, an economic boom, and the Welfare State formed part of the natural order of things as they experienced it. Their perspectives were no doubt affected by other factors too – lengthier education, expansion of electronic communications media, an autonomous youth culture. Some observers argued that their whole experience of life was governed by a sense of insecurity produced by the nuclear threat. This may have applied to an aware minority. For many others, insecurity was heightened by extreme pressures towards a narcissistic pursuit of individual gratification. But to the vast majority the concept of economic insecurity had little meaning.

The immediately preceding generation had experienced the 1930s Depression and a world war, insecurity and hardship, followed by peace and unimagined prosperity. Their sense of social involvement and political loyalty were enhanced in the post-war period. But the bases on which this increased social integration – or at least their wish for it – were occurring for the older generation were almost without meaning for their own children.

We can easily define the general cultural change that affected the post Second World War generation. Some have called it the onset of 'post-materialism', others that of 'post-industrialism'. No one has yet hit on quite the right term. But, at this remove, what is remarkable is the degree to which the last remnants of Victorianism were discarded. Middle-class respectability in ways of living and thinking, long questioned in artistic circles, was rapidly discarded after 1960. By the end of the decade, it was publicly disparaged. In this *post-bourgeois* syndrome, themes like the unguilty gratification of desire, distrust of all authority, aversion to formality, and anti-productivism – rejection of economic growth at all costs – mingled with a search for new forms of sociability, demands for sexual and racial equality, and belief in the imperative of *self-actualization*.[5]

All these themes are clearly visible in the various causes and protest movements that burgeoned between 1968 and 1973. What stunned the older intellectuals was not just the scale of this revolt but the apparently overriding need that the post-bourgeois protesters felt to justify and *theorize* what they were doing. This was a startling departure from tradition in English-speaking countries, but before long even rock papers like the *New Musical Express* were carrying articles that wove radical-sounding theoretical terms like alienation into record reviews or reports of concerts. The expansion in political literature was prodigious, as the older traditions of anarchism and Marxism sprouted inventive new variants, and were joined by orientations such as Green politics. The doctrine of the end of ideology – it was of course itself an ideology – was, to put it mildly, disconfirmed.

The story of how this change affected social science is far too complex even to trace summarily here. For some time, turmoil persisted in subjects like sociology, where several brands – and even bands – of radical sociologist vied with each other in smoking out 'bourgeois' and 'reactionary' elements that were as often as not chimerical. On balance, the chaos was productive. Most radicals declared themselves Marxists. The old thick-hided dialectical materialists of the Communist hard core regarded many of the neo-Marxists as opportunist dabblers.

True enough, to embrace Marxism did not automatically imply acceptance of traditional Marxism in its theoretical mode. Nor did it imply any regular political activity in a recognized Marxist party. A common pattern was a *marxisant* ('Marxising') one, with Marxist concepts or theories being utilized in a sometimes undiscriminating way. Some Marxizing radicals had personal magnetism, and a few could make themselves sound like Zarathustra, anathematizing the work of rivals, excommunicating each other with all the doctrinal certainty of a Counter Reformation pope. The strength of these *gauchiste* elements forced liberal, social-democratic and even some traditional Marxist social scientists on to the defensive.

Their influence on the study of economic life was overall a tonic one in so far as they drew attention to underlying realities of the wages–effort bargain, the systemic nature of the socio-economic whole, the role of coercion in economic relationships, and the power of ideology. There was a serious attempt, too, to break down the compartmentalism of the social sciences, and a critique of the very notion of science itself – in which the Marxizers were joined by subjective sociologists (see chapter 27). The drive towards trans-disciplinary social science was very welcome. It produced, it is true, some sociologists who babbled amateur economics, and some economists who came out with sociological clichés as if they had just discovered the wheel. But there has occurred real progress and the pay-off in the form of new ideas and research is still coming.

A marked impact has thus been produced on industrial sociology in particular. It is appropriate to talk of a New Wave of research, ideas, and theories – though some of these turn out to have a rather longer pedigree than some New Wave researchers imagine. How much this matters is not something easily agreed. What is refreshing is the vigour of the debates that have resulted. We shall focus on two, both of which relate to the *division of labour*.

The first focuses on the *labour process*, a useful concept. It is no longer closely identified with a partisan Marxist interpretation of economic life. There has always been a distinct risk of that occurring.[6] 'Work', as we have repeatedly seen, is an ambiguous concept. We often need to designate the broad, characteristically human, activity embodying: (1) deliberate physical actions or mental operations organized into *tasks* performed by persons; (2) transformation by the 'labourers' of raw materials into finished products; (3) utilization of equipment and tools, which extend, simplify, lighten, and thus make more productive the activity as a whole.

Some philosophers call work 'purposeful human activity'. But such a term could include creative play. Why not just say 'production'? Production, though, has the disadvantages of what might be called a compression word. It cuts down any sense of the chain-like quality of purposeful productive activity. It focuses narrowly on a final outcome, leaving in the dark whatever has led up to it. On the other hand, when we talk about a labour process, we are reminded that the act of production comprises the three elements (operations, material, tools) listed above, stretches over a period of time, and – above all – demonstrates forethought. In other words, the term lays stress on something that is *systematic* and *purposeful*.

This is not how all labour process theorists would justify the term. For many of them, the prime virtue of the concept is that it is located within the overall framework for analysing the capitalist economy put forward by Marx.[7] For some of these people, it evokes all the other Marxian conceptual apparatus and requires them never to lose sight of the political implications of the Marxian framework. For other investigators, it is unnecessary to accept the linked Marxian analysis wholesale and unquestioningly. Rather, this second group aspires to adapt, update or otherwise remodel Marx's approach in order to produce explanations of economic behaviour which are first and foremost *materialist*; that is to say, rest on economic pressures or constraints.

For this latter perspective, the labour process must be given priority: organized productive activity is the main datum point in mapping any modern society, and offers the best means of accounting for a society's past and future development. This may be a pragmatic position, chosen on account of the greater penetrativeness of the notion, not for any political reasons. The labour process approach (LPA) has generated enormous controversy and much useful research. No one can understand this properly unless they appreciate these differences in outlook among exponents of the LPA. Luckily, it is easy to fix the essential disagreements in mind.

The LPA intersects with the second New Wave problematic at many points, which also focuses on the division of labour. According to these *segmented labour market* theories, the allegedly free, rationally operating market for labour of advanced capitalism is carefully managed. It is not even a single, unified market, but a whole series of partial markets dominated by large employers. The segmentalists agree with LPA investigators that large employers develop strategies in order to control the labour force more closely, and utilize the division of labour for this purpose. But the core of the LPA is the *degradation hypothesis*, which states that the aim of capitalist control strategies is to eradicate skill in all sections of the labour-force. The segmentalists, however, believe that strategies aim to sectionalize the labour force by deliberately creating different levels of skill.

This is a very schematic initial statement of the position. We shall also find, predictably, that some of the more impressive New Wave investigators cannot be classified neatly as either degradationists or segmentalists, and that their work shows continuities with some of the other traditions examined in the book – even though they themselves may sometimes be unaware of these similarities.

I shall take up relatively more space discussing the work of these latter investigators than in presenting that of the more schematic thinkers. These have by now been widely documented in many easily available sources. So they will be noted more briefly in the following account of New Wave thinking about industrial behaviour. We shall, however, need to spend rather more time on a complication that has largely gone unnoticed till now. It occurs in the central study of the LPA literature, Harry Braverman's *Labor and Monopoly Capital*, to which we first turn. It is of unusual interest and importance to the theme of this book and in the light of the comments on the political allegiance of New Wave thinkers sketched in the foregoing section.

30

The Degradation Problem

Only a few paragraphs could be given over in the previous chapter in trying to communicate the extraordinary atmosphere that brewed up in the protest peak years of 1968–73. At the very end of this period Harry Braverman's *Labor and Monopoly Capital*[1] appeared and insisted that the issue of what he characterized as the *degradation of work* should be made a priority for social scientists.

In fact, it already was one. I noted earlier that the issue of subdivided work had been growing in intensity since the early 1960s in orthodox industrial sociology, and it was increasingly debated as social-science teaching expanded later in that decade. Other ways in which the question was recognized have been noted, for example, in chapters, 19, 22, 23, and 28. We saw that Warner and Low had also examined what they regarded as the historic decay of craft skill in the 1930s. Braverman's essay caught the 'work woes' tide just before the flood, and was well designed to sail on that tide. The 'revolt against work' was articulated in a language that clearly bears the imprint of debates already in progress among social scientists.

Nor is it entirely true to say that the book revived concern with subdivided work among Marxists. The rediscovery of the theme of alienation (in the correct Marxian sense) was led by ex-Communists of the New Left, who saw themselves as engaged in the regeneration of Marxism. But Braverman was correct in saying that some Marxists had devoted far more energy to what seemed to them the politically more urgent and profitable questions bearing on social class structure and consciousness. Vigorous debates were then raging between Marxist and 'bourgeois' sociologists about whether the working class was becoming middle class (*embourgeoisement*), obsessed with goods (*consumerism*), and withdrawing from public life (*depoliticization*).[2]

To summarize in Marxist terms, the question of class domination, which applies to relationships in the spheres of politics and culture, had come to overshadow the question of class exploitation, which occurs in the sphere of production. Braverman insisted that the balance ought to be tipped the other way.

It is interesting to situate Braverman's intervention in this way – as an event in the development of Marxism in the latter part of the twentieth century. But is not necessary to do so. To anticipate: it may be that the work is really less of a Marxist one than has been supposed. What makes a work Marxist is not how hard its writer thumps a clenched left fist on the table and holds forth in an eloquent Marxist vocabulary. The world-view and values implicit in what the writer is saying are what counts. I shall take up this theme again shortly. First, Braverman's argument must be outlined.

Braverman's basic assumption is that private employers, which he always refers to by the abstract category Capital, aim to establish complete control over the employed workforce. Pursuit of control may begin as a means of increasing profit by extracting more labour; but Braverman clearly believed it also embodied the political aim of subduing the working class, and reflected an ingrained mentality in which the need to control became an end in itself. Control over labour was to be exerted above all by the *separation of conception and execution*, that is by Capital appointing managers whose task was to plan exactly how work was to be done, by appropriating craft knowledge, developing machinery that required no craft skill to operate, and thus stripping formerly skilled workers of any responsibility or initiative, leaving the latter as unskilled executants of detail tasks – monotonous, subdivided work. To achieve this, Capital promoted the scientific management movement, which has successfully de-skilled craft work and created new occupations in the office, which are themselves non-skilled, to administer de-skilled manual work. This overall process was to be characterized as the *degradation* of work because labour not only lost its skill status but was socially humiliated: the attack on craft knowledge and craft organization was also an attack on the self-respect of craftsmen.

Braverman could hardly have stated his message more eloquently or more persuasively. *Labor and Monopoly Capital* has many passages that remind its readers of a brilliant advocate brimming with conviction for the case he is putting. Its verve, wit and commitment struck a perfect echo among radical social scientists. Moreover, it came from the hand of a man who was himself an ex-craftsman, a 'real worker' who proudly proclaimed his lifelong Marxist loyalty. Its success was thunderous.

Then people began to think. For a Marxist, this was an odd work indeed, on further consideration. One essential feature of Marx's own thought is the inevitability, the pervasiveness, and the transforming power of working-class resistance and struggle against the drive of capital to exploit its labour. Braverman's Labour, on the other hand, has always seemed to me peculiarly unresistant, even submissive. What is certain, as commentators soon began to observe, was that Braverman had not only edited out of his account the recalcitrance of individual workers faced with attempts to control their effort but also the entire trade-union movement. Surely he must acknowledge that in certain places labour had successfully evaded the tentacular control of the scientific managers?

Of course, if the scientific managers were as clever as Braverman suggested, if Capital was always so well attuned to its own interests, so capable of devising foolproof methods of pursuing them, and so crushingly powerful in imposing them, then it might well be pointless for labour to invite a thrashing by taking on Capital. But is Capital, or the managers it appoints to run its affairs, quite so knowledgeable and quite so strong? The image of Capital as omniscient and omnipotent simply did not square with the real world either. Along with Braverman's dismissal of worker resistance, this was a prescription not for action but for resignation, however resentful. A Marxist analysis? Marxists are historical optimists, not fatalists, as this doctrine risked inviting its readers to become.

After these logical doubts came the empirical ones. Was the central thesis true? How justified was the portrayal of the fate of craft work that it offered? Might there be just a touch of romanticism in its implied vision of the pre-industrial situation, for example? Was it in fact an analysis, or a jeremiad?

The degradation thesis states that skilled work has declined in importance since the rise of capitalist industrialism, being sharply accentuated from around 1900 following the rise of the scientific management movement. Most of the evidence we need to settle the first part of this claim, that for a pre-industrial idyll, does not exist or is not agreed. The popular image is a compelling one of joyous pastoralism mixed with cheery artisanship. Enter the capitalist with his factories and suddenly the cottage industry of the handloom weavers, like that of nail-makers, stocking-knitters or potters, was swept aside by standardized, factory-made products.

We must beware of too elegiac a view of pre-industrial craft labour: Touraine's queries about it (see chapter 28) are worth recalling here. Handloom weaving may be creative when it involves producing highly patterned one-off luxury articles as a hobby. It was sheer drudgery for the weavers who had to toil long hours producing very simple fabrics to make a living. Apprentices and journeymen in the more noble traditional crafts like metalworking, bricklaying or printing also spent much of their time on miserable, dirty tasks, under the capricious discipline of masters who were frequently drunk and typically extortionate in their view of the wages–effort bargain.

Most of the pre-industrial labour-force were not employed as coppersmiths, masons, cabinet-makers, or as farriers or thatchers, but as farm-labourers and domestic servants. Certainly, very substantial elements of skill may be called on at times in these occupations. The exhausting tasks of following a horse-plough through the winter mud or mucking out a pigsty in a heat-wave might seem preferable to work on a Ford assembly-line. Factually, wisely or less than wisely, country people often thought otherwise, voting with their feet for the dark satanic mills. Let us keep a hold on pastoral romanticism when this question comes up.

Industrialization boosted the number of factory workers and

increased the proportion of the labour-force who worked in factories and in those workplaces that increasingly imitated the factory regime. Equally clearly it created dozens of new occupations – boilermakers, machinery fitters, locomotive drivers, electricians, etc. – whose work was at least as skilled, inherently interesting, and prestigious as that of the longstanding traditional crafts. In the present century, some of the skilled occupations created by the industrial revolution began to contract as products and the pattern of demand altered. These changes were aggravated in some cases by rationalization, scientific management, and a managerial quest for greater control of exactly the kind Braverman depicts. Many of his examples are totally appropriate for documenting the case for degradation, and we are in his debt for describing them so eloquently and in such rich detail. Here, however, in the very exactness of Braverman's documentation of the particular, is one secret of the spurious verisimilitude, the mere semblance of truth, of his thesis as a whole.

Braverman refused to admit that any new occupations have been created equivalent to the skilled occupations degraded by rationalization, or that work in some longer-standing occupations has been upgraded. There are numerous examples of both kinds of occupation: nurses, electronics engineers, typists. I have just seen the results of an inquiry among several thousand employed people in Britain. Those who claim that their tasks have been subject to simplification or other kinds of 'degradation' in the last five years are far outnumbered by those who claim to have experienced a growth in the skill and responsibility expected of them.[3] This does not mean that these jobs are becoming 're-skilled', in the sense of becoming like craft work. They are probably not. It merely suggests that the process is an infinitely more complex one than Braverman suggests.

Debate about such empirical questions has provoked much new research, and some valuable ideas such the notion of *tacit skill* explored by researchers like Jones and Wood building on the ideas of M. Polanyi.[4] Some of this work will be briefly explored in chapter 29 (on British LPA). The most relevant reports and studies are readily available, and summarized in such useful examinations of the LPA as Paul Thompson's *The Nature of Work*.[5] The present book is not primarily concerned with the empirical validity of such hypotheses, but with the approach to work that they embody and their relationship with other schools of thought. In this respect I find the degradation hypothesis unusually interesting. I have already remarked that in some important respects it goes against the very Marxist world-view that it professes to exemplify. The contradictions are far deeper than those already noted.

In talking of Touraine in chapter 28, I mentioned the work of the veteran French sociologist, Georges Friedmann. In his first book, *La crise du progrès*, published in 1936,[6] Friedmann took up the theme that was to run throughout a series of gradually more pessimistic books on the theme of work and social change. As a young fellow traveller of the PCF who had visited the USSR several times, Friedmann lashed the 'odious puerilities' of the bourgeois scientific managers, notably Taylor and Ford.[7] Fragmented work, he affirmed, was a characteristic of capitalism, produced by the drive to separate execution from control and thus de-skill craft workers.

Ten years later, Friedmann was acknowledging that his hopes of the USSR had been too high. The Soviets also seemed set on degrading work. Friedmann's books were now being translated into English, with titles like *The Anatomy of Work* and *Industrial Society*.[8] His following in the English-speaking world became considerable, but he had become convinced that there was little hope of reversing the tendency towards the shattering of skill into meaningless fragments. In the 1960s, he was probably the most widely read author on this subject in the world. He was not encouraged, as we saw, even by Touraine's thesis that automation would result in work regaining a meaning. He was not only sceptical about it: I suspect he did not even *want* to believe it.

For this aversion there was a fundamental reason. Friedmann was obsessed with skilled work and the craft, not simply because craft work was 'more interesting' but because such work, learned as an apprenticeship, resulted in a *moral* and *ethical* transformation of the individual who performed it; Friedmann believed strongly enough in this doctrine actually to take an apprenticeship himself as a metal-worker. Pierre Rolle, a specialist observer of French ideologies of work, unhesitatingly places Friedmann in a long tradition of thinkers and labour activists who have been moved by such ideas.[9] The intellectual source of these ideas is the work of Pierre-Joseph Proudhon, the printer-philosopher and Utopian socialist whose followers dominated the French socialist movement until 1900.[10] For this 'microcosm of the French people', craft knowledge was the touchstone of human work, training in a craft should form the core of all public education, and the craft workshop offered the model for rebuilding society – the Workshop Republic would be constituted from the mini-republics of craft workshops.

However one reads *Labor and Monopoly Capital*, one impression is inescapable: for Braverman, traditional craft labour is an absolute value. And the basis for its superiority is *moral* and *intellectual*. Here are two passages, drawn almost at random from the book:

> From the earliest times to the Industrial Revolution the craft or skilled trade was the basic unit, the elementary cell of the labor process. In each craft, the worker was presumed to be the master of a body of traditional knowledge, and methods and procedures were left to his or her discretion. In each such worker reposed the accumulated knowledge of materials and processes by which production was accomplished in the craft. The potter, tanner, smith, weaver, carpenter, baker, miller, glassmaker, cobbler, etc., each representing a branch of the social division of labor, was a repository of human technique for the labor processes of that branch. The worker combined, in mind and body, the concepts and physical dexterities of the speciality: technique, understood in this way, is, as has often been observed, the predecessor and progenitor of science.[11]

> Before the assertion by management of its monopoly over science, craftsmanship was the chief repository of scientific production technique in its then existing form, and historical accounts emphasize the origins of science in craft technique.[12]

The tone of these comments is characteristic. Yet they could be found anywhere in Friedmann's books. Braverman, however, explicitly disparages Friedmann's work – not for its detail, nor for his view of craft, but for its lack of a Marxist perspective. I am not sure why Braverman should have wished to attack Friedmann so sharply and, in a sense, so gratuitously. But to accuse Friedmann of lacking a Marxist perspective is a rare piece of irony.

I have given an account of Marx's debate with Proudhon over the consequences of machinery in another place.[13] Proudhon hoped machinery would evolve so as to restore what he regarded as the *natural division of labour*, which was expressed in the divisions between traditional crafts. Marx regarded this as at best rather backward looking. We must expect technical innovation finally to allow us to recompose labour along entirely novel lines, Marx suggested, although these could hardly be glimpsed in the middle of the nineteenth century. Work in its earlier forms would therefore be transcended. Craft might well become a quaintly anachronistic notion, outdated by the shift in all human frames of thought once socialism was attained. In this regard, we should perhaps recall Touraine's remarks on skill and the future of work. These are closer to the spirit of Marx.

I think it is worth pointing this out to put the record straight. Whatever we choose to call it, a preference for inherently challenging work, for work demanding a high level of intellectual involvement on the part of the worker, is one that most of us must share. It seems to me that Braverman's dedication to the preservation of the craft, Proudhonian or not, is a defensible position too. But it is not the same as the first position. To adopt it brings a risk of falling into craft romantic[14] nostalgia, however, which hampers any ability to contribute seriously to a debate about the desirable future shape of work in industry.

While it is possible to preserve most of the ancient crafts as hobby activities, many of the more skilled industrial tasks that exist today are likely to be modified in ways that organized labour, if it can win more allies among work designers, or develop its own technical resources, may be able to influence no less decisively than it has influenced some task structures in the past. But this will require a readiness to envisage the future, and to write an agenda for work that is technically appropriate to conditions as they are at the end of the twentieth century, not as we like to believe they were at the end of the eighteenth century.

The work culture and values so valiantly defended by Proudhon in his time, and by Braverman and Friedmann in our own, may serve anyone who sets out to invent this future less well as a model than one they might develop from an understanding of the position taken by Marx, or for that matter, by Touraine, on these matters.

Another feature of Braverman's thesis, already noted in chapter 29, is that wholesale degradation cannot be squared with most theories of *labour market segmentation*. The context in which the latter appeared must also be appreciated. It is set out in the following chapter.

31

Segments and Struggles

From an early point in the post-Second World War period, sociologists of work began to take an especially close interest in one aspect of the development of the large modern firm. This was the growth of white-collar workforces. Until this point, the term *bureaucracy* had been reserved for the staff of a government department. Now it was realized that private firms were also building up their internal bureaucracies, and were doing so in more than one sense. It was not just that office staffs were rapidly growing. Their conditions of work, and their employment contracts, were similar in some respects to those of civil servants. The work that many of them did was highly routine and subject to all kinds of rules of procedure.

The radical sociologist C. Wright Mills caused a stir around 1950 when he observed that, despite advantages such as greater security, many office workers were performing very routine tasks, that machine-paced work was growing, and that the status of white-collar work must fall. His book *White Collar*[1] was a best-seller. An argument over whether office-workers might become 'proletarianized', merging socially and politically with semi-skilled manual-worker strata, which began then is still continuing. British researchers like Rosemary Crompton who have taken a cue from Braverman, report finding among office staff substantial work degradation, for example.[2]

The book thus provoked some sociologists to focus on the implications for class structure of the spread of white-collar employment. Others more concerned with intervention began to ask what effects bureaucratization would have on motivation and performance, especially as Mills had pointed out that the work of managers themselves was becoming increasingly bureaucratized. This branch of inquiry produced such classics as W. H. Whyte's *The Organization Man*,[3] which bewailed the strangulation of the Protestant work ethic in the toils of the organization.

But another implication of Mills's work was neglected by the sociologists. The advantages of white-collar employment such as security and the opportunity to move upwards in grades according to seniority or experience were also being awarded or won by many groups of manual workers. Mills had noted these changes in passing. A labour economist, Clark Kerr, had already claimed that American job markets were becoming so fragmented because some large employers were developing internal career ladders for skilled workers that normal economic theory was being outdated by events.[4] This observation was of the utmost importance to the theory of social class because it pointed to lines of division within the working class additional to those of skill levels. But sociologists largely overlooked it.

The new breed of political economist, briefly mentioned in chapter 29, that began to appear in the USA in the late 1960s took up this insight and developed it into the *segmented labour-market* theory – abbreviated to *segmentalism* here. I will not consider segmentalism at length, since our interest is primarily in its contribution to understanding work behaviour, not issues that are more strictly economic ones. But its relationship to degradation theory also needs noting.

The immediate precursor of the segmentalist approach was an analysis published in 1971 of the operation of what its authors, Peter Doehringer and Michael Piore, called *internal labour markets* (ILMs).[5] Other noteworthy contributors to the perspective have been Catherine Stone, Richard Edwards, Michael Reich, and David Gordon.[6]

Was it useful to look at large modern firms as smaller, private versions of the State, exercising within their 'territory' an authority akin to the political sovereignty of an independent country? The authors did not go quite as far as that, nor as far as those economists who had talked about the growth of 'feudal' institutions in the employment practice of large firms. But by allocating better jobs to workers on the grounds of personal characteristics, rather than on those of skill, such employers were breaking the rules of economics textbooks which see labour markets as relationships between large numbers of workers offering skills of varying scarcity and large numbers of employers seeking such skills, such that both skills and rewards can be rationally allocated only through the market mechanism.

Only a minority of employers, usually the larger private firms, or public organizations, were seen as having ILMs, of course. Just how many there were, depended in part on what was regarded as the core feature of an ILM. This can be either a job ladder, that is a set of posts arranged vertically, thus providing a *mobility cluster* or set of *career lines*; or it can be *seniority entitlements*, which provide access to a wider set of better jobs within the organization.[7] The extent to which either of these arrangements, or some combination of them, are used, and how far they are formalized, varies greatly. But clearly many employers do not offer any such advantages at all. Thus a further distinction was soon drawn. Not only was there segmentation *within* firms with ILMs, but there was a further division between such employers and the remainder. The result is the division of employment by the *dual labour market*.

In the segmentalist perspective, any external labour market is split between two sectors, a *primary*, generally large-firm sector, and a *secondary* or mostly small-firm sector. Primary-sector workers are awarded many advantages: higher pay; better terms of employment; safer working conditions; interesting work-tasks; promotion opportunities; fringe benefits; thoughtful supervisors; security of employment.[8] The position of secondary-sector workers almost amounts to a straightforward inversion of these advantages. Overall, the contrast is a violent one between privilege and security on the one side, and deprivation and insecurity on the other. Some sociologists of work find this either/or way of looking at employment structures rather schematic. On the other hand, sociologists have never managed to systematize their observations about the operation of labour markets. We shall come back to the point.

One important elaboration, however, was soon introduced, as segmentalists came to make a distinction between sets of *upper-tier* and *lower-tier* posts within primary-sector employment. Upper-tier posts, occupied by the higher flying executives or experts, have very low security, and their incumbents do not consider them as part of a career ladder inside the firm. If they produce results, they move on to a better job in another firm. If they fail to, they are dismissed.

The behavioural assumptions behind this conceptual framework are not obvious, however. Of course, primary-sector firms can pay out much more per worker. They may be able to do this partly because they have built up a monopoly position. But segmentalists do not rely as heavily as traditional economists on a vocabulary of incentives to explain behaviour. The benefits of primary employment are seen as encouraging workers to acquire stable, dependable work habits; whereas secondary-sector jobs do not require such stability and may actively discourage it – to illustrate this rather crudely, employers do not want a labour force that will stage a sit-in when redundancy threatens.

But there is more to it than this. There are two supplementary arguments. Firstly, primary-sector employment is said to be reserved for individuals who possess 'appropriate' characteristics. The stereotyped image of a primary-sector worker is of a thirty-three-year-old white male, married with two children, who has a big mortgage on a house in a pleasant suburban area. Secondary-sector workers are filled mainly, but not exclusively, by women, ethnic-minority members and younger workers. These characteristics are thought to be those likely to accompany the type of work involvement that back-street employers seek. Secondly, however, segmentalists hold that primary-sector work should reinforce desired personal behaviour patterns and in many workers lead to a sense of commitment, of identification with the firm.

Because they adopt the employer's framework of interpretation, committed workers are easier to manage. They take the initiative, solve problems as they arise without waiting to check their solution with a manager. They get on with their work, not necessarily at a frantic pace but steadily. They do not take days off just because they 'feel off'. They turn up at work on time and they stay there until the end of the work-period. They will stay on after the end of the work-period too, when asked to do so, or even, in a few cases, because they feel they should.

Primary-sector firms thus cream off the highest quality labour. Here, however, 'quality' does not refer to technical competence, or not to that alone. Rather, as Blackburn and Mann put it in their study of the labour market in a British town, employers offering 'primary' type advantages are less interested about the *ability* of their workforce than about its *stability* – that is, its regularity in attendance, its timekeeping and its turnover-rate, which they hope to keep low in order to minimize training costs.[9]

There are some details that we have ignored that might be significant for sociological research. For example, an important strand in the explanation for the growth of the ILM is that training is increasingly firm-specific. Thus employers seek to prevent turnover by tying workers to the firm with 'golden chains', to spread average training costs as low as they can. Stable workers can also absorb training from co-workers, and a steady induction into higher level tasks and responsibilities. These are just hypotheses – the segmentalists are very short on organized empirical data to substantiate their claims – but they seem plausible enough to be worth testing whenever data are collected.

Likewise, there are some criticisms of segmentalism by economists that could be important for economic sociology. For instance, Althauser and Kalleberg have pointed out that the segmentalists have never spelled out the relationship between segmented markets and economic sectors.[10] But the following remarks are made from the point of view of a sociologist of work.

Firstly, if labour markets are becoming more differentiated then the character of the socio-economic system is undergoing an important modification and sociologists of work cannot afford to ignore whatever ways are suggested for understanding this change, which could significantly affect work behaviour. We must look very closely at this work for what it can give us. Some of the ideas outlined above are clearly as original for sociologists as they have been for economists.

However, we should not have unreal expectations. Clearly, some of the ground covered by segmentalist theory is similar to that dealt with by sociologists of work. If we think in terms of the five dimensions of control outlined in the Introduction, the segmentalist contribution is mainly in the area of the conditions of employment, though it also says something about work operations and their design. When we turn to work done by sociologists on employment structures we find a mass of theorization, especially about bureaucratic forms of employment relationship.[11] In many of these, there is a distinct social-psychological bias. Thus, a stress on (probable) structural economic factors provides a welcome and long overdue counterbalance.

When it comes to exploring the subtler aspects of organizational attachment, I do not think the segmentalist work has yet anything to offer which compares with the statements to be found in any handbook of organization theory. Why should it have any? It is not its purpose to generate such ideas. What is perhaps regrettable is how little of this work the segmentalists are, apparently, aware of. The same comment applies to their account of how structures of control develop and change. There must be, I would have thought, many ideas in classic studies of changes in forms of control in work organizations – for example, in Gouldner's *Patterns of Industrial Bureaucracy*,[12] or in Burns and Stalker's *The Management of Innovation*[13] – that the segmentalists would find valuable. Occasionally, segmentalists make it sound as though they were inventing the field already well filled with such studies. This is irritating because unnecessary duplication should be avoided.

Other aspects of the perspective need clarifying. There was originally a tendency for segmentalists to project an image of employers as rational and omnipotent controllers of their environment that was reminiscent of Braverman. Later, as they took account of the fact that some segmental features are produced through trade-union pressure, they began to provide an antidote to the superbosses assumptions in degradation theory. But the break has never been complete.

It is, of course, quite clear, and always has been, I think, that it is inconsistent to hold the full version of the degradation theory at the same time as a segmentalist perspective. For Braverman, the drive towards degradation is comprehensive: capital sets its scientific managers to rationalize all types of work. At the heart of the segmentalist perspective is the claim that any such campaign operates highly selectively. Segmentalism also makes the assumption that employers are politically motivated to *divide and rule* the working class by reinforcing sectionalist tendencies in the labour movement: this policy allegedly operates not only in a general way, through the creation of primary and secondary sectors, but within organizations.

In a politically radical mode, some segmentalists can make almost as much use of Marxist vocabulary as does Braverman. They also have their roots in the protest peak radicalism. In many eyes, including those of several of its adherents, the whole political economy movement was virtually synonymous with a Marxist political commitment. As noted with regard to Braverman, to utilize Marxian categories does not automatically indicate adoption of a position that is either intellectually or politically consistent with that of Marxism. I am not sure how important such a point is nowadays, when so much of the dust of old ideological battles has settled. But it is worth getting the record straight.

Let us note just a couple of points. It may be, as Blackburn and Mann suggest,[14] that individual capitalist employers exploit chances to create divisions between worker groups in their plants as these occur. But any opportunist and surreptitious wedge-driving of this sort is a very different process from the strategic planning and implementation of a campaign of division by capitalists as a *class*. No convincing evidence for such a campaign is available. It would be far truer to Marxian theory at least to portray division as an unforeseen consequence of the development of the forces of production, which constantly adds new elements to the labour force, thus maintaining its heterogeneity.

And the term 'maintaining' in that last sentence has been put there deliberately, to drive home a further point these authors make. Marx may have believed that a homogeneous proletariat would be produced by capitalist development, but he never claimed that it actually existed, either objectively or in terms of consciousness. Professional Marxist revolutionaries have been seeking it ever since, unsuccessfully. It is thus incorrect to talk as if, at some point in the past, a unified, homogeneous proletariat existed. This is sociology fiction. There never was such a class to be divided.[15] The use of Marxist terminology by some segmentalists, therefore, is uncomfortably reminiscent of the Marxizing that obstructs rather than advances understanding of the work domain. In the next chapter a specific example will be reviewed.

32

Divisions Evolve

For a sociologist of work, one of the most challenging applications of segmentalist theory was that developed by Richard Edwards in his book *The Contested Terrain*,[1] published in 1979. In it, Edwards further developed the distinction between the three major or *macro* labour markets (a two-tiered primary sector, and a homogeneous secondary sector) defined in earlier segmentalist literature. (These earlier definitions were quickly outlined in the preceding chapter, and familiarity with them will have to be assumed here.) Edwards linked each one of them to a particular form or *system of management control* and a characteristic type of organization of industry. On this basic framework he proceeded to draw an ambitious, even grandiose, portrayal of capitalist industrial development, including an analysis of technical invention, which, Edwards stated, could account for patterns of class consciousness, and, through them, political action in the twentieth-century USA.

A tall order, probably destined to fall short of its aims. But in doing so, it provides some instructive reading. A problem that Edwards had to face up to in his avowedly Marxist essay was the chronic disunity of the American working class. In a sense, he willed this on himself through adopting a neo-Marxist definition of the working class. In orthodox Marxism, this has always comprised manual workers. But neo-Marxist investigators were beginning to follow Eric Olin Wright in regarding all employed people except top managers as 'labour'.[2] True, this scheme of analysis does recognize *structural faults* or *divides* among labour. Indeed, these are created by the employment systems and control strategies that

Edwards claims American bosses have utilized for achieving – or, rather, for attempting to achieve – a capacity to determine the work-effort of employees.

These systems are, in order of historical appearance: (1) *simple control*; (2) *technical control*; and (3) *bureaucratic control*. Edwards recognizes also three main areas to which control applies: *direction*; *evaluation* and monitoring; and *discipline*. (The latter are not as crisply defined as they might be, but, maybe significantly, they are somewhat reminiscent of three of the four functions of foremanship set down by F. W. Taylor, see chapter 2. We shall come back to them later.)

As noted, Edwards claimed that each form of control had emerged at a definite historical moment, reflecting the needs of capital for novel control technique following the growth of organizations and changing occupational structures. *Simple control* is the easiest pattern to visualize, being based on the personal and often capricious 'bossing' of the small employer and his henchmen. Edwards tells us that it was characteristic of Victorian industry but is still to be found widely today in secondary-sector firms with their largely unskilled workforces – he labels them the 'working poor'. From the early part of the century, however, a movement arose to exert control less directly, removing the stress in personal relations and the antagonistic class-imagery experience of *simple* control created in the minds of those exposed to it.

This new technique set out to exploit the potentialities of technology as a control medium. Employers commissioned production-engineering specialists to design production-lines and machinery that would operate so as to oblige workers to keep pace with them. Tension with foremen was reduced because 'the track is boss' – as workers sometimes say in such plants. The army of semi-skilled and skilled workers subject to this 'technical' form of control constituted the *subordinate primary* labour market and in class terms form the *traditional proletariat*.

Finally, technical and white-collar grades of labour expanded, partly reflecting the spread of technical control. These employees, having a longer education, do not respond to harsh management methods. They have been controlled by the subtle pressures of *bureaucratic* rules and procedures. They thus constitute the *independent fraction* of the primary labour market and the *middle layers* of the class system.

The real world that looks back when social scientists observe it often seems hopelessly complicated and confused. We have to reduce this complexity, by finding the underlying components of society and the essential processes that are occurring under the confused surface of short-run events. Any attempt to undertake the task of reduction is laudable but one danger is that, because of the scale of the task, reduction is pressed too far. It then becomes *reductionism*. Reductionism is widespread in popularized scientific accounts, especially behavioural ones. The pattern of behaviour is simplified almost to a caricature and explained by reference to a small number of causes, or even a single one.

Edwards comes uncomfortably close to reductionism in several respects. This was less well recognized by his fellow economists than by such industrial sociologists as Roger Penn.[3] This reductionism can be illustrated by looking at the role ascribed to technology in the analysis. Edwards does not claim to have originated his view, but largely accepts the accounts of the process of technical invention under capitalism put forward by other scholars. In the main, it is a 'made-to-measure' view, which argues that the production technology used by capitalists is in essence a set of inventions customized to their control needs.

As noted, this doctrine originated with social historians like Stephen Marglin and David Noble.[4] Marglin had studied the abandonment of craft-based production and the introduction of the factory system in Britain. Why had concentration of production in larger units occurred? Not necessarily because of economies in scale or because the old division of labour was inefficient, he replied. The real motivation was the desire of employers to exert closer control over workers. In answering his own celebrated question 'What do bosses do?', Marglin gave an answer that can be summarized as: 'Capitalist bosses develop machinery and work processes linked to it in order to check workers' solidarity, even at the expense of profit.'[5]

There must be incontestable cases where this motivation has

been stronger among employers than any others, though it is not clear that they are the cases put forward by Marglin. But even when the existence of such a motivation seems likely, it is risky to assume that a suitable solution is feasible in engineering terms. The *direct* control option – to use a vocabulary we shall examine in the next chapter – might be less effective or more costly than a *responsible autonomy* alternative solution.

We know that employers pursued their control aims at an earlier period of capitalist development, and they are doing so again today by means of subcontracting. The notion of technological choice is an attractive one. Edwards's book has helped to popularize it. But it is unproven that employers have exercised choice always in the direction indicated. On the other hand, the most pressing incentive for a capitalist to seek technical innovation is to make more money by cutting costs. That at least is what most capitalists seem to think they are doing. That is what they say they are doing when you ask them, and they seem to mean what they say.

Next, while there is much evidence that smaller workplaces are less formal and run less often according to a rule-book, there is no problem finding many which are bureaucratically controlled; similarly, many large firms operate a form of paternalist control. This may not fit the template of 'simple' control, with its arbitrary and autocratic petty bossdom. But research by such investigators as Scase and Goffee shows that in Britain at least, many such firms are notable for the 'fraternalist', the genuinely or phoney 'matey', tone of relations between bosses and workers.[6] This is also one of the chief points Sabel has been making about artisan-type organization,[7] as we shall see in Chapter 36.

As the title of his book shows, Edwards recognizes the workers' will to resist employers' efforts to control them. However imperfectly, unions have expressed opposition to many of the practices and principles of capitalist business. But have unions always been tamed so readily by tough or seductive managers as he claims? Is this true even for the USA? I am sure Edwards exaggerates the extent of co-optation of unions, while overlooking the frequency with which individual groups of workers may well continue to resist control pressures by covert means.

Nor has labour been divided simply as a result of employers' action. Penn points out that the fact has to be faced that in some circumstances the labour movement becomes disunited through internal tensions that have nothing to do with employer action.[8] It is also wrong to assume that employers always welcome the friction that arises between occupational and skill groups. Indeed, the prerogatives that craft workers establish make it altogether more difficult for production managers to meet targets. That is why there now exist employer drives to establish single-status employment grades which abolish occupational distinctions, and encourage flexibility in job and task allocation.

In placing the problem of control at the centre of his analysis, Edwards overlooked the extent to which workers comply voluntarily with managerial goals. This does not mean that such workers become committed to such goals or integrated into the firm as a social system, though some may. Workers may dispute the level of effort expected of them at any one time by managers. But most do not dispute the existence of an effort *bargain*, which states an implicit moral obligation on their part to 'labour'.

In these two senses, in the recognition of the existence of a bargain and in the existence of standards applying to expected effort, workers can have a *normative rapport* with the employer. This may be fragile: normative rapport falls short of normative involvement; it is merely an agreement about how to proceed, and what action is, for the time being, fair and reasonable. But the relationship is not a purely, or even primarily, coercive, manipulative, or calculative one. Conflict over underlying interests, which may remain dormant, is paired with co-operation. In some cases, situations in which a genuine *trust relationship*, in the sense defined some years ago by Alan Fox,[9] come about. These are complexities that industrial sociologists are bound to point to when they encounter an analysis such as that offered by *The Contested Terrain*. As we have seen, there is no shortage of studies, going back over a half-century, that should have provided Edwards with the material to offer a more penetrative examination of the operation of worker-manager and union-employer relationships. If he had been able to incorporate some of these findings in that examination it would have been the better for it.

An omission that I particularly regret is a proper treatment of the fifth dimension of control in work organization, defined in the Introduction. Employers often make an effort to mould employee behaviour through altering the *interpretative frames* employees have of the employment relationship, management action, etc. It is surprising that a Marxist author should overlook the importance of ideology. But whether they see themselves as Marxist or orthodox in their approach, this is a characteristic oversight among economists. It is difficult even for recent, consciously radical, economists to recognize the *moral* aspect of control structures. These are the traditional speciality of sociology. Sociologists perhaps need also to study ways of achieving better communication with their economist colleagues, not just of findings relevant to the work they have begun in the last decade, but of elementary concepts as well.

A final remark. Edwards once set his name to this statement: 'Labor market segmentation arose and is perpetuated because it is *functional* – that is, it facilitates the operation of capitalist institutions.'[10] The word 'functional' was heavily stressed in the original. It is revealing, for this analysis is a functionalist one. In several places (the Introduction, the discussion of Touraine) I have pointed out the problems of a functionalist theory, whether it is the orthodox ('bourgeois') theory of Talcott Parsons or some of the neo-Marxist theories. Institutions and practices as they exist are attributed with functions, and it is assumed that they discharge these functions predictably, or sufficiently well to ensure continuity.

This is a teleological trap. In *The Contested Terrain* Edwards comes close to falling into it. The theoretical framework he favoured had too great an influence on what counted as evidence and how evidence was used. The investigator's assumptions were not tested by the evidence. This also threatened to negate the logic of the evolutionary theory. One characteristic of a developmental approach is that it highlights qualitative changes in social and economic life. Edwards was concerned with demonstrating capital's ability always to keep a hold on workers. He succeeds in showing the resourcefulness of large private employers as controllers at the expense of overlooking a mass of changes affecting the system and the way it is experienced by the people living under it. Surely a Marxist analysis would also distinguish a creative *dialectic* in history?

An alternative way some economists have taken in characterizing the forms of management control over labour has been to portray control as a reflection of levels of economic activity. As the next chapter argues, this brings with it the risk of putting forward a rather different kind of over-schematization.

33

Campaigning for Control

Supporters of the labour process approach (LPA) had to give way on many of the objections to the degradation thesis listed in chapter 30. Undogmatic Marxists like the social anthropologist Michael Burawoy (whose contribution will be examined more fully later) and the economist Andrew Friedman pointed out that Braverman equated all capitalist management technique with Taylorism and grossly overstated the penetration of the Taylor System, or rather of versions of scientific management inspired by Taylorism. In rallying to the restricted diffusion view of scientific management, they improved on ideas Braverman had introduced, or which can be clearly read between the lines of his polemic. Of these, the most contentious was that of *strategy*.

Before examining how the strategy concept has been used in the LPA, some further comment on the penetration of Taylorism is worthwhile, since it bears closely on the question of employer strategies. The first edition of this book claimed, as against Braverman, that Taylorism achieved its greatest impact not as an integrated set of production techniques that successfully ousted traditional methods, but as an ideology for professional engineers and modernizing managers. In this new edition I have further underlined its attractions as a doctrine sustaining *productivism* – that is, the conviction that the overriding business of life is to produce more goods more efficiently – and that both right-wing and left-wing radical technocrats have been inspired by it, albeit for different reasons.

But in other respects, the Taylor System, whether in the integral version which Taylor himself regarded as indispensable to its success, or in its modified forms, had been adopted only very patchily even in the USA by 1930, and, after that, was restricted mainly to sweatshops utilizing piece-rates. In this sense, as a productivist programme for industry facilitated by the consensus of a Mental Revolution, Taylorism failed and failed abysmally.

As an implicit theory of industrial behaviour – always the main concern of this book – its inadequacies were apparent right from the start, and became dramatically visible whenever managers were reckless enough to model workplace regimes closely in line with it. In this sense too, Taylorism failed. As we saw in Part III, psychological research from an early date began to disprove, in controlled laboratory experiments, its mechanistic view of effort and fatigue, and this process of disconfirmation was accelerated by field studies from the mid 1920s. Scientifically, the image of the workers as a greedy robot was shown to be trash. Yet again, Taylorism failed.

Craig Littler, a British colleague resident in Australia in the 1980s, objected to these conclusions some time ago.[1] It was, he objected, misleading to state that scientific management, or even Taylorism more narrowly, had failed. Rather, revised or negotiated versions of the system continued to be adopted at an increasing tempo and in a greater range of industries in the 1920s and 1930s. In particular, Littler pointed out, piece-rate methods allied to time-and-motion studies like the Bedaux System, on which he had undertaken a research project,[2] were popular with managers in the interwar period.

While some of this is a tenable argument, the evidence hardly shows that neo-Taylorite methods penetrated very widely in countries like Britain, whose employers had ignored Taylorism proper before 1914. A popular history of Britain in the 1930s estimates that 240 firms were operating mass-production methods along scientific management lines, notably the Bedaux System,[3] towards the end of the decade. Two hundred and forty cases adds up to only a tiny minority of all manufacturing firms operating in Britain at the time. Paul Thompson concludes otherwise in his persuasively restated case for a degradationist position.[4] He must have overlooked the statistics for the base population of eligible firms.

Littler's argument did not take up the point – in my own case it was the main one, for others it might be less important – that the utility of the greedy robot image of the worker was undermined in the interwar period as its scientific emptiness was, albeit imperfectly, documented in the laboratories and field tests carried out by the human factor psychologists discussed in Part II, and, after the Western Electric studies, in factories too. It is no doubt correct and significant that this kind of regime was imposed mainly in newly established plants producing goods designed to be mass-produced on assembly-lines. But to call it 'neo-Taylorism' begs a number of questions, the most important of which is whether Taylorism can be reduced to subdivided work and payment by results. One of the things that is significant about such schemes is that they omitted key elements of the Taylor System as propounded by Taylor. One of the most important of these were the productivist and managerialist doctrines that cemented together the technical proposals.

It should be further noted that the introduction of these work systems in newly established plants, rather than in those already operating along traditional lines, weakens the Braverman thesis, to the extent that any degradation thus affected *jobs* not persons. This is a vital distinction that has been developed to great effect by David Lee.[5] In any case, we cannot take the heavy rationalization of one or two expanding industries as a sign that British industry adopted scientific management. Possibly for the worse, the reverse is true, as even Marxist economic historians like Eric Hobsbawm have maintained for some time when assessing early twentieth-century British economic performance.[6]

But let us suppose that the evidence indicated the existence of a growing interwar management movement, reflected in an increase in the number of attempts to organize the labour process in line with an aforethought policy – with a *strategy*. There are clearer signs of this in countries like Germany, but even in Britain, with its by then inbuilt backwardness in economic culture, we can detect a rising aspiration for management to become less of a 'guess and boss' activity, but based more closely on a systematic body of knowledge that should be transmitted in formal training courses. Though it fell a long way short of a stampede, there was a move away from amateur management in these years.

In the sense that it would reflect formally trained competence, rather than 'leadership quality' or other vague personal attributes, the reformers expected to make the management function more scientific. But this is not the same impulse as a will to adopt scientific management in the guise of Taylorism. The desire to be more rational or systematic did not automatically imply the adoption of this increasingly dated system of rationalization.

It is difficult to pin down the idea of *management strategy*, as we shall soon see. Yet it seems clear that, in any sphere of life, a strategy is a campaign plan resulting in patterned action of an unmistakable sort: namely, action that is rational in spirit, consistent over time, coherent in reconciling various aims, costed before it is undertaken, and evaluated after it has occurred. The plan of campaign may or may not embody a list of intermediate aims or subsidiary targets. But it has a definite *mission* from which such explicit goals can be deduced.

On the other hand – and to forget this is to court trouble – we cannot say a strategy exists simply because we observe that certain specific goals are pursued, and even attained, in practice. Pursuit of such goals may merely reveal behaviour built on either habit, intuition or opportunism. In other words, strategy is confirmed by demonstrating the existence of clear and rational intentions behind behaviour. An ostensibly clear and seemingly rational shape to patterns of behaviour is insufficient proof of a strategically determined orientation. Many organizations draw up plans for some aspects of their activity, and a few no doubt attempt do create comprehensive 'game plans'. But to state that any given branch of activity is strategically planned without better evidence than observed behaviour is careless.

So far so good. We agree on what a strategy is like in the abstract. Can we now pin down what a *management* strategy is like? Surely we can, without risking serious disagreement. Whatever else management may or may not be concerned with, it is always concerned with the *control* of business activity. Industrial control is concerned with the cost-effective production of goods and services. One department of strategy has to do with the development of these products, another with marketing them. But the area that is our concern here covers the control of production, and that means control of the tasks, tools, and – above all – people that are brought together in the labour process.

It will save an enormous amount of trouble in grasping what is at stake in the strategy debate if we can agree, for the moment, that control of the labour process has the five main aspects that were first sketched in the Introduction, on pages 10–12. In simplified form, these were given as: (1) the *employment* contract; (2) work *operations* and organization; (3) the *supervision* system; (4) employee *representation* arrangements; and (5) frameworks of *interpretation* held by personnel. These are the five main logical strands in the concept of control of the labour process. Logically, also, the following possibilities occur with regard to a strategic effort by an employer to exert control: (1) all five areas are covered by a campaign plan; (2) none of the five areas are affected by such a plan: (3) one or more are affected by a strategy, but one or more are not.

Additional complications are quite possible in practice. Between those areas affected by strategic management designs, the level and type of control sought may vary sharply. For example, a militantly anti-union or open-shop policy in the *representation* area may be paired with an indulgent pattern of supervision. Again, a nannying extension of the employment contract which guarantees all employees a bundle of perks, frills and fringe benefits so long as they maintain a 'deserving' loyalty to the employer may go along with a happy-go-lucky treatment of manning levels, performance standards, methods, and quality in the field of operations. Failure to specify to which areas a strategy is meant to apply has resulted in a great deal of noisy cross-purposes argument among those people who have embroiled themselves in the strategy debate. For confirmation of this, readers will need to consult the specialist literature.[7]

First, there has been the exposure of what has been called the *monism*[8] of the degradationist conception of strategy, by which is meant the habit of reducing all employer policies and management actions to a common set of simple, single-minded intentions. The original degradation thesis obviously provides the rawest example of this, with its attribution to Capital of an obsessive campaign to de-skill the craftsman. Braverman's immediate followers supplied almost equally caricatural descriptions of employers' allegedly strategic aims and intentions. To adopt the language utilized by some of them, the long-term logic of this strategy was to produce a coincidence between the *theoretical* and the *real subordination* of labour. In blunt, uncoded terms, this meant that bosses were operating a successful plan to instigate a complete system of wage-slavery in which any employed person would not possess even the capacity to imagine any other set of arrangements than the one in which they toiled and grovelled.

The first serious attempt to offer a more nuanced characterization of management strategy was made by the political economist Andrew Friedman, a young North American who had settled in Britain. As Friedman was then working within the LPA, and was a member of the Conference of Socialist Economists (see chapter 34), his readiness to attack the simplifications of Braverman's view of capital's campaign for control is all the more remarkable. This risked a charge of political treason. He also saw that industrial sociology already offered material of which political economists should take account if they are to offer a more convincing analysis of employers' behaviour.

As some observers noted, there is some similarity between Friedman's contrast between strategies of *direct control* (imposition of rigid control structures) and *responsible autonomy* (encouraging workers to police their own effort) and the dichotomy proposed by the veteran Oxford sociologist Alan Fox between *low-trust* and *high-trust* methods of control.[9] Likewise, Friedman supported his contrast by citing the accounts of scientific management and human relations provided in the first edition of this book, which, he argued could provide *ideological* support for each of these two modes of strategy.

While I have, of course, always been glad that Friedman found my material useful, I do not go along with the view that management strategy can be reduced to the simple alternatives he puts forward. In fact, nearly all the trouble with that analysis lies in the either/or nature of his model. It will not do to argue that any *dualist* view of strategy is better than Braverman's *monism*. Any pattern of control we discover in the real world has to be allocated to one or the other of just two boxes. This involves some forcing, because, as was noted above, it is vital to recognize at least five dimensions to the concept of control.

More awkwardly, any change in a pattern can only be registered as one of a move towards its opposite, or towards a more intense form of itself, which may create the illusion that there is simply a long-term oscillation between the two basic forms, which – mistakenly – can be characterized as a *cycle*. Here, there is a similarity between Friedman's and other either/or schemes. For example, the sociologist Harvey Ramsay once characterized workplace democracy in terms of 'more' or of 'less' as economic circumstances change.[10] The result he saw was a historical pattern of *cycles of control* – a curiously un-Marxist characterization because it recognizes no developmental, no *dialectical* pattern in employer–worker relations.

In his examination of British industrial history, Friedman almost followed a similar procedure, with the conceptual alternatives of his theory being shown as the empirical alternates of reality. But he broke what could have been a very obvious storyline in three interesting ways. Firstly, he perceived a long-term historical shift towards responsible autonomy. Secondly, he pointed out sharp countertrends in given trouble-prone industries, analysing the declining British motor industry in this light. As the motor industry can no longer be taken automatically either as the typical or the most important activity of industrial countries, it is mistaken to argue that the case of motor manufacturing necessarily contradicts Friedman's main conclusion.[11] Thirdly, Friedman argued that worker resistance – a better term might be recalcitrance – can successfully undermine direct-control policies. Obviously, shortage of labour strengthens the capacity of workers to do this but labour supply is not the only determinant. Tight control over some areas is expensive in management time and nervous energy. It is counter-productive for worker motivation. Factors like these grow important in those industries where products or equipment are becoming more intricate or technically complex, or where higher-quality workmanship is demanded. There appear to be more industries where such an upgrading is occurring – or at least there are more of them in industrially successful countries. Nor does such a trend exclude the possibility that control may have been *tightened* in other industries: there may be fewer industries in the middle, as it were, subject to moderately tight control.

The limitations of an either/or conceptualization of strategy are clear. If Friedman had dug a little deeper into orthodox industrial sociology he would have unearthed Gouldner's study of a gypsum mine, which contrasts patterns of what Gouldner called 'industrial bureaucracy'.[12] (Bureaucracy was a 'sunrise' topic in the early 1950s: in the late 1970s Gouldner would have talked of strategy.) Gouldner identified no less than three control patterns, which rapidly succeeded one another within a single firm as the employer sought to get a grip of a particularly obstreperous group of mine-workers. The exact characteristics of each pattern – *indulgency*, *punishment-centred*, and *representative* – do not matter here. What does, is the way that Gouldner was able to infer them from objective evidence and to establish the distinctiveness of each one. And he does this by unpacking the idea of control along lines similar to those suggested earlier.

This was the main lesson to be learned from the treatment of the strategy problem by the mid 1980s. In so far as the LPA still remained self-consciously anchored in a Marxizing political economy outlook and suspicious of orthodox ('bourgeois') industrial sociology, it seemed likely to continue to be plagued by simplifications that limited its capacity to penetrate behind the wall of everyday reality.

The main alternative to it is not one that readily fires many people with enthusiasm. Yet it has something to offer. As we saw in Part IV, sociologists once believed technology narrowly restricts choice of structures in control areas like operations, supervision, and even representation. This technological determinism was gradually discredited. It is now accepted that while technical factors set some limits on these structures, scope for real choice does arise.

In the early 1970s, J. Child argued strongly that other factors – the balance of power between groups, workplace traditions, or other local peculiarities – specific to individual firms or sites produce forms of organization different from those predicted by technology theory.[13] This does not mean that local peculiarities really determine structure. Rather, they show how far any determining factors can be stretched. This in turn suggests that, in principle, organizational designers have considerable scope to make choices, though in practice they may make them unconsciously in blind response to immediate pressures. How far this is so may vary from one country to another.

Such societal factors operate strongly in Britain. Two out of five British companies report they have no definite policy covering such a vital aspect of operations as the introduction of new technology.[14] Organizational inertia, dynamic conservatism, or other cultural factors may no doubt go some way to explaining such findings. What is clear in other studies of British work organizations is that the extent to which any one of the five main control areas is subject to strategic planning varies enormously between organizations, and within organizations over time.[15] The lesson is clear. Never assume a strategy exists until presumptive evidence is available to make it worthwhile looking for one more carefully.

The caveat is especially valid for Britain. Because of its special place in the history of capitalism, no less than for its importance in the 1980s as an economic laboratory, the relevance of New Wave thinking to British circumstances needs special examination.

34

Dividing Labour Differently in Britain

While New Wave ideas encouraged a vigorous international discussion and reinforced the welcome trend towards internationally comparative research, we can distinguish clear differences between some countries in the way the new lines of analysis developed. The British case is particularly instructive here. There are two main reasons for this. The first is an institutional one. In Britain, there already existed a particularly well implanted and internally diverse tradition of research on work and organizations. At a time of accelerated British industrial decline, British industrial sociology was going through a growth period. As the first edition of this book pointed out, this effort was not easy to characterize or sum up: in a word, it lacked shape. But there could be no doubt about the wealth of material that was being generated from the late 1950s onwards. One consequence of this was obvious. However much some British industrial sociologists admired the efforts of the American segmental theorists to broaden the conceptual base of labour economics, they were conscious from the start that the grasp of the available research material on work behaviour and industrial relations of some of these colleagues, even for the USA itself, was a modest one. For Britain, it was simply inadequate.

This brings us to the second source of difference. Britain is *different* as an industrial society. It bears, in particular, the marks of early industrialization, the priority of financial power over manufacturing, marked industrial decline, and an exceptionally powerful labour movement with its own pronounced idiosyncrasies. True enough, the British economy is subject to many processes identical or analogous to those occurring in other capitalist societies. But British societal specificity mediates in sometimes drastic ways the forms in which they actually occur. I will illustrate this distinctiveness shortly.

What was true for segmentalism applied with added force for degradation theory. Industrial sociologists, even Marxist industrial sociologists, at first treated Braverman's thesis with guarded enthusiasm. This was not simply because they were aware from the start of the simplification of historic trends in the book, at least when they were applied in a British context – and this sometimes raised the suspicion that the American evidence itself had passed under the hands of a vigorous masseur.

If Britain was different, its exceptionalism seemed to be confirmed by the turn of industrial politics. For the two or three years after 1974, Britain hardly offered a textbook instance of a country where Capital was definitively vanquishing labour. In 1970, organized labour had indirectly procured the fall of a government, and was to do so again in 1979. In 1974 it had toppled the Heath government directly. The incoming Labour government was forced to make considerable concessions to the unions in its Social Contract. Anyone with a passing knowledge of British workplaces knew that union influence over a broad range of matters, from work organization to hiring and dismissal, could be massive and exercised firmly. It was widely assumed that labour's power would be legitimized in a new set of worker-participation institutions: the Bullock Committee recommended this in early 1977. In sum, if British Capital was degrading British labour then it was doing so in a singularly indirect way.

The first real effort to get Braverman taken seriously in Britain was made by the Conference of Socialist Economists (CSE) in their journal *Capital and Class*, in 1977. This organization formed a rallying point for young radicals in all the social sciences, though economists predominated. The tone of its politics was noticeably affected at first by a Maoist tendency – that is to say, by strong support for the interpretation of Marx offered by Chairman Mao Zedong and applied, with mixed results, in China. Maoists violently loathed the USSR, and therefore all Communist parties in communion with Moscow. Mao's thought was believed to supply an alternative, coherent system of Marxist analysis and political action (*praxis*). Its main signs were an inclination towards an emphatic style of speech and a heavy use of such phrases as 'it will come as no surprise that in the Soviet Union' and 'what more could Capital ask?'

The flavour is conveyed by the keynote article, 'The Capitalist Labour Process'.[1] Written by a collective author, the Brighton Labour Process Group, it consisted largely of a synopsis of Braverman. While writing off industrial sociology – without showing much sign of familiarity with it – on the grounds that it must be ideologically unsound, these writers showed little awareness of the real complexities of work life and industrial politics. In a piece of virtuoso Marxist argumentation, Andrew Friedman put his own case for a more complex view of capitalist management strategy in the same issue.[2] A riposte, however, from the sternly academic Marxist journal *Economy and Society* was to hit the nail on the head several months later: the degradation thesis depended on an idealized and backward-looking view of skill and technical change, the journal's reviewer objected, though he stopped short of characterizing it as Proudhonian.[3]

The scent of controversy was now in the air. By late 1977, the industrial sociology section of the British Sociological Association had held a special conference on the Braverman thesis at the London School of Economics. It was a lively occasion, with the CSE belief in degradation vociferously represented. During the afternoon debate, the suggestion that Braverman had regurgitated many of the arguments put forward much earlier in France, and held an equally romantic set of illusions about pre-industrial craftsmanship, had 'Braverman's parrot' squawking.

The positions people took up at public events like this in the immediately following years were not always identical to what they were saying in private. Among sociologists, acceptance of the degradation thesis in its integral form was limited to a small but extremely dedicated network of people. Many of the others, whatever their politics, were irritated by the prospect of research and debate being dominated by 'Bravermania', and regretted that their desire to communicate better with economists might be short-circuited owing to the uncritical acceptance among the latter of a thesis they regarded as wrong and wrong-headed. Only a few relished the thought of confronting the degradationists. But it was clear that such a collision was inevitable and nobody could escape it. Whoever looked on these things as an entrepreneur would also have remarked that some academic reputations are made, and many academic books sold, thanks precisely to intellectual feuds, artificial or not, such as the one that was looming.

So it proved. Let us quickly list some important ensuing events. A research workshop on de-skilling sponsored by the Nuffield Foundation in December 1978 resulted in some forthright exchanges and helped to define new research directions. A standard collection edited by Stephen Wood, *The Degradation of Work?*,[4] arising from this first appeared in 1982. The University of Aston, which had recently been made the centre of an officially funded research programme on work organization, collaborated with the University of Manchester Institute of Science and Technology (UMIST) in establishing an annual conference on the labour process in 1983. From the start, it attracted distinguished contributors, and provided some, at times, invigorating hand-to-hand intellectual engagements – not merely between degradationists and their critics. The book *Job Redesign*, edited by Knights, Willmott and Collinson,[5] which resulted from the 1983 conference, was the first of a whole series.

A kind of *modus vivendi* with the economists was being reached by the mid 1980s. The latter had become much more interested in segmentalist ideas than in degradation. The main forum for the latter became the *Cambridge Journal of Economics*. This was based at the university's Department of Applied Economics. While its editorial board was dominated by Marxists in the early days, this review was far more exigent in its rules of evidence (and writing style) than *Capital and Class*. A team of researchers gathered around one of its editors, Frank Wilkinson, soon embarked on a programme of research notable for its strict methodology. From the late 1970s an international seminar on segmented labour markets was organized by it. Some industrial sociologists took a close interest in this work, and economists like Elizabeth Garnsey,

Jill Rubery, and Shirley Dex were for their part so thoroughly familiar with sociological work on economic life as to be considered largely transdisciplinary researchers.[6]

By the late 1980s, the term labour-process approach, though still widely used, no longer designated anything in any sense theoretically controversial or politically daring. Certainly since the early Aston–UMIST conferences, degradation theory had been largely abandoned by nearly all British researchers. There seemed to exist a reassuring capacity to continue communicating even when serious differences remained on this score. The climate never turned into one of sour distrust between a half-dozen ideologically incompatible factions, though that had seemed a real possibility in the mid 1970s. Undoubtedly one reason for this was the growing crisis in British higher education, which the Thatcher government attacked with a will from 1979 onwards. But the need to make a common front cannot alone explain the prompt manner in which New Wave thinking was assimilated in Britain.

Assimilated . . . and possibly neutered too in the process? Not really. Books such as Nichols and Armstrong's *Workers Divided* or Willis's *Learning to Labour*[7] became standard, internationally admired works, which anticipated some of the conclusions later to be urged upon American New Wave thinking by Burawoy and by Sabel respectively (see chapters 35 and 36). No one could question the commitment of either of these works. Yet both were concerned with showing how Capital evoked the assent of workers as much as with phrasing ringing condemnations of the system. This concern to explain the subtler forms of domination and exploitation of labour met a readiness on the side of more politically mainstream writers to present to readers of the textbooks they published what seemed most positive in New Wave thinking. The results can readily be inspected in such books as Stephen Hill's *Competition and Control at Work* or Tony Watson's *Sociology, Work and Industry*.[8]

As noted in an earlier chapter, both strands of the New Wave are concerned with the division of labour, and the radical forms of segmentalism attribute to employers the political motive of 'divide-and-rule'. The core idea had been developed originally in France, by de Stephanis around 1960 – it was on one of his visits that Piore, a francophile, was first inspired by it but it gained most currency thanks to Piore's own work, which was based mainly on an American experience. We need to take up once again here the question of British specificity – of whether those main lines of segmentation that exist in the British labour force have implications different from those they have in other countries for employees' working lives, and for their behaviour. To put it in a nutshell: is British labour divided differently?

As yet, there are no full comparative data which would tell us in exactly what ways, and how far, the lines of labour-market cleavage in Britain correspond with or diverge from patterns in other countries. Yet those data we have are good enough to point to clear conclusions on three or four counts.

As a backcloth to them, several points need to be remembered in the British case. To begin with, the Welfare State grew sooner and became bigger in Britain than in the USA – though not than in all continental European countries – making illness and unemployment less serious personal hazards. This left less scope for those large employers who could have done so to create an 'internal welfare state' to woo the loyalty and commitment of their workers. Again, the seller-buyer ideology was always a dominant influence in Britain over the whole vision possessed by both bosses and workers of the employment relationship.[9] Union power was trained on targets like winning higher money wages or policing work methods for those *sections* of a workforce they represented, not on exacting packages of seniority rights, promotion routes, or in-house training for a workforce *as a whole*. The quirks of occupational structure and the rivalry between unions resulting from this 'spontaneous' working-class sectionalism could obviously be exploited by employers: British engineering, Raymond Loveridge noted, rejected paternalism; its giant federated firms exemplified narrow market-based employment relationships.[10]

British variants of paternalism have been for the most part odd, unsystematic, and infused with religious ideology. Joyce chronicles the very single-minded drive among some Victorian northern mill-owners to bind their employees to the firm, morally above all.[11] This local tradition of a rather lordly concern for 'the good of our people' is evident in such cases as that examined by Martin and Fryer.[12] But only a minority of British private employers ever modelled themselves on this pattern.

Systematic paternalism did not create the ingrained deference of the British working class which historians are fond of detecting. In any case, these observers overlook that a surface 'respectfulness' often coexisted with concealed defiance. Rebellion could suddenly erupt among a paternalist's hitherto docile workforce: Lane and his colleagues describe an exemplary case.[13] In rare instances, like the Cambridge electronics workers described by Anthony Lawson,[14] a large employer could elicit a dependent attachment while withholding from his employees any primary sector advantages at all.

To sum up, native British paternalism is eccentric and has no clear link with the creation of labour segments through internal labour markets. Whether recently arrived transnational corporations, especially Japanese ones, will, at a time when welfare is being rolled back, spearhead the development of more systematic internal labour markets was still largely unforeseeable when White and Trevor undertook a survey of Japanese employers in Britain.[15]

Historically speaking, we might find clearly defined internal labour markets outside the manufacturing sector – and outside the civil service or the military. The railway companies are an obvious candidate for close examination. This is probably an academic question, in the full sense. But segmentation based on other characteristics than the employment sector is worth noting. After doing so, it will be useful to discuss some evidence on how closely the market for labour in Britain, if it does not reflect the simple play of employers' power, actually corresponds to the rational model of action held by orthodox economists.

A valuable summary treatment of this was offered in Blackburn and Mann's *The Working Class in the Labour Market*.[16] Two findings, on race and gender, stand out. First, race *per se* does not result in systematic segregation into occupations by ethnic group. Distinct immigrant groups may be concentrated in some trades or activities, partly because these trades are highly localized and the immigrants were originally recruited to staff them at a time of labour scarcity. Thus males from the Indian subcontinent constitute almost 30 per cent of employees in some textile trades. A few plants in this and other trades are virtually all-brown, and many more may be perceived as such by prejudiced locals in high-immigration areas. Yet the microstudies of individual workplaces cited by Blackburn and Mann show that ethnic concentrations of above 12 per cent of a workplace labour-force are very rare; British employers seem to have regarded this as some kind of 'safe limit' only to be exceeded at the risk of antagonizing their white British workers or some other British-born ethnic group.[17] Where immigrants can show they possess similar experience or qualifications to native-born workers they have been fairly readily recruited. Linguistic ability can, of course, be used as a pretext for exclusion in some such jobs. Nor do studies of pay show systematic discrimination in pay rates awarded and earnings made.

Most of these studies, it is worth mentioning, were undertaken before race relations legislation came into force or had been long in operation. It may be, as some claim, that the economic crisis has enabled subtler forms of illegal discrimination to be practised. Nor has there been any doubt that educational or cultural deprivation upstream of entry to the jobs market produces similar effects to some kinds of open discrimination. Again, as Mann and Blackburn show clearly, immigrants and black Britons are not promoted into supervisory positions or technical grades in anything like the numbers that they should be. But despite these facts, and others that a race relations expert could readily list, no systematic ethnic principle structures the British labour market.

Most emphatically, this cannot be said of sex. It is still possible to point to dozens of jobs that are regarded either as 'women's work' or as jobs 'only men' can do, despite legislation and slowly changing public attitudes. Where jobs are in practice equally open to both sexes, men earn significantly more, are promoted far more often, and made redundant less often and later than women co-workers. If the women's job market has been growing faster than the total job pool in recent years, that is because there has been a disproportionate growth in part-time or in *precarious* jobs, typical slump jobs that are also miserably paid.

There is something faintly archaic about the notion that to be a 'proper job' a job must be done full time. Some women prefer part-time work (the number of men who would prefer to work part-time is also persistently underestimated[18]) but women who want or need full-time work are far less likely to find it even than are men, especially if they expect similar rewards to men. Reports in the 1980s[19] did little to brighten the sombre picture offered by Blackburn and Mann, though observers like Rosemary Crompton pointed out oncoming breakthroughs for women in some professional or technical occupations.[20]

Blackburn's and Mann's own immensely detailed study of a local labour market supplied striking case material on this issue. This is what they say:

> We note that in the town of Peterborough [site of their inquiry] occupational segregation is virtually complete – men and women are almost never interchangeable as individuals in the manual labour market. Of course sexual discrimination is too obvious really to need specialized sociological investigation. It is so uniform that *everyone knows* [emphasis in original] that women are rarely allowed to do men's jobs, and where they are they are paid less, that their shifts are restricted, that they are rarely allowed to supervise men.[21]

If orthodox economic theory is correct, then the British labour market was failing to allocate resources of inherent skill and aptitude as between the sexes in a rational way. But was the market even functioning rationally in allocating the labour of semi-skilled *male* workers? This set of employees made up the core of the working class until recently. Special study of the behaviour of men in it was still well justified in the mid-1970s.

None of 951 currently employed men interviewed in Peterborough had an employer with an internal labour market neatly fitting the textbook model. Nor were tasks or responsibilities tailored by work designers to call for abilities narrowly specific to given employers, thus cutting down workers' scope for moving away to other jobs. On the contrary, the most striking feature of these jobs was their underlying similarity. This could be shown objectively. All jobs at every workplace were rated on each of a set of thirty-one technical and other characteristics. This showed that *nine out of ten* of these workers had virtually interchangeable jobs, nearly all equally devoid of real skill – on the same measures of skill, over ninety per cent of men exercised more skill in driving to work than they needed to expend once they arrived at the workplace.

Some employers might have questioned the extent of this interchangeability or whether only low-level skill was developed. One in eight of the sample, after all, *had* acquired some real skill through experience at work, not through apprenticeship. Employers offered promotion to such tasks. But these ladders were ill-defined, and so were selection procedures. A large element of chance governed an upward move to a better job inside a firm. This points to the prevalence of a slip-shod folk-method for developing competence and loyalty, not any kind of strategic manpower policy. In some British firms, managers may disguise archaic practice in an up-to-date business school rhetoric. Many Peterborough employers talked of their search for 'worker quality' in recruitment and promotion, as if they had genuine strategies for adding to their *human capital*. Blackburn and Mann comment:

> However, when we investigated what they meant by this [worker quality], we found that they were worried not by intelligence or manual dexterity, but about *worker co-operation* [stress in original]. Responsibility, stability, trustworthiness – such are the qualities by which (reasonably enough) they wish to select and promote. From the employer's point of view, the internal labour market allows workers to demonstrate these qualities (if they have them) over a period of years before they reach jobs where mistakes would matter.[22]

Now although these authors rightly pointed out that this emphasis on *stability* rather than *ability* gives the segmental theorists, especially the more radical ones like Richard Edwards, the edge over human capital theorists in exposing the underlying process of allocation, it takes the eye of segmentalist faith to spot here any skilfully rationalized management strategy for provoking division and nurturing loyalty. What we have, rather, is an *unsystematized* policy, leading to a pattern of management action which employees must often experience as capricious, since rules are not clear and can be changed at will to suit circumstances or 'personalities'.

In other words, it was to be seen as an extemporized, pragmatic form of organization and style of management action. It was hard to resist the conclusion that just as British industrialists had generally fallen behind their foreign counterparts in developing new products or introducing new technology they had also failed to rationalize their internal supplies of labour and of loyalty. What certainly becomes clear in the light of cross-national comparison of internal labour markets in Western European countries, such as that undertaken by Loveridge or by Child and his associates,[23] is that in Britain occupational groups, mobilized by competing unions, have had a much greater effect on the ability of management to organize internal labour markets according to their own view of rationality.

This is not the place to prolong such reflections. Rather, I think it is appropriate to close this chapter with a few final comments about the issue of segmentation by gender in Britain. As noted, Blackburn and Mann confirmed its rigidity in their local labour market. There are other peculiarities of female employment in Britain. In particular, there is a particularly high incidence of part-time women's work in Britain compared to the USA and other European countries.[24] One reason for this is the lack of official nursery provision or the award of tax relief for the payment of childcare. But there is no mistaking the historic trend towards greater female participation in the labour market, which is now over 60 per cent of women of working age. (Men's participation has fallen modestly.)

It has to be acknowledged that the issue of gender was not taken seriously by sociologists until the 1970s, and has still to make a proper impact on economists. True enough, women worker groups have often been studied by industrial sociologists. But *gender* as an explanatory variable or as a set of *theoretical* problems has until lately been largely ignored. Many of the groups studied by the human factor researchers (see Part II) were women. Several of the experimental groups studied by the Western Electric researchers were all-women. Generalizations about 'the worker' were derived from these studies. Yet, for most social scientists, like most members of the public, 'the worker' has usually conjured up the image of a male manual worker with a home-making wife. We cannot regard the treatment of the women-worker studies as the product of an unconsciously – and laudably – non-sexist form of analysis. It occurred by default. From the vantage point of the present it comes over, at best, as sloppy and naïve.

Parts of the separatist wing of the feminist movement, which regards women as subject to quite distinct motivations from those that they see as affecting men, would prefer to build an entirely distinct social science of women and work. Most feminists do not subscribe to this extreme view. The relationship of some women to the work domain is no doubt utterly unlike that of many males. But it seems reasonable to suppose that, just as we know the approach to work of males varies enormously from one class or occupation to another, so will that of women also. Between some groups of males and females there will be considerable overlaps.

But this is only to consider the most elementary aspect of the problem. To unpack, or, to use the right technical term, to disaggregate the concept of the worker does little more than remove a certain absurdity from our mental set. But it does permit us to get closer to the real problems. Let us take one of the simpler ones. We know that the so-called *traditional household* – a wage-earning male with a dependent housekeeping wife – used to be the most common form of household by far. Nowadays, there is a wider spread of domestic circumstances. In many households, more than one member is in paid employment. There is an interaction between the broad economic behaviour of cohabiting couples especially. They often arrive at agreements about their respective work involvement through a process of negotiation. These couples are, in effect, inventing new social structure. This adds enormous difficulty to dealing with the question of what the role of women is in contemporary economic life. Simultaneously we are asking about the role of men, too.

Numerous writers have now grappled with these issues. If one British treatment is to be singled out for its contribution to defining the new problematics of gender emerging in the 1980s then it should be Shirley Dex's *The Sexual Division of Work*.[25] Dex brought an exceptional combination of qualities to her task. Though her background was in economics, she not only recognized the importance of social factors but utilized existing material on gender in the sociology of work with shrewd discrimination, combining it with recent economic research and a creatively feminist critique. She went beyond registering yet another call for a conceptual revolution in economic sociology but actually tried to show where progress could be made.

The limits she came up against were similar to those confronting people dealing with different problems. Presenting evidence for the USA and Britain, she noted the marked societal differences between women's economic roles in the two countries, but decided that any satisfying explanation for them was beyond the scope of her review.[26] To stress the primary importance of societal factors was perceptive. Any sexual division of labour is strongly affected by them. A shorthand way of accounting for this is to put the peculiarities down to the effect of national culture. But in one sense the peculiarities *are* the culture: they are what makes a society distinctive.

Yet there are several sets of objective factors which can help us to define societal specificity in socio-economic organization. I shall review some of them more fully in the final chapter of the book. One of them derives from previous economic development: which industries have been important, where they were located, and how organizers sought to marshal competence and effort. Another is the role in economic life taken by the state. The political power of the nation-state has been largely concerned with regulating the economy, either directly or indirectly. The way in which this may affect gender at work is illustrated most dramatically during the two world wars – and in their sequel, too, when Rosie the Riveter was usually encouraged to rediscover her 'natural place' behind the kitchen sink.

True enough, the nation-state, especially in Western Europe, is in decline. British women have felt the effects of this through the imposition of European laws on equality of treatment in employment. They at least have been benefited by the erosion of British sovereignty movingly bewailed by old male politicians. But the effects of national specificity in the economic domain will be perpetuated for the foreseeable future. It is clear that national individuality in social structure and in value systems bearing on the sexual division of labour interacts closely with special features of economic organization in any historic industrial country. We need to understand British individualism in this sphere, and its causes, much better than we have done to date. Indeed, only then will we be able to come to more valid conclusions about the general, or universal features of economic life.

This selective review of the impact in Britain of the segmented labour market approach shows how rapidly new thinking has been assimilated and developed. A rapid internationalization of debates in the social sciences occurred in the 1970s and 1980s. The special conditions of a country can none the less affect the way concepts and theories are understood or developed. American industrial relations law and practice, for example, have strongly encouraged the spread of segmented labour markets, and bureaucratic employment rules in large American firms. British Institutions make for a more intricate pattern. Similar comments apply to the subject of the next chapter.

35

Saying Yes to the System

Numerous books on work were published around 1980 whose titles rang the changes around the concept of *division*.[1] Then a rival trend set in more recently making equal play on the term *consent*. As we saw in the foregoing chapters, many segmentalists seem to hold the view, which they often characterize as Marxist, that control must normally be *imposed* on workers. Thus subdivided tasks, bureaucratic rules, and tough supervision, in various blends, govern relations at the point of production. Strategies for control within the workplace are reinforced by a wider ideological campaign mounted on behalf of capitalist employers by the state and the media.[2]

Evidence of such activities can always be produced. Other, more complex material can be accommodated in this theoretical mould without squeaking. But some data cannot, and these may be overlooked. I do mean *overlooked*, of course. We are talking about the effect of adopting an inadequate perspective, not of deliberate suppression. Theories often trick the people who hold them. One class of data that has habitually been overlooked by political economists bears on the way workers as persons *experience* the employment relationship and the wages–effort bargain. What we know of this subjective consciousness suggests that most workers accept their situation in the capitalist economic system, where 'accept' means something between grudgingly acquiesce and keenly consent to it.

Raising this problem of consent leads straight towards aspects of motivation and awareness with which a resolutely materialist approach to behaviour has enormous trouble dealing. Defining an ideology, mapping a social doctrine, exploring the contours of collectively held imagery – the task of capturing frameworks of interpretation requires not just a recognition of the importance of symbols, values, and mind-pictures in human life but patience, sensitivity, and vigilant scepticism. It should come as no surprise, then, that the way such frames underpin involvement in work has in the USA been most thoroughly – and brilliantly – explored not by an East Coast political economist but by a globe-trotting social anthropologist.

I have decided to discuss the work of Michael Burawoy in this Part because he sees himself as contributing to a radical political economy of contemporary capitalism mainly by complementing segmentalist theory. In fact, he presents his work as establishing a 'reverse problematic' for these fields. But I am not sure it is right to pigeonhole him in this school of thought. To be candid, it is increasingly difficult to view his intellectual and value position as in any way commensurate with that of the segmentalists. I will go further. His work is a refreshing antidote to the ingrained dogmatism and schematization of some segmentalist theory.

However, Burawoy does not lack competent and vocal critics. For example, the British LPA writer Paul Thompson devotes a very substantial fraction of his *The Nature of Work* to a critique of Burawoy's position, and I suggest readers consult Thompson's spirited but thoughtful commentary as an antidote to what is said here.[3]

An intriguing current in contemporary Marxism – and the capital 'm' is justified because it has directly influenced the behaviour of the Italian Communist Party – is that arising from the doctrines of Antonio Gramsci (1891–1937). Gramsci is noteworthy on at least two counts: first, as a keen exponent of *modernism*, even the modernism of the Ford assembly-line; and secondly, for the stress he placed on the importance for radical politics of winning the ideological commanding heights, or *hegemony*.

Gramsci was surely correct about the importance of winning hearts and minds. Capitalism is not simply a crude system of domination. It has an elaborate framework of organized meanings, ways of looking at the world, conventional attitudes, preferred modes of thought, and subtle justifications. These meanings can permeate the consciousness of workers – sometimes more thoroughly than they can that of well-educated sons and daughters of the bourgeoisie. Many of them are deeply enough embedded to seem beyond doubt to any sane individual. To put it another way, they make up a substantial portion of everyday common-sense thinking, of the feelings of 'normal people', and of most of what politicians call 'our cherished beliefs'.

To sound an early note of caution, we must never overstate the degree of acceptance, by any group of people, of any such framework of meaning. But unless we recognize its influence, some aspects of workers' compliance with an employer's demands seem puzzlingly aberrant. Burawoy's aim is to show, however, something more than the influence *on* work behaviour of capitalist hegemony. He wishes to demonstrate that workplace behaviour itself generates and maintains submission to hegemony. This is a tall order. And to anticipate one conclusion, I do not think he has succeeded in doing so for work in general. But it is an instructive failure.

After anthropological research in the central African copper belt, Burawoy, who is a British citizen, went to do a doctoral project in the sociology of work in Chicago. Searching for an appropriate plant to study, he reports that he stumbled on the very metal-cutting factory where Donald Roy undertook his classic studies of 'making-out' in piece-work (see p. 158f). His book *Manufacturing Consent*[4] embodies his main findings – empirically, they were strikingly similar to those Roy reported thirty years earlier. But it is most stimulating for his contentious interpretation of them.

Like Roy before him, Burawoy was struck by the ability of the piece-workers at the Geer factory to convert the apparently tedious challenge of *making-out* – reaching an output target necessary to earn a bonus – into an exciting game. He soon found himself experiencing the work in a similar way. The interaction between workers promoted by these output games was increased by other forms of horseplay and by joking rituals. The close workplace culture, with games as its backbone of activities, was facilitated by management, who operated an indulgent pattern of supervision, which ran to connivance in various production fiddles.

What have we here? Jolly tribesmen in overalls? No. The surface mateyness of the workplace culture disguised a deeply ingrained individualism, Burawoy argues. His reasoning here recalls another remarkable Gramscist study of the late 1970s, Paul Willis's *Learning to Labour*, which plots the economic socialization of youths from the deprived end of the British working class.[5] Underlying the solidarity of the youths' delinquency, their taste for turning everything into 'a laugh', all their racist and sexist hee-hawing, was a squarely individualistic view of work as a place for proving their personal identity and masculinity, for showing they could 'take it' and bring back money to the household. In acting out what they took to be their freedom from the conventional school world, with its despised lefty teachers and bookish, middle-class swots, they were grooming themselves in the most narrowing core-values of the system.

Of the function of work-games, Burawoy writes: 'One cannot play a game and question the rules at the same time; consent to rules becomes consent to capitalist production.'[6] Now of course, the games we are talking about here are not games in the same sense as beach cricket or shove ha'penny. They *are* about making work more interesting but more fundamentally they are about making the pressure to make money more interesting. In a tough urban-American context, making a living is a particularly isolated act. The workplace culture of Geer, which deflected conflict with management into conflict with fellow workers, clearly supplied a set of values that were at the same time useful for survival in that milieu and likely to make the Geer workers more loyal to capitalism in so far as capitalism means beady-eyed individualism.

There is an obvious objection to this claim. The behaviour patterns of Geer operatives, as reported, do not seem to me to demonstrate any obvious general *consent* to capitalist or any other economic values if the term is meant to carry positive force and not simply mean *compliance*. We are bound to go along with Burawoy's opinion on this matter since he must have come to know his informants thoroughly enough to have insight into their most strongly held values. But proof we do not have – at least, *Manufacturing Consent* does not provide it. What we have is a plausible series of extrapolations. This becomes important when we consider the broader question of *commitment* to work in recent times. But there is a point which needs making first.

In 1961 Dennis Wrong wrote a classic article called 'The Oversocialized Conception of Man'[7] which attacked the sociological theory of Talcott Parsons. Simplified, Parsons's doctrine is that we learn our society's core-values as children and this socialization process results in our not only becoming familiar with moral codes and normative standards of behaviour but in wishing to adhere to them. But, complained Wrong, modern societies have competing sets of values, the socialization process is incompletely achieved, and much action is manifestly produced by pressures from other people, financial need or economic bait, the law, and other factors that are not moral or normative. Following Parsons, it is hard to account for social change, except as the doing of misfits or wreckers.

Wrong was right. Some behaviour is produced by values, but not all behaviour. One of the tasks of the sociologist is to determine such questions empirically for named groups of people in named societies at a given point in time. There is an evident quasi-Parsonian bias in Burawoy's application of the notion of capitalist hegemony. Even if their work experiences do tend to implant – or, more likely, reinforce – free market thinking and ideals among the Geer workers, we have no reason, on the evidence to hand, to conclude that it is those perspectives and values as such which mainly determine their behaviour and attitudes.

Let us return to the problem of consent. I made the point earlier that while Burawoy shows a high degree of *compliance* with managers' aims and own attributed values, this does not prove consent to these frameworks in the sense of personal *commitment*. Now in fact we know that a crisis of workers' commitment occurred in the 1970s, being signalled by the kind of events and behaviour – the revolt against work – discussed in the introduction to Part VI (see pp. 307–11). Many American commentators saw this revolt as a rejection of traditional economic values, notably those of the work ethic, thought necessary for dynamizing a capitalist economy.

I have examined this moral panic elsewhere, concluding that commentators usually overstate the role of economic values in work discipline and productivity.[8] But there *is* evidence of a real change in work involvement and commitment, and a large part of this change *can* be put down to a shift in economic mentality in the labour forces of advanced societies in recent years. The value-change can best be thought of as a move away from some characteristically bourgeois values, notably the readiness to save up money (*deferred gratification*) or the belief that work is the main business of life for the male (*work-centredness*), which marked an earlier phase of capitalist development. Patterns such as the 'hedonist' readiness to prefer leisure to work, the ecology-minded suspicion of the cult of economic growth at all costs (*anti-productivism*), or the suspicion of anyone claiming to wield authority, have also strengthened.

These changes have not affected all sections of the working population equally. Their incidence varies somewhat from one advanced country to another. It is just possible – though most unlikely – that the changes merely reflect attitudes learnt in the Growth Era and thus may be merely a passing event, historically speaking. But for the foreseeable future they will continue to affect the ways in which managers can manage, and even, since some managers are themselves affected by them, the ways in which managers are prepared to manage. The post-bourgeois attitude is hostile to impersonality, the sense of being utilized purely as an instrument or a resource, and to any form of autocratic direction or supervision.

In that sense, it is incompatible with the experience of capitalist exploitation in its traditional raw form. But otherwise, it is not inconsistent with strong *abstract* support for capitalism as an economic system and the presumed buttress of political democracy. The inference to be drawn is clear. Management structures and personnel policies will need to become far more subtle if they are to motivate employees to adequate levels. For reasons including greater product and service complexity or the spread of 'high-tech peril', which cannot be explored here, employers will have a rising need to elicit positive commitment from their workers. How far this can be done through shaping the activities of the workplace is thus becoming a crucial management question.

Whether Burawoy's book will figure prominently on business-school reading-lists, because it is thought to give a reassuring answer, is anybody's guess! It is coy about predicting how managers might try to modify task-structures and control methods in order to exploit post-bourgeois attitudes. But the question is worth raising, and it seems to me that there is only one avenue that they will find it worthwhile to explore for such a purpose, and that is the one defined in the mid 1970s by the QWL movement (see pp. 245–8). Critics of QWL like Ivar Berg are probably correct in judging that, so far, it has served mainly as a prop to managerial legitimacy without producing many tangible changes in compliance or productivity.[9] It is also possible that wider management support for QWL would enhance the pull on employees of new values.[10]

If a pattern of activities at work can produce a significantly closer identification by workers with the system as a whole, then it probably does so mainly in this way: namely, via gain in the prestige of workplace managers thanks to their sponsorship of work-practices more closely in line with the expectations and values people already hold. Experience of being managed in a preferred way may enhance support for the wider system.

But this can occur only when managers explicitly make the link between the *implied culture* of workplace experience and the core economic values of the capitalist system in its contemporary, post-bourgeois, guise. Burawoy's notion that face-to-face *activities* create loyalty to broader economic values is one that I join his harshest critics in rejecting. It reminds me uncomfortably of the old applied anthropologists, whose nonsensical doctrines – how much you like a person depends on how often he grabs hold of your hand and shakes it, but not vice versa.[11]

More recently, Burawoy states a belief that there is now occurring what amounts to a worldwide campaign by employers to constrain the consent of workers. A new, 'despotic' version of the 'hegemonic' control pattern[12] he found at Geer was emerging in the early 1980s. In *The Politics of Production*,[13] he contrasts this with earlier types of *factory regime* thrown up by interacting workplace struggles and government policies – the core of his politics of production. Despite its ugly-sounding name, *hegemonic despotism* is not an arbitrary tyranny like Victorian paternalist despotism, but under it, workforces that formerly gained concessions from employers were being forced to hand them back under the threat of job losses or close-downs.[14]

There was no shortage in the 1980s of examples to fit this model, certainly in Britain: British Leyland, British Steel, British Coal. Yet here is an immediate difficulty. It is not just that these were nationalized firms: the more important fact is that they operated in smokestack or metal-bashing branches that were experiencing difficulties throughout industry. The record of a boss like Michael Edwardes at British Leyland or Ian MacGregor in the other two undertakings could be described as despotic – in fact, some would say the term is too mild – but there has not occurred any *general* adoption of such methods in any other industry except newspapers, though political support for a more widespread employers' offensive would be forthcoming.

Better evidence for such a general campaign exists in the USA and in France. But even in those countries, the picture is a variegated one. In every country, we find an astonishing range of employer policies for coping with the new economy and the new work culture. Rather than knowing where they want to go, most employers are dithering. Burawoy could just as well have pointed to the alteration of the employment relationship towards a 'Californian' pattern, i.e. personalized and brittle, or a Japanese one that is formalized and stable. He could also remember that managers vary from one country to another, and one industry to another within countries, in their readiness to act as despots. For that matter, equally fortunately for workers, their native ability or acquired competence to act as despots varies too. It needs to be borne in mind, however, that Burawoy is concerned with manufacturing industry, with factories, and factories in the more threatened branches of manufacture. He has not attempted to talk about what experiences the workers may have outside these workplaces. In that sense, there is sometimes, in reading his work, a curious sense that we have come across some of this before. And so we have. It is appropriate that his best-known study should have been undertaken in Chicago, before his move to the West Coast. It was here after all, as we saw in chapter 14, that W. F. Whyte, another brilliant anthropologist, whose own early work stressed the role of games in integrating groups, developed one of the most distinguished strands of research in the human relations tradition.

Rather different resonances are given out by the work to be reviewed in the next chapter.

36

The Artisans are Coming Back

Despite their common aim of clarifying the capitalist division of labour there had always been a severe tension between the degradation thesis in its integral version and segmentation theory. The central claim of segmentalists is that employers deliberately *preserve* a hierarchy of job-quality, in order to divide and rule the working class. Some New Wave investigators managed to overlook this inconsistency or stressed the overlap of the two problematics in their belief that capital always knows what it wants, knows how to get it, and then gets it.

In Charles Sabel's first book, *Work and Politics* (1982), he attacked the idea that the labour force has ever been shaped passively by capital.[1] Rather, groups of workers possess differing wants and expectations, which are socially distributed according to their position in an overall division of labour. Managers, he agreed, in building task-structures and systems of work discipline, may play on the cleavages that result in the working class. But these job-structures are dynamic or, at least, potentially so; workers may seek to freeze them in a form they find advantageous.

This sounds rather like standard industrial sociology, drawing on Michel Crozier's notion of *bounded rationality*.[2] But there was a surprise in store. When, in their daily routine dealings with plant managers, worker groups resist the control exerted over them, they alter the picture both they and their managers hold of their relationship, generating new aims on both sides and new methods of pursuing them. Work is inherently political – that too sounds like Crozier – but the political struggle is partly determined by the alteration of frameworks of interpretation. Though he is not a

Marxist, Sabel thus makes use of two Marxist notions conspicuously absent from the work of some writers regarded as Marxists – notably Richard Edwards, see chapter 32 – that of *consciousness*, and that of *dialectic*.

Forms of collaboration in production also express past struggles and point to new lines of cleavage. These may reach relative stability in some communities, yielding a subculture which is passed on to the next generation. This is clearly a very different evaluation of the relative importance of community factors from that of Michael Burawoy (see chapter 35). Overall, the employment relationship and shop-floor relations are many-sided, tied to a place, yet fluid. What counts is exactly how that context is structured.

This way of seeing things simultaneously challenged standard perspectives in both segmentalism and labour-process theory. Sabel was able to do this precisely because he took note of standard literature in industrial sociology. (Compare his bibliography with the lists of works cited by the two other political economists whose work has been reviewed in depth in earlier chapters.) Most political economists seem to have been unaware of it. We have already touched elsewhere on one feature of the segmentalist description of the employment relationship. The stress on the supposed significance of hierarchical sets of job titles, pay, security, prescribed work content, and mobility prospects amounts in effect to a rediscovery of *industrial bureaucracy*.

Utilizing a new range of terms, the segmentalists have partly redescribed, but mainly relabelled, many structures and processes extensively mapped by organizational sociologists over the last forty or so years. This striking duplication needs no further comment. But it is easier to understand the irritation some sociologists feel when political economists lecture them on the importance of understanding the formal internal structure of work organizations.

Segmentalism and orthodox organizational sociology likewise share a stress on the capacity of Capital (as segmentalists would say) or organizational controllers (as organization theorists would) to shape as it pleases the internal environment of firms. The important historical dimension of Sabel's book helped throw more doubt on this assumption. Here, it converged with a critique mounted against labour-process theory by sociologists of work who had been reacting against 'Bravermania', and was to lead in a very fruitful direction, as we have seen in chapter 32, by focusing upon the concept of *strategies of control*.

First it is necessary to say something more about the implications of *Work and Politics* for the labour-process approach. It is this. Although the book further discredited the Braverman thesis, it plainly drew some of its great energy from a sympathy with Braverman's *values*. This is most clear in discussion of artisanal work.

Though the book reworked a mass of published findings from economics to social history as well industrial sociology, it also incorporated findings from Sabel's own case-study work on what has come to be termed the Emilian model of neo-industrialism. In the little towns inland from the northern Adriatic coast of Italy, a host of small manufacturing firms specializing in high-quality, small-volume runs of products sprang up in the early 1970s. Some were started, ironically enough, by militant trade unionists thrown out of the large factories in the northern Italian industrial towns like Turin. Moreover, these entrepreneurs were given strong support by local authorities that more often than not were dominated by left-wing political parties. Operated by proprietors who themselves worked alongside maybe a half-dozen, rarely more than two dozen, employees, many of them close friends or family members, and using the most modern equipment the artisan-entrepreneur could afford, these new plants – often occupying part of the artisan-entrepreneur's own home – heralded, Sabel declared, a prototypical *high technology cottage industry*. Yes, he agreed, some were sweatshops. But the majority he eulogized:

> If you had thought so long about Rousseau's artisan clockmakers at Neuchatel or Marx's idea of labor as joyful, self-creative association that you had begun to doubt their possibility, then you might, watching these craftsmen at work, forgive yourself the sudden conviction that something more utopian than the present factory system is practical after all.[3]

Sabel recognized that some of these firms led an extremely precarious existence. That is a feature of such artisanal organization. But, he observed, it is reassuring that types of artisanal firm that we think of as having been destroyed by the mass-production regimes can none the less continue under modern conditions.

With an Italian colleague, Sebastiano Brusco, Sabel had identified three types of artisanal production in contemporary Italy. The *traditional artisan* firm, to be found in towns like Puglia or Sardegna, continued to produce speciality goods for a local market. In the shadow of the giant car factories and chemical plants of Lombardy and Piedmont, *dependent decentralized* firms were to be found living off the giant firms – subject to them in many respects, but with the chance in some cases of making the transition to what the authors depict not just as the most modern kind of artisan firm, but one that is perhaps prototypical of a future neo-industrial revival. This *independent decentralized* firm, common in the vicinity of Bologna, is remarkable for its ability to control some of its customers, because '. . . it invents new needs and satisfies them at the same time. The secret of this trick lies in the particulars of the firm's internal organization, its close relations with its clients and its collaboration with other firms in the sector'.[4]

In the mid 1980s, Sabel collaborated with Michael Piore – Piore had supervised some of Sabel's graduate work – on an ambitious international review of the possibilities for neo-industrialism based on the Emilian model. It is interesting to observe the intellectual shift involved for Piore. Though the book was entitled *The New Industrial Divide*,[5] it undertook a revision of segmentalism that explicitly severed the former link with Marxist class analysis, substituting an explicit stress on the *moral* as well as social and economic superiority of craft culture: we shall come back to this Proudhonian emphasis.

Work and Politics had questioned whether Fordist mass-production methods ever possessed the economic advantages claimed for them, suggesting that over the long term their effects on labour quality and worker commitment were self-defeating. This attack was renewed with added zip in *The Second Industrial Divide*. The corporate giants, the authors note, have been seeking new methods of control, through smaller units, 'intrapreneurship', worker involvement, and experiments in work enrichment. Equally important, decentralization and flexibility are demanded by emerging patterns of consumer demand. High-spending young consumers in advanced countries demand products that are, or that appear, crafted and customized, and these Yuppies are increasingly emulated by other groups. This imposes rapid changes in styling, increasing technical sophistication, and high-quality finish. Such products by definition are not made in mass-production factories.

This was a fascinating piece of reasoning, mixing cultural insight with economics. Their argument even incorporates a sociology of technical knowledge. This is woven around a lively attack on technological determinism in management thought and production-engineering practice. The mass-production factory became the model for industrial development between 1860 and 1960, they allege, although its universal superiority had never been demonstrated. These were not the infinitely resourceful engineer bosses of Marglin's, Braverman's, or Noble's account, but ordinary men who accepted without blinking an eyelid what they were taught in the technical institute. Engineers and managers propagated a production engineering orthodoxies whose real strength was their ability to drill the technologist's mind until it could roll down only the approved tramines. In other words, much of such knowledge was *normative* not technical.

Thus, new ways of organizing were ignored though they had always been technically possible. Such arguments have been familiar enough to industrial sociologists since the first Tavistock mining studies were reported almost forty years ago (see chapter 17). It is eloquent of the failure of sociologists of work to communicate such ideas among their economist colleagues that Sabel and Piore need to document their case so carefully.

Their analysis of the work reform or QWL movement is equally interesting. Acknowledging that QWL experiments sometimes aim to smash union power, they reject the idea – hitherto often held by radical political economists – that QWL is a new version of Mayoite manipulation and ideology, and nothing more than that.

On the contrary, they claim, where experiments have proceeded successfully they do break barriers between narrow labour segments in large firms. This raises the possibility that new forms of solidarity may replace tight segment loyalties. I am convinced that this courageous judgement is essentially correct. The work-reform movement, though no doubt it has some dubious operators in its midst, has been propagating and reinforcing new values about work which will help to alter its culture – albeit very slowly. In any case, the organizational changes of QWL schemes also presage the emergence of the new, post-Fordist economy. In this economy, Piore and Sabel predict, mass-production will be largely displaced by *flexible specialization* – small, high-tech units able to switch rapidly from one customized product to another. These units will be operated by versatile, or *polyvalent*, workers capable of managing their own work. The resulting broader socio-economic organization they label *yeoman democracy*, because assets would be operated in conjunction with the state or local community. (The state might meet start-up costs and retain ownership of some of the plant; it would supply specialist advisory and training services, just as it does already for farmers.) The authors term this a republic of small-holders; Proudhon termed his Utopia the Workshop Republic.

These claims must be tested by time. Nor is there space here to pursue some obvious questions: is the portrait that of a genuinely resurgent craft culture, or of the revival of primitive capitalist rugged individualism? Wasn't there always an ambiguity in the very notion of craft culture, meaning at one time a concern with skill and quality of output, and at another the restrictive regulation of work by craft members? Such questions ought to provoke controversy and new research. Irrespective of the soundness of the verdicts and accuracy of the book's projections, it condenses many of the debates of the last decade into a new set of issues. It should contribute to a more constructive collaboration between economists and sociologists in the study of the new forms of economic life that are emerging in the advanced societies.

From the viewpoint of industrial sociology, the authors performed one very signal service by clarifying and putting into perspective the debates on segmentalism and the labour process that were discussed above. At times, these had produced some very schematic and doctrinaire work. In moving away from strictly economic categories, political economists have often done so, lacking adequate awareness of existing sociological findings. Alternatively, they have made use of such findings in an *ad hoc* manner, without any feel for the concepts underlying them.

For their part, sociologists excited by segmentalist findings have concluded, prematurely, that they have gained comprehensive understanding of how the modern capitalist economy is structured and operates, when what they have really acquired is merely a glimpse of the outlines of a novel and unproven paradigm. Many of the unanswered questions raised by it are, as we have seen, sociological. Yet the urgency of dealing with such issues fades away once the sociologist has fooled himself into believing that the factors that really count are to do with economic structure. The extra-economic pretensions of the political economists, then, have been matched by an amateurishly self-confident economic reductionism among some sociologists.

On the issue of the future of craft labour, the treatment here deals a double blow to the Marxizing simplifications of degradation theory. Firstly, the degradation thesis is inverted without committing the authors to acceptance of the facile formulas of human capital theory. Moreover, workers and unions, they show, can take positive steps to extend job quality: they need not wait for Capital to do them any favours. Secondly, the spuriousness of the Marxism in labour-process analysis becomes apparent: however many deep red stickers are pinned on it, Braverman's approach is governed down to its smallest details by a conspicuously Proudhonian world-view and value system. It is the height of irony that Proudhon's ideas, so poorly known outside Latin countries, should have spread so widely in the English-speaking world in the last decade, masquerading as those of his old arch-enemy!

What, however, does this book suggest will be the most productive area for collaboration between the disciplines that study work? This is answered in the limitations of the treatment itself. The greatest of these is apparent enough: Piore and Sabel recognize different patterns in the handling of economic change between countries, and explicitly compare moves in five of them towards *flexible specialization.* In the comparative sections, they point out the role of societally specific factors in shaping the course of organizational innovation. In this sense, their analysis is carefully linked to given places and given groups of persons.

These then are the economists with whom sociologists should have no trouble in beginning a more constructive dialogue. And they point towards some of the questions that should come high on the agenda for inquiry, collaborative or not, in the years until the turn of the century. We shall take that question up again after a few final comments on the New Wave studies of production and its social concomitants.

37

In the Wake of the New Wave

Around 1985, a critical attitude towards New Wave theories such as those reviewed was setting in. Orthodox industrial sociologists had for years been overawed by the sheer volume of New Wave output, and the insistent way in which some of the new voices talked to win arguments. On all sides, people had at first identified the New Wave with the labour-process approach, and the latter with the ideas of Harry Braverman. I hope this Part has at least provided a corrective to the latter misunderstanding. Criticism is of course due and to be expected at this stage in the life-cycle of these theories but it should be properly targeted. It would be regrettable if the reaction against the New Wave, however understandable, were to obliterate most of its positive achievements. Let me remind readers what I see them as being.

First, it restated the ideal of an integrated theory of economic life and work behaviour. It is to be deplored that academic social science runs along disciplinary and departmental lines. There are numerous explanations for this. The most creditable, and credible, is that specialization improves the quality of research and teaching. But this often results in specialists who have an intense knowledge of insignificant problems.

In fact, academic boundaries have far too much to do with a quasi-feudal power game in which existing fiefdoms and baronies in universities are utilized as bases for extending influence, and ferociously defended from what are seen as the attacks of 'rival subjects'. As noted at many points in this book, the no-go line between economics and sociology – and the common condescension of politics specialists who mutter about protecting the 'queen of the social sciences' from contamination by these allegedly lower-order disciplines – are to be particularly deplored. By reaffirming the interdisciplinary credo of classical political economy, New Wave theorists gave all the specialisms concerned with economic life a shot in the arm.

Next, the New Wave added to the agenda of questions on which useful research could be done. True, the prominence of the degradation problematic, which as we saw merely duplicated work done by Georges Friedmann in particular, might seem to offset any other gains in this area. But even there, once it had been accepted that there was no simple, unilinear trend of the kind Braverman had so boldly traced, curiosity about the historical record and future trends in key occupations was increased. If we take craft engineering work – selected by Braverman as the exemplar and prototype of the degradation and proletarianization of skilled workers – the historical work of Roger Penn on Victorian engineers and of Bryn Jones on the contemporary impact of computer-controlled machine tools gains added topicality.[1]

A strong case can be made out for a third contribution of the New Wave, though perhaps I am not the best person to make it. Here, I am thinking of the value, for some people, of simply being confronted, at certain moments, with a viewpoint that is stated forcefully. To be challenged with a set of new ideas, or even when they are old ideas expressed in novel language, can have a very tonic effect on the sense of purpose both of those who accept them and of those who are sceptical of them or who consider their empirical grounding insufficient.

Those enthusiasts of the New Wave who insisted that its ideas should not be rejected simply because conventional empirical backing for them might be inadequate, in this light, need to be judged more sympathetically than they have been by their more traditionally minded colleagues, who write them off as incompetent or naïve. Sure enough, some of them could be merely an annoyance when they set about the task of stimulation. After all, there is a difference between challenging people with new ideas and belabouring them with them. They were liable to forget also that many of their colleagues like to think of themselves as self-starters so far as intellectual stimulation goes. Some of their more reserved admirers did not appreciate being bombarded with a stream of what often seemed just new words, anyway, not new ideas, by people who lacked information on the topics on which they were claiming to be experts. It occasionally gave them the unpleasant feeling of being patronized by morons.

But in one respect there can be no doubt whatsoever that the New Wave initiated a debate that should prove valuable far beyond the empirical controversies about trends in control patterns, employer strategies, and work-tasks, which it has excited. This relates to the balance between Marxian and Proudhonian themes and perspectives in the more radical versions of the work reform movement. We have, as I noted earlier, experienced the strangest of flesh and blood ironies in that people whose declared or apparent political commitment was frequently explicitly Marxist have, in effect, been advocating a position championed by Marx's most important rival as guru to the nineteenth-century labour movement. This peculiar aberration occurred, I believe, not simply because Proudhon's ideas are so poorly known in the English-speaking world but because changes in the modern political economy are reviving the topicality of some of the issues that fired these writers.

There is a final contribution of the New Wave that I wish to mention. It is more important than all of the preceding ones. But it will be best to come to it only after summarizing what I see as the failings frequently met in work of this kind. I do not propose to dwell on them, however, as they have already been noted in individual chapters, and it is important to remember that most of its critics would regard the achievements of the New Wave work as positive all round.

I have already noted what might be called its *confirmation bias* in many places. The early Braverman devotees exemplified this in their apparently in-built ability to assimilate only that evidence which confirmed the picture of long-term workforce de-skilling. Those whose interest in radical political economy was not merely political were far less likely to disregard or massage counter-evidence. But on all sides there was a tendency to treat disagreement as equivalent to bad faith or as the sign of a politically reactionary value position. And this merged with a similar trait, a tendency to stress the political implications of some finding or conclusion, which was habitually done in places that were inappropriate for communicating such explicit opinions, or, much more embarrasingly, when there was no need to do so because the political implications were obvious. The subculture of the New Wave, it has to be said, discouraged subtlety in such matters, just as it virtually tabooed lightheartedness even out of business hours.

It has always been baffling, though, that one of the most commonly advocated political conclusions was of the resilience and resourcefulness of the capitalist system. To Capital was attributed a quite extraordinary ability to recognize its interests and act to achieve them. You could put the suggestion to a New Wave devotee that if Capital was quite so clever and well organized as some New Wave analysis declared, then one astute move would be to recruit precisely such experts as themselves to disguise pro-system propaganda as table-thumping critique. Any suggestion that a Marxist vocabulary might be utilized to demonstrate not just the political irrelevance of Marxism but the impossibility of any radical change always caused offence. Of course, if New Wave theories *did* constitute an ideological danger to capitalism, we would have to abandon the image of Capital as all-knowing and all-controlling.

This is not the place to become embroiled in another of the interminable arguments between different interpretations of Marx, but what is striking about the version ostensibly held by many New Wave writers is their apparent foreclosure of the possibility of significant social change. Yet we have been living at a time when capitalism has been undergoing substantial changes, some of which have greatly modified the forms taken by the employment relationship and authority patterns. For every New Wave investigator capable of exploring imaginatively the possible consequences of this there have been five incapable of doing anything but repeating a new schematic orthodoxy in which occasions for significant change in the system are treated as rare and peripheral.

One reason for this stress on the containment of change no doubt lies in the social and political climate of the hangover years following the growth era. Depressions conservatize radical thought, just as the growth years artificially sustained neo-revolutionary theories like the new working-class hypothesis (see chapter 22) and put worker's participation and self-management on to the political agenda. But we would do well to remember that some of the changes in social relations and values at that time are still at work because they were not simply a reflection of prosperity but had a deeper structural cause.[2] While change following the old scenarios must now be excluded, it is wrong to assume that almost all change must.

There is another problem, which has to do with mental sets and paradigms of knowledge. Several influential New Wave writers have a technical training in standard economics. As somebody who has undergone such a training, I can testify that one result is an in-built reflex to reduce the complexity of real economic life to a set of models and formulae. It is then an easily taken step to regarding what does and can occur in the real world as equally axiomatic, equally schematized. To rectify this bias requires very deliberate effort. Such trained minds find everyday life implausibly complete.

Those two or three New Wave figures whose work is outstandingly interesting either lack this background or have complemented it with wide reading in orthodox industrial sociology – Michael Piore even presents the interesting case of an economist who appears to have become acquainted with such material only after developing his theory of the internal labour market. I find his more recent work far more impressive than his earlier output as a way of describing and explaining work behaviour and its context. There is a visible cleavage, also, among the *Cambridge Journal* economists between those who know the industrial sociology most relevant to their interests and those who do not. The work of the latter lacks verisimilitude beside that of the former, but for all I know it may be better economics, technically speaking.

This unfamiliarity with material directly relevant to what they were trying to talk about – and sometimes this material anticipated their conclusions – becomes lamentable, and made some followers of the New Wave appear simultaneously objectionable and ludicrous, when it was paired with a self-confident mishandling of what are low-level sociological problems. For example, group behaviour would be regarded automatically as a product of the play of material incentives, not, in part at least, of moral pressures: for such economists, a *norm* meant nothing more than an output target in a Soviet factory. Fortunately, however, we are talking about only a fringe here, and it is appropriate at this moment to revert to the credit column.

By far the greatest single service done by the New Wave is its insistence on situating particular phenomena within an overall model of the economic system, and one that is seen as developing along a traceable historical path. Agreement on a single model of the system, and certainly on crucial details of any given model, has always been lacking within the New Wave itself. Most New Wave models I find biased towards a minimalist, not to say reductionist, account of capitalism as a system which understates the cleavages and contradictions within it. I likewise consider some of its historical generalizations too schematic, or based on an overselective use of evidence. Both the models and the histories, nevertheless, have an incitative value: they encourage constructive argument and new investigations. They serve also as a reminder that treatment even of very narrow technical questions – rates of absenteeism, the award of fringe benefits, provision of childminding services – always embody assumptions about these overall or *macro* properties of the system and its history. Far too often industrial sociologists and psychologists have ignored these matters or discounted their relevance. Unconsciously held assumptions about such them have as a result biassed the work of some of them. In other cases, they have missed opportunities to give their work added significance. We have seen that what made the work of such investigators as Eli Chinoy (see chapter 22) or W. Lloyd Warner (see chapter 14) outstanding for its time, and led each of them to write a classic, was just such an awareness of the influence of system and history.

Anyone who thinks about such questions can set themselves the task of writing what they hope will be the definitive history of that aspect of economic life that concerns them most. Or, taking up the system issue, they can attempt to produce what might be the definitive account of employment relationships based on the wages–effort bargain. However, they ought to take two things seriously into account. Firstly, the reasons for which any history is written change, and they do so in line with the interests and world-view of key groups. Secondly, accumulated change itself alters the exact nature of a system and relationships within it: it thus alters the key groups. For these reasons, it may be impossible to envisage *definitive* treatments of such questions. On the other hand, societies face a range of problems, which alters with time.

In the economic sphere, these problems are not only the obvious ones of employment and industrial structure, but also of how problems are themselves conceived, and indeed, of what constitutes a *problem*. Here, there is a rough parallel between the material infrastructure of the economy – the division of employment between sectors, the strength of a given branch of production, the location of workplaces and markets, etc. – and the theories we have about these structures. The material structures change, often barely perceptibly, occasionally very fast. Our mental infrastructure, our theories, interpretations, doctrines, and ideologies about them can change more slowly than does the material infrastructure. By this, I do not mean that our stock of facts about them is necessarily out of date but our way of interpreting those facts may well be; and we often collect the wrong facts, anyway, because we have never thought hard enough about what facts we most need.

Social and economic inquiry undertaken in line with the time-bound way of looking at things has no pretensions to offering definitive accounts or final answers. It is merely concerned with choosing the most relevant questions for the period of historic time being lived through, and examining these in the most penetrating way, with regard to the material and moral needs of one's society at the given *historic moment*.

Much of New Wave research can be looked on as an indirect corroboration of this perspective. This is paradoxical, since some of its exponents may have aimed to produce definitive theories, or to sound as if they were doing so. But their most instructive, and creditable, failure has been precisely here. If some of them had been better aware of work done previously by industrial sociologists, they might never have pursued aims of comprehensiveness and universalism that are intrinsically over-ambitious. By the same token, outstanding New Wave contributors quite obviously have read more widely in economic sociology and harbour fewer grandiose ideas.

Yet most earlier industrial sociology was also locked into a perspective that limited its contribution to well below what it could have been. By its tendency to take the economic system, and its history, as given facts, and thus to view the future, in so far as it was ever concerned with the future, as a prolongation of the trends recognized in conventional thinking, it could not deal as penetratively as it should have done with many of the issues which arose in the world of work in the period after 1965. That is one reason for the rise and success of the New Wave writers. The culmination of the post-Second World War boom in a strike wave and change in work-values was exactly the opposite of what was predicted by such wider theories as orthodox economic sociologists utilized.

However, I do not wish to minimize the achievements of earlier approaches to industrial behaviour. It should be clear that they provide, at the very least, an immensely rich stock of information about how economic life was lived throughout the twentieth century. We discover, in the literature, descriptions of situations and events that resemble, closely or otherwise, most of those that can be found in workplaces today. We are in no way bound to accept the interpretations put on these observations by the investigators who reported them but we should try to develop understanding of how the investigators arrived at their interpretations. In this way we not only learn something important about the past, but something immediately relevant for understanding the present better.

This book is now nearing its close. In it, my overriding aim has been to encourage precisely such an appreciation. I have, I think, used some fairly plain words at times to describe what seem to be lapses in research procedure, naïveté in interpretation, or bias in theory. But I hope I have never been dismissive about any work plainly undertaken in good faith, although I may be appalled by it. The record that has been presented may have its piebald stretches but even these can be instructive and surprising. I wish to state again the view put forward in the Introduction that the interpretative frameworks created in social science do not simply change randomly between a limited number of possible views. A qualitative alteration towards more sophistication can and does occur, however slowly, and despite temporary regressions. Critique like that offered here aids that process. It is impossible to predict what kinds of interpretative ideas will be influential in ten years' time. But I think it is worthwhile trying to suggest which ones *ought* to be influential.

At the very least, some open debate on this question is always necessary. This branch of social science is more closely connected than are many with policy questions in organizations and political issues in public life. Researchers and their assistants, teachers and their students, cannot live in an ivory tower. But those who wish to minimize their involvement in such matters must still cope with pressures from those who take a different view. The *purists'* best answer to these *interventionists* is to be certain of what they are doing and why it is important to be doing it. They have a right to put the interventions themselves under exactly such an obligation too.

For such reasons as these, we have to discuss what to do next and how to set about doing it. The last chapter will contribute to this effort by being relatively prescriptive. In it, I shall present a case for a particular emphasis in research and theory, which can be labelled the *historic societal* approach. But I wish to make it clear that I am not putting forward an approach I regard, in any sense, as definitive. The historic societal approach is intended to help define a way of trying to understand economic life over the next twenty years or so of development in the more advanced societies. It is less concerned with the eternal than with the *interim* aspects of economic life in a societal whole. It falls squarely within Type III theory as defined in the Introduction.

Space to justify it adequately is not available here. All the same, it will be clear that some of its elements have been suggested by the material covered in this last Part, as well as by one or two of the classic studies reviewed earlier. In recent years, there have been a number of other studies, which so far have been neglected as pointers to the way ahead in the next couple of decades. I shall back up my case by referring to these studies, which I consider good illustrations of the points I am trying to make, in a necessarily rather selective way.

CONCLUSION

38

Nations, Work and History

I ended the Introduction by noting that inquiry into any aspect of human behaviour should be *penetrating*. To be penetrating means more than being able to get beyond the surface appearances of behaviour. We have now seen how language itself, including the language of social science, and sets of received ideas can mask the meaning of a pattern of work behaviour. The approach also should be *relevant*, that is, an aid to mastering the economic process in ways that most benefit the greatest number of people.

These requirements sound reasonable enough. But applying them raises problems. Much hinges on the definition of relevance. Judgements of relevance ultimately depend on ideals and values. Part of the public responsibility of the researcher is to put current debates about social values into perspective. How closely do values recommended to people in fact correspond with the aspirations that people have, or with ambitions they could pursue with hope of success? Answers to such questions can be provided, at least partly, in the light of available evidence. They may reflect the observer's values, it is true, but they do not need to do *just* that.

For example, any explanation of work behaviour that takes account of the influence of gender is more relevant than one that fails to do so. This is not because most women have a feminist attitude about employment. Very few do, though many women are now aware of these ideals. But, in every advanced economy, a growing number of women seek paid employment. Many are far better qualified to do certain jobs than some men now doing them. More of the highly qualified women are developing the aspiration to move into those jobs. That aim is realistic in some occupations, but not in others, however well qualified the excluded women are.

These are facts. We can grasp them without sharing feminist ideals. If better-qualified women were to take over such jobs, resulting in their competence being fully used, an overall gain would occur to the economy. Women who are excluded from these jobs, when they are competent to do them, have an obvious grievance. The rest of us share that grievance, however, in the sense that we must, as a community, pay for sex discrimination in lost output. Some feminists complain that capitalism exploits women by pushing them into low-grade work. Wrong. The real problem is, in a sense, one of *under*-exploitation.

Observers may have strong personal feelings on an issue such as this. Some male observers might consciously suppress or hide them – or try to do so. Some women might openly declare the feminist ideal, but mis-state their observations, thanks to the understandable strength with which they hold it. More worryingly, though, a few observers are unaware or uncritical of the effect on their work of their social prejudices and political tastes. This book supplies many examples of the lapses which result from this naïveté. But, however strong their values, irrespective of how aware of them they are, most observers would have to agree on the present priority of gender questions in the study of work-behaviour. They have gained the highest relevance. In accounting for this, real events 'out there' are as important as the personal values of social radicals who are appalled by sex discrimination, and social reactionaries who want to 'protect' women by sending them back into the home.

Some particular questions – unemployment, the effects of automation, the growth of a career orientation among women – are obviously important everywhere. However, the *context* in which priority issues are investigated can alter the way in which they are treated. Context – special features of place, space, or culture – has often been overlooked by social scientists. Sociologists have often been addicted to producing conclusions or *models* that, supposedly, are good for all times and all places.

When the issue of Third World economic development became urgent after the Second World War, the experts, economists and sociologists alike, at first worked with a model of development based on ideas about *natural stages* of economic growth. Later, a model of *pluralistic industrialization* replaced it. Though this model listed six alternative paths to industrialism, these were based on historic cases – England, Japan, the USSR, etc. Theorists of industrialism or development in more recent years have been far more careful to delimit their conclusions as to time and place. Consider two examples.

Ronald Dore's *British Factory, Japanese Factory*, a report of the mid 1970s, was based on case studies of large firms manufacturing washing-machines. Each employer was fairly typical of the large-firm employment sector in each country.[1] Dore builds up a characterization of the employment relationship and industrial relations in each country on this basis. People have quibbled over some details of his portrayal of these institutions but his contrast between an employment relationship based in Britain on the *individualistic labour market* and in Japan on a *mutual lifetime commitment* is argued convincingly. So is his contrast between the logic of industrial relations – adversarial, fragmented, preoccupied with pay rates in Britain; collaborative, company-based, concerned largely with fringe benefits in Japan. In any case, the precision of his observation is not important here.

A second example, drawn from the political economy tradition, is *Unions, Change and Crisis*, by Peter Lange, George Ross and Maurizzo Vanicelli of the Harvard Centre for European Studies.[2] The Harvard team compare French and Italian trade unions as political actors in the period 1945–80. Once, industrial sociologists and political theorists lumped together the French and Italian trade-union movements as instances of a southern European pattern: internally divided, ideological, given to abrupt spasms of rebellion, and low in membership. In the period examined, large parts of the French movement continued to support a *maximalist* strategy of sudden radical political change, while the Italian unions became increasingly *interventionist*, that is, ready to collaborate with the State and employers if they were granted at least some key demands. Close similarities between these movements existed in 1945. By 1980 they had almost disappeared.

Most social scientists feel such comparisons are uniquely informative. And they are. But why? It is not for the local colour that they can introduce into what might otherwise be much duller books. To be sure, it is easier to picture Dore's blue-overalled English Electric workers with their shop stewards and tea-breaks when they are set beside their sprucely uniformed, company-song singing opposite numbers from Hitachi. In the Harvard Team book, we can get a better sense of events in the long hot autumn of 1969 in Italy because it contrasts with the national strike in France in May and June 1968. But by focusing on local peculiarities we may conclude there is no common denominator at all between such cases.

It is tempting to account for the worker–large firm relationship in Japan as an updated form of the Japanese version of the feudal relationship between a patron and his client. The client might even be adopted as the son of a childless patron in Japan. Perhaps the employer and the worker are bound by a similar moral and emotional bond? Could that be why the employer rarely sacks a worker, or will pay him according to his age and family circumstances not his effort, promote him for length of service not merit, and otherwise repeatedly cross the logic of capitalist market relations? At the same time, it may be that the honour of being engaged by a prestigious firm is such that the employee feels overwhelmed with a sense of moral obligation to return good service.

Some such values and perspectives, no doubt, powerfully affect behaviour. There may come a point, too, when an attempt to account for an institution or a pattern of action in other terms than culture reaches a dead end. That is the moment to start examining cultural peculiarities. Dore by no means ignores Japanese culture and history but he never assumes that national difference can be explained *only* by the oddities of national culture. To do so is to adopt a circular form of reasoning. We end by saying: Japanese firms developed differently because they were Japanese; Italian unions adopted interventionism because they were Italian. Culturalism decays rapidly into explanation by means of the inspired tautology. (There is a parallel here, at the societal level, with the interactionism of the Chicago branch of human relations, or the subjectivist sociology of organizations examined in chapter 27.)

Because of their convenience, culturalist explanations are often used as a substitute for institutional analysis. In many British workplaces, the relations between managers and workers have certain properties – a forced affability, an ironic use of terms like 'squire', a sort of familiarity at a safe distance – which seem peculiarly British, or maybe we should say English. In fact, these patterns can be defined and subjected to a culture-free analysis in terms of the elements of submissiveness (*deference*) and conflict (*defiance*) involved in them.

There is another common form of culturalism. Many of us believe there exists a typical personality structure for every society – or, anyway, a typical social actor who has characteristic ways of thinking, viewing situations, and responding. Entire national institutional complexes, including political culture, have been explained – or rather, explained *away* – by referring to *national character*. It is foolish to deny that everyday national stereotypes – the Hardworking German, the Go-Getting American, etc. – lack *any* basis but any such national character may be more the product of institutions, than the reverse.

Within any society, organizers assume they must handle persons of one type more often than any other. They build control structures accordingly. These structures may then actually begin *producing* people of the expected type. At the same time, the industrial workplace also has disseminated a culture that has some similar properties wherever industrialism is adopted. National personality types have to adapt to it.

But institutions themselves are not produced by a *modal personality* or a *typical social actor*. Rather, insitutions are produced by groups of men and women trying to collaborate with one another. The solutions these real people, acting in real historical circumstances, arrive at can, of course, have a long-term effect on personality. But it is *institutions* – stable complexes of rules about correct ways of behaving – that are the real immediate reproductive agency of culture. Social and economic institutions are themselves created by forces we still cannot delineate fully. But it is not difficult to see some ways in which they operate. The historic development of economic life in any nation-state provides a mass of informative clues to the structure of its institutional DNA.

Dore's account combines analysis of economic and institutional history. As the first nation to undergo capitalist industrialization, he contends, Britain saddled itself with a model for the employment relationship, and with sets of industrial relations practices, that reflected the toughness and short-sightedness of the primitive capitalist economy. Later industrializing countries often tried to bypass its uglier ('English') sides by planning industrial development and adopting enlightened social policies. The circumstances in which they arrived at the threshold of industrialization were vital for their success in so doing. Japan was – and is – a homogeneous, very stable society; the *samurai* warrior élite, who had seized power in the last quarter of the nineteenth century determined to adopt Western technology, but to keep at arm's length the social and political practices of Western bourgeois society, was overthrown at the end of the Second World War.

The Harvard Team's approach lays much more stress than Dore's on political events. Patterns of economic development in the post 1945 period in their two countries differed greatly. In Italy an already glaring inequality between the north and south of the country was accentuated, resulting in a tidal wave of migration towards the northern industrial cities. Union leaders set out to fight for very different benefits from those sought by their French counterparts. They behaved entirely differently towards their members as a result. When strong shop-floor movements, in which southern immigrant workers figured prominently, sprang up in the giant northern factories, Italian union leaders encouraged this local activism, while putting a great stress on member education and after-work social activity.

Similar movements in French plants were suppressed by the largest French union confederation. Yet it continued to call for a revolution that meant little to a growing number of workers. The Italian movement had a growing membership it could control through persuasion. It could bargain therefore with the State for general advantages. Many large French unions could not adopt this strategy, even if they had wanted to, because they had antagonized so many potential members.

History and politics within the context of the *nation-state* thus modify, imperceptibly much of the time, now and then abruptly, the institutions through which behaviour is shaped. True enough, the fundamental economic system, the *market* economy of capitalism or the *command* economy of State socialism does create some similarity between the institutions and the way of life of those societies grouped into each system. But what is instructive is not this similarity, which is so general we can only talk about it in clichés: the challenging task is to characterize and interpret what is specific about the institutions a society develops.

At the risk of being dangerously misleading, let me point out an analogy between institutions and technology. The institutions of economic life incorporate a social technology, a set of 'transmission-belts', 'presses', 'moulds', and even 'production-lines'. It is no accident that we actually do use such terms in everyday life. Just as productive technology can be developed and applied in more than one way, so may institutions. The existence of the principle of technological choice certainly does not mean that choices are actually made consciously. We are often not aware of alternatives, or we do not allow ourselves to consider them. Similarly, institutional solutions may develop in an adventitious, 'just-happened-that-way' fashion.

They *may* do so. But, since its historical rise, the nation-state has striven to select, or at least to shape, its economic institutions and practices. A centralized government and national law, backed by a massive bureaucracy, enabled the State to enact the general will of the nation as the latter was interpreted by politicians and their advisers. In doing so, countries often acquired institutions produced by accident when bold experiments went wrong. Such unintended results add to national peculiarities. In practice, too, national governments always had less, much less, sovereignty over the economy than they thought they had, and the historic nation-states of Western Europe have been losing still more economic independence since 1945. But this erosion *increases* the need to situate (or, to use the correct technicality, to *locate*) an analysis of work behaviour within a national context. I shall come back to this point briefly before closing.

The cases examined by Dore and by the Harvard team are excellent illustrations of how a *societal* perspective clarifies analysis, irrespective of whether some statements made by the authors in their analysis are justifiable. The same goes for the next example, which takes us still closer towards the approach we should endorse.

This is a comparison of the structure of firms in France and West Germany undertaken by the Aix Group (Marc Maurice, François Sellier, and Jean-Jacques Silvestre) mentioned towards the close of chapter 21. Two features of the Aix version of *societalism* (as the group term their approach) make it exceptionally interesting. Firstly, it has been worked on by a group of collaborating economists and sociologists. Secondly, it is highly theory-conscious as well as being based on well-designed fieldwork. Lengthier examinations of the societalist approach to economic life are available elsewhere;[3] only a sketch of the Aix analysis is necessary here. (Since 1986, a translation of the main Aix work, *The Social Foundations of Industrial Power*[4] has been available and this is indispensable for fuller study of the societalist problematic.)

When people attempt to control organizations, what, essentially, are they trying to do? What blocks their aims? In making control their main problem, the Aix researchers follow many other recent investigators. In manufacturing industry, control should have the overriding aim of ensuring that goods are produced economically. Control techniques *may* also have the aim of subduing workers' resistance, or wooing them into a positive feeling about the workplace. What most affects the *shape* and complexity of control systems, is not such 'commitment', or the general willingness to accept industrial discipline, but the mix of *competence* – real skills not paper ones – available to production managers. The stock of skills, training and qualifications puts strict limits on how a work process is designed, supervised and operated.

A low-skilled workforce needs closer supervision, even if composed of workers eager to co-operate with management. Newly recruited cabbage-patch workforces may be respectful towards anybody in authority, but they are also notorious for their two-thumbed hands. Any untrained, barely competent workforce may rapidly increase its productivity if set to work on simplified, repetitive tasks. But Taylorized work calls for elaborate back-up services and staff, increasing bureaucracy, paperwork, and supervision. Moreover, early rapid gains in productivity tail off as workers react against tasks well below their potential abilities.

Training provision can thus become a battlefield in the politics of the workplace, but technical training is organized very differently from one country to another; and these training systems are likely to produce, within each country, conventional recipes for utilizing the stockpile of competence and capturing a measure of employee commitment. Inevitably this produces very different ways of organizing workplace control systems. The Aix Group point out some sharp contrasts in organization between French firms and West German ones of the same size making similar products.

In Germany, training agencies, methods, and ideology always were structured entirely unlike those in France. Apprenticeship remained the keystone of German industrial training. The apprenticeship diploma is still awarded by bodies independent of firms, not by employers. It carries some of the prestige of craftsmanship, although craft union *organization*, with its petty snobberies and blinkered world-view, is absent from German industry. Most workers in a typical workplace have taken at least one apprenticeship. Some have collected several. (Apprenticeship training can be taken at any stage of work-life except the pre-retirement period.)

Training for managerial and technical occupations also has been founded on apprenticeship. This provides managers and workers with a common fund of *technical culture*. German industrial ideology stresses technical competence as a qualification for promotion and the basis of authority, while doubting the value of academic qualifications, even those in a technological subject. West German unions endorse this stress on 'hands-on' competence, and know-how gained from work experience. Yet union officials often can argue on the same technical level as managers about work-study or job-design; they are thus able to win points by objective discussion that would result in a strike elsewhere. Unions are also readier than they would otherwise be to seek an extension of their involvement in *Mitbestimmung* – the co-management system that gives German workers a say in important decisions in their employing firm. But trade unionists and workers both identify strongly with an occupation, not with an employing firm. Having credentials valid throughout industry, they can move easily between firms when they wish to. In practice, most do not switch employers frequently.

While competence is created in Germany in the educational and training domain, in France, in very sharp contrast, it is created within the organizational domain. Apprenticeship was banned during the French Revolution because the guilds or artisan *corporations* that provided it were regarded as oppressive agencies of the old regime. It revived in a half-hearted way later on, but the French state decided that it should provide technical training through formal courses in technical institutes. But the institutes never trained enough technicians. The training they provided had a strong academic bias, towards general principles and mathematics, not towards problem-solving through practical experience. This forced large employers to devise their own training programmes. And these were in turn biased towards the peculiarities of the employer's product, labour process, and technology.

The technical competence of staff trained by employers was often narrow. They lacked an ideology of professionalism. Nor could they communicate easily with technologists recruited into management positions because these outsiders were steeped in the academic ethos of the training institutes. Moreover, French bosses promulgated a social doctrine among their workforces that harped on the uniqueness of each firm as a 'working family'. Workplace particularism was magnified by the peculiarities of work organization. Individual competence was lacking because of the general low level of technical training. So it had, as it were, to be *organized into* the labour process. French employers always have been keen on scientific management. They were the first in Europe to seize at Taylorism as a method of tightening work organization. This is not because of some supposed Gallic obsession with logical structures, as culturalists would claim. It reflected the defects of the training system.

Despite reforms of training, and an attempt by some French employers to introduce modern forms of organization, management, and ideology, these features linger on. French organizations are often over-governed. French workers have always detested what they experience, justifiably, as the semi-feudal nature of authority as it is exercised by their bosses.

Their lack of widely applicable training, it would seem, ought to prevent them escaping from it. In fact, French workers change employers more often than their German counterparts. Younger workers who want to broaden their skill seek to do so by starting their career again in another firm. Others detest the cloying paternalism of many firms. French trade unions have often played on these discontents. Yet, the strongest of the union groupings scorned local bargaining or calls for trade unions to gain a voice in the operation of the firm. For the most part, as the Harvard Team demonstrate, they encouraged the belief that any change short of a political revolution was not worth pursuing.

Yet the French system has been a viable one. In fact, in the later years of the post-1945 growth era, the French economy was expanding faster than the West German miracle. The Aix group leave it to others to draw what conclusions they wish about the desirability of each form of the industrial relationship they define.

Industrial structures and procedures, which result from sharply different philosophies about skill and training, feed back into the education system, industrial relations practices, and workers' attitudes. They sustain certain types of behaviour and exclude others. Over time, then, there have emerged coherent and stable industrial institutions peculiar to each of these societies.

The production and delivery of competence is organized in still other ways elsewhere: the Aix analysis has been applied to other countries.[4] It has become more evident how far, within nations, relatively fixed sets of institutions mediate, qualify, and complicate the universal effects of the employment relationship of a capitalist economy. To mediate these effects does not, of course, mean to override or neutralize them. But nobody can read off patterns of industrial behaviour within any historic nation-state simply specifying the abstract properties of the capitalist wages–effort bargain. On the contrary, to adopt another metaphor we can understand such behaviour by mapping out the institutional geography that shapes action within the societal locality.

Not everyone would agree that the salient features of such a geography have so much independent influence on behaviour. Undoubtedly, too, the economic autonomy of the nation-state has been eroded by the growth of international trade and the rise of multinational business. Likewise, there has been a sharpening within many countries of internal *economic* differences. The backwater areas hit by the decline of smokestack industry often seem to belong to different societies from the booming hi-tech and plate-glass regions. Economic geographers have been creating a valuable descriptive vocabulary for defining how previous rounds of investment result in geographical space itself becoming implicated in the growth and maintenance of local subcultures – behaviour, values, world-views – at variance with national patterns.[6]

Social scientists usually have overlooked or understated local variations such as these. But there is no evidence that such variations were ever bigger within nations than they were between nations.

Many studies examined in this book – for example, Warner's shoe-operatives in Yankee City, Chinoy's automobile assemblers, the money-men of Luton, Gallie's petrochemical workers – presented groups living in regions or communities with a sometimes marked local identity. Each one of these investigations carefully targeted the locality where inquiries were to occur. Yet, in each case, the employee groups themselves show attitudes and behaviour that are characteristic primarily of the *national* society in which they are located.

In Chinoy's study, it is striking how the hold of the American Dream was as hypnotic in a remote area as in its suburban heartlands. One of Gallie's British refineries was in Scotland, the other in the socially dissimilar South of England. His French refineries likewise were separated by the enormous geographical and social gaps between Dunkirk, in the dour Pas de Calais, and

Fos, on the coast just outside the typically Mediterranean port of Marseille. In each case, for the behaviour and attitudes that mattered most, regional variations from the nationally specific patterns could be discounted.

Possibly, occupational differences modify societal patterns more heavily than do regional ones. This is what some classic American studies, as well as more recent studies by investigators such as Howard Davis or Graeme Salaman in Britain suggest.[7] But it makes sense to keep a very open mind on this question for the time being. As far as the internationalization of the capitalist economy goes, the conclusions of *spatial theory* geographers seem to point to existing differences in economic specialization between countries remaining at least as pronounced as they are now. Growing specialization, with a given country producing certain products and not others, may result in forms of the employment relationship, occupational structures, and industrial relations patterns, within any nation-state, becoming still *more* uniform than they now are.

Long ago Geoffrey Ingham made a very astute comparison between Scandinavian and British industrial-relations patterns, which he traced not only to what might be called the *sedimented* institutions and practices produced in the years when industrialization first occurred, but also to the mix of industries that emerged at that fatal moment.[8] Some Type-II sociological theories of *structuration*, clearly benefiting from work such as Ingham's, have also made this point.[9]) Sedimented industrial structures have been relatively enduring. They reinforce the institutional factors discussed earlier in the creation of country-based behaviour and attitudes.

Yet, as noted earlier, penetration of national economies by multinational corporations, and, in Western Europe, the growth of EC law and regulations, together with other voluntary or forced reductions in national sovereignty, could produce an exactly opposite result. In this region, which already operates, however creakily, as a confederated state, *homogenization* – the growth in similarity – of at least *some* key industrial institutions is a possibility. But monolithic uniformity can be discounted.

The conclusion to be drawn is clear. Nobody yet knows how the capitalist world economy will evolve in the next two decades. But the concept and reality of the national society has been under growing stress for a half-century: not only from economic integration, but from developmens in travel, the media, popular culture, and the threat of nuclear annihilation. Those born before 1950 find the current wave of flag-waving populism, in some countries, a strange counterpoint to the underlying reality: a steady decay in the effective sovereignty, as well as in the military and economic independence, of the historic European nation-states.

This drama, played out where the systemic tendencies of the international market economy intersect with the societal sedimentation of nationally anchored institutions, will haunt the underlying economic life of the capitalist world for the immediate future. For the student of work behaviour it will become a central issue. Investigations of particular work situations will have increasingly to relate to this central problem. We should make such links explicitly.

Notes

PART I: THE GREEDY ROBOT

2. *Rational Workmen, Incompetent Managers*

1. H. Braverman, *Labor and Monopoly Capital: The Degradation of Work in the Twentieth Century* (New York, Monthly Review Press, 1974). Braverman's own ideas, a version of work-degradation theory, will be examined in chapter 30.
2. Revulsion from Taylor's methods, or a readiness to equate scientific management, as a movement or as an ideology, with capitalism, prevents analysis from coming to grips with it. Many Marxists fail to apply a Marxian analysis to the movement or its ideas.
3. Quoted by C. S. Maier, 'Between Taylorism and Technocracy: European Ideologies and the vision of industrial harmony in the 1920s', *Journal of Contemporary History*, 5, 2 (1970), 27–61.
4. This 'revolt against work' is discussed in chapter 29.
5. F. W. Taylor, *The Principles of Scientific Management* (New York, Harper and Row, 1947), p. 19.
6. Ibid. p. 20.
7. F. B. Copley, *Frederick Winslow Taylor: Father of Scientific Management* (New York, Harper and Row, 1923), vol. I, p. 155.
8. A. Fox, *Beyond Contract: Work, Power and Trust Relations* (London, Faber and Faber, 1974).
9. Taylor, op. cit.
10. C. Littler, *The Development of the Labour Process in Capitalist Societies: A Comparative Study of the Transformation of Work Organization in Britain, Japan and the USA* (Heinemann, 1982) pp. 52–3.
11. Ibid.
12. Braverman, op. cit., chapter 4.
13. F. W. Taylor, *Testimony Before the Special House Committee* (New York, Harper and Row, 1947), p. 109.
14. Taylor, *Principles*, p. 60.
15. Taylor was not well served by his biographer Copley. In a characteristic passage, Copley enthuses over Taylor's selection of horses when he purchased a mansion, Bloxley, on the outskirts of Philadelphia, and set about the redesign

of an extensive classical garden laid out by a certain Comte du Barry, a French émigré occupier of the 1800s – operations that called for the levelling of a hill: 'We found out', Taylor wrote, 'just what a horse will endure, what percentage of the day he must haul with such a load, how much he can pull, how much he should rest.' Copley comments: 'His standard was set by the best heavy-draft horses of the locality, and he used his keen eyes to chase all others off the job.' (Copley, *op. cit.*, vol. II, p. 197.)

16. Especially H. L. Gantt and R. Feiss, with their New Machine movement. For an account, M. J. Nadworny, *Scientific Management and the Unions, 1900–1932* (Cambridge, Massachusetts, Harvard University Press, 1955), chapter 7.

3. Taylor, the Tory Radical Technocrat

1. C. S. Maier, 'Between Taylorism and Technocracy: European ideologies and the vision of industrial harmony in the 1920s', *Journal of Contemporary History*, 5, 2 (1970), pp. 27–61.
2. M. J. Nadworny, *Scientific Management and the Unions, 1900–1932* (Cambridge, Massachusetts: Harvard University Press, 1955), chapter 1.
3. Reprinted in *Economic Studies*, 1 June 1896.
4. F. B. Copley, *Frederick Winslow Taylor: Father of Scientific Management* (New York, Harper and Row, 1923), vol. II, p. 146.
5. F. W. Taylor, *Shop Management* (New York, Harper and Row, 1947).
6. F. W. Taylor, 'On the Art of Cutting Metals', *Transactions of the American* Society of Mechanical Engineers, 28 (1907), p. 19.
7. S. Haber, *Efficiency and Uplift* (Chicago, Illinois, University of Chicago Press, 1964), chapter 4.
8. *Ibid.* 51ff.
9. Nadworny, *op. cit.*, chapter 3, provides numerous examples.
10. H. G. J. Aitken, *Taylorism at Watertown Arsenal* (Cambridge, Massachusetts, Harvard University Press, 2nd edition 1986), provides a full account.
11. *Ibid.* p. 32.
12. F. W. Taylor, *Testimony Before the Special House Committee* (New York, Harper and Row, 1947) p. 21.
13. *Ibid.* p. 43.
14. E. Cadbury, 'Some Principles of Industrial Organization', *Sociological Review*, 7 (1914), 99–117; C. B. Thompson, 'The Case for Scientific Management', *Sociological Review*, 7 (1914), 315–327.

4. The Roots of Taylorism

1. D. Montgomery, *Workers' Control in America* (Cambridge, Cambridge University Press, 1979); the same author's 'The "new unionism" and the transformation of workers' consciousness in America, 1909–1922', *Journal of Social* History, 7, 3 (1974), pp. 509–29; M. J. Nadworny, *Scientific Management and the Unions, 1900–1932* (Cambridge, Massachusetts, Harvard University Press, 1955).

2. C. Littler, *The Development of the Labour Process in Capitalist Societies: A Comparative Study of the Transformation of Work Organization in Britain, Japan and the USA* (London, Heinemann, 1982).
3. S. Kakar, *Frederick Taylor: A Study in Personality and Innovation* (Cambridge, Massachusetts, MIT Press, 1970), provides a psycho-biographical treatment of Taylor.
4. C. S. Maier, 'Between Taylorism and Technocracy: European ideologies and the vision of industrial harmony in the 1920s', *Journal of Contemporary History*, 5, 2 (1970), pp. 27–61.
5. Quoted in R. Bendix, *Work and Authority in Industry: Ideologies of Management in the Course of Industrialization* (New York, Harper and Row, 1963), p. 255.
6. G. Friedmann, *La crise du progrès* (Paris, Gallimard, 1936), pp. 76ff.
7. Bendix, *op. cit.*, p. 265.
8. H. G. Gutman, *Work, Culture and Society in Industrialising America: Essays in American Working Class and Social History* (Oxford, Basil Blackwell, 1977).
9. Bendix, *op. cit.*, pp. 257–67.
10. Nadworny, *op. cit.*, chapters 7–9.
11. *Ibid.* Nadworny points out that many of the New Machine's ideas were revived during the 1930s by the Technocracy Movement.
12. M. L. Cooke, and S. Gompers (special eds.), 'Labor, Management and Productivity', *The Annals of the American Academy of Political and Social Science* (September 1920).
13. Nadworny, *op. cit.*, 119ff.
14. *Ibid.*, chapter 8.
15. *Ibid.*
16. *Ibid.*, pp. 138ff.

PART II: HAPPY HUMANS RUN SMOOTHER

5. *The Human Factor*

1. E. Farmer, 'The Method of Grouping by Differential Tests', *Fourth Report of the Industrial Fatigue Research Board* (London, HMSO, 1924).
2. *Ibid.*
3. L. S. Hearnshaw, *A Short History of British Psychology, 1840–1940* (London, Methuen, 1964), pp. 275–82, gives a summary account.
4. C. S. Myers, *An Account of Work Carried Out by the National Institute of Industrial Psychology during the Years 1921–34* (London, NIIP, 1934).
5. C. S. Myers, *Industrial Psychology in Great Britain* (London, Cape, 1924).
6. *Ibid.* pp. 35–6.

6. *War and Fatigue*

1. C. S. Myers, *Industrial Psychology in Great Britain* (London, Cape, 1924), p. 74.
2. E. P. Cathcart, *The Human Factor in Industry* (Oxford, Oxford University Press, 1928), p. 17.

3. *Ibid.* p. 20.
4. Myers, *op. cit.*, p. 40.
5. E. Farmer, 'The Interpretation and Plotting of Output Curves', *British Journal of Psychology*, 13 (1923), 308–14.
6. G. Friedmann, *Industrial Society: The Emergence of the Human Problems of Automation* (Glencoe, Illinois, The Free Press, 1955), pp. 70ff.
7. *Ibid.*
8. S. Wyatt, *et al.*, *The Effects of Monotony in Work* (London, HMSO, 1929), list them in an appendix.
9. H. M. Vernon, 'The Use and Significance of the Kata Thermometer' (London, HMSO, 1924).
10. H. M. Vernon and T. Bedford, *A Study of Absenteeism in a Group of Ten Collieries* (London, HMSO, 1928).
11. *Ibid.* p. 50.

7. Explorations in Monotony

1. See, for example, R. G. Stansfield, review of T. O. Kvalseth, *Ergonomics of Workstation Design*, in *British Sociological Association Network*, 29 (1984) 19.
2. H. M. Vernon *et al.*, *Two Studies of Rest Pauses in Industry* (London, HMSO, 1924).
3. H. M. Vernon *et al.*, *On the Extent and Effects of Variety in Repetitive Work* (London, HMSO, 1924).
4. S. Wyatt and A. D. Ogden, *Rest Pauses and Variety in Work*, HMSO, 1926.
5. S. Wyatt and J. A. Frazer, *The Comparative Effects of Variety and Uniformity in Work* (London, HMSO, 1928).
6. S. Wyatt, G. L. Stock and J. A. Frazer, *The Effects of Monotony in Work* (London, HMSO, 1929).
7. *Ibid.* p. 2.
8. *Ibid.* p. 5.
9. *Ibid.* p. 43.
10. *Ibid.* p. 40.
11. M. Smith, 'General Psychological Problems Confronting the Investigator' (London, HMSO, 1924).
12. M. Smith *et al.*, *A Study of Telegraphists' Cramp* (London, HMSO, 1927).
13. M. Culpin and M. Smith, *The Nervous Temperament* (London, HMSO, 1930).

8. The Myers Group in Perspective

1. S. Wyatt and J. N. Langdon, *The Machine and the Worker* (London, HMSO, 1938).
2. W. Baldamus, *Efficiency and Effort* (London, Tavistock Institute of Human Relations, 1961), is milestone work locating the problems of fatigue and monotony within a conflictual perspective.

3. Wyatt and Langdon, *op. cit.*, p. 45.
4. C. S. Myers (ed.), *Industrial Psychology* (London, Home University Library, 1929).
5. *Ibid.* chapter 2.
6. *Ibid.* pp. 33–4.
7. *Ibid.* p. 32.
8. E. P. Cathcart, *The Human Factor in Industry* (Oxford, Oxford University Press, 1928).
9. *Ibid.* p. 93.
10. *Ibid.* p. 91.
11. *Ibid.* pp. 13–15.
12. G. Friedmann, *Industrial Society: The Emergence of the Human Problems of Automation* (Glencoe, Illinois, The Free Press, 1955), p. 84.
13. C. S. Myers, 'The Efficiency Engineer and the Industrial Psychologist', *Journal of the National Institute of Industrial Psychology*, 1 (1921), 168–72; F. Gilbreth and L. Gilbreth, 'The Efficiency Engineer and the Industrial Psychologist – Reply', *Journal of the National Institute of Industrial Psychology*, 2 (1922), 40–45.
14. Gilbreth and Gilbreth, *op. cit.*
15. *Ibid.*
16. *Ibid.*
17. C. S. Myers, *Industrial Psychology in Great Britain* (London, Cape, 1924).
18. *Ibid.* p. 83.
19. *Ibid.* p. 29.
20. *Ibid.* p. 25.
21. E. Farmer, 'The Interconnections between Economics and Industrial Psychology', *Journal of the National Institute of Industrial Psychology*, 2 (1922), 78–83.
22. Friedmann, *op. cit.* p. 125.
23. *Ibid.*

9. *Human Factors in the USA*

1. S. R. Cohen, 'From industrial democracy to professional adjustment: The development of Industrial Sociology in the USA, 1900–1955', *Theory and Society*, 12, 1 (1983), 47–67.
2. The experimental design of the lighting studies at Western Electric can be compared with a human-factor study reported in H. C. Weston *et al.*, *The Relation between Illumination and Efficiency in Fine Work* (London, HMSO, 1926).
3. E. Mayo, *The Human Problems of an Industrial Civilization* (New York, Macmillan, 1946), p. 1.
4. The conference was held in Toronto in August 1924; see E. Mayo, 'Day-Dreaming and Output in a Spinning Mill', *Journal of the National Institute of Industrial Psychology*, 2 (1923), 203–9. C. S. Myers's *Industrial Psychology in*

Great Britain (London, Cape, 1924), was based on lectures given at Columbia University, New York City.

5. L. Baritz, *The Servants of Power* (New York, Wiley, 1965), chapters 1–4.
6. W. McDougall, *An Introduction to Social Psychology* (London, Methuen, 1908).
7. O. Tead, *Instincts in Industry* (Boston, Massachusetts, Small, Maynard, 1918).
8. Baritz, *op. cit.* p. 31.
9. D. Scott, *The Psychology of Advertising* (Boston, Massachusetts, Small, Maynard, 1908).
10. E. Mayo, 'Day-Dreaming and Output in a Spinning Mill', *loc. cit.*; 'The Irrational Factor in Society', *Journal of Personnel Research*, 1 (1923), 419–26; 'Irrationality and Revery', *Journal of Personnel Research*, 1 (1923), 477–83; 'Revery and Industrial Fatigue', *Journal of Personnel Research*, 3 (1924), 273–81; *Human Problems of an Industrial Civilization*, pp. 40ff.
11. Mayo, 'Revery and Industrial Fatigue', *ibid.*
12. A. Carey, 'The Hawthorne Studies: A Radical Criticism', *American Sociological Review*, 32 (1967), 403–16.
13. J. Smith, 'Elton Mayo and the Hidden Hawthorne', *Work, Employment and Society*, 1, 1 (1987), 107–20; 'Elton Mayo and the English Dream', *The Sociological Review*, 35, 3 (1987), 603–21.
14. 'Indeed, sometimes the mere presence of the Institute's investigators and the interest they have shown in the employees' work has served to send up output before any changes have been introduced.' (C. S. Myers, *Industrial Psychology in Great Britain*, p. 28). Well into the 1940s, American applied social scientists were to discover the human-factor school: see C. F. Harding, 'Uniformities in Human Relations Tentatively Established', *Applied Anthropology* (January–March 1944) 37–44. Harding was in no two minds over the verdict that 'the British studies reviewed demonstrate the extreme importance of social behaviour in determining output'.

10. In Conclusion

1. J. Child, *British Management Thought* (London, Allen and Unwin, 1969), chapters 3 and 4.

PART III: THE TRIBAL FACTORY

11. The Six Sides of Human Relations

1. I. Berg, M. Freedman and M. Freeman, *Managers and Work Reform: A Limited Engagement* (New York, The Free Press, 1978); P. Goldman, and D. R. Van Houten, 'Uncertainty, Conflict, and Labor Relations in the Modern Firm', Parts I and II, *Economic and Industrial Democracy*, 1, 1 and 2 (1980), 63–98, and 263–87; W. A. T. Nichols, 'Management Ideology and Practice', in G. Esland, and G. Salaman, (eds.), *The Politics of Work and Occupations* (London, Open University Press, 1980); A. Friedman, 'Responsible Autonomy versus Direct Control over the Labour Process', *Capital and Class*, 1 (1977) 43–58; C.

F. Sabel, Review of *Managers and Work Reform*, *Challenge* (July–August 1979), 64–6; R. Sennett, 'The Boss's New Clothes', *New York Review of Books* 26 (22 February 1979), 42–6.

2. See H. A. Landsberger, *Hawthorne Revisited: 'Management and the Worker'. Its Critics and Developments in Human Relations in Industry* (Ithaca, New York, Cornell University Press, 1958); C. Kerr and L. Fisher, 'Plant Sociology: The Elite and the Aborigines', in M. Komarovsky (ed.), *Common Frontiers of the Social Sciences* (Glencoe, Illinois, Free Press, 1957); W. H. Whyte, *The Organization of Man* (Harmondsworth, Penguin Books, 1960), chapters 3–5. More specialized criticisms will be noted below.
3. L. Baritz, *The Servants of Power* (New York, Wiley, 1965), chapter 5 onwards; and R. Bendix, *Work and Authority in Industry* (New York, Harper and Row, 1963) pp. 287ff.
4. Whyte, *op. cit.*
5. H. A. Landsberger, *op. cit.* was the first to point out the importance of the differences between Mayo's treatment of the Hawthorne data and that of F. Roethlisberger, and W. J. Dickson, in *Management and the Worker* (New York, Wiley, 1964 edition).
6. Baritz, *op. cit.* and Bendix, *op. cit.*
7. Roethlisberger and Dickson, *Management and the Worker* (New York, Wiley, 1964), p. 21.
8. Landsberger, *op. cit.* p. 21.
9. Roethlisberger and Dickson, *op. cit.* p. 604, their emphasis.
10. H. L. Wilensky, and K. L. Wilensky, 'Personnel Counselling: The Hawthorne Case', *American Journal of Sociology*, 57 (1952), 265–80.

12. What Did Mayo Do?

1. J. Smith, 'Elton Mayo and the Hidden Hawthorne', *Work, Employment and Society*, 1, 1 (1987), pp. 107–20.
2. Biographical source material on Mayo is cited and discussed in Smith *op. cit.* and in J. Smith, 'Elton Mayo and the English Dream', *Sociological Review*, 35, 3 (1987), 603–21. R. Trahair, *The Humanist Temper* (New Brunswick, Transaction Books, 1985), is concerned largely with Mayo's Australian years.
3. E. Mayo, *Democracy and Freedom* (Melbourne, Macmillan, 1919).
4. *Ibid.* p. 5.
5. Especially in E. Mayo, 'The Irrational Factor in Society', *Journal of Personnel Research*, 1 (1923), 419–26.
6. Henderson's fascination with Pareto is documented from first-hand experience in the Autobiographical Introduction to G. C. Homans, *Sentiments and Activities* (London, Routledge, 1962); see also the same author's *Coming to my Senses* (New Brunswick, Transaction Books, 1984); and B. S. Heyl, 'The Harvard Pareto Circle', *Journal for the History of the Behavioural Sciences*, 4 (1968), 316–34.

7. Smith, *Sociological Review*, pp. 608–9.
8. E. Mayo, 'Maladjustment of the Industrial Worker' in O. S. Beyer, *et al.* (eds.), *The Wertheim Lectures on Industrial Relations, 1928* (Cambridge, Massachusetts, Harvard University Press, 1929). (Interestingly, another participant in this series was J. P. Frey, a veteran union opponent of Taylorism.)
9. *Ibid.*
10. P. Goldman, and D. R. Van Houten, 'Uncertainty, Conflict, and Labor Relations in the Modern Firm', Parts I and II, *Economic and Industrial Democracy*, 1, 1 and 2 (1980), 63–98, and 263–87.
11. Smith, *Work, Employment and Society*, p. 114.
12. John Smith's new evidence (*ibid.* p. 114) also suggests that Mayo indeed had to expend considerable effort at times to keep the company interested in the research. This must have left even less time for leg-work in the plant. Smith also talks of Roethlisberger taking steps to protect Mayo from the consequences of Mayo's own 'indifference to detailed academic reportage'. I think the term 'reporting', might have been a happier one, but that chosen by Smith may be more appropriate. But I accept his finding that Mayo spent more time in Chicago than his academic colleagues.
13. Smith, *ibid.*
14. F. J. Roethlisberger, and W. J. Dickson, *Management and the Worker* (New York, Wiley, 1964), p. 389.
15. E. Mayo, 'The Hawthorne Experiment', *Human Factor*, 6 (1930), pp. 8–15.
16. Roethlisberger and Dickson, *op. cit.* pp. 53–5, 60ff, and 133.
17. *Ibid.* chapter 15.
18. E. Mayo, *The Human Problems of an Industrial Civilization* (New York, Macmillan, 1946), pp. 96–7: all quotations refer to this edition.
19. *Ibid.* p. 116.
20. *Ibid.* p. 147.
21. *Ibid.* p. 175.
22. B. Adams, *The Theory of Social Revolutions* (London, Macmillan, 1913), quoted in Mayo, *Human Problems*, p. 165.
23. Mayo, *ibid.* p. 171.
24. E. Mayo, *The Social Problems of an Industrial Civilization* (London, Routledge, 1949); all references are to this edition. A reprinted edition, with a Foreword by John Smith, was issued by the same publisher in 1975.
25. *Ibid.* p. 21, Mayo's italics.
26. Mayo in Beyer, *op. cit.* p. 185; and Mayo, *Social Problems*, p. 27.
27. Mayo, *Social Problems*, pp. 74–5.
28. *Ibid.* pp. 80ff which refers to Mayo's report (with G. F. Lombard) *Teamwork and Labour Turnover in the Aircraft Industry of Southern California* (Cambridge, Mass. Harvard Business School, 1944).
29. Mayo, *Social Problems*, pp. 93–5.
30. *The Political Problem of Industrial Civilization*, intended to complete the trilogy, was published by Routledge in an unfinished form in 1947.

13. The Harvard Group

1. S. R. Cohen, 'From industrial democracy to professional adjustment: The Development of Industrial Sociology in the United States, 1900–1955', *Theory and Society*, 12, 1 (1983), 47–67.
2. H. A. Landsberger, *Hawthorne Revisited: 'Management and the Worker'. Its Critics and Developments in Human Relations in Industry* (Ithaca, New York, Cornell University Press, 1958).
3. W. L. Warner, and J. O. Low, *The Social System of the Modern Factory* (New Haven, Connecticut, Yale University Press, 1947).
4. A. Carey, 'The Hawthorne Studies: A Radical Criticism', *American Sociological Review*, 32 (1967), 403–16.
5. F. J. Roethlisberger, and W. J. Dickson, *Management and the Worker* (New York, Wiley, 1964), pp. 22 and 180. In fact, the original observer was eventually promoted and given the assistance of a *second* observer. It is difficult to determine the timing of this change and others connected with it.
6. G. C. Homans, 'The Strategy of Industrial Sociology' in G. E. Swanson *et al.* (eds.), *Readings in Social Psychology* (New York, Holt, Rinehart, 1952 edition), pp. 637–49; H. A. Landsberger, *op. cit.*
7. T. N. Whitehead, *The Industrial Worker* (London, Oxford University Press, 1938), is informative here. Whitehead comments (vol. I, p. 104) that at first 'it was not clearly realized that full co-operation and typical supervisory techniques were mutually incompatible'.
8. H. M. Parsons, 'What happened at Hawthorne?', *Science*, 183 (1974), 922–32. See also R. Franke, and J. Kaul, 'The Hawthorne Experiments: First Statistical Interpretation', *American Sociological Review*, 43 (1978), 623–43; and R. Franke, 'The Hawthorne Experiments: A Review', *American Sociological Review*, 47 (1979), 858–66.
9. A much more generous commentary is J. Madge, *The Origins of Scientific Sociology* (London, Tavistock Institute of Human Relations, 1963), chapter 6, 'Pioneers of Industrial Sociology'.
10. A. V. Cicourel, *Method and Measurement in Sociology* (London, Collier-Macmillan, 1967), chapter 3.
11. Roethlisberger and Dickson acknowledge the advice given to them by the anthropologist W. L. Warner, but it is difficult to estimate how actively he took part in the work. But see Smith, *Work, Employment and Society*.
12. H. A. Landsberger, *op. cit.* p. 22.
13. Roethlisberger and Dickson, *op. cit.* pp. 391–2.
14. Madge, *op. cit.*
15. Roethlisberger and Dickson, *op. cit.* pp. xiii and 184.
16. *Ibid.* pp. 578ff.
17. Madge, *op. cit.* makes some useful introductory comments, but lacked the benefit of more recent research.
18. Landsberger, *op. cit.* p. 64.

19. *Ibid.* p. 67.
20. H. L. Wilensky, and K. L. Wilensky, 'Personnel Counselling: The Hawthorne Case', *American Journal of Sociology*, 57 (1952), 265–80.
21. Landsberger, *op. cit.* p. 86.
22. *Ibid.* pp. 96–7.
23. Roethlisberger and Dickson, *op. cit.* p. 568.
24. *Ibid.* p. 553.
25. Mayo wrote to his daughter Patricia about Whitehead in the following terms: 'He illustrates the diplomatic manner by permitting some of us to talk in his presence. Or if we do manage to rush in a word or two, our errors are graciously explained to us.' Smith, 'Elton Mayo and the English Dream', *Sociological Review*, 35, 3 (1987), 615.
26. T. N. Whitehead, *Leadership in a Free Society* (Cambridge, Massachusetts, Harvard University Press, 1936).
27. T. N. Whitehead, *The Industrial Worker: A Statistical Study of Human Relations in a Group of Manual Workers*, (2 vols. London, Oxford University Press, 1938).
28. *Ibid.* Vol. I, chapter 16 covers the initial impact made by operator 2.
29. *Ibid.* pp. 127 and 233.
30. *Ibid.* p. 161.
31. H. Braverman, *Labor and Monopoly Capital: The Degradation of Work in the Twentieth Century* (New York, Monthly Review Press, 1974).
32. Braverman mentions Warner once only, on p. 28, and only incidentally, in a passage criticizing the measurement of social class by pollsters.
33. W. H. Whyte, *The Organization Man* (Harmondsworth, Penguin Books, 1963), Part I.
34. W. L. Warner, and J. O. Low, *op. cit.*
35. In particular W. L. Warner, and P. S. Lunt, *The Social Life of a Modern Community* (New Haven, Connecticut, Yale University Press, 1941).
36. W. H. Whyte, *op. cit.* quite wrongly states that Warner allocated only 'a couple of sentences to the logical, economic factors' behind the strike. This kind of misconception of Warner's work is typical.
37. Warner and Low, *op. cit.* p. 65.
38. *Ibid.* pp. 172ff.
39. *Ibid.* pp. 188–9.
40. *Ibid.* p. 195.
41. What this proposal highlights is the scale of Warner's ambivalence towards his 'Yankee City' material, and, *a fortiori*, to the turn of socio-cultural change in America, as instanced in W. L. Warner, *American Life: Dream and Reality* (Chicago, Illinois, University of Chicago Press, 1953). Warner is a better analyst of dream than reality, but that is the strength of an anthropologist. Of all the Harvard Group he seems to have possessed the most independent and critical mind. This is all the more remarkable in view of his academic background and training. As a functional anthropologist (he was a graduate

pupil of the arch-Durkheimian Radcliffe-Brown) he went to Harvard determined to apply in an industrialized setting the anthropological techniques he had mastered in his study of Australian aborigines, the Murngin: W. L. Warner, *Black Civilization: A Social Study of an Australian Tribe* (New York, Harper and Row, 1937). Certainly, his functionalist training pushed him into overstating the similarities between the Murngin and the citizens of Newburyport, especially the importance of kinship ties, social rank and general community attachment and cohesion to the latter.

14. Storytellers of Chicago

1. P. W. Bridgman, *The Logic of Modern Physics* (New York, Macmillan, 1928).
2. See the 'Autobiographical Introduction' to G. C. Homans, *Sentiments and Activities* (London, Routledge, 1962). W. F. Whyte, 'From Human Relations to Organizational Behaviour: Reflections on the Changing Scene', *Industrial and Labor Relations Review*, 40, 4 (1987), 487–500.
3. C. M. Arensberg, and S. T. Kimball, *Family and Community in Ireland* (Cambridge, Massachusetts, Harvard University Press, 1940).
4. E. D. Chapple, and C. M. Arensberg, *Measuring Human Relations: An Introduction to the Study of the Interaction of Individuals* (Provincetown, Massachusetts, Journal Press, 1940).
5. C. M. Arensberg, 'Behaviour and Organization: Industrial Studies', in J. H. Rohrer, and M. Sherif (eds.), *Social Psychology at the Crossroads* (New York, Harper and Row, 1951), p. 345.
6. Homans, *op. cit.* p. 37.
7. E. D. Chapple, 'Editorial', *Applied Anthropology*, 1, 1 (1941), 1–3.
8. See the review of Mary Parker Follett's *Dynamic Administration* in *Applied Anthropology*, 1, 3 (1942), 50.
9. O. Collins, M. Dalton and D. Roy, 'Restriction of Output and Social Cleavage in Industry', *Applied Anthropology*, 5, 1 (1946), 1–14.
10. M. Dalton, 'The Industrial Rate-Buster: A Characterization', *Applied Anthropology*, 7, 1 (1948), 5–18.
11. C. M. Arensberg, 'Editorial', *Applied Anthropology*, 6 (1947), 1.
12. R. F. Bales, *Interaction Process Analysis* (Reading, Massachusetts, Addison-Wesley, 1951).
13. Compare E. D. Chapple, 'Applied Anthropology in Industry', in A. L. Kroeber (ed.), *Anthropology Today* (Chicago, Illinois, University of Chicago Press, 1951), with C. M. Arensberg, and G. Tootell, 'Plant Sociology: Real Discoveries and New Problems' in M. Komarovsky (ed.), *Common Frontiers of the Social Sciences* (Glencoe, Illinois, The Free Press, 1957).
14. T. Nichols, *The British Worker Question: A New Look at Workers and Productivity in Manufacturing* (London, Routledge, 1985, p. 29) recognizes the importance of this work, for example.

15. For example, W. F. Whyte, *Organizational Behaviour: Theory and Application* (Homewood, Illinois, Irwin, 1969).
16. W. F. Whyte, *Street Corner Society*, 2nd edition (Chicago, Illinois, University of Chicago Press, 1955).
17. Whyte, *Organizational Behaviour*, pp. 18–19.
18. W. F. Whyte, and B. B. Gardner, 'Facing the Foreman's Problems', and 'The Position and Problems of the Foreman', *Applied Anthropology*, 4, 1 (1944), 1–28.
19. *Ibid.*
20. W. F. Whyte and B. B. Gardner, 'From Conflict to Co-operation', *Applied Anthropology*, 5 (1946), 1–45.
21. W. F. Whyte, *Pattern for Industrial Peace* (New York, Harper and Row, 1951).
22. W. F. Whyte, and B. B. Gardner, 'Methods for the Study of Human Relations in Industry', *American Sociological Review*, 11 (1946), 506–12.
23. W. F. Whyte, *Human Relations in the Restaurant Industry* (New York, McGraw Hill, 1948).
24. W. F. Whyte, 'The Social Structure of the Restaurant', *American Journal of Sociology*, 54 (1949), 302–10.
25. *Ibid.*
26. W. F. Whyte, 'Small Groups and Large Organizations', in J. H. Rohrer, and M. Sherif, *Social Psychology at the Crossroads* (New York, Harper and Row, 1951).
27. W. F. Whyte, *Money and Motivation: A Study of Incentives in Industry* (New York, Harper and Row, 1955).
28. *Ibid.* pp. 208–9.
29. *Ibid.* chapter 6. Whyte relied here extensively on M. Dalton, 'The Industrial Rate-Buster: A Characterization', *Applied Anthropology*, 7, 1 (1948), 5–18.
30. See D. Roy, 'Quota Restriction and Goldbricking in a Machine Shop', *American Journal of Sociology*, 57 (1952), 427–42.
31. Whyte, *Money and Motivation*, p. 227.
32. *Ibid.* p. 233.
33. *Ibid.* p. 260.
34. I. Berg, M. Freedman, and M. Freeman, *Managers and Work Reform: A Limited Engagement* (New York, The Free Press, 1978).

5. The Psychological Puppeteers

1. H. Feldman, *Problems in Labor Relations* (New York, Macmillan, 1937).
2. R. Lippitt, 'An Experimental Study of the Effect of Democratic and Authoritarian Group Atmospheres', *University of Iowa Studies in Child Welfare*, 16 (1940), 43–195; R. Lippitt, and R. K. White, 'An Experimental Study of Leadership and Group Life', in G. E. Swanson *et al.* (eds.), *Readings in Social Psychology* (New York, Holt, Rinehart and Winston, 1952).
3. K. Lewin, 'Group Decision and Social Change', in G. E. Swanson *et al.* (eds.),

Readings in Social Psychology (New York, Holt, Rinehart and Winston, 1952).
4. L. Coch and J. P. French, 'Overcoming Resistance to Change', *Human Relations*, 1 (1948), 512–32.
5. For a sympathetic review of the Harwood investigations, see M. Viteles, *Motivation and Morale in Industry* (New York, W. W. Norton, 1953); for a more recent evaluation of the Coch and French study, M. Warner, *Organizations and Experiments: Designing New Ways of Managing Work* (Chichester, Wiley, 1984), p. 76ff.
6. Warner, M., *Organizations and Experiments* (Chichester, Wiley, 1985).
7. D. Katz, N. Maccoby and N. Morse, *Productivity, Morale and Supervision in an Office Situation* (Ann Arbor, Michigan, University of Michigan Survey Research Center, 1950).
8. D. Katz, N. Maccoby and N. Morse, *Productivity, Supervision and Morale amongst Railroad Workers* (Ann Arbor, Michigan, University of Michigan Survey Research Center, 1951).
9. D. Katz and R. L. Kahn, *The Caterpillar Tractor Company Study* (Ann Arbor, Michigan, University of Michigan Survey Research Center, 1951).
10. M. Argyle, *Social Interaction* (London, Methuen, 1969) pp. 302–3.
11. F. C. Mann, 'Changing Supervisor-Subordinate Relationships', *Journal of Social Issues*, 7 (1951), 56–63.
12. C. Arensberg and A. B. Horsfall, 'Teamwork and Productivity in a Shoe Factory', *Human Organization*, 8 (1949) 13–26.
13. Viteles, *op. cit.* gives a full list.
14. S. Seashore, 'Group Cohesiveness in the Industrial Work Group', in W. A. Faunce (ed.), *Readings in Industrial Sociology* (New York, Appleton, Century, Crofts, 1967).
15. Viteles, *op. cit.* is the outstanding example, but a close, more sociological, runner-up is B. B. Gardner and D. G. Moore, *Human Relations in Industry*, 3rd edition (Homewood, Illinois, Irwin, 1955).
16. C. Kerr and L. Fisher, 'Plant Sociology: The Elite and the Aborigines', in M. Komarovsky (ed.), *Common Frontiers of the Social Sciences*, (Glencoe, Illinois, Free Press, 1957).
17. C. Arensberg and G. Tootell, 'Plant Sociology: Real Discoveries and New Problems', in Komarovsky, *ibid.*

16. Overview

1. S. Ackroyd, 'Sociological Theory and the Human Relations School', *Sociology of Work and Occupations*, 3 (1976), 279–410.
2. G. C. Homans, *Sentiments and Activities* (London, Routledge, 1962) p. 4.
3. See E. Freeman, *Social Psychology* (New York, Holt, Rinehart and Winston, 1936), pp. 323–66; R. S. Lynd, review of T. N. Whitehead, *Leadership in a Free Society*, in *Political Science Quarterly*, 52 (1937), 590–2: M. Gilson, review

of *Management and the Worker*, in *American Journal of Sociology*, 46 (1940), 98–101.

4. C. W. M. Hart, 'The Hawthorne Experiments', *Canadian Journal of Economics and Political Science*, 9 (1943), 73–87; D. Bell, 'Adjusting Men to Machines', *Commentary*, 3 (1947), 79–88; H. Blumer, 'Sociological Theory in Industrial Relations', *American Sociological Review*, 12 (1947), 271–8; W. E. Moore, 'Industrial Sociology: Status and Prospects', *American Sociological Review*, 13 (1948), 382–91; C. W. Mills, 'The Contribution of Sociology to the Study of Industrial Relations', *Proceedings of the Industrial Relations Research Association*, 1 (1948), 199–222; E. V. Schneider, 'Limitations on Observations in Industrial Sociology', *Social Forces*, 28 (1950), 279–84; J. T. Dunlop, 'A Framework for the Analysis of Industrial Relations: Two Views', *Industrial and Labor Relations Review*, 3 (1950), 383–93; R. C. Sorensen, 'The Concept of Conflict in Industrial Sociology', *Social Forces*, 29 (1951), 263–7.
5. A. Carey, 'The Hawthorne Studies: A Radical Criticism', *American Sociological Review*, 32 (1967), 403–16.
6. See the listings in J. Smith, 'Elton Mayo and the Hidden Hawthorne', *Work, Employment and Society*, 1, 1 (1987), 107–20; and J. Smith, 'Elton Mayo and the English Dream', *Sociological Review*, 35, 3 (1987), 603–21.
7. R. Bendix and L. Fisher, 'The Perspectives of Elton Mayo', *Review of Economics and Statistics*, 31 (1949), 312–19.
8. Mills, *op. cit.*
9. C. Kerr and L. Fisher, 'Plant Sociology: The Elite and the Aborigines', in M. Komarovsky (ed.), *Common Frontiers of the Social Sciences* (Glencoe, Illinois Free Press, 1957); W. H. Whyte, *The Organization Man* (Harmondsworth, Penguin Books, 1960).
10. C. Arensberg and G. Tootell, 'Plant Sociology: Real Discoveries and New Problems', in Komarovsky, M., ed., *Common Frontiers of the Social Sciences* (Glencoe, Illinois Free Press, 1957); C. M. Arensberg, 'Behaviour and Organization: Industrial Studies', in J. H. Rohrer and M. Sherif (eds.), *Social Psychology at the Crossroads* (New York, Harper and Row, 1951); W. F. Whyte, 'Human Relations – A Progress Report', *Harvard Business Review*, 34 (1956), 125–32; G. C., Homans, 'The Strategy of Industrial Sociology', *American Journal of Sociology*, 54 (1949), 330–37.
11. M. Viteles, *Motivation and Morale in Industry* (New York, W. W. Norton, 1953); B. B. Gardner and D. G. Moore, *Human Relations in Industry*, 3rd edition (Homewood, Illinois, Irwin, 1955).

PART IV: IMPERATIVES OF THE MACHINE

17. *Credo for an Age of Growth*

1. S. M. Lipset, *Political Man* (London, Heinemann, 1960).
2. C. Kerr *et al.*, *Industrialism and Industrial Man* (Cambridge, Massachusetts, Harvard University Press, 1960).

3. E. L. Trist and K. W. Bamforth, 'Some Psychological and Social Consequences of the Longwall Methods of Coal-Getting', *Human Relations*, 4 (1951), 3–38.
4. E. L. Trist, *The Evolution of Socio-Technical Systems: A Conceptual Framework and an Action Research Program* (Toronto, Ontario Ministry of Labour, Occasional Paper no. 2, 1981).
5. R. K. Brown, 'Research and Consultancy in Industrial Enterprises', *Sociology*, 1 (1967), 33–60.
6. Trist and Bamforth, *op. cit.*
7. J. N. Morris, 'Coal Miners', *The Lancet*, 2 (1947), 341.
8. Trist and Bamforth, *op. cit.*
9. *Ibid.*
10. *Ibid.*

18. The Technological Countryside

1. C. R. Walker and R. H. Guest, *The Man on the Assembly Line* (Cambridge, Massachusetts, Harvard University Press, 1952).
2. C. R. Walker, R. H. Guest and A. N. Turner, *The Foreman on the Assembly Line* (Cambridge, Massachusetts, Harvard University Press, 1956).
3. G. Friedmann, *Où va le travail humain?* (Paris, Gallimard, 1950).
4. Walker and Guest, *op. cit.*, p. 4.
5. *Ibid.* p. 2.
6. *Ibid.* p. 3.
7. *Ibid.* p. 20.
8. *Ibid.* p. 80.
9. *Ibid.* p. 160.
10. *Ibid.* p. 66.
11. *Ibid.* p. 134.
12. *Ibid.* p. 66.
13. *Ibid.* p. 161.
14. *Ibid.* p. 156.
15. M. Dalton, 'The Industrial Rate-Buster: A Characterization', *Applied Anthropology*, 7 (1947), 323–32.
16. This theme will be developed more fully in chapter 26.
17. R. H. Guest, 'Job Enlargement: A Revolution in Job Design', *Personnel Administration*, 20 (1957), 13–15.

19. Organizational Engineering and the Self

1. See D. Silverman, *The Theory of Organizations* (London, Heinemann, 1970), chapter 4.
2. For a brief statement, A. Maslow, 'A Theory of Human Motivation', in V. Vroom, and E. L. Deci (eds.), *Management and Motivation* (Harmondsworth, Penguin Books, 1970).

3. Maslow's ideas were propagated enthusiastically, even entrepreneurially, in the 1970s by Frederick Herzberg and guided the research reported in F. Herzberg, *Work and the Nature of Man* (St Albans, Staples Press, 1968).
4. Maslow, *op. cit.*
5. D. McGregor, *The Human Side of the Enterprise* (New York, McGraw-Hill, 1960); for a succinct statement, see 'The Human Side of the Enterprise' in Vroom and Deci, *op. cit.*
6. R. Likert, 'New Patterns of Management' in Vroom and Deci, *op. cit.*
7. See especially C. Argyris, *Personality and Organization* (New York, Harper and Row, 1957).
8. C. Argyris, 'Understanding Human Behaviour in Organizations', in M. Haire (ed.), *Modern Organization Theory* (New York, Wiley, 1959), p. 115.
9. *Ibid.* p. 119.
10. J. Scott, *Corporations, Classes and Capitalism* (London, Hutchinson, 1981); G. Salaman, *Class and the Corporation* (Glasgow, Fontana, 1979).
11. Argyris, *Modern Organization Theory*, p. 120.
12. *Ibid.* p. 145.
13. C. R. Walker and R. H. Guest, *The Man on the Assembly Line* (Cambridge, Massachusetts, Harvard University Press, 1952); W. Baldamus, *Efficiency and Effort* (London, Tavistock Institute of Human Relations, 1961).
14. A. Kornhauser, *Mental Health of the Industrial Worker* (New York, Wiley, 1965).
15. Baldamus, *op. cit.*
16. R. Blauner, 'Work Satisfaction and Industrial Trends in Modern Society', in W. Galenson, and S. M. Lipset, *Labor and Trade Unionism* (New York, Wiley, 1960).
17. Silverman, *op. cit.* pp. 87–8.
18. M. J. Rose, *Reworking the Work Ethic: Economic Values and Socio-Cultural Politics* (London, Batsford Academic, 1985).

20. Designing Aggravation Out

1. L. R. Sayles, *The Behaviour of Industrial Work Groups: Prediction and Control* (New York, Wiley, 1958).
2. Sayles even slips into saying occasionally that technology *moulds* group behaviour, *op. cit.* p. 4.
3. *Ibid.* p. 39.
4. *Ibid.*
5. *Ibid.* p. 42.
6. *Ibid.* pp. 58–9.
7. D. Lockwood, *The Blackcoated Worker*, 2nd edition (London, Allen and Unwin, 1987).
8. Sayles, *op. cit.* p. 70.
9. *Ibid.* p. 93.
10. *Ibid.* p. 94.

11. *Ibid.* p. 135.
12. *Ibid.* p. 156.
13. Sayles, *op. cit.* p. 166.

21. Organization, Technology and National Culture

1. J. Woodward, *Management and Technology* (London, HMSO, 1958).
2. See J. Woodward, *Industrial Organisation: Theory and Practice* (Oxford, Oxford University Press, 1965).
3. M. Albrow, *Bureaucracy* (London, Macmillan, 1970), pp. 37–40.
4. J. Woodward, *Industrial Organisation*, p. 40.
5. *Ibid.* p. 50.
6. *Ibid.* p. 72.
7. *Ibid.*
8. On the other hand, the extent of conscious experimentation with organization has perhaps been seriously underestimated. The best study of this question is M. Warner, *Organizations as Experiments: Designing New Ways of Managing Work* (Chichester, Wiley, 1984).
9. J. Woodward, *Industrial Organization*, p. 249.
10. See, for example, B. Jones and P. J. Scott, '"Working the System": The Management of Work Roles in British and American Flexible Manufacturing Systems' in C. Voss (ed.), *Managing Advanced Manufacturing Technology* (Bedford, IFS Publications, 1986).
11. See J. Woodward and J. Rackham, 'The Measurement of Technical Variables' in J. Woodward (ed.), *Industrial Organization: Behaviour and Control* (Oxford, Oxford University Press, 1970).
12. For a full review and critique, see M. J. Rose, 'Universalism, culturalism and the Aix Group: Promise and problems of a societal approach to economic institutions', *European Sociological Review*, 1, 1 (1985), 65–83.
13. F. A. Richardson, 'Organisational contrasts on British and American Ships', *Administrative Science Quarterly*, 1, 2 (1956), 189–207.
14. M. Crozier, *The Bureaucratic Phenomenon* (London, Tavistock Institute of Human Relations, 1964).
15. M. Brossard and M. Maurice, 'Is there a universal model of organisation structure?', *International Studies of Management and Organisation*, 6, 1 (1976), 11–45; their original article in French was published two years earlier in *Sociologie du Travail.*
16. M. Maurice, F. Sellier, A. Sorge, and M. Warner, 'Societal differences in organizing manufacturing units: A comparison of France, West Germany and Great Britain', *Organization Studies*, 1, 1 (1980), 59–86.
17. Rose *op. cit.* M. Maurice, F. Sellier, and J.-J. Silvestre, *The Social Foundations of Industrial Power: A Comparison of France and Germany* (MIT Press, 1986): this is a good translation of their monograph in French, *Politique d'éducation et organisation industrielle en France et en Allemagne* (Paris, Presses Universitaires de France, 1982).

22. Automating for Harmony – or Revolution

1. For an account of the first bout of 'automation hysteria', see M. J. Rose, *Computers, Managers and Society* (Harmondsworth, Penguin Books, 1969).
2. R. Blauner, *Alienation and Freedom: The Factory Worker and his Industry* (Chicago, University of Chicago Press, 1964).
3. *Ibid.* p. 6, Blauner's emphasis.
4. R. Schacht, *Alienation* (London, Allen and Unwin, 1971).
5. Blauner, *op. cit.* p. 15.
6. *Ibid.* p. 24.
7. *Ibid.* pp. 202–4.
8. See D. McLellan, *Marx Before Marxism* (Harmondsworth, Penguin Books, 1970) pp. 213f.
9. E. Chinoy, *Automobile Workers and the American Dream* (Garden City, Doubleday, 1955).
10. If Blauner had followed a similar course he would have had less difficulty explaining the responses of his textile workers. It is possible to interpret their 'insulation' from work deprivation, because of their acceptance of values that clashed with their own underlying interests, as an aspect of alienation in the stricter, historically established sense of the term.
11. S. Mallet, *La nouvelle classe ouvrière* (Paris, Éditions du Seuil, 1965); references are to the 2nd French edition, 1969. English translation *The New Working Class* (Nottingham, Spokesman Books, 1975).
12. *Ibid.* pp. 74–6.
13. *Ibid.* p. 46.
14. B. C. Roberts *et al.*, *Reluctant Militants* (London, Heinemann, 1972); S. Low-Beer, *Protest and Participation: The New Working Class in Italy* (Cambridge, Cambridge University Press, 1978).
15. Low-Beer *op. cit.*; M. J. Rose, *Servants of Post Industrial Power?: Sociologie du Travail in Modern France* (London, Macmillan, 1979) chapter 6.
16. D. Gallie, *In Search of the New Working Class: Automation and Social Integration in the Capitalist Enterprise* (Cambridge, Cambridge University Press, 1978).

23. Socio-Technical Visionaries

1. E. L. Trist *et al.*, *Organizational Choice* (London, Tavistock Institute of Human Relations, 1963), p. 6.
2. *Ibid.*
3. Quoted *ibid.*
4. *Ibid.* p. 8.
5. See E. L. Trist, *The Evolution of Socio-Technical Systems: A Conceptual Framework and Action Research Programme* (Toronto, Ontario Ministry of Labour, 1981), pp. 24ff.
6. The most noted experiments were to occur in the Scandinavian motor industry, in the Saab-Scania and Volvo companies. The Volvo plant at Kalmar was

intensively studied. For a review, S. Hill, *Competition and Control at Work* (London, Heinemann, 1981).

7. M. Warner, *Organizations and Experiments* (Chichester, Wiley, 1984); Trist, *op. cit.* (1981), p. 42.
8. I. Berg *et al.*, *Managers and Work Reform: A Limited Engagement* (New York, The Free Press, 1979).
9. P. Goldman, and D. R. Van Houten, 'Uncertainty, Conflict, and Labor Relations in the Modern Firm', Parts I and II, *Economic and Industrial Democracy*, 1, 1 and 2 (1980), 63–98, and 263–87.
10. Berg, *op. cit.*
11. S. Marglin, 'What Do Bosses Do?', in A. Gorz (ed.), *The Division of Labour: The Labour Process and Class Struggle in Modern Capitalism* (Brighton, Harvester, 1976); D. F. Noble, 'Social Choice in Machine Design: The Case of Automatically Controlled Machine Tools', in A. Zimbalast (ed.), *Case Studies on the Labor Process* (London, Monthly Review Press, 1979).

PART V: ACTION THAT MEANS SOMETHING

24. *Work as Social Action*

1. For example, see S. Hill, *Competition and Control at Work* (London, Heinemann, 1981), pp. 118ff; and T. J. Watson, *Sociology, Work and Industry* (London, Routledge, 1980), pp. 48ff.
2. M. Weber, *The Methodology of the Social Sciences* (New York, The Free Press, 1949).
3. P. S. Cohen, *Modern Social Theory* (London, Heinemann, 1968), chapters 3–6.
4. M. Dalton, 'The Industrial Rate-Buster: A Characterization', *Applied Anthropology*, 7 (1948), 5–18.
5. E. Chinoy, *Automobile Workers and the American Dream* (New York, Doubleday, 1955).
6. *Ibid.* p. 133.
7. F. Parkin, *Class Inequality and Political Order: Social Stratification in Capitalist and Communist Societies* (London, McGibbon and Kee, 1971).
8. A. W. Gouldner, *Patterns of Industrial Bureaucracy* (New York, The Free Press, 1964); A. W. Gouldner, *Wildcat Strike* (New York, Harper & Row, 1965).
9. A. W. Gouldner, 'Cosmopolitans and Locals: Towards an Analysis of Latent Social Roles', Parts I and II, *Administrative Science Quarterly*, 2 (1957–8), 281–306 and 444–80.
10. M. Dalton, *Men Who Manage* (New York, Wiley, 1959).
11. J. C. Abegglen, *The Japanese Factory* (Glencoe, Illinois, The Free Press, 1958); C. Kerr, and A. J. Siegel, 'The Interindustry Propensity to Strike – An International Comparison', in C. Kerr (ed.), *Labor and Management in Industrial Society* (New York, Doubleday, 1964).
12. A. Etzioni, *A Comparative Analysis of Complex Organizations*, 2nd edition (New York, The Free Press, 1975).

25. The Money Men of Luton

1. The earliest critic was J. Westergaard, 'The Rediscovery of the Cash nexus' in R. Miliband and J. Saville (eds.), *The Socialist Register 1970* (London, Merlin Press, 1970); also still stimulating is G. Mackenzie, 'The "Affluent Worker" Study: An Evaluation and Critique' in F. Parkin (ed.), *The Social Analysis of the Class Structure* (London, Tavistock Institute of Human Relations, 1974).
2. J. H. Goldthorpe, D. Lockwood, F. Bechhofer and J. Platt, *The Affluent Worker: Industrial Attitudes and Behaviour* (Cambridge, Cambridge University Press, 1968).
3. J. H. Goldthorpe, D. Lockwood, F. Bechhofer and J. Platt, *The Affluent Worker in the Class Structure* (Cambridge, Cambridge University Press, 1969). Chapter 1 provides a review of these claims.
4. J. H. Goldthorpe and D. Lockwood, 'Affluence and the British Class Structure', *Sociological Review*, 11 (1963), 133–63.
5. D. Lockwood, *The Black-coated Worker*, 1st edition (London, Allen and Unwin, 1958), (2nd edition, 1987); J. H. Goldthorpe, 'Technical Organization as a Factor in Supervisor-Worker Conflict', *British Journal of Sociology*, 10 (1959), 213–30.
6. J. H. Goldthorpe, 'Attitudes and Behaviour of Car Assembly Workers: a Deviant Case and Theoretical Critique', *British Journal of Sociology*, 17 (1966), 227–44.
7. Compare Goldthorpe, *ibid.*, with J. H. Goldthorpe, D. Lockwood, F. Bechhofer and J. Platt *The Affluent Worker: Industrial Attitudes and Behaviour*, pp. 175–8.
8. Notably H. Behrend, 'The Effort Bargain', *Industrial and Labor Relations Review*, 10 (1957), 503–15, for an exposition of the concept.
9. See J. H. Goldthorpe, *op. cit.*
10. J. H. Goldthorpe, D. Lockwood, F. Bechhofer and J. Platt, *The Affluent Worker: Industrial Attitudes and Behaviour*, p. 183, emphasis in original.
11. R. M. Blackburn and M. Mann, *The Working Class in the Labour Market* (London, Macmillan, 1979), pp. 277ff.
12. J. H. Goldthorpe, D. Lockwood, F. Bechhofer and J. Platt, *The Affluent Worker: Industrial Attitudes and Behaviour*, pp. 146–7.
13. See F. Bechhofer, 'The Relation between Technology and Shop-Floor Behaviour' in D. O. Edge and J. N. Wolfe (eds.), *Meaning and Control* (London, Tavistock Institute of Human Relations, 1973).
14. J. H. Goldthorpe, D. Lockwood, F. Bechhofer and J. Platt, *The Affluent Worker: Industrial Attitudes and Behaviour*, chapter 12, and p. 167 especially.
15. G. K. Ingham, *Size of Industrial Organization and Worker Behaviour* (Cambridge, Cambridge University Press, 1970), barely avoids some of the risks.
16. Bechhofer, *op. cit.* helped to reduce the risk of such a misunderstanding.
17. W. W. Daniel, 'Industrial Behaviour and Orientation to Work – A Critique', *Journal of Management Studies*, 6 (1969), 366–75.

18. W. A. T. Nichols and P. Armstrong, *Workers Divided* (Glasgow, Fontana, 1976).
19. Blackburn and Mann, *op cit.*
20. A. W. Gouldner, *Wildcat Strike* (New York, Harper & Row, 1965); T. Lane and K. Roberts, *Strike at Pilkington's* (Glasgow, Fontana, 1971).
21. J. H. Goldthrope, D. Lockwood, F. Bechhofer and J. Platt, *The Affluent Worker: Industrial Attitudes and Behaviour*, pp. 40–41.
22. These themes recurred in M. Bulmer (ed.), *Working Class Images of Society* (London, Routledge, 1975).
23. R. K. Brown and P. Brannen, 'Social Relations and Social Perspectives Amongst Shipbuilding Workers – A Preliminary Statement', Parts I and II, *Sociology*, 4 (1970), 71–84 and 197–211.
24. J. H. Goldthorpe, D. Lockwood, F. Bechhofer and J. Platt, *The Affluent Worker in the Class Structure*, chapter 6.
25. A view put forward by A. Glyn and B. Sutcliffe, *British Capitalism, Workers and the Profits Squeeze* (Harmondsworth, Penguin Books, 1972).
26. J. H. Goldthorpe, *Order and Conflict in Contemporary Captialism* (Oxford University Press, 1984).

26 *Talking of Situations*

1. M. Poster, *Existential Marxism in Postwar France: From Sartre to Althusser* (Princeton, New Jersey, Princeton University Press, 1975).
2. K. Marx, *The Eighteenth Brumaire of Louis Bonaparte in Karl Marx and Frederick Engels: Selected Works* (London, Lawrence & Wishart, 1970), p. 96.
3. Still the best advocate for the approach is A. M. Rose (ed.), *Human Behaviour and Social Processes: An Interactionist Approach* (London, Routledge, 1962).
4. B. Hindess, 'The "Phenomenological" Sociology of Alfred Schutz', *Economy and Society*, 1 (1972), 1–27.
5. D. Silverman, *The Theory of Organizations* (London, Heinemann, 1970).
6. *Ibid.* chapter 2, but see L. Haworth, 'Do Organizations Act?', *Ethics*, 70 (1959), 59–63.
7. M. Albrow, 'The Study of Organizations – Objectivity or Bias?' in J. Gould (ed.), *Penguin Social Sciences Survey* (Harmondsworth, Penguin Books, 1968).
8. Silverman, *op. cit.*, p. 14.
9. *Ibid.* pp. 127–8.
10. *Ibid.* pp. 139–40.
11. *Ibid.* p. 172.
12. *Ibid.* pp. 224–5.
13. *Ibid.*
14. G. Salaman, *Class and the Corporation* (London, Fontana, 1981); J. Scott, *Corporations, Classes and Capitalism* (London, Hutchinson, 1979).
15. Some subjectivists even extended the principle to cover the 'realities' of individual physical strength: for example, D. Atkinson, *Orthodox Consensus*

and Radical Alternative: A Study in Sociological Theory (London, Heinemann, 1971), pp. 192ff.

16. A. Etzioni, *A Comparative Analysis of Complex Organizations*, 2nd edition (New York, The Free Press, 1975).
17. Quoted in Silverman, *op. cit.*, p. 138: from P. L. Berger and T. Luckmann, *The Social Construction of Reality* (Harmondsworth, Penguin Books, 1971), p. 101.
18. See the review by J. Platt in *British Journal of Sociology*, 21 (1970), 466–7.
19. Silverman, *op. cit.* pp. 130 and 132.
20. *Ibid.* p. 134.
21. Ibid. p. 216.
22. Hindess, *op. cit.* Hindess also makes the following comment: 'If some of Schutz's followers in sociology use the "commonsense" categories of a somewhat more radical audience that in no way alters the general character or the scientific status of their stories.'
23. G. Burrell and G. Morgan, *Sociological Paradigms and Organizational Analysis* (London, Heinemann, 1979); M. Read, *Redirections in Organizational Analysis* (London, Tavistock Institute of Human Relations, 1985).
24. S. Clegg and D. Dunkerley, *Organization, Class and Control* (London, Routledge, 1980).

27. *The Ultimate Artisan*

1. A. Touraine, *Sociologie de l'action* (Paris, Éditions du Seuil, 1965). Touraine's book is not available in English and makes difficult reading even in French. Alfred Willener, one of Touraine's greatest admirers, once remarked that Touraine's writing 'can be as confused as it is brilliant and original': A. Willener, *The Action-Image of Society* (London, Tavistock Institute of Human Relations, 1970). But the effort to understand can be rewarding.
2. M. J. Rose, *Servants of Post-Industrial Power? Sociologie du Travail in Modern France* (London, Macmillan, 1979), chapter 7; and M. J. Rose (ed.), *Industrial Sociology: Work in the French Tradition* (London, Sage, 1987).
3. These models are set out respectively in C. Kerr *et al.*, *Industrialism and Industrial Man* (Cambridge, Massachusetts, Harvard University Press, 1960); and H. Marcuse, *One-Dimensional Man* (London, Routledge, 1964).
4. P. Berger, *The Capitalist Revolution* (Aldershot, Hants, Wildwood House, 1987).
5. A. Touraine, *L'évolution du travail ouvrier aux usines Renault* (Paris, Centre National de la Recherche Scientifique, 1955).
6. For instance in C. R. Walker (ed.), *Modern Technology and Civilization* (New York, McGraw-Hill, 1962).
7. G. Friedmann, *The Anatomy of Work: The Implications of Specialization* (London, Heinemann, 1961).
8. Rose, *Servants of Post-Industrial Power?*, chapter 5 for an account.

9. Touraine, *op. cit.*, p. 112, trs. M. Rose, Touraine's own stress.
10. *Ibid.* p. 181.
11. A. Touraine, *Sociologie de l'action* (Paris, Éditions du Seuil, 1965), p. 123; trans. M. J. Rose, Touraine's stress. *Dépasser* in French philosophical discourse – where it is regarded as the equivalent of the German *aufheben* – implies 'going beyond' some state, typically after struggling with it, in order to reach a novel and superior state.
12. *Ibid.* p. 54.
13. *Ibid.* pp. 38–9.
14. *Ibid.* pp. 134ff.
15. *Ibid.* p. 133f.
16. *Ibid.* p. 143.
17. *Ibid.* pp. 253–4.
18. *Ibid.* pp. 338 and pp. 407ff.
19. E. J. Hobsbawm, 'Karl Marx's Contribution to Historiography' in R. Blackburn (ed.), *Ideology in Social Science* (Glasgow, Fontana, 1972).
20. M. J. Rose, *Servants of Post-Industrial Power?*, chapter 7.

28. Structure, Action, Consciousness

1. R. M. Blackburn and M. Mann, *The Working Class in the Labour Market* (London, Macmillan, 1979).
2. See T. Watson, *Sociology, Work and Industry* (London, Routledge, 1980), pp. 116ff.
3. R. K. Brown and P. Brannen, 'Social relations and social perspectives amongst shipbuilding workers', Parts I and II, *Sociology*, 4, 1 and 2 (1970), 71–84 and 197–211.
4. W. A. T. Nichols and P. Armstrong, *Workers Divided* (Glasgow, Fontana, 1976); M. J. Burawoy, *Manufacturing Consent: Changes in the Labor Process under Monopoly Capitalism* (Chicago, University of Chicago Press, 1979).
5. A. Etzioni, *A Comparative Analysis of Complex Organizations*, 2nd edition (New York, The Free Press, 1975).
6. H. Beynon and R. M. Blackburn, *Perceptions of Work* (Cambridge, Cambridge University Press, 1972).
7. H. H. Davies, *Beyond Class Images: Explorations in the Structure of Social Consciousness* (London, Croom Helm, 1979).
8. M. Rose, 'Class Versus Nation Amongst French and British Union Activists' in G. Spyropoulos (ed.), *Trade Unions in a Changing Europe* (Maastricht, European Centre for Work and Society, 1987).
9. M. Mann, *Consciousness and Action Among the Western Working Class* (London, Macmillan, 1973).
10. D. Gallie, 'Social radicalism in the French and British Working Classes: Some Points of Comparison', *British Journal of Sociology* 30, 4 (1979), 500–24.
11. A. Touraine, *La conscience ouvrière* (Paris, Éditions du Seuil, 1966).

12. M. J. Rose, *Servants of Post-Industrial Power? Sociologie du Travail in Modern France* (London, Macmillan, 1979), pp. 109ff.
13. W. A. T. Nichols, *Ownership, Control, and Ideology* (London, Allen and Unwin, 1969).
14. J. Scott, *Corporations, Classes and Capitalism* (London, Hutchinson, 1979). G. Salaman, *Class and the Corporation* (Glasgow, Fontana, 1981).

PART VI: DIVIDING THE LABOURERS

29. *Protest Peak and the New Wave*

1. See the essay 'Two Roads from Marx' in D. Bell, *The End of Ideology* (New York, The Free Press, 1960).
2. A. Zimbalast (ed.), *Case Studies on the Labor Process* (New York, The Monthly Review Press, 1979), xi–xii.
3. M. J. Rose, *Reworking the Work Ethic* (London, Batsford Academic, 1985).
4. D. Lockwood, 'Social Integration versus System Integration' in G. K. Zollschan and W. Hirsch (eds.), *Explorations in Social Change* (New York, Houghton Mifflin, 1964).
5. Rose, *op. cit.*, pp. 53–63.
6. In Britain, one of the earliest attempts to spread its use was made by the Brighton Labour Process Group: see chapter 34.
7. K. Marx, *Capital*, vol. I (Harmondsworth, Penguin Books, 1976), chapters 13–15.

30. *The Degradation Problem*

1. H. Braverman, *Labor and Monopoly Capital: The Degradation of Work in the Twentieth Century* (New York, Monthly Review Press, 1974).
2. M. Mann, *Consciousness and Action among the Western Working Class* (London, Macmillan, 1973) is a concise account.
3. From the *Work Histories and Attitudes Survey* of the research initiative on Social Change and Economic Life (SCELI) begun in 1985 with support from the Economic and Social Research Council (ESRC). Reports based on the data appeared from 1986 onwards, and the data themselves were deposited in the Survey Research Data Archive at the University of Essex at the end of the programme. They are useful for evaluation of some of Braverman's claims.
4. B. Jones, and S. Wood, 'Qualifications tacites, division du travail et nouvelles technologies', *Sociologie du Travail*, 26, 4 (1984), 407–21. The notion of *tacit skills* was canvassed earlier, in M. Polanyi, *Personal Knowledge* (London, Routledge, 1958), and given an interesting application in H. M. Collins, 'The T-Set: Tacit Knowledge and Scientific Networks', *Social Studies of Science*, 4 (1974), 165–86. The drift of these authors' arguments suggests that Braverman greatly *understated* the absolute level and general dispersion of skills utilized in everyday life by the population as a whole, while simultaneously *overstating* the

capacity of experts or specialist organizers to gain access to it and to reduce it to a form they could use to exert control or cut costs.

5. P. Thompson, *The Nature of Work: An Introduction to Debates on the Labour Process* (London, Macmillan, 1983).
6. G. Friedmann, *La crise du progrès* (Paris, Gallimard, 1936), chapter 2 especially.
7. M. J. Rose, *Servants of Post-Industrial Power? Sociologie du Travail in Modern France* (London, Macmillan, 1979), chapter 3 for an account of Friedmann's early career and own involvement with Marxism.
8. G. Friedmann, *Industrial Society: The Emergence of the Human Problems of Automation* (Glencoe, Illinois, 1964) and *The Anatomy of Work* (London, Heinemann, 1961).
9. P. Rolle, 'Proudhonism and Marxism in the Origins of the Sociology of Work', in M. J. Rose (ed.), *Industrial Sociology: Work in the French Tradition* (London, Sage, 1987).
10. B. Moss, *The Origins of the French Labor Movement, 1830–1914* (Berkeley, California, University of California Press, 1976).
11. Braverman, *op. cit.* p. 109.
12. *Ibid.* p. 131.
13. For a short account, Rose, *Servants of Post-Industrial Power?*, chapter 5; also Rolle, *op. cit.*
14. A. Cutler, 'The Romance of Labour', *Economy and Society*, 7, 1 (1978), 75–95.

31. Segments and Struggles

1. C. W. Mills, *White Collar* (New York, Oxford University Press, 1953).
2. R. Crompton and S. Reid, 'The De-Skilling of Clerical Work', in S. Wood (ed.), *The Degradation of Work?* (London, Hutchinson, 1982).
3. W. H. Whyte, *The Organization Man* (Harmondsworth, Penguin Books, 1961).
4. C. Kerr, 'The Balkanization of Labor Markets', in E. W. Bakke *et al.*, *Labor Mobility and Economic Opportunity* (Cambridge, Massachusetts, MIT Press, 1954).
5. P. B. Doehringer and M. J. Piore, *Internal Labor Markets and Manpower Analysis* (Lexington, Massachusetts, D. C. Heath, 1971).
6. See especially R. C. Edwards, M. Reich and D. M. Gordon (eds.), *Labor Market Segmentation* (Lexington, Massachusetts, D. C. Heath, 1975).
7. R. P. Althauser, and A. L. Kalleberg, 'Firms, Occupations, and the Structure of Labor Markets: A Conceptual Analysis', in I. Berg (ed.), *Sociological Perspectives on Labor Markets* (New York: Academic Press, 1981).
8. M. Reich, D. M. Gordon, and R. C. Edwards, 'A Theory of Labor Market Segmentation', *American Economic Review*, 63, 2 (1973), 359–65; reprinted in A. H. Amsden (ed.), *The Economics of Women and Work* (Harmondsworth, Penguin Books, 1980).

PRAISE BE TO JESUS OUR LORD. AMEN.

9. R. M. Blackburn and M. Mann, *The Working Class in the Labour Market* (London, Macmillan, 1979).
10. R. P. Althauser and A. L. Kalleberg, *op. cit.*
11. This pattern was set in R. K. Merton *et al.* (eds.), *Reader in Bureaucracy* (New York, The Free Press, 1952). But a powerful reaction to it occurred in the 1970s. For an account see M. Reed, *Redirections in Organizational Analysis* (London, Tavistock, 1985).
12. A. W. Gouldner, *Patterns of Industrial Bureaucracy* (New York, The Free Press, 1964).
13. T. Burns and G. M. Stalker, *The Management of Innovation* (London, Tavistock, 1961).
14. R. M. Blackburn and M. Mann, *op. cit.* pp. 32–33.
15. This is a theme of M. Mann, *Consciousness and Action among the Western Working Class* (London, Macmillan, 1973).

32. Divisions Evolve

1. R. C. Edwards, *The Contested Terrain: The Transformation of the Workplace in the Twentieth Century* (London, Heinemann, 1979).
2. E. O. Wright, *Classes, Crisis and the State* (London, New Left Books, 1978).
3. R. D. Penn, '*The Contested Terrain*: A Critique of R. C. Edwards' Theory of Working Class Fractions and Politics', in G. Day (ed.), *Development and Decomposition in the Labour Market* (Aldershot, Gower, 1982).
4. S. Marglin, 'What Do Bosses Do? The Origins and Functions of Hierarchy in Capitalist Production', in A. Gorz (ed.), *The Division of Labour: The Labour Process and Class Struggle* (Brighton, Harvester, 1976); D. Noble, 'Social Choice in Machine Tools: The Case of Automatically Controlled Machine Tools', in A. Zimbalast (ed.), *Case Studies in the Labour Process* (London, Monthly Review Press, 1979).
5. S. Marglin, *op. cit.*
6. R. Scase and R. Goffee, *The Real World of the Small Business Owner* (London, Croom Helm, 1980).
7. C. Sabel, *Work and Politics* (Cambridge, Cambridge University Press, 1982).
8. R. Penn, *op. cit.*
9. A. Fox, *Beyond Contract: Work, Power and Trust Relations* (London, Faber and Faber, 1974).
10. See M. Reich, D. M. Gordon and R. C. Edwards, 'A Theory of Labor Market Segmentation', *American Economics Review*, 63, 2 (1973), 359–65; reprinted in A. H. Amsden (ed.), *The Economics of Women and Work* (Harmondsworth, Penguin Books, 1980).

33. Campaigning for Control

1. C. J. Littler, 'Understanding Taylorism', *British Journal of Sociology*, 29, 2 (1978), 185–202.
2. See chapters 5 and 8 in C. J. Littler, *The Development of the Labour Process in*

Capitalist Societies (London, Heinemann, 1982). Littler's treatment of some of his data, especially the records of the British branch of the Bedaux Company, is in certain respects incautious: more allowance might have been made for the fact that they were produced by hard-selling executives of a consultancy organization which, as Littler himself reports, was prepared to sail very close to the commercial wind.

3. N. Branson and M. Heinemann, *Britain in the 1930s* (St Albans, Panther Books, 1971, p. 96; cited by P. Thompson, *The Nature of Work* (London, Macmillan, 1983), p. 131.
4. Thompson, *ibid.*
5. D. Lee, 'Skill, Craft and Class: A Theoretical Critique and a Critical Case', *Sociology*, 15, 1 (1980), 56–78.
6. E. Hobsbawm, *Industry and Empire* (Harmondsworth, Penguin Books, 1969).
7. K. Thurley and S. Wood, *Industrial Relations and Management Strategy* (Cambridge, Cambridge University Press, 1983).
8. J. Storey, 'The Means of Management Control', *Sociology*, 19, 2 (1985), 193–211.
9. For example, P. Thompson, *op. cit.* p. 138.
10. H. Ramsay, 'Cycles of Control: Worker Participation in Social and Historical Perspective', *Sociology*, 11, 3 (1977), 481–6.
11. P. Thompson, *op. cit.* p. 136, who wished to vindicate Braverman, ought to have been more wary of this risk.
12. A. W. Gouldner, *Patterns of Industrial Bureaucracy* (New York, The Free Press, 1964).
13. J. Child, 'Organisational Structure, Environment and Performance: The Role of Strategic Choice', *Sociology*, 6, 1 (1972), 1–22.
14. This and similar findings are itemized in J. Child, 'Organisational Design for New Manufacturing Technologies', in T. D. Wall, C. W. Clegg, and N. J. Kemp, *The Human Aspects of New Manufacturing Technology* (Chichester, Wiley, 1986).
15. M. J. Rose, and B. Jones, 'Managerial Strategy in Trade Union Responses in Work Reorganization Schemes at Establishment Level', in D. Knights *et al.* (eds.), *Job Redesign* (Aldershot, Gower, 1985); B. Jones and M. J. Rose, 'Re-Dividing Labour: Factory Politics and Work Reorganization in the Current Industrial Transition', in S. Allen *et al.* (eds.), *The Changing Experience of Work* (London, Macmillan, 1986).

34. Dividing Labour Differently in Britain

1. Brighton Labour Process Group, 'The Capitalist Labour Process', *Capital and Class*, 1, 1 (1977), 3–26. This collective author included at least ten persons. The actual writing was undertaken by John Mepham.
2. A. Friedman, 'Responsible Autonomy versus Direct Control over the Labour Process', *Capital and Class*, 1, 1 (1977), 43–58.

3. T. Cutler, 'The Romance of Labour', *Economy and Society*, 7, 1 (1978), 74–95.
4. S. Wood, (ed.), *The Degradation of Work?* (London, Hutchinson, 1982).
5. D. Knights, H. Willmott and D. Collinson (eds.), *Job Redesign: Critical Perspectives on the Labour Process* (London, Heinemann, 1984).
6. See, for example, S. Dex, *The Sexual Division of Labour: Conceptual Revolutions in the Social Sciences* (Brighton, Harvester, 1985); E. Garnsey, 'Women's Work and a Theory of Class Stratification', *Sociology*, 12, 2 (1978), 223–43; J. Rubery, 'Structured Labour Markets, Worker Organization and Low Pay', *Cambridge Journal of Economics*, 2, 1 (1978); 17–36.
7. W. A. T. Nichols and P. Armstrong, *Workers Divided* (Glasgow, Fontana, 1976); P. Willis, *Learning to Labour* (Farnborough, Saxon House, 1977).
8. S. Hill, *Competition and Control at Work* (London, Heinemann, 1981); T. Watson, *Sociology, Work and Industry* (London, Routledge, 1980).
9. Writers like Ronald Dore bring this out when making international comparisons; see R. Dore, *British Factory, Japanese Factory: The Origins of National Diversity in Industrial Relations* (London, Allen and Unwin, 1973).
10. D. Lane, *The Union Makes us Strong* (London, Arrow, 1974). R. Loveridge, 'Labour Market Segmentation and the Firm', in J. Edwards *et al.*, *Manpower Strategy and Techniques'* (Chichester, Wiley, 1983).
11. P. Joyce, *Work, Society and Politics: The Factory North of England in the Second Half of the Nineteenth Century* (Brighton, Harvester, 1980).
12. R. Martin and R. H. Fryer, *Redundancy and Paternalist Capitalism* (London, Allen and Unwin, 1973).
13. T. Lane and K. Roberts, *Strike at Pilkington's* (London, Fontana, 1971).
14. A. Lawson, 'Paternalism and Labour market Segmentation Theory', in F. Wilkinson (ed.), *The Dynamics of Labour Market Segmentation* (London, Academic Press, 1981). It is true, however, that the town in question falls in a region of England noted by labour activists as a cabbage patch. East Anglia is rewarding territory for those sociologists who chart the parameters of deference among agricultural workers: see H. Newby, *Property, Paternalism and Power* (London, Hutchinson, 1978).
15. M. White and M. Trevor, *Under Japanese Management* (London, Heinemann, 1983).
16. R. M. Blackburn and M. Mann, *The Working Class in the Labour Market* (London, Macmillan, 1979).
17. *Ibid.* p. 27.
18. S. Dex, *op. cit.*
19. J. Martin and C. Roberts, *Women and Employment: A Lifetime Perspective* (HMSO, 1984).
20. R. Crompton, 'Gender, status and professionalism', *Sociology* 21, 3 (1987), 413–28.
21. *Op. cit.* p. 24.
22. *Ibid.* p. 280.
23. R. Loveridge, 'Sources of Diversity in Internal Labour Markets', *Sociology*, 17,

1 (1983), 45–62; J. Child, M. Fores, I. Glover and P. Lawrence, 'A Price to Pay? Professionalism and Work Organization in Britain and West Germany', *Sociology*, 17, 1 (1983), 63–85.

24. S. Dex and L. B. Shaw, *British and American Women at Work* (London, Macmillan, 1983).
25. S. Dex, *The Sexual Division of Work: Conceptual Revolutions in the Social Sciences* (Brighton, Harvester, 1985).
26. *Ibid.* p. 2.

35. *Saying Yes to The System*

1. For example, W. A. T. Nichols and P. Armstrong, *Workers Divided* (Glasgow, Fontana, 1977); R. Gordon, R. Edwards and M. Reich, *Segmented Work, Divided Workers* (Cambridge, Cambridge University Press, 1982); W. Form, *Divided We Stand: Working Class Stratification in America* (Urbana, Illinois, University of Chicago Press, 1985); R. Pahl, Divisions of Labour (Oxford, Blackwell, 1984); M. Piore and C. Sabel, *The Second Industrial Divide: Possibilities for Prosperity* (New York, Basic Books, 1984).
2. R. Miliband, *The State in Capitalist Society* (London, Weidenfeld and Nicolson, 1969); W. A. T. Nichols and H. Beynon, *Living with Capitalism* (London, Routledge, 1977).
3. P. Thompson, *The Nature of Work: An Introduction to Debates on the Labour Process* (London, Macmillan, 1983), pp. 157–78 especially. Thompson seems to have something of an obsession with Burawoy's position – almost an heretical one for Thompson: there are almost thirty references to Burawoy in the index. Burawoy has published another important book recently, *The Politics of Production: Factory Regimes under Capitalism and Socialism* (London, Verso, 1985).
4. M. Burawoy, *Manufacturing Consent: Changes in the Labour Process under Monopoly Capitalism* (Chicago, University of Chicago Press, 1979).
5. P. Willis, *Learning to Labour* (Farnborough, Saxon House, 1977).
6. M. Burawoy, 'Terrains of Contest: Factory and State under Capitalism and Socialism', *Socialist Review*, 11, 4 (1981), 10–26 (cited by Thompson, p. 161).
7. D. Wrong, 'The Over-socialized Conception of Man', in A. Inkeles (ed.), *Readings on Modern Sociology* (Englewood Cliffs, New Jersey, Prentice-Hall, 1966).
8. M. J. Rose, *Reworking the Work Ethic: Economic Values in Socio-Cultural Politics* (London, Batsford Academic, 1985).
9. I. Berg, M. Freedman and M. Freeman, *Manager and Work Reform: A Limited Engagement* (New York, The Free Press, 1978).
10. This is argued in M. Rose, *op. cit.* chapter 8.
11. This is unfortunate. Burawoy is nobody's historical *doppelgänger*, though often his detailed analysis – his ethnographic flair is always apparent here – of micro-relationships and everyday events is reminiscent of W. F. Whyte at his best.

12. In 1981 Burawoy distinguished such variants of the hegemonic factory regime as the bureaucratic (mainly in the USA), the anarchic (UK), and the corporatist (Japan); see Burawoy, 'Terrains of Conquest', p. 100.
13. M. Burawoy, *The Politics of Production: Factory Regimes under Capitalism and Socialism* (London, Verso, 1985).
14. *Ibid.* pp. 150f.

36. *The Artisans are Coming Back*

1. C. F. Sabel, *Work and Politics* (Cambridge, Cambridge University Press, 1982).
2. M. Crozier, *The Bureaucratic Phenomenon* (London, Tavistock Institute of Human Relations, 1964).
3. C. F. Sabel, *op. cit.* p. 220.
4. S. Brusco and C. F. Sabel, 'Artisanal Production and Economic Growth', in F. Wilkinson (ed.), *The Dynamics of Labour Market Segmentation* (London, The Academic Press, 1981).
5. M. J. Piore and C. F. Sabel, *The Second Industrial Divide: Possibilities for Prosperity* (New York, Basic Books, 1984).

37. *In the Wake of the New Wave*

1. R. D. Penn, *Skilled Workers in the Class Structure* (Cambridge, Cambridge University Press, 1985); B. Jones, 'Destruction or Redistribution of Craft Skills? The Case of Numerical Control' in S. Wood (ed.), *The Degradation of Work?* (London, Hutchinson, 1982); B. Jones and S. Wood, 'Qualifications tacites, division du travail et nouvelles technologies', *Sociologie du Travail*, 26, 4 (1984), 407–21; B. Jones and M. J. Rose, 'Re-Dividing Labour: Factory Politics and Work Reorganization in the Current Industrial Transition', in S. Allen *et al.* (eds.), *The Changing Experience of Work* (London, Macmillan, 1986); B. Jones and P. J. Scott, '"Working the System": The Management of Work Roles in British and American Flexible Manufacturing Systems', in C. Voss (ed.), *Managing Advanced Manufacturing Technology* (Bedford, IFS Publications, 1986).
2. M. J. Rose, *Reworking the Work Ethic: Economic Values and Socio-Cultural Politics* (London, Batsford Academic, 1985).

CONCLUSION

38. *Nations, Work and History*

1. R. Dore, *British Factory, Japanese Factory: The Origins of National Diversity in Industrial Relations* (London, Allen and Unwin, 1974).
2. P. Lange, G. Ross and M. Vanicelli, *Unions, Change and Crisis: French and*

Italian Union Strategy and the Political Economy, 1945–1980 (London, Allen and Unwin, 1982).

3. M. J. Rose, 'Universalism, Culturalism and the Aix Group: Promise and Problems of a Societal Approach to Economic Institutions', *European Sociological Review*, 1, 1 (1985), 65–83.
4. M. Maurice, F. Sellier and J.-J. Silvestre, *The Social Foundations of Industrial Power* (trans. A. Goldhammer: MIT Press, 1986).
5. M. Maurice, A. Sorge and M. Warner, 'Societal Differences in Organizing Manufacturing Units: A Comparison of France, West Germany and Great Britain', *Organization Studies*, 1, 1 (1980), 59–86.
6. See J. Urry, 'Making Space for Space', *Economy and Society*, 15, 2 (1986), 273–80.
7. H. H. Davis, *Beyond Class Images* (London, Croom Helm, 1977); G. Salaman, *Community and Occupation* (Cambridge, Cambridge University Press, 1974). See also Salaman's recent *Working* (London, Tavistock, 1986).
8. G. K. Ingham, *Strikes and Industrial Conflict* (London, Macmillan, 1974).
9. A. Giddens, *The Constitution of Society: An Outline of the Theory of Structuration* (Cambridge, Polity Press, 1984).

Bibliography

The following suggestions are works concerned primarily with the schools of thought, management movements, or ideologies that mark the history of inquiry into work behaviour. In notes to individual chapters full bibliographic information is provided on several hundred further monographs, reports or theoretical works.

Ackroyd, S., 'Sociological Theory and the Human Relations School', *Sociology of Work and Occupations*, 3 (1976), 279–410. Proposes rehabilitation of some human relations ideas.

Arensberg, C. M. and Tootell, G., 'Plant Sociology: Real Discoveries and New Problems', in M. Komarovsky (ed.), *Common Frontiers of the Social Sciences* (Glencoe, Illinois Free Press, 1957). Vigorous defence plea for interactionist approach to workplace behaviour.

Bendix, R., *Work and Authority in Industry: Ideologies of Management in the Course of Industrialization* (Berkeley, University of California Press, 1974). Taylor and Mayo figure prominently as rival creators of managerial legitimation.

Berg, I., Freedman M. and Freeman, M., *Managers and Work Reform: A Limited Engagement* (New York, The Free Press, 1978). The work reform movement of the 1970s viewed as a self-interested managerial doctrine.

Braverman, H., *Labor and Monopoly Capital: The Degradation of Work in the Twentieth Century* (New York, Monthly Review Press, 1974). Classic recent English language statement of the Proudhonian view of work.

Brossard, M. and Maurice, M., 'Is there a universal model of organisation structure?', *International Studies of Management and Organisation*, 6, 1 (1976), 11–45. First formulation of the societal approach to work behaviour.

Brown, R. 'Research and Consultancy in Industrial Enterprises', *Sociology*, 1, 1, 1967, (33–60). Insider's report on the Tavistock Institute of Human Relations.

Burawoy, M. *Manufacturing Consent: Changes in the Labor Process under Monopoly Capitalism* (Chicago, University of Chicago Press, 1979). In effect, a restatement of the interactionist approach, integrated in a superb research report.

Chapple, E. D., Arensberg, C. M. and Tootell, G., 'Plant Sociology: Real Discoveries and New Problems' in M. Komarovsky (ed.), *Common Frontiers of the Social Sciences* (Glencoe, Illinois, The Free Press, 1957). Unapologetic defence plea by champions of applied industrial inquiry.

Child, J., *British Management Thought* (London, Allen and Unwin, 1969). The story of the early management movement, its ideologies and views of social science in Britain.

Cohen, S. R., 'From industrial democracy to professional adjustment: The development of Industrial Sociology in the USA, 1900–1955', *Theory and Society*, 12, 1 (1983), 47–67. Condemnation in the radical tradition of orthodox industrial sociology.

Cutler, A. 'The Romance of Labour', *Economy and Society*, 7, 1 (1978), 75–95. Marxist attack on degradation hypothesis of Braverman school.

Dex, S., *The Sexual Division of Work: Conceptual Revolutions in the Social Sciences* (Brighton, Harvester, 1985). Traces treatment of the gender dimension in industrial studies and persuasively argues for closer integration of sociological and economic perspectives on work.

Fox, A., *Beyond Contract: Work, Power and Trust Relations* (London, Faber and Faber, 1974). Examines link between work design and management ideologies.

Franke, R., 'The Hawthorne Experiments: A Review', *American Sociological Review*, 47 (1979), 858–66. Recent methodological and theoretical critique.

Friedmann, G., *Industrial Society: The Emergence of the Human Problems of Automation* (Glencoe, Illinois, The Free Press, 1955). A more searching statement of the degradation thesis to be revived by Braverman in the 1970s.

Goldman, P. and Van Houten, D. R., 'Uncertainty, Conflict, and Labour Relations in the Modern Firm', Parts I and II, *Economic and Industrial Democracy*, 1, 1 and 2 (1980), 63–98, and 263–87. Documents the spread of revived human-relations practices after the end of the economic Growth Era.

Goldthorpe, J. H., 'Attitudes and Behaviour of Car Assembly Workers: A Deviant Case and Theoretical Critique', *British Journal of Sociology*, 17 (1966), 227–44. The most explicit statement of a 'middle range' action approach.

Haber, S. *Efficiency and Uplift* (Chicago, Illinois, University of Chicago Press, 1964). An hilarious study of scientific management thought as a general social doctrine.

Heyl, B. S., 'The Harvard Pareto Circle', *Journal for the History of the Behavioural Sciences*, 4 (1968), 316–34. Explores intellectual background to the Harvard branch of human relations.

Homans, G. C., *Coming to my Senses* (New Brunswick, Transaction Books, 1984). Characteristically frank, personal account of how politics affected social theories of human relations exponents.

Kerr, C. and Fisher, L., 'Plant Sociology: The Elite and the Aborigines', in M. Komarovsky (ed.), *Common Frontiers of the Social Sciences* (Glencoe, Illinois, The Free Press, 1957). Attack on human relations from perspective of free-market economic liberalism.

Landsberger, H. A., *Hawthorne Revisited: 'Management and the Worker'. Its Critics and Developments in Human Relations in Industry* (Ithaca, New York, Cornell University Press, 1958). Classic analysis and critique of the varying strands of human relations.

Mackenzie, G., 'The "Affluent Worker" Study: An Evaluation and Critique' in F. Parkin (ed.), *The Social Analysis of the Class Structure* (London, Tavistock, 1974). Lists a number of limitations with the action approach to work behaviour.

Madge, J., *The Origins of Scientific Sociology* (London, Tavistock Institute of Human Relations, 1963). Chapter on 'Pioneers in Industrial Sociology' presents defence for Western Electric studies as a research programme.

Maier, C. S., 'Between Taylorism and Technocracy: European ideologies and the vision of industrial harmony in the 1920s', *Journal of Contemporary History*, 5, 2 (1970), 27–61. How spread of Taylorism to Europe was filtered by local conditions, especially strength of productivist doctrines.

Maurice, M., Sellier, F. and Silvestre, J.-J., *The Social Foundations of Industrial Power: A Comparison of France and Germany* (MIT Press, 1986). Fully developed specification from the Aix Group of a societal approach linked to empirical analysis and integrated application of sociological and economic approaches to work behaviour.

Mayo, E., *The Social Problems of an Industrial Civilization* (London, Routledge, 1975). See especially chapters on human factor psychology.

Mills, C. W., 'The Contribution of Sociology to the Study of Industrial Relations', *Proceedings of the Industrial Relations Research Association*, 1 (1948), 199–222. Calls for reacknowledgement of conflict of interest as a factor in workplace relationships.

Moore, W. E., 'Industrial Sociology: Status and Prospects', *American Sociological Review*, 13 (1948), 382–91. Review by middle-of-the-road participant.

Nadworny, M. J., *Scientific Management and the Unions, 1900–1932* (Cambridge, Massachusetts, Harvard University Press, 1955). How scientific management ideas penetrated many American unions following campaign by Taylor's consciously technocratic and productivist heirs.

Poster, M., *Existential Marxism in Postwar France: From Sartre to Althusser*, (Princeton, New Jersey, Princeton University Press, 1975). Enthusiastic exposition of links between theme of alienation in social science, change in the workplace, and French radical politics during Growth Era.

Rolle, P. 'Proudhonism and Marxism in the Origins of the Sociology of Work', in M. J. Rose (ed.), *Industrial Sociology: Work in the French Tradition* (London, Sage, 1987). One of the few informed accounts of Proudhonian ideas about work available in English, by well informed French authority.

Rose, M. J., *Servants of Post-Industrial Power? Sociologie du Travail in Modern France* (London, Macmillan, 1979). Development of the French School in the sociology of work and its relations with politics in the years after 1945.

'Universalism, Culturalism and the Aix Group: Promise and problems of a societal approach to economic institutions', *European Sociological Review*, 1, 1 (1985), 65–83. Exposition and critique of the Aix version of the societal approach.

Reworking the Work Ethic: Economic Values and Socio-Cultural Politics (London, Batsford Academic, 1985). Work as cultural politics: see especially chapters on work and post-bourgeois values, and the work-reform movement.

Rose, M. J. (ed.), *Industrial Sociology: Work in the French Tradition* (London, Sage, 1987). Recent history of French School related to decay of technocratic management of economy, recounted by leading French researchers.

Sabel, C. F., *Work and Politics* (Cambridge, Cambridge University Press, 1982). Interesting combination of disciplines produces coherent account of politics of the workplace consistent with a societal approach.

Simpson, R. and Simpson, I. H. (eds.), *Research in the Sociology of Work*, (Greenwich, Connecticut, JAI Press, 1981). Several useful theoretical chapters.

Silverman, D., *The Theory of Organizations* (London, Heinemann, 1970). Bold statement of the radical subjectivist approach to work behaviour, and valuable examination of organization theory prior to 1970.

Smith, J., 'Elton Mayo and the Hidden Hawthorne', *Work, Employment and Society*, 1, 1 (1987), 107–20. Defends Mayo's record as a researcher from attacks of Landsberger and other critics.

'Elton Mayo and the English Dream', *The Sociological Review*, 35, 3 (1987), 603–21. How Mayo's work may have been affected by his itinerant life.

Thompson, P., *The Nature of Work: An Introduction to Debates on the Labour Process* (London, Macmillan, 1983). Spirited defence of degradationist view of the workplace.

Trist, E. L., *The Evolution of Socio-Technical Systems: A Conceptual Framework and an Action Research Program* (Toronto, Ontario Ministry of Labour, Occasional Paper no. 2, 1981). Includes historical account of the British version of the technological-implications school.

Warner, M., *Organizations and Experiments* (Chichester, Wiley, 1985). Interprets history of social science as an aspect of broader human effort to achieve organized control of work process. Informative.

Whyte, W. F., 'From Human Relations to Organizational Behavior: Reflections on the changing scene', *Industrial and Labor Relations Review*, 40, 4, (1987), 487–500. Characteristically frank account by someone who was there from the start.

Index